THE RISE AND FALL OF IMPERIAL CHINA

PRINCETON STUDIES IN CONTEMPORARY CHINA

Mary Gallagher and Yu Xie, Series Editors

The Rise and Fall of Imperial China

THE SOCIAL ORIGINS OF STATE DEVELOPMENT

YUHUA WANG

PRINCETON UNIVERSITY PRESS

PRINCETON & OXFORD

Published by Princeton University Press
41 William Street, Princeton, New Jersey 08540
99 Banbury Road, Oxford OX2 6JX

press.princeton.edu

All Rights Reserved

Library of Congress Control Number 2022941962

ISBN 978-0-691-21517-4
ISBN (pbk.) 978-0-691-21516-7
ISBN (e-book) 978-0-691-23751-0

British Library Cataloging-in-Publication Data is available

Editorial: Bridget Flannery-McCoy and Alena Chekanov
Production Editorial: Jill Harris
Cover Design: Karl Spurzem
Production: Lauren Reese
Publicity: Kate Hensley and Charlotte Coyne

Cover image: *The Kangxi Emperor's Southern Inspection Tour, Scroll Three: Ji'nan to Mount Tai* by Wang Hui and assistants. Datable to 1698 (Qing Dynasty). Metropolitan Museum of Art - New York / Purchase, The Dillon Fund Gift, 1979.

This book has been composed in Arno

10 9 8 7 6 5 4 3 2 1

For Boyang

CONTENTS

PART V. CONCLUSION

APPENDICES

FIGURES

TABLES

PREFACE

THIS IS my dream book.

I've always been interested in history, and have dreamed of writing a book about Chinese history. In 2014, after I submitted the final draft of my first book, the time finally came. I decided to start writing a book that introduces Chinese history to the social sciences and brings social sciences to Chinese history.

I sat down and began to read what social scientists, mostly economic historians, had written about Chinese history. Each piece of the puzzle told an interesting story, but I struggled to get a sense of the bigger picture. Most of the works focused on China's economic and fiscal decline in the nineteenth and twentieth centuries, in an attempt to explore the roots of the "Great Divergence" in economic development between China and Europe. I was eager to instead find out the *political* story. I wanted to understand why the elites did not implement policies that promoted economic development and fiscal capacities. Were they not able to? Or did they not want to? Searching for the political backstory, I discovered another literature that studies the formation of the Chinese state. That literature portrays the Chinese state as a strong and centralized entity that was forged in iron and blood two millennia ago. But what happened in between?

I was trying to connect the dots. A sabbatical in 2016 gave me the opportunity to dive into China's history. I decided to put aside my other research projects and read. It turned out to be my least productive year with respect to writing, but the most stimulating in terms of generating new ideas. I read historians' works and official Chinese histories, dynasty by dynasty. What struck me the most, among the hundreds of books scattered around my office, was the work by social historians. Hilary Beattie, Beverly Bossler, Chung-li Chang, Yinke Chen, Prasenjit Duara, Patricia Ebrey, Robert Hartwell, Ping-ti Ho, Robert Hymes, David Johnson, Hanguang Mao, Nicolas Tackett, Yuqing Tian, Ying-shih Yu, and others have traced the evolution of China's political elites, from the Han Dynasty to the Qing Dynasty, paying special attention to their social relations. A great insight from these works is that Chinese elites became more localized over time in their social relations, which greatly changed how they viewed the state and their relationship with the ruler.

I became convinced that if I could understand how elite social relations were structured and how they changed over time, then I could begin to unscramble the many puzzles in China's political development. For instance, why did the Tang emperors die so young when China was the world's dominant empire? Why did some Qing emperors stay in power so long, while their government struggled to collect taxes? How did every dynasty in the late imperial era last hundreds of years, while their economies were stagnant, their treasuries empty, and their armies inept? And more fundamentally, what explains the gradual decline and the eventual fall of a political system that had endured for over two thousand years?

A broad narrative started to form in my head. Chinese rulers faced a fundamental trade-off in state building, which I call the *sovereign's dilemma*: a coherent elite that could take collective actions to strengthen the state was also capable of revolting against the ruler. This dilemma existed because strengthening state capacity and lengthening ruler duration required different *elite social terrains*—the type of social networks in which the central elites were embedded. In the beginning, China's social terrain featured central elites with an encompassing interest in strengthening the state, but they were also coherent enough to topple the emperors. Large-scale violence in the medieval era destroyed the old elites and provided an opportunity for the ruler to reshape the elite social terrain to one in which the central elites were fragmented enough for the emperor to divide and conquer; but they pursued their own narrow interests and sought to hollow out the state from within. Long-reigning emperors ended up ruling a weak state. In essence, over two thousand years of China's state development can be boiled down to the history of its rulers struggling with the sovereign's dilemma—pursuing state capacity *or* personal survival. The emperor's relentless pursuit of power and survival through fragmenting the elites is the final culprit for the decline and fall of imperial China.

———

While researching and writing this book, I have accumulated many debts to individuals and institutions whose generous support I will never be able to repay.

My mentor and colleague, Liz Perry, provided initial encouragement and pointed me in the right direction whenever I got lost. A pioneer in using history to understand politics herself, she helped me navigate every turn of the journey and cheered me up when I failed to see the light at the end of the tunnel. Another mentor and colleague, Steve Levitsky, kept reminding me of the big picture and helped me appreciate the book's broader contributions before I even knew what they were. Several outstanding scholars read an early version of the book and participated in a book workshop sponsored by the Faculty of Arts and Sciences and the Fairbank Center for Chinese Studies at Harvard. These scholars are Lisa Blaydes, Nara Dillon, Prasenjit Duara, John Ferejohn, Anna Grzymala-Busse, Steve Levitsky, Liz Perry, Frances Rosenbluth, and David Stasavage. Their feedback improved the manuscript in crucial ways, and their continuous support has given me the strongest motivation I could ever ask for.

My colleagues in the Department of Government at Harvard University have provided an intellectually vibrant and inspiring home over the last six years. My "office neighbor" Bob Bates took me to lunch almost every week and generously shared his knowledge of European and African history. He tried to teach me how to ask big questions and write short books (I have miserably failed to achieve at least one of these tasks, as you will soon find out, through no fault of his own). Peter Hall helped me identify ideas that were worth pursuing, carefully read an earlier draft, and provided detailed and constructive comments. Daniel Ziblatt gave me the best example of how to integrate historical insights into cutting-edge political science work. The semester teaching the Comparative Politics Field Seminar with Torben Iversen reshaped my understanding of the intellectual history of the discipline. Conversations over the years with Eric Beerbohm, Melani Cammett, Dan Carpenter, Tim Colton, Christina Davis, Nara Dillon, Grzegorz Ekiert, Ryan Enos, Jeff Frieden, Fran Hagopian, Jennifer Hochschild, Alisha Holland, Iain Johnston, Gary King, Susan Pharr, Ken Shepsle, James Snyder, and Dustin Tingley have provided enduring inspiration and encouragement. The late Rod MacFarquhar encouraged me to study elite networks in historical times and led by example through his own work. An internal workshop attended by Matt Blackwell, Stephen Chaudoin, Sarah Hummel, Josh Kertzer, Horacio Larreguy, Christoph Mikulaschek, Pia Raffler, Jon Rogowski, and Dan Smith provided me with helpful advice on key empirical chapters.

Since this book took me beyond my area of training, I also relied on many colleagues who helped steer me to what I needed to read in fields they knew far better than I did. Peter Bol, Mark Elliot, Arunabh Ghosh, and Michael Szonyi helped me understand key debates among historians and identify works that offer the best insights on each dynasty. The late Ezra Vogel was always a warm cheerleader and taught me how to ask a question that became important before everyone else realized it. Arunabh Ghosh, Daniel Koss, Yawen Lei, Meg Rithmire, David Yang, and Xiang Zhou provided a community that I can rely on for mutual support.

A great privilege as an academic is to work with and learn from a large number of talented students. Steve Bai, Chris Carothers, Nora Chen, Cheng Cheng, Caterina Chiopris, Iza Ding, Josh Freedman, Chengyu Fu, Jany Gao, Yichen Guan, Qiang Guo, Jeff Javed, Andrew Leber, Handi Li, Jialu Li, Yishuang Li, Tao Lin, Dongshu Liu, Daniel Lowery, Shiqi Ma, Shom Mazumder, Brendan McElroy, Shannon Parker, Jingyuan Qian, Matt Reichert, Basak Taraktas, Saul Wilson, Saul Yang, Fu Ze, Yu Zeng, Helen Zhang, and Zelda Zhao have taught me things that I wish I had learned in graduate school. My undergraduate students in large lecture halls and small seminar rooms alike asked me questions that kept pushing my intellectual boundaries.

Along the way, I have talked about the book's ideas and presented various aspects of the project to many colleagues and friends outside my home institution. Scott Abramson, Daron Acemoglu, Chris Atwood, Carles Boix, Bruce Bueno de Mesquita, Xun Cao, Brett Carter, Erin Baggott Carter, Volha Charnysh, Hao Chen, Ling Chen, Shuo Chen, Bill Clark, Gary Cox, Jacques deLisle, Bruce Dickson, Mark Dincecco, Iza Ding, Greg Distelhorst, Peter Evans, Mary Gallagher, Scott Gehlbach, Dan Gingerich, Avery Goldstein, Jean Hong, Yue Hou, Yasheng Huang, Saumitra Jha, Atul Kohli, Stephen Krasner, Guillermo Kreiman, James Kung, Pierre Landry, Melissa Lee, Zhenhuan Lei, Lizhi Liu, Xiaobo Lü, Debin Ma, Xiao Ma, Eddy Malesky, Melanie Manion, Isabela Mares, Dan Mattingly, Andy Mertha, Blake Miller, Carl Müller-Crepon, Kevin O'Brien, Jean Oi, Christopher Paik, Jen Pan, Margaret Pearson, Didac Queralt, Molly Roberts, Jeff Sellers, Ian Shapiro, Victor Shih, Dan Slater, Hillel Soifer, Hendrik Spruyt, Danie Stockmann, Rory Truex, Lily Tsai, Erik H. Wang, Yu Xie, Yiqing Xu, Dali Yang, John Yasuda, Changdong Zhang, Taisu Zhang, Congyi Zhou, and Boliang Zhu have invariably provided useful feedback. Special thanks go to Mark Dincecco, who has collaborated with me on various projects. His thinking on the role of violence in state building has shaped my own.

I am grateful for the participants at workshops where I have presented my work, including seminars and conferences at Huazhong University of

Science and Technology (Wuhan, China), Johns Hopkins University, Korea University, New York University, New York University in Abu Dhabi, Northwestern University, Peking University (Beijing, China), Penn State University, Princeton University, Renmin University (Beijing, China), Stanford University, Texas A&M University, University of Oxford, University of Pennsylvania, University of Southern California, University of Virginia, Yale University, and the Zoom in China Webinar Series.

I have relied on a team of excellent research assistants for data collection and coding: Nora Chen, Cheng Cheng, Yusi Du, Maggie Huang, Shiqi Ma, Jia Sun, Patricia Sun, Yihua Xia, and Siyao Zheng. Two of my research assistants deserve special thanks: Ce Gao and Jialu Li, who formed a formidable research team at an early stage to help collect the bulk of the biographical data used in the book. I also thank James Cheng and Xiaohe Ma at the Harvard Yenching Library, Lex Berman at the China Historical GIS Project, and Ji Ma and Hongsu Wang at the China Biographical Database for their guidance. I could not have finished the book without their help.

Several institutions at Harvard have provided generous financial support: the Faculty of Arts and Sciences, the Fairbank Center for Chinese Studies, the Weatherhead Center for International Affairs, the Asia Center, the Harvard Academy for International and Area Studies, the Harvard China Fund, the Institute for Quantitative Social Sciences, and the Department of Government.

Kelley Friel has provided outstanding copyediting and greatly improved my writing over the years.

At Princeton University Press, I thank Bridget Flannery-McCoy for her enthusiastic support of the book. Alena Chekanov has provided timely and helpful editorial assistance. Wendy Washburn carefully copyedited the book manuscript. I also want to thank Brigitta van Rheinberg for an earlier conversation that convinced me to publish with Princeton. Six anonymous reviewers offered overgenerous compliments and thoughtful comments. I am grateful to Mary Gallagher and Yu Xie who kindly offered to include my book in their Studies in Contemporary China series.

Parts of different chapters of this book were first published in the *American Political Science Review* and *Comparative Politics* and are reprinted with the journals' permission.

My personal debts are no smaller than my professional ones. Much of this book was written during the COVID-19 pandemic when I could not visit my parents, Shulan Yin and Yanli Wang, who have provided the most important spiritual support that I could ever imagine. My lovely daughter, Yushi, who grew faster than the pages of this book, sustained my curiosity about the world and made me laugh every day. My wife Boyang has given me unconditional understanding, patience, and love, and often had to endure an absent-minded husband who worried more about the Ming Dynasty than dinner plans. As a small gesture of appreciation, I dedicate this book to her.

Somerville, Massachusetts
July 2021

PART I

Introduction

1

Elite Social Terrain and State Development

1.1 Not All Roads Lead to Rome

The state is the most powerful organization in human history. Since the formation of the first states in Mesopotamia, Egypt, the Indus Valley, and the Yellow River around 4000 to 2000 BCE, the state as an organization has undergone numerous transformations in form and strength. It has become an institution we cannot live without.

Why did some states stay intact for centuries, while others fall relatively soon after they were founded? Why are some strong, and others weak? Why are some ruled by a democratically elected leader, and others by an autocrat? These are among the most time-honored questions that have produced generations of remarkable scholarship.

Yet, much of our understanding of how the state as an organization develops is based on how states evolved in Europe. The centuries after the fall of the Roman Empire laid the foundation for Europe's distinctive path of political development.[1] Political fragmentation led to competition and conflicts between states, creating a dual transformation.[2] On the one hand, rulers' weak bargaining power vis-à-vis domestic elites gave rise to the creation of representative institutions, which constrained executive power and enabled the ruler to tax effectively.[3] On the other hand, frequent (and increasingly expensive) interstate conflicts advantaged large territorial states that centralized the bureaucracy and eliminated rival domestic organizations.[4]

The literature treats the European model as the benchmark and asks why states in other regions have failed to follow suit. Representative institutions, effective taxation, and what Max Weber calls a "monopoly over violence"[5] have become universal criteria for evaluating states across the world. This convergence paradigm has also influenced policy makers. Many of the policy interventions carried out by the international community, such as the World Bank and the International Monetary Fund, focus on strengthening tax capacities and building "Weberian" states, in the hope that countries in the Global South will approach their European counterparts.[6]

For most of human history, the majority of the world's population, however, has not been governed by a European-style state.[7] Some non-European states have achieved incredible durability and effective governance by pursuing their own approach.

Clearly, not all roads lead to Rome. Rather than treating non-European states as underdeveloped cases that will eventually converge to the European model, we should take these durable and alternative patterns of state development seriously in their own right. Most developing countries have not created a rule based on consent, but are still run by autocrats. Even after a hard-fought process of national independence, the odds are that a developing country will not establish a European-style nation state. Sticking with the convergence paradigm is holding back evolution in the field of comparative political development and leading policy makers astray. It is time to recognize that there is more than one state development pattern, and to look for a new lens with which to analyze these new models.

1.2   Why China?

China represents an alternative—and incredibly durable—pattern of state development. Since its foundation around 200 BCE, Chinese imperial rule remained resilient for over two thousand years until its fall in the early twentieth century. Especially in the second millennium, a long-lasting equilibrium seems to have emerged. While many studies have lauded European rulers' exceptionally long tenures thanks to the emergence of representative institutions, from 1000 to 1900 CE Chinese emperors on average stayed in power as long as European kings and queens. With the exception of the Yuan (1270–1368), every Chinese dynasty in the second millennium lasted for roughly three hundred years—longer than the United States has existed. Yet durability does not mean stability: dynasties eventually changed, rulers altered, rebellions erupted, and enemies invaded. But the pillar of imperial rule—a monarchy governing through an elite bureaucracy and in partnership with kinship-based organizations—remained intact; the basic form in which the state was organized was exceptionally resilient.

While European states had become more durable and better able to achieve their main objectives by the modern era, the Chinese state seemed to have gained durability at the expense of state strength. Chinese emperors became increasingly secure, and the dynasties endured for longer. But the country's fiscal capacity gradually declined. In the eleventh century, for example, the Chinese state (under the Song Dynasty) taxed over 15 percent of its economy. This percentage dropped to almost 1 percent in the nineteenth century (under the Qing Dynasty).[8]

Exploring how the state maintained its durability *despite* declining strength, and what explains its eventual fall, helps broaden our understanding of alternative patterns of state development. China's different, but durable, patterns of state development demand a new approach that goes beyond simply testing Europe-generated theories in a non-European context, which has produced fruitful results, but not a new paradigm. The intellectual payoffs of departing from the Euro-centric approach are great if it enriches our repertoire of paradigms and approaches to the study of the state.

1.3   What Needs to Be Explained

A central puzzle that motivates this book is why short-lived emperors often ruled a strong state while long-lasting emperors governed a weak one. Previous scholarship has not provided a satisfactory answer.

A static origin story has dominated popular understandings of the Chinese state. Starting with Karl Marx, and popularized by Karl Wittfogel, this story features an "oriental state" that was formed to control floods and manage irrigation.[9] According to this explanation, the Chinese state—a despotic monster—has been stuck in an inferior equilibrium from its inception. Headed by an autocratic monarch, and too centralized and too strong, the state squeezed the society for more than two thousand years until its eventual collapse: it was doomed to fail.

A similar static approach emphasizes political culture and ideology. Confucianism, which emerged during the Warring States period (475–221 BCE) and became institutionalized in the Han Dynasty (202 BCE–220 CE), legitimized imperial rule and created China's "ultra-stable equilibrium structure" for two millennia.[10] By treating two thousand years of Chinese history as a single equilibrium, this cultural account vastly underestimates changes in the country's political structure.[11]

Historians' earlier work, by contrast, examined China's political development through the lens of dynastic cycles. Dynastic cycle theory states that each dynasty usually started with strong leaders, but subsequent emperors' quality gradually deteriorated and lost the "Mandate of Heaven."[12] The peasants would then rebel, and the dynasty would decline and fall, and be replaced by a new one. According to this view, Chinese history can be explained by repetitions of recurring patterns. However, such an approach overlooks key features of these dynasties. In the second millennium, for example, ruler duration steadily lengthened, while fiscal revenue continuously declined, despite the rise and fall of dynasties.

Recent social science scholarship on China's state development has focused on either the beginning or the end—state formation during the Qin era (221–206 BCE) or state collapse during the Qing (1644–1911 CE). The scholars who study the beginning treat China's early state formation as a finite, complete process without examining how the state was sustained and how it changed over the next two millennia.[13] The scholars who study the end focus on China's declining fiscal capacity without discussing the system's exceptional durability until the early twentieth century despite fiscal weakness, foreign invasions, and internal rebellions.[14]

It is time to account for the entire trajectory of China's state development and to consider these seemingly contradictory trends—longer ruler duration and declining fiscal revenues—not as paradoxes, but as interconnected manifestations of an underlying political equilibrium. Only when we take a holistic view can we start to explore the conditions that led to the emergence, durability, and fall of different political equilibria in China's political development.

In this book, I will explain *state development*, which I define as a dynamic process in which the state's *strength* and *form* evolve.[15] A state's strength refers to its ability to achieve its official goals—particularly collecting revenue and mobilizing the population.[16] State form is a product of two separate relationships. The first is between the ruler and the ruling elite: is the ruler *first among equals*, or does he or she *dominate* the ruling elite? The second relates to the relationship between the state and society—defined as a web of social groups: does the state *lead* or *partner with* social groups to provide basic services? While the first relationship concerns what Michael Mann calls despotic power, the second reflects the degree of infrastructural power.[17]

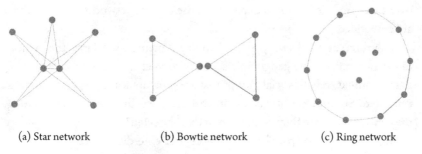

(a) Star network (b) Bowtie network (c) Ring network

FIGURE 1.1: Three Ideal Types of Elite Social Terrain

1.4 My Argument

My overarching argument is that whether the state is strong or weak (state strength) and how it is structured (state form) follow from the network structure that characterizes state-society relations. Among various aspects of state-society relations, I emphasize *elite social terrain*: the ways in which central elites connect local social groups (and link to each other).[18] When elites are in geographically broad and densely interconnected networks, they prefer a strong state capable of protecting their far-flung interests, and their cohesiveness constrains the ruler's power. When elites rely on local bases of power and are not tightly connected, they will instead seek to hollow out the central state from within and prefer to provide order and public goods locally; their internal divisions will enable the ruler to play competing factions against each other and establish absolute power. Elite social terrain, therefore, makes the state by creating a trade-off that the ruler must face: state strength and ruler duration are incompatible goals; one can be achieved only at the expense of the other.

1.4.1 Elite Social Terrain

Building on social network theories, I use three graphs in figure 1.1 to characterize three ideal types of elite social terrains.[19] In each graph, the central nodes are state elites, defined as politicians who work in the central government and can influence government policies. The peripheral nodes represent local-level social groups. Each peripheral node represents a social group, such as a clan, in a specific geographic location. The edges denote connections, which can take multiple forms, such as membership in a clan, social ties, or family ties.[20]

Central elites are agents of their connected social groups; their objective is to influence government policies to provide the best services to their groups at the lowest possible cost.[21] Whether elites cooperate with each other or clash over their preferred policies depends on the type of networks in which they are embedded.

The three networks vary along two key dimensions.[22] First, the *vertical* dimension reflects the geographic scope of each elite's social relations: is he or she connected with social groups that are geographically dispersed or concentrated? Second, the *horizontal* dimension reflects the cohesiveness among the central elites: are they connected or disconnected?

In a *star network* (panel (a)), each central elite directly connects every social group located in different geographic areas. The central elites are also connected with each other: because elites link various social groups, their networks are likely to be overlapping, generating lateral ties between the elites. An approximate example of a star network is England after the Norman conquest. In 1066, a team of Norman aristocrats connected by (imaginary) kinship links conquered England and formed a coherent elite.[23] Although these elites had disagreements, they were all centrally oriented because they owned land and were embedded in social relations throughout the country.[24] Geographically dispersed social relations and internal cohesion are the defining features of the star network.

In a *bowtie network* (panel (b)), each central elite is connected to a set of social groups in a confined geographic area, but not to any groups in distant areas. Nor are the central elites connected with each other: because elites' social relations are localized, they are also less likely to be in each other's social networks. An example of a bowtie network is feudal France. In response to the chaos of the last years of the Carolingian Empire (800–888), the elites banded together in regional military alliances to protect themselves.[25] The French aristocrats were therefore "tribal," and each was attached to a certain locality.[26] Geographically concentrated social relations and internal divisions among the elites are the defining features of the bowtie network.

In a *ring network* (panel (c)), central elites are not connected with any social groups, or with each other. For example, in kingdoms in pre-colonial sub-Saharan Africa, such as the Kongo, the Kuba, and the Lunda, the center struggled to control its periphery. Traditional leaders, often called chiefs, governed these peripheral regions and connected adjacent communities through kinship ties. These outlying territories could easily escape central control.[27] Disjunctures between state elites and social groups and internal divisions among elites are the defining features of the ring network.

The three forms of elite social terrains are archetypes; the reality is messier. The vertical dimension of elite social terrains (geographic dispersion vs.

concentration) conditions elite preferences regarding the ideal level of state strength, while the horizontal dimension (cohesion vs. division) conditions how the state is organized. Each ideal type produces a steady-state equilibrium of state-society relations; they vary in their durability and are powerful in describing and explaining a wide range of outcomes in China and beyond.[28]

China's state development, for example, started as a star network, transitioned to a bowtie network, and ended as a ring network. The star network created a strong state but short-lived rulers. The bowtie network contributed to the country's exceptional durability but also undermined state strength. The ring network preluded state collapse.

Below I discuss how elite social terrains help us understand changes in state strength and form over the long run.

1.4.2   State Strength

Elite social terrain provides micro-founded insights about elite preferences regarding the ideal level of state strength. Each central elite is mainly interested in providing services to the social groups to which he or she is connected and not necessarily to the whole nation. Central elites can use a variety of governance structures to service their connected social groups. The most popular such structures are public-order institutions, such as the state, and private-order institutions, such as clans, tribes, or ethnic groups.[29] These structures provide services such as protection and justice, including defense against external and internal violence, insurance against weather shocks, justice in dispute resolution, and social policies that protect people from risks. Central elites embedded in the star network have the strongest incentive to use the state to provide these types of services to their connected social groups.

Two considerations drive elites' choices. The first is economic. In the star network, elites are connected to multiple social groups that are geographically dispersed. It is more efficient to rely on the central state to provide services because it enjoys economies of scale and scope.[30] With a strong central state, it is much cheaper to cover an additional territory in which a connected social group is located than to rely on the social group to provide its own security and justice. In the bowtie network, where elites only need to service a few groups in a relatively small area, private service provision is more efficient because the marginal costs of funding private institutions to service a small area are lower than the taxes that elites would be required to pay to support the central state. The ring network represents an extreme case in which central elites are not connected to any social groups; they have lost control over society and cannot mobilize the necessary social resources to strengthen the state. Therefore, they choose to allow social groups to provide services through their own tribes, clans, or ethnic groups.

The second consideration that motivates elites' decisions is social. Tribes, clans, and ethnic groups that are concentrated in a certain locality often care a lot about their local interests but little about national matters. They oppose paying taxes to the central state, because the state will provide services to all parts of the country, and these specific social groups would end up paying for services to others. These geographically defined social groups hence create regional cleavages that produce distributive conflicts. Nevertheless, if central elites can connect multiple social groups that are geographically dispersed, as in a star network, this social network will cross-cut regional cleavages.[31] These cross-cutting cleavages incentivize the central elites to aggregate the interests of multiple localities and groups and scale them up to the national level. The star network therefore transcends local interests and fosters a broad state-building coalition.[32]

In the bowtie network, however, each central elite represents only a small number of localities. Social networks in this case *reinforce* existing regional cleavages. The central government then becomes an arena in which these elites compete to attract national resources to serve local interests.[33] Elites in the bowtie network would oppose strengthening the central state because such policies would divert resources from social groups to the state and weaken their local power bases. For example, during an eleventh-century state-strengthening reform in China's Northern Song Dynasty, opponents worried that creating a national standing army would threaten the power of "well-established local families," which controlled local private militias, and leave local communities powerless.[34] The ring network is an extreme case in which central elites pay no attention to regional cleavages and have no way of uniting different groups.

The elites embedded in these different types of networks follow patterns that are similar to those of what Mancur Olson describes as encompassing versus narrow interest groups.[35] Elites in the star network have an encompassing interest as they represent multiple groups in multiple locations. Cross-pressures arising from encompassing networks incentivize elites to form a coalition pursuing national, rather than sectarian, goals. Elites embedded in the star network prefer to strike a Hobbesian deal with the ruler to pay taxes in exchange for centralized protection. The central state, represented by the ruler, provides an institutional commitment device between the elites and their groups. Supporting state building allows the elites to credibly commit to protecting their groups because it is harder for the central state, compared with private-order institutions, to exclude specific group members as beneficiaries from a distance. Those in the bowtie and ring networks become a narrow interest group.

In sum, the vertical dimension of elite social terrain that characterizes how central elites connect social groups conditions elite preferences regarding the ideal level of state strength. Their incentive to strengthen the central state weakens as we move from a star network to a ring network.

1.4.3   State Form

Network structures that characterize elite social terrains are also a principal factor that shapes how the state is structured and the development of state institutions. Elite social terrain shapes state institutions through two relationships: (1) between the ruler and the ruling elite and (2) between the state and society. This section discusses each relationship in turn.

RULER AND ELITES

In the relationship between *the ruler and the ruling elite*, the star network represents a centralized and coherent elite that can constrain the ruler in two ways. First, the elites are embedded in a centralized social structure in which they can use their cross-cutting ties to mobilize a wide range of social forces across regions. Second, the cooperative relations among the central elites in the star network make them a coherent group, which helps overcome collective action and coordination problems if they decide to rebel against the ruler. In this scenario, the ruler is only *first among equals* and is thus more likely to share power with the elites.

In the bowtie network, because central elites have regional bases of power, they can mobilize some (regionally based) social groups against the ruler. But it is easier for the ruler to quell challenges that are concentrated in certain areas. In addition, the lack of a dense network among the central elites provides what the sociologist Ronald Burt calls "structural holes" that allow the ruler to divide and conquer.[36] As Burt argues, if parts of a community are not directly connected with one another (i.e., structural holes separate them), an outside player can gain an advantage by playing the clusters against each other.

In this scenario, the ruler is more likely to establish absolute rule to *dominate* the elites.

Central elites' bargaining power is the weakest in the ring network since they cannot find allies within the society or coordinate among themselves against the ruler. The ruler's absolute power therefore reaches its zenith in this scenario.

STATE AND SOCIETY

In the relationship between *the state and society*, the star network represents the *direct rule of the state*. The ruler includes representatives from local groups in the national government in part to collect information about local societies and economies. With a centralized social network, the ruler can rely on central elites to collect revenue for the state and to mobilize the population. In this scenario, the state often takes a leading role in initiating and funding public goods provision, the most important of which include security, justice, and public works.

The bowtie network represents the *state-society partnership*. Central elites, embedded in local social relations, often compete for national resources to channel to their own localities. They prefer to allocate national resources and to outsource public goods provision to their own social groups. Connected social groups can seek rents from these projects and enhance their status within the local community. The result is often a partnership between the state and society in which the state delegates part of its functions, such as organizing defense and public works, to social groups. Social groups in this case would still depend on the state for resources and legitimacy, but would enjoy considerable autonomy.

The ring network is an example of what the historian Prasenjit Duara terms "state involution,"[37] in which the formal state depends on society to carry out many of its functions, but loses control over it. As the state descends further into involution, social groups replace it as the leader in local defense and public goods provision and threaten the state's monopoly over violence.

1.4.4   *Three Equilibria*

I argue that each of the three ideal types of elite social networks creates its own corresponding *steady-state equilibrium*.[38] For each network type, both sets of actors—the ruler and central elites—find it in their best interest, *absent an exogenous shock*, to maintain the current steady state.

The ruler faces a fundamental trade-off that I term *the sovereign's dilemma*: state strength versus personal survival. The ruler seeks to maximize state strength, which can best be achieved by facilitating the creation of a star network. But he also seeks to maintain his grip on power, which is easier if elites are fragmented, for instance if they are disconnected as in the bowtie or ring network. Depending on initial conditions, the ruler attempts either to strengthen the state or to maximize personal survival, but not both. A coherent elite helps the ruler strengthen the state, but threatens his survival.

Exogenous shocks, however, sometimes allow the ruler to reshape the elite social terrain to escape from the equilibrium of low survival to one of high survival, at the expense of state strength. The ruler survives by fragmenting the elite. A fragmented elite weakens the state, but must overcome insurmountable collective action and coordination problems to revolt against the ruler. Hence a fragmented elite structure undermines state infrastructural power, and contributes to despotic power.

In each type of network, the objective of the central elites is to economize the provision of services for their social groups. In the *star network*, elites seek to mobilize society to strengthen the state by, for example, contributing monetary and human resources to it. A strong central state provides efficient national coverage to protect their social groups if elites are linked in this way. In the *bowtie network*, however, elites prefer to delegate state functions to their social groups, which can provide the services privately at a much lower price than paying taxes to the national government. But the society in the bowtie network still has an interest in keeping the state "afloat." A state with a moderate level of capacity can help protect society from existential threats, such as external invasions and large-scale natural disasters. In the *ring network*, the central elites can no longer use their ties to mobilize social groups, which are independent from the state. Rather than contributing resources to keep the state alive, social groups prefer to retain resources for themselves and start to play a leading role in local defense and public goods provision. The state in this equilibrium has minimal power to control society and is on the verge of collapse.

Table 1.1 summarizes the implications of the three equilibria for state strength and form.

The star network creates an equilibrium, which I label "State Strengthening under Oligarchy." In this equilibrium, the ruler and the central elites jointly control the state in an oligarchy in which the ruler is first among equals. The elites can credibly threaten a revolt, which prevents the ruler from seizing absolute power. The elites in this equilibrium prefer a strong state because

TABLE 1.1: Three Steady-State Equilibria

| | | | State Form | | |
| | | State | Ruler vs. | State vs. | |
Network	Equilibrium	Strength	Elite	Society	Example
Star	State Strengthening under Oligarchy	High	First among equals	Direct rule	Medieval China; England after the Norman Conquest
Bowtie	State Maintaining under Partnership	Moderate	Dominant	Partnership	Late imperial China before the Opium Wars; feudal France; sub-Saharan Africa and Latin America under colonial rule; the Islamic world during the Classical Period; the Ottoman Empire
Ring	State Weakening under Warlordism	Low	Dominant	State involution	Imperial China after the Opium Wars; sub-Saharan Africa in the pre-colonial era; part of the Middle East in the post-colonial era

they want to exploit its scale economies to offer services to their respective social groups. Private-order institutions are not desirable for the central elites in this case, because it is redundant for each geographic region to set up its own local defense and provide its own public goods. This equilibrium best characterizes medieval China during the Tang era (618–907) and England after the Norman Conquest (1066).

I call the bowtie network equilibrium "State Maintaining under Partnership." In this equilibrium, the ruler uses a divide-and-conquer strategy to dominate a fragmented central elite and establish absolute power over this group. The elites choose not to threaten the ruler's power because such collective action and coordination are too costly; they prefer a moderately strong state that can protect their social groups from existential threats. But they do not want the state to be strong enough to extract all resources from the society, since this would undermine their social groups' efforts to establish private-order institutions. The ruler accepts this moderate level of state authority because further strengthening the state would require a more coherent elite, which would threaten his personal power and survival. The state outsources some of its functions to social groups, which partner with the state to provide public goods.

This equilibrium best describes late imperial China before the Opium Wars (tenth to mid-nineteenth century), feudal France (tenth to mid-fifteenth century), sub-Saharan Africa and Latin America under colonial rule (eighteenth to early twentieth century), the Islamic world during the Classical Period (seventh to twelfth century), and the Ottoman Empire (fourteenth to early twentieth century). In these cases, a central state assembled different social groups and relied on them to rule. These social groups included lineage organizations (in imperial China), feudal lords (in France), regional elites (in Latin America), and tribes or ethnic groups (in sub-Saharan Africa and the Middle East).[39]

In the ring network's equilibrium, "State Weakening under Warlordism," the state, ruled by an autocratic leader, is too weak to control the society. Social groups therefore establish private-order institutions to provide security and justice. The state loses its monopoly over violence and is on the verge of collapse. This equilibrium approximates imperial China after the Opium Wars (mid-nineteenth to early twentieth century), sub-Saharan Africa in the pre-colonial era (pre-nineteenth century), and part of the Middle East in the post-colonial era (mid-twentieth century).[40]

1.4.5   Social Terrains Make the State, and Vice Versa

The three equilibria are steady, and each steady state represents a unique equilibrium during a certain historical period. Exogenous shocks, however, can disrupt an existing equilibrium and provide opportunities for the state to reshape the society. I assume the ruler has a "first-mover advantage," which he can exploit to restructure the elite social terrain in his favor to ensure his own survival—even if this involves creating an elite network that jeopardizes state strength.

A polity can suffer from various exogenous shocks. Over the long term, the most important shock to dynasties is climate change, which leads to large-scale conflict. Here, I focus on two sorts of conflicts: external conflicts with foreign rivals, and internal conflicts during mass rebellions. Warm weather, for example, improves crop yields, making the territory a more attractive target for external attack. Greater yields should in turn reduce the likelihood of famine, making internal rebellion less appealing. Cold weather, by contrast, should decrease the odds of external attack by making the territory less valuable. It should also increase the threat of internal rebellion, since famine is more likely.

In the next chapter I demonstrate empirically that foreign rivals and the masses respond to exogenous climate shocks. When most external threats originate from the steppe nomads, and peasants live below the subsistence level, a climate shock can exogenously increase the odds of violence.

The violence induced by climate shocks provides an opportunity for the ruler to reshape the elite social terrain. Large-scale violence can destroy or weaken the old elite. If the old elite threatens the ruler's survival, he may take advantage of this power vacuum to recruit a new elite that is more fragmented and less threatening. A fragmented elite, however, will lead to declining state strength and a weak state. If large-scale violence erupts when the state is weak, the ruler may choose to relinquish the monopoly over violence and delegate the country's defense to social groups to quell rebellions. Such delegation, however, will empower society and create autonomous social groups that are independent from the state.

Social terrains make the state, and the state makes social terrains. While elite social terrains generate certain state development outcomes, the state led by the ruler can exploit exogenous shocks to reshape elite social terrains, facilitating transitions of equilibria.

A central theme of this book is that the Chinese ruler's pursuit of power and survival by reshaping the elite social terrain so that he could divide and conquer the elites created a great paradox in Chinese history: imperial rule endured, but the imperial state lost strength.

1.4.6   Durability of Equilibria

The three equilibria vary in their durability because some elite social terrains are more vulnerable to exogenous shocks than others. The star network is generally durable because the ruler can mobilize social resources through the central elites to cope with any challenges. But it is vulnerable to a particular type of violence: attacks on the center. If the central nodes are removed in a star network, the whole network will collapse. This type of network is prone to attacks on the center because centralized politics also funnels contentious politics to the center. When power comes from the center rather than the local level, people are more likely to direct their grievances toward the central government. This is consistent with a well-established relationship between political opportunity structure and contentious politics. Charles Tilly, for example, argues that the centralization and strengthening of the

State Strengthening under Oligarchy	State Maintaining under Partnership	State Weakening under Warlordism
7th to 10th Century	10th to Mid-19th Century	Mid-19th to Early 20th Century
Star Network	Bowtie Network	Ring Network
High State Strength	Medium State Strength	Low State Strength
Low Ruler Survival	High Ruler Survival	High Ruler Survival
Direct Rule	State-Society Partnership	State Involution
Medium Durability	High Durability	Low Durability

FIGURE 1.2: Summary of Argument

British state between 1758 and 1834 disseminated mass popular politics on "a national scale."[41] Daron Acemoglu and James Robinson term this the "mobilization effect of state centralization" in which a centralized state attracts mobilization against the center.[42] The star network, therefore, produces a medium degree of durability, and is vulnerable to violence targeting the capital.

The bowtie is the most durable network structure. Because politics is compartmented, internal conflicts tend to be geographically concentrated. Rebel groups find it difficult to coordinate cross-regionally due to a lack of lateral ties. Even if an attack destroyed part of the network, such as half of the "bowtie," the other half would remain intact. A foreign enemy may leverage domestic factionalism and play one bloc against another. This strategy, however, rarely works. A foreign ruler does not have the reputation established in repeated interactions to credibly commit *ex ante* to giving the defected faction the same power it currently enjoys. The bowtie network, therefore, produces a high degree of durability.

In the ring network, internal rebellions led by social groups are more likely to succeed in overthrowing the state, because the state cannot leverage state–society linkages to quell such rebellions or mobilize one part of the society against another. External attacks are also more likely to destroy a ring network for the same reason that the state is unable to mobilize sufficient resources for national defense. Although the ruler in a ring network is safe from elite coups because the central elites are disconnected and hence find it difficult to cooperate, a state built on a ring network is vulnerable to both internal mass rebellions and external invasions. The ring network, therefore, has low durability.

I summarize my arguments in figure 1.2. While the change from a star network to a bowtie network marks an important transition, the shift to a ring network is often a prelude to state collapse. The crucial difference therefore lies between the star and bowtie networks on the one hand, where state elites are socially embedded, and the ring network on the other hand, where state elites are disconnected from society.

1.5   Intellectual Lineages

My argument is built on a long tradition of social science literature, but also advances it in significant ways. Modern social scientific studies of the state have followed three broadly defined traditions. The first, represented in pluralist, structural-functionalist and neo-Marxist approaches, takes a *society-centered* perspective and views the state as an arena in which different social groups and classes vie for power. The second tradition, best reflected in the movement to "bring the state back in," takes a *state-centered* perspective and treats the state as an actor that is autonomous from society. The third tradition takes a *state-in-society* approach and views the state and society as competing forces. I discuss each tradition in turn and elaborate on how I advance their study.

1.5.1   Society-Centered Theories

After World War II, modern social sciences began shifting away from legal-formalist studies of constitutional principles in favor of more empirically focused investigations of human behavior. Society-centered approaches to explaining politics and government activities dominated the study of political science and sociology in the United States during this behavioral revolution in the 1950s and 1960s. These approaches treated government as an arena in which social and economic groups compete for power and influence. Scholars of this generation treated government decisions and public policies as the major outcomes of interest. Accordingly, they examined who participates in decision-making processes, how their "inputs" are translated into government "outputs," and whose interests the government represents. Society-centered theories fall into three broad categories—pluralist, structural-functionalist, and neo-Marxist.

The pluralist tradition offers a group interpretation of politics. In a seminal contribution, Robert Dahl investigated how different groups participated in and influenced decision-making; he argued that power was dispersed among a number of groups that competed with each other.[43] In a theoretical synthesis,

David Truman provided a framework on how interest groups make certain claims upon both other groups and government institutions. He explicitly dismissed the idea that the state has a single, unified interest and viewed individuals belonging to the same groups as the fundamental actors in politics.[44]

The structural-functionalist tradition employs a more macro-level analysis. Deeply rooted in sociology, adherents of this family of theories view society as a complex system that resembles a "body"; the various parts are like "organs." Institutions exist to perform certain functions, and government institutions are parts of the system: each unit has its own role. Social and economic groups provide their inputs to the government, which then produces outputs.[45]

Lastly, neo-Marxists view the state as an instrument of class domination. As the mode of production changes, the composition of (and power relations between) classes in a society evolve, and the dominant class uses the state apparatus to dominate the other classes and preserve its favored mode of production. Perry Anderson, in a grand tour of European historical development, argues that landed elites created and used the "absolutist state" to exploit the peasantry.[46] Applying a class-centered perspective to the international arena, Immanuel Wallerstein developed World Systems Theory, in which "core" countries are dominant capitalist countries that exploit "peripheral" countries for their labor and raw materials. Industries in peripheral countries remain underdeveloped because they are dependent on core countries for capital.[47]

In all three theoretical perspectives, the state is not an independent actor: it is either an arena in which social groups compete (according to the pluralists), an organ that translates inputs into outputs (according to the structural-functionalists), or an instrument of class struggle that reflects the interests of the dominant class (according to the neo-Marxists).

1.5.2   State-Centered Theories

As the postwar era unfolded, society-centered perspectives increasingly failed to explain the social and political changes emerging in both developed and developing countries. Many developed countries continued pursuing their wartime Keynesian approach to macroeconomic management after the war ended.[48] They grew more independent of particular social influences and continued to increase public expenditures as the state became a main provider of welfare and services for multiple social classes.[49] Waves of independence produced scores of new states in Africa, Asia, Latin America, and the Middle East, which strived to shed their colonial pasts and build their own nation states.

Developed countries in Europe and North America began to face stiff competition from newly industrialized countries in East Asia, which relied on a "developmental state" to steer their economies.[50]

In 1983, the New York–based Social Science Research Council established the Research Planning Committee on States and Social Structures. This committee was given the responsibility to "foster sustained collaborations among scholars from several disciplines who share in the growing interest in states as actors and as institutional structures."[51] Its first publication was a field-changing book—*Bringing the State Back In.*

In the book's preface, Peter Evans, Dietrich Rueschemeyer, and Theda Skocpol state that "Until recently, dominant theoretical paradigms in the comparative social sciences did not highlight states as organizational structures or as potentially autonomous actors."[52] In the introduction, Skocpol contends that states formulate and pursue goals that do not simply reflect the demands of social groups, classes, or society. States achieve autonomy when "organizationally coherent collectives of state officials" that are "insulated from ties to currently dominant socioeconomic interests" launch distinctive state strategies.[53]

Once the state can be modeled as a coherent collective of officials, researchers can analyze it as a unitary actor. The rewards of such an approach are enormous. Otto Hintze put forward one of the most influential arguments in this camp, which Charles Tilly later popularized—the notion that interstate competition drives state building. It has since become a widely held belief that external war incentivizes state elites to develop a centralized fiscal system, a modern bureaucracy, and a standing army.[54] As Tilly succinctly summarized, "war made the state."[55]

This bellicist argument has set the agenda; much of the follow-up work has centered on how war (or its absence) has affected state building beyond Europe. For instance, scholars have applied the bellicist theory in Asia and indirectly proved Tilly's argument using negative cases in sub-Saharan Africa and Latin America, where there were no (large-scale) wars and no state building.[56] Over time, much of the scholarship in this camp has evolved from a state-centered structuralist to a historical-institutionalist approach that emphasizes the importance of critical junctures and path dependence.[57]

Another branch of this state-centered camp advocates an institutional approach that takes a rational choice perspective and focuses on state elites and their bargaining power vis-à-vis the ruler. Margaret Levi labeled the impulse behind this approach "bringing people back into the state."[58] For rationalist theorists, the agents who constitute the state, rather than the state itself, are the actors. This agency focus differentiates the rationalists from the structuralists, who concentrate on macro-level factors such as population, geography, and geopolitics.

In an influential study, Douglass North and Barry Weingast argue that England's Glorious Revolution established parliamentary sovereignty, which cemented the Crown's commitment to the elites, whose financial support was urgently needed to finance wars.[59] Robert Bates and Donald Lien examine how asset specificity conditions elites' bargaining power; they show that while taxing commerce produced early democracy in England, taxing land produced absolutism in France.[60] For Margaret Levi, the ruler is a revenue maximizer, but is constrained by bargaining power, transaction costs, and their time horizon.[61]

Bellicist and institutional accounts have both analyzed state building independently of society. Since state elites are autonomous from society, interstate relations and within-state bargaining ultimately determine how the state is organized—and how strong it is.

1.5.3   State-in-Society Approach

During the heyday of the state-centered approach, another group of scholars that studied the newly independent countries in Africa, Asia, Latin America, and the Middle East observed that these states often struggled to establish authority in competition with strong social forces. These social forces— tribes, clans, or chiefdoms—were either a historical legacy or recently empowered by colonial regimes. Although these countries had established central governments with well-staffed bureaucracies in the capital, the centers often found it difficult to project their power to remote corners, where traditional authorities still dominated people's lives.

In a seminal book, *Strong Societies and Weak States*, Joel Migdal argues that many Third World states struggle to become the organization in society that effectively establishes the rules of behavior. According to his model of state-society relations, a state does not exist in isolation: it coexists with other social organizations, all of which strive to exercise social control by using a variety of sanctions, rewards, and symbols to induce people to follow certain rules or norms. These social organizations range from small family and neighborhood groups to mammoth foreign-owned companies. Strong states emerge only when "massive dislocation" weakens the social organizations.[62]

The state-society approach has generated a fruitful literature. One strand of this literature examines how social forces constrain state power. Vivienne Shue argues that the Chinese imperial state's "reach" was limited by the rural "honeycomb" structure of gentry families.[63] Another strand of the literature investigates how incorporating social forces into the state shapes its goals and capacities. Elizabeth Perry, for example, shows that the Chinese state incorporated the working class into its leadership during the communist revolution, which influenced the state's goals after the founding of the People's Republic.[64] Joel Migdal, Atul Kohli, and Vivienne Shue further developed the state-in-society approach in an edited volume that showcases the approach's ability to explain a wide variety of phenomena in the developing world.[65] Daron Acemoglu and James Robinson recently built on the traditional state-society approach to model the state and society as competing actors that produce different scenarios in which the state becomes despotic, shackled, or absent.[66]

1.5.4   Situating the Argument

My framework combines insights from state-society scholars who emphasize interactions between the two types of actors, borrows the pluralists' notion that society consists of competing groups, and builds on the rational choice approach's agency-centered microfoundations. However, my argument also diverges from traditional works in some respects. At the conceptual level, Max Weber defines the state in terms of its monopoly over violence.[67] I consider a state's monopoly to be a *choice* rather than a given: a state becomes a monopoly when both political elites and social groups choose it to be *the* provider of security. In this sense, Weber's definition of the state is only an ideal type. The boundary between the state and society is often blurred in practice; the state may partner with society to provide protection and justice. Similarly, in contrast to traditional state-society scholarship, I do not think society is necessarily in competition with the state.[68] A more useful conceptualization, following the sociologist Georg Simmel, is to view society as "a web of patterned interactions" that highlights its relational features, including its linkages to the state.[69]

I build on Margaret Levi's notion that the ruler is a revenue maximizer, but add that he or she is also a *survival* maximizer.[70] Moreover, in non-European states that lack representative institutions, these two objectives compete against each other because they require different elite structures.

This capacity-survival trade-off—the sovereign's dilemma—echoes what Barbara Geddes calls the "politician's dilemma," in which strengthening the state jeopardizes the ruler's chances of survival.[71]

My focus on violence as a driving force for transitions in state development is inspired by the bellicist approach, which Otto Hintze and Charles Tilly first proposed and has been more recently articulated by Dan Slater and Douglass North, John Wallis, and Barry Weingast.[72] Robert Bates' discussion of the tension between prosperity and violence in stateless societies and Avner Greif's analysis of private-order institutions are especially helpful for thinking about the differences between state- and society-provided order.[73] However, I depart from this violence-centered literature in at least one crucial way. While previous works have found a straightforward association between war (external or internal) and state building,[74] I argue that how conflict shapes state development depends on *prior state-society linkages*. War may either strengthen or weaken the state, depending on the country's elite social terrain.

As I describe it, China's path toward state development is fundamentally different from that of Europe. Unlike Europe, where political order and economic development evolved at the same time, durability fostered economic and fiscal stagnation in China. My depiction thus challenges the linear progression of human societies found in various versions of classic modernization theory, which tend to be based on European case studies. Classic modernization theorists tend to believe all good things go together.[75] My discussion of the different paths of state development resonates with Perry Anderson's and Barrington Moore's observation that there are different paths of political development.[76] While Anderson and Moore emphasize the importance of social class, however, I focus on state-society linkages. I echo Samuel Huntington in pointing out that if there are no strong institutions, political order and economic success are often incompatible goals.[77]

My account of China's alternative patterns of state development parallels a large literature that examines the "Great Divergence" in economic development between China and Europe. Several important works seek to explain why Western Europe took off economically by the mid-eighteenth century, while China did not. These studies advance several explanations of why this may be, citing the roles of colonial exploitation and natural resources,[78] Atlantic trade,[79] domestic price conditions,[80] generalized morality,[81] a culture of scientific inquiry,[82] political fragmentation,[83] sovereign scope,[84] and mercantilist policy.[85] My argument does not explain China's economic development *per se*. But my exploration of its long-term state development, especially its declining fiscal capacity in the late imperial era, casts new light on China's economic downturn in the premodern era. My interpretation joins the spirit of the "California school," as articulated especially by Kenneth Pomeranz and Bin Wong, by pointing out that scholarship should branch out from Euro-centric perspectives and view China not as an aberration, but as an alternative—maybe a leading alternative—to the rise of Europe. However, while scholars in this school generally argue that China's economy declined in the eighteenth century,[86] some recent estimates show that the stagnation occurred much earlier—in the fourteenth to fifteenth centuries.[87] My finding that China's state weakened during the Song-Ming times is consistent with this new evidence.

The state-society relations literature is the most relevant to my approach.[88] My proposed framework builds on the contention of these studies that state-society interactions are a fundamental driving force of political development. But rather than treating the state as a unitary actor (e.g., the ruler), I disaggregate its elements and emphasize ruler-elite relationships within the state. Departing from the assumption that the state and society are separate and competing entities, I emphasize the blurred boundary between the two and analyze how state-society linkages through elite networks drive state development.[89] While state-society scholars believe that traditional social organizations, such as kinship-based institutions, undermine state building, I argue that kinship networks, when geographically dispersed, align the incentives of self-interested elites in favor of state building. Therefore, the relationship between social forces and the state depends on the type of elite social terrain.

1.6   How Is It Done?

State development is a slow-moving process that requires an in-depth examination of history. This book starts with the seventh century—a critical era in which the Chinese state consolidated as a centralized, bureaucratic entity. This was roughly the same time that Europe started to fragment after the fall of the Roman Empire. I did not go back earlier, for example to the Qin and Han times, because we know less about the politics of these earlier dynasties beyond the official histories. The Chinese state was also in the early process of formation and did not establish a political equilibrium of internal spatial integration until the early seventh century.

I end in 1911, which marks the fall of the dynastic state, in order to maintain a temporal distance from the events and people I study. Examining a series of events that ended over a century ago allows me to disregard unnecessary details, place events and people within a longer time frame, and uncover previously undetectable patterns. As Hegel's maxim goes, "The owl of Minerva begins its flight only with the onset of dusk."[90]

My analysis is based on two methods. First, I use what Robert Bates, Avner Greif, Margaret Levi, Jean-Laurent Rosenthal, and Barry Weingast call "analytic narratives" to provide an overarching description of the development of the Chinese state over a millennium.[91] I rely heavily on historians' work and my own reading of the archival materials. Second, I have collected and compiled a large amount of original data for this book—most notably a dataset of all Chinese emperors, a longitudinal dataset of taxation from the seventh to the early twentieth century, a large geo-referenced dataset of over seven thousand military conflicts, a large geo-referenced dataset of over fifty thousand genealogical records compiled from 1005 to 2007 CE, and various biographical datasets that include information on major central elites and their marriage networks from the seventh century. Upon publication of this book, I will make all the data publicly available to facilitate future research.[92]

I acknowledge that historical data are imperfect for many reasons. For example, some individuals and events were better documented than others; some documents have survived, while many were destroyed during wars; and even among those that have survived, some are better digitized than others. Mindful of these biases, I triangulate different sources of data and interpret my findings with caution. More importantly, I am transparent about how these biases could influence my conclusions. I use modern econometrics, with attention to causal inference, to analyze these data. I present the analyses and results in an accessible way in the main text, and relegate all technical details to the appendix.

While the historical discussions will provide a continuous narrative, the empirical analysis will focus on key moments of state making—such as fiscal reforms, military restructuring, and internal rebellions—to provide an in-depth examination of critical historical episodes.

1.7   A Roadmap

The book comprises nine chapters, which proceed chronologically. Together they probe the social foundations of China's long-term state development.

Chapter 2 provides an overview of China's state development. I draw attention to an important puzzle in Chinese history that motivates the rest of the book: short-lived emperors often ruled a strong state; long-lasting emperors governed with a weak state. Using analytic narratives and descriptive statistics, I present a bird's-eye view of China's fiscal and military institutions, external and internal warfare, elite structure, ruler duration, and development of social organizations over a millennium. My descriptive analysis demonstrates that the Chinese elites transitioned from an encompassing interest group with geographically dispersed social relations to a narrow interest group with localized social relations. The fragmentation and localization of elite social networks contributed to long durations of Chinese emperors but also weakened the imperial state.

Chapter 3 examines the State Strengthening under Oligarchy era during the Tang Dynasty (618–907). Tang China was governed by a national elite connected by dense marriage ties, which spread out across the entire country. This national social network incentivized the Tang elites to build a strong central state. The geography of the elites' social network facilitated China's rise as a superpower in the early medieval era. The empirical analysis in this chapter focuses on one of the most important fiscal reforms in historical China— the Two-Tax Reform—which influenced the structure of taxation over the next millennium. I conduct a social network analysis of 141 major politicians from the mid-Tang era (779–805), and show that the elites during this period formed a star-type network with a coherent center and ties reaching out to the periphery. This centralized elite network helps explain both the success of the fiscal reform and the short duration of Tang emperors. The star network also made the Tang state vulnerable to violent attacks on the center, which is the focus of the next chapter.

Chapter 4 studies the transition from the first to the second eras by focusing on the elite transformation from the Tang to the Song dynasties (960–1279). While Tang China was governed by a hereditary aristocracy connected by cross-regional marriage ties, a mass rebellion in the late ninth century induced by climate changes occupied the capitals and destroyed the aristocracy. The early Song emperors exploited this power vacuum and expanded the competitive civil service exam to prevent the formation of a new aristocracy, which led to the emergence of a new class of elites—the gentry. Using an original biographical dataset of over three thousand major politicians from throughout the Tang and Song eras, I show that elite social networks became increasingly local and fragmented. As a result, the post-Song elites created a bowtie-style network. This elite transformation helps explain the change in ruler survival: Chinese emperors since the Song era became more secure and less threatened by the elites. The transformation also marked the beginning of a new era in Chinese political development in which the state partnered with society to govern, creating a durable equilibrium in the next millennium.

Chapter 5 discusses the early stage of the second era, State Maintaining under Partnership, by examining politics during the Song Dynasty (960– 1276). I show that the Song emperors took advantage of a fragmented elite to concentrate monarchical power in the bureaucracy, which was staffed by the newly expanded civil service examination system. The empirical analysis focuses on an unsuccessful state-strengthening reform in the Northern Song Dynasty. In 1069, a Song politician—Wang Anshi—implemented a series of reforms to strengthen the state's fiscal and military capacities. Politicians fiercely opposed these reforms and orchestrated their abolishment in 1085. I use tomb epitaphs to construct the kinship networks of 137 major politicians to analyze why some supported the reform while others opposed it. I show that the politicians who were recruited through the civil service exam were embedded in local marriage networks, which incentivized them to oppose the reforms in order to protect their local interests. By contrast, the politicians who inherited their positions were embedded in a national elite network, which incentivized them to support the reforms. The failure of state activism led to the development of social organizations, especially the lineages, which collaborated (and sometimes competed) with the state in local governance.

Chapter 6 investigates the consolidation of the second era during the Ming Dynasty (1368–1644). The founding Ming emperor fundamentally reorganized the bureaucracy to finally establish an absolute monarchy. Throughout the Ming era, the fragmented and locally oriented elites sought to maintain the status quo: they wanted to keep the state minimally functional, and opposed any attempts to strengthen it. Meanwhile, they built lineage organizations to consolidate their local power bases and negotiated with the state to protect their local interests. The empirical analysis in this chapter examines a critical fiscal reform—the Single Whip—which provides a useful lens through which to analyze the behavior of the Ming elites. I show that politicians with localized kinship networks—the majority of Ming-era politicians—represented local interests and influenced central policy making to protect their kin's economic interests and autonomy. The empirical analysis draws on an original biographical dataset of 503 major officials under Emperor Shenzong (1572–1620) and historical data on local implementation of the Single Whip reform. I demonstrate that the more national-level politicians a prefecture produced, the slower its adoption of the Single Whip, if it was adopted at all.

Chapter 7 assesses another aspect of State Maintaining under Partnership by analyzing how private-order institutions emerged in the late imperial era. I first show that Chinese elites invented private-order institutions—lineage organizations and lineage coalitions—which helped them overcome commitment problems in a weak state in three ways. First, by worshipping a common ancestor, lineage organizations spiritually bonded people who belonged to the same descent group. Second, by compiling genealogy books, lineage organizations could reward well-behaved members and exclude free-riders. Third, through intermarriages, lineage coalitions helped exchange "mutual hostages" between lineages. I then support these arguments using an original dataset of historical conflicts, civil service examination success, and lineage organizations identified from genealogical records. The development of private-order institutions and their partnership with the state help explain China's durable political order in the late imperial era, despite a weakening state and frequent challenges from foreign invaders and internal rebels.

Chapter 8 examines the transition from the second era to the third—State Weakening under Warlordism. The early Qing period was characterized by an unusually high degree of centralization for late imperial China. Emperors during the High Qing era in the eighteenth century enforced policies to diminish the power and privileges of the gentry, simplified tax collection by merging land and labor taxes, and delineated central and local revenues. The early Qing emperors were state builders, but they strengthened the central state by circumventing the civil bureaucracy. With the deterioration of the Eight Banners (a state army) and the Manchus' increasing corruption and ineptitude, however, later Qing rulers increasingly relied on the civil bureaucracy, which was staffed by members of the narrowly interested gentry. The Qing Dynasty could not escape the inevitable fate of fiscal and military decline that its predecessors had experienced. The Western intrusion in the mid-nineteenth century led to an unprecedented financial crisis in the Qing Dynasty. The effects of cold weather exacerbated by droughts triggered the Taiping Rebellion. Qing emperors, focused on ensuring their personal survival, delegated local defense to gentry leaders. Using data on the locations of rebellions and lineage activities, I show that internal rebellions significantly increased lineage collective action and tilted the balance of power from the imperial state to local society. The abolishment of the civil service examinations further cut the ties between the state and society, and created a state that was disconnected from an increasingly autonomous society. I show that the counties that experienced more post-rebellion lineage collective action were more likely to declare independence from the Qing government in 1911.

Chapter 9 concludes by discussing the broader implications of the findings for our understanding of the developing world. My China-based theory resonates with state-building experiences observed in Africa, Latin America, and the Middle East, and generates an important lesson: state weakness is a social problem that cannot be resolved with a bureaucratic solution. State-building projects should extend beyond a narrow focus on reforming the bureaucracy to include efforts to make incentives related to the social structure compatible with a strong state. China's imperial state development and its legacies also help us understand the challenges of modern state building. One of the secrets to the Communist Party's success in state building was the transformation of Chinese society through a social revolution, which paved the way for the formation of a modern Chinese state.

2

China's State Development over the Last Two Millennia

2.1 Patterns Show Themselves at a Distance

China's state has developed over the last two millennia in a fundamentally different way from European states. While European rulers relied on representative institutions to stay in power and build an effective state at the same time, Chinese rulers faced a trade-off between personal survival and state strength. This chapter provides an overview of its distinctive path. I save stories of sage rulers, loyal servants, and brave warriors for other chapters. Here I take a step back to highlight broad historical patterns.

I characterize Chinese state development from the early seventh to the early twentieth century as comprising three phases: (1) State Strengthening under Oligarchy, (2) State Maintaining under Partnership, and (3) State Weakening under Warlordism.

The first phase, State Strengthening under Oligarchy, best describes the Tang era (618–907). During the Tang times, an aristocracy ruled China. This aristocracy was a semi-hereditary caste that consisted of several hundred noble clans. These families formed a close-knit marriage network in which status endogamy persisted for centuries. Through marriage alliances made in the capitals, Changan and Luoyang, the aristocracy connected different corners of the empire. The social terrain that formed among the Tang aristocratic families hence resembled a star network: a coherent center connected to the periphery. The Tang aristocrats were dedicated to strengthening the state to protect their kinship networks, which spanned the entire empire. They nearly unanimously implemented a historic fiscal reform—the Two-Tax Reform—which influenced China's fiscal development for the next

millennium. Aristocratic interests constituted a credible check on monarchical power by institutionalizing the office of the chief councilor, which was
almost on a par with the emperor. It was a rare time in Chinese history when
the emperor ruled *with* the elites. Yet the star network was vulnerable to rebellions against the center. In the late ninth century, a mass rebellion stormed the
capitals and physically destroyed the aristocracy.

The second phase, State Maintaining under Partnership, characterizes the
almost millennium-long period from the mid-tenth to the mid-nineteenth
century. This is the most stable chapter in Chinese history; it consisted of four
unified dynasties—Song (960–1276), Yuan (1276–1368), Ming (1368–1644),
and Qing (1644–1911). Starting in Song times, the emperors took advantage
of the power vacuum left by the Tang aristocracy and reshaped the elite social
terrain. They expanded the civil service examinations to identify bureaucratic
talent on a relatively meritocratic basis. With its competitiveness and focus
on learning, the examinations brought selected members of local gentry families to the center and prevented them from forming a new aristocracy. The
central elites in this era thus became representatives of local interests. They
sought to influence central policies to benefit their home societies and kin
groups. Despite severe external threats from the steppe nomads, the Chinese elites sought to maintain a state with only mediocre strength. Several
state-strengthening attempts failed; one reform succeeded, but took more
than a century to be implemented due to political opposition. The emperors
exploited the fragmented and localized elite to establish an absolute monarchy at the expense of a much contracted state. With the rapid development
of corporate clans, the state often outsourced local public goods provision,
including defense and public works, to local elites. During this period, monarchical power greatly expanded, while the Chinese state gradually became
weakened.

The third phase, State Weakening under Warlordism, describes the last
episode of the country's dynastic history from the mid-nineteenth century
to the fall of the empire in the early twentieth century. The Western intrusion starting with the Opium Wars significantly weakened the central state's
ability to provide public goods and protect its citizens from violence. To survive during the Taiping Rebellion (1850–1864)—the deadliest civil conflict
in recorded Chinese history—the Qing rulers allowed social elites to form
private militias. The state defeated the Taiping rebels with the help of these
private militias, but the growth of autonomous social forces tilted the balance
of power away from the state and towards society. Private-order institutions

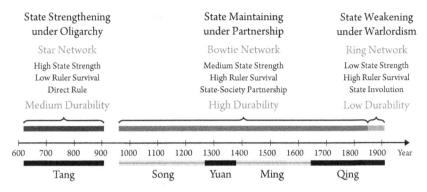

FIGURE 2.1: Timeline of China's State Development (618–1911)

organized along lineage lines took over local administration, taxation, and defense. In the early twentieth century, when the Qing state finally decided to reform its political system by installing a new army and local assemblies, these organizations soon fell into the hands of local strongmen. The abolishment of the civil service examinations further cut the ties between central elites and local social groups. The Qing state could no longer control these social forces, which co-opted local military officers and declared independence in 1911.

Figure 2.1 summarizes the timeline and phases of China's state development. A defining feature of China's state development is that ruler duration and state strength were like the two ends of a seesaw: as one went up, the other went down.

————

The rest of the chapter proceeds in three parts. First, I offer a bird's-eye view of the Chinese state over the last two millennia, starting with how climate change triggered violent conflicts that altered state-society relations by either eliminating a certain class of elite or cutting central elites' ties with society. In either case, large-scale violence provided political opportunities for the ruler to transform the elite social terrain. Social terrains were in turn associated with outcomes of state strength and form. Second, I provide an analytic narrative for each of the three phases of China's state development, focusing on how rulers, central elites, and social groups interacted, which generated different equilibrium outcomes for the state and society. Third, I conclude by discussing how China's path of state development differs from Europe's.

2.2 Climate Change and Violence

The Earth's temperature varies on a wide range of timescales and for a variety of reasons.[1] Scientific studies have yielded a generally consistent picture of temperature trends during the preceding millennia, including relatively warm conditions centered around 1000 CE—the "Medieval Warm Period"—and a relatively cold period—the "Little Ice Age"—from roughly 1500 to 1850.[2]

I collect data from a recent authoritative study published by the Chinese Academy of Sciences that reconstructs a composite series of temperature variations in China at the decade level over the past two thousand years.[3]

Figure 2.2 (upper panel) presents a time series of temperature anomalies from 0 to 1900 CE.[4] This period approximately spans the middle of the Han Dynasty to the downfall of the Qing. Positive numbers indicate warmer-than-normal temperatures, and negative numbers colder-than-normal temperatures.[5] Consistent with global evidence from the Northern Hemisphere, China's surface temperature fluctuated considerably during the study period: three warm intervals during 1–200, 551–760, and 951–1320, and four cold intervals in 201–350, 441–530, 781–950, and 1321–1900.

Social scientists have established an association between climate and conflict.[6] A climate shock can exogenously raise the odds of violent conflict. Here, I focus on two sorts of violent conflict: internal conflicts triggered by mass rebellion and external conflicts with foreign rivals.

I construct the historical conflict data relying on the *Catalog of Historical Wars* produced by the Nanjing Military Academy.[7] This catalog contains detailed information including the dates, locations of individual battles, and leaders for each major internal and external conflict that took place in China from approximately 1000 BCE to 1911.[8] The *Catalog* derives this information from China's official historical books, known as the "twenty-four histories." Traditionally, each dynasty in China compiled a standardized history of its predecessor, typically based on official court records. The twenty-four histories are among the most important sources of systematic data on Chinese history.[9] Given the historical nature of these data, however, there may be measurement errors. Smaller and local conflicts, for example, were less likely to be recorded. We should therefore assume that the conflicts in the data were above a certain threshold of significance since they merited recording by historians.[10]

I define "mass rebellion" as a violent conflict between a government force and a mass rebel group (e.g., peasants, artisans). I identify a rebel group

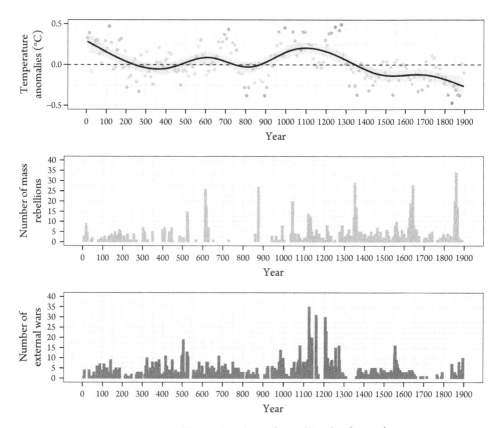

FIGURE 2.2: Temperature Anomalies and Conflict (0–1900)

as a mass organization as long as its leadership did not hold any official government positions according to the *Catalog*.[11] The Huang Chao Rebellion in the late Tang era and the Taiping Rebellion in the late Qing era are two examples of mass rebellions included in the *Catalog*.

My sample data consist of 1,586 individual battles linked to 789 recorded mass rebellions between 0 and 1900. Figure 2.2 (middle panel) presents the number of mass rebellion battles in each year during this period.

I define "external warfare" as a violent conflict between a China-based dynasty and a non-Han state or state-like power.[12] Thus, for example, battles between the Manchu invaders and the imperial Ming state were categorized as "external," while those between the subsequent imperial Qing (i.e., Manchu) state and mass rebel groups were classified as "internal."

There were 2,214 individual battles linked to 989 recorded external wars during my sample period. Most external conflicts were fought against nomads from the Eurasian Steppe. Figure 2.2 (lower panel) presents the number of external war battles in each year during this period.

Theoretically, a positive climate shock (i.e., warmer temperature) should improve crop yields, making the territory a more attractive target for external attack from the nomads. An agricultural state after harvest time is a juicy site for plunder and tribute—what James Scott calls the "golden age of barbarians."[13] The concentration of settled people with their grain, livestock, manpower, and goods represents a ripe target for more mobile predators. Greater yields should also reduce the likelihood of famine, making internal rebellion less appealing. A negative climate shock (i.e., colder weather), however, should decrease the odds of external attack (because the territory becomes less valuable) and increase the threat of internal rebellion (since famine becomes more likely).[14]

The patterns shown in figure 2.2 are consistent with these theoretical predictions. For example, during a period of exceptionally cold weather, mass rebellion reached a historical high in the late ninth century. Many rebel groups at the time joined forces under the leadership of Huang Chao, a salt merchant, and occupied the capitals of the Tang Dynasty, slaughtering most of their aristocratic residents.[15] The mass violence of this period directly led to the collapse of the Tang Dynasty; it also destroyed the medieval Chinese aristocracy and ended the State Strengthening under Oligarchy era—the first equilibrium in Chinese state-society relations.

External warfare peaked during the "Medieval Warm Period" from 951 to 1320. Over one-third of all the external war battles in the sample occurred during this exceptionally warm period. The majority of these battles were between a Han regime and various nomadic regimes, including the Khitan Liao, Jurchen Jin, Tangut Xixia, and the Mongol Empire. This period ended with the Mongolian conquest of China and the establishment of the Yuan Dynasty in 1279.

During the "Little Ice Age" from 1321 to 1900, external threats abated. Internal rebellions, however, became frequent, including three waves of large-scale, dynasty-ending mass rebellions. The first wave happened in the mid-fourteenth century, culminating in the great anti-Mongol revolt led by Zhu Yuanzhang, who founded the Ming Dynasty in 1368. The second wave took place in the early to mid-seventeenth century, reaching its climax during the Li Zicheng Rebellion, which ended the Ming Dynasty and created an opportunity for the Manchus to conquer China and establish the Qing Dynasty. During these rebellions, although the dynastic state sometimes outsourced its local defense to private, clan-led militias, the state was still able to control these militias. Social groups partnered with the state to provide security. Most private militias disbanded after the rebellions and hence did not threaten the state's monopoly over violence.[16]

The third wave broke out in the mid-nineteenth century and reached a pinnacle during the Taiping Rebellion. Private militias organized by gentry clans again flourished during this rebellion. But this time, the central state was too weak to control them. The Taiping Rebellion tilted the state-society balance away from the state and ushered in the final equilibrium of China's state-society relations—State Weakening under Warlordism.

To examine the association between climate shocks and violence more systematically, I also carry out a regression analysis. Using a time-series dataset at the decade level, my quantitative results are largely consistent with the patterns shown in figure 2.2. Estimates from my preferred specifications suggest that a one degree Celsius increase in temperature is associated with, on average, almost fourteen more external war battles and twelve fewer mass rebellion battles in any given decade.[17]

It is important to note that a climate shock is neither a necessary nor sufficient condition to trigger conflict. Mass rebellions broke out in warmer periods, just as external enemies attacked during colder times. Other factors that social scientists use to explain conflict—such as grievances, political opportunity structure, communication network, international tribute and treaties, and political leaders—certainly add explanatory power.[18] But climate shock provided a precondition for these structural and leader effects to apply, and increased the odds of conflict when these other factors were held constant.

2.3   Elite Social Terrain

The elite social terrain—the ways in which central elites connect to local social groups and to each other—took three forms in China. In each phase of state development, a certain form of elite social terrain became self-perpetuating, and shaped state strength and form. The elite social terrain proved to be resilient; rulers were only able to alter it during or after large-scale violence.

2.3.1   Elite Data

The following analysis examines original data that I collected on China's political elites and their kinship networks in various dynasties. I define state elites as

central-level politicians of vice-ministerial rank or above who had the authority to influence government policies. These officials were the most powerful
political elites: they could attend palace meetings and discuss policies with
the emperor.[19] This narrow definition excludes local officials, who had less
power to influence government policies, and local elites, who I consider to be
leaders of local social groups. This narrow definition helps me examine and
operationalize a comparable group of individuals over time.

I first constructed a biographical dataset of these major officials using a variety of archival and documentary sources.[20] I then mapped these officials' kinship networks using a unique archaeological source: tomb epitaphs (square
slabs of limestone on which biographies of the deceased were inscribed).[21]
The texts of tomb inscriptions contain lengthy eulogistic passages, which
almost always include the surnames of officials' wives and generally provide
the names and, if applicable, ranks of their sons, as well as the names and
ranks of their daughters' husbands. These conventions—especially where
more than one member of the network is eulogized—allow us to reconstruct
descent lines and affinal connections over several generations.[22] Figure 2.3
shows an example of the tomb epitaph of Fu Bi, a chief councilor (宰相) in
the eleventh century.

Figure 2.4 defines the scope of an individual's kinship network, which
included two components: his nuclear family and all in-laws who were connected by marriage to the individual's son(s) or daughter(s). Due to cost
limitations, I limited the scope of my data collection to three generations—the
politician's parents' generation, the politician's generation, and the politician's
children's generation. I then geocoded each kin member using the China Historical Geographic Information System, which provides the latitudes and longitudes of historical localities.[23] Missing data is an inevitable problem when
dealing with historical data. We should therefore consider the geographic span
of the sample network to be the lower bound of the true network.

2.3.2 Measuring Elite Social Terrain

Elite social terrain exhibits two dimensions. The horizontal dimension characterizes how central elites connect to each other; the vertical dimension characterizes how central elites connect to local social groups. I use two metrics to
measure these two dimensions.

To measure how central elites connect to each other (horizontal dimension), I use network density. In a network of central elites, I consider two politicians, e.g., Zhang and Liu, to have a tie if Zhang is in Liu's kinship network,

(a) Fu Bi's tomb stone   (b) Transcription of Fu Bi's tomb epitaph

FIGURE 2.3: Tomb Epitaph Example

English Translation: His excellency (Fu Bi) married the daughter of **Yan Shu**. She was virtuous, calm, and restrained. They had three sons: **Fu Shaoting**, Gentleman of Court Service; **Fu Shaojing**, Deputy Commissioner of Storehouse; **Fu Shaolong**, Aide in the Court of Imperial Entertainments. They had four daughters: the first married **Feng Jing**, Scholar at the Institute for the Extension of Literary Arts; after she died, the second daughter married Feng Jing; the third daughter married **Fan Dazong**, Court Gentleman for Instruction; the fourth daughter married **Fan Dagui**, County Magistrate of Huoqiu. They have three grandsons and three granddaughters.

or vice versa.[24] Density is the proportion of observed ties in a network up to the maximum number of possible ties.[25] In various analyses, I also use a more sophisticated measure—social fractionalization—which gauges how fragmented the network of central elites is.[26]

To measure how central elites connect to local social groups (vertical dimension), I differentiate geographically dispersed versus concentrated networks. In the former, central elites have kin all over the country, while in the latter their kin are located nearby. I construct a localization score using

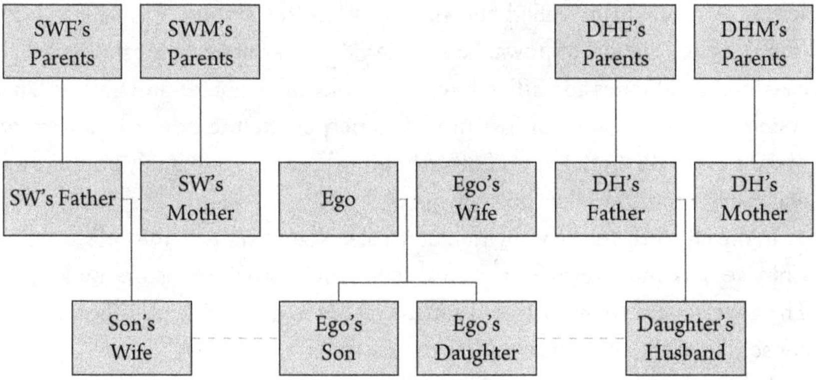

FIGURE 2.4: Example of a Kinship Network

Notes: SW = son's wife; SWF = son's wife's father; SWM = son's wife's mother; DH = daughter's husband; DHF = daughter's husband's father; DHM = daughter's husband's mother. Solid lines represent blood relations, and dashed lines denote marriage ties.

the "market potential" approach, which the economic geography literature employs to measure market localization.[27] The underlying logic is that this localization score increases as all kin move closer to the politician.

I then use these measures to distinguish between different types of elite social terrains. A star network features a high network density among central elites and geographically dispersed networks between the central elites and their kin. A bowtie network features a medium to low network density among central elites and geographically concentrated networks between central elites and their kin. A ring network features a low network density among central elites, who are disconnected from the society at large. Locally powerful social groups, such as clans, no longer have members serving in the central government and thus do not develop ties with state elites.

2.3.3   Star Network

A star-like network emerged during the Han Dynasty (206 BCE–220 CE). Han emperors' policy of recruiting Confucian scholars into the bureaucracy created a class of scholar-bureaucrats. These scholar-bureaucrats then exploited their political power to strengthen their economic power, which further contributed to the education of their sons and their families' political power.[28] In 220 CE, the new ruler of the Wei regime introduced a political selection mechanism called the nine-rank arbiter system (九品中正) to gain the cooperation of powerful families.[29] The arbiter—a local notable—classified candidates for office into nine ranks of character and ability. The system rapidly became an instrument to perpetuate the power of a narrow social class.[30] Birth, status, and office holding became inseparably bound, and many aristocratic families began to form.[31]

In the late fifth century, the nomadic ruler Xiaowen (471–499) placed elite Chinese clans into one of four classes, depending on their ancestors' ranking.[32] The government then examined a man's family to determine his office, which consolidated the self-perpetuating aristocracy.[33]

These eminent families were similar enough to aristocracies elsewhere, such as the medieval European nobility, to merit the description "aristocrat." But their eagerness to be associated with the imperial court in order to perpetuate their social status countered any tendencies for aristocratic families to become feudal lords with proprietary control over sections of the country.[34] Many of the great clans managed to survive for five, six, or even seven hundred years and maintain a position in the elite. The secret to their success was family practices that sustained a continuous descent line. While the medieval European Church engaged in a vigorous campaign against aristocratic reproductive behavior by prohibiting endogamy, adoption, polygyny, concubinage, divorce, and remarriage,[35] men in imperial China could take as many concubines as they could afford.[36] Wealthier elites reproduced faster than their poorer counterparts because they could afford more concubines and support more children.[37] The most successful clans therefore reproduced more quickly, allowing them to occupy an ever greater share of government positions.[38] While in Europe a 50 percent rate of attrition among aristocratic families every century was common,[39] the same group of great clans dominated China for centuries.

By the Tang period, the aristocratic families had become a status group that was sustained by marital exclusiveness. The core male members of the aristocratic clans congregated to the capital cities of Changan and Luoyang and often held office for successive generations.[40] Their geographic proximity to the emperor certainly helped them obtain desirable positions. But as the historian Nicolas Tackett pointed out, the key to their political success was their social networks. The geographic concentration of dominant political elites in the two capitals both reinforced and was reinforced by a tightly knit and highly circumscribed marriage network. Members of this network constituted the dominant political elites who monopolized power during the

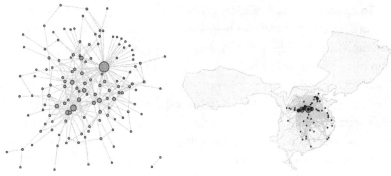

(a) Tang elite marriage network (750–850)   (b) Tang elites and their kin (779–805)

FIGURE 2.5: Tang Elite Social Terrain

late Tang era. The social capital embedded in the capital-based elite marriage network allowed these elites to control both bureaucratic recruitment and appointment to the highest posts.[41] There are countless examples of chief councilors intervening to promote a clansman, son-in-law, or sister's son.[42]

With capital elites moving throughout the empire to serve in top local positions, the Tang political center maintained a colony-like relationship with other parts of the empire. Capital-based bureaucrats were sent out to all corners of the empire, monopolizing all of the top civilian posts for three- to four-year tenures.[43]

The marriage network that was facilitated by capital interactions and regional rotations also created a colony-like relationship. A central family located in the capital connected through marriage ties with multiple families with home bases in the provinces to form a star network.[44]

Scholars of social network analysis often use images of such networks to gain insights into network structures.[45] The most common form of display is based on points (which represent social actors) and lines (which denote connections among the actors). Throughout the book, I will use point and line graphs to illustrate the network structures of Chinese elites.

Figure 2.5 (panel (a)) shows the marriage network of Tang aristocratic families during 750–850.[46] Each node represents a single patriline, and the ties denote marriage connections. Almost all of these families had members who were high-ranking officials in the Tang government.[47] The graph demonstrates that the aristocratic network featured high levels of connectedness and centralization.[48] Every family was connected with almost every other family, at least indirectly.

To examine how central elites connected local kin groups, I also created an original dataset that includes biographical information on all the major officials and their kinship networks during Emperor Dezong's reign (779–805). Figure 2.5 (panel (b)) traces the kinship networks of these major officials. Each large, central node represents a major official. Smaller nodes represent these officials' kin connected by marriage or blood ties. While the central officials were concentrated in the capital area, their kin were dispersed across the country.[49] The graph approximates a star network in which a group of well-connected elites in the center have ties to social groups in the periphery.

2.3.4   Bowtie Network

The star network is vulnerable to violence that targets the center.[50] During the late Tang period, China—and much of the Northern Hemisphere—experienced an unusually severe period of cold and dry weather.[51] The prolonged period of drought ignited rebellions in multiple places. Huang Chao, a salt merchant, gradually united the rebel forces and captured the capital city of Changan in 880.[52] During two years of occupation, the rebels killed all the aristocrats in the city.[53] Once the central nodes were removed, the star network collapsed.

The succeeding Song emperors seized the opportunity to reshape the elite social terrain. They began to rely on an expanded civil service examination system to recruit bureaucrats.[54] Candidate numbers grew dramatically, as did the examinations' competitiveness. E. A. Kracke and Ping-ti Ho have demonstrated the meritocratic nature of the examination system and how it increased social mobility.[55] While in the Tang era several hundred aristocratic clans held all the offices, the exam system during the Song period significantly broadened the social basis of bureaucratic recruitment. Although locally powerful families enjoyed an advantage in grooming their sons for the exam, they still needed to compete with thousands of other families across the country to obtain the advanced scholar degree in order to be placed in the higher echelon of the bureaucracy.

The "Tang-Song transition," first described by Naito Konan[56] in the 1920s, involved the transformation of the elite social terrain. Since then, historians have reached a near consensus on what happened.

The story goes something like this.[57] During the Tang Dynasty, office holding was the single most important determinant of family status. Every elite family sought to place as many of its sons in the bureaucracy as possible.

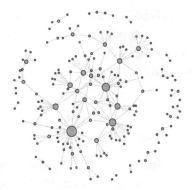 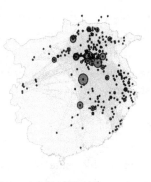

(a) Song elite marriage network (997–1022)   (b) Song elites and their kin (997–1022)

FIGURE 2.6: Song Elite Social Terrain

Building a marriage coalition with other powerful families at the national level hence provided insurance against uncertainties (such as the death of an important family patron) and represented the most effective way to exploit the patronage system.

During the Song era, the expanded exam system made it more competitive to obtain a position. Thus pursuing a bureaucratic career became a risky investment with uncertain returns. Meanwhile, rising trade, marketization, and urbanization gave men more occupational options. Consolidating a local power base with solid properties and close-knit networks with other powerful neighbors became the best way to perpetuate elite families' status.

When the elites scattered and married locally, multiple communities emerged with their own centers connected to their own neighbors but not with other parts of the network. This resembles a bowtie network in which each central node connects with its own community, but different communities are not connected.

Figure 2.6 (panel (a)) illustrates the marriage network among the major officials under the Song emperor Zhenzong (997–1022). Each node indicates a major official, and a tie denotes a marriage link between two officials' families. This network is much less connected than that of Tang aristocrats. The network density of the Song officials is less than half that of the Tang aristocrats (0.011 vs. 0.028, respectively). Figure 2.6 (panel (b)) presents the kinship networks of these major officials. In contrast to the Tang star network, the Song network has multiple centers, denoted by the larger nodes (major officials), which connect to multiple smaller nodes (officials' kin). The average standardized localization score of the Song officials' kinship networks is more than twice (i.e., more localized) that of the Tang officials (0.102 vs. 0.044, respectively). This pattern is closer to the bowtie network, in which central elites are less connected, and each central node is connected to a regional cluster of social groups.

2.3.5   Ring Network

The bowtie-like elite social terrain was consolidated after the Song era. Gentry families perpetuated their power by investing in land and their sons' educations.[58] The civil service examinations sent the sons of these locally entrenched families to the central government. In the capital, these local "representatives" advocated their local interests and allocated national resources to benefit their hometowns.[59]

Britain's victory over China in the First Opium War (1839–1842), along with the Taiping Rebellion (1850–1864), was a turning point that fundamentally changed how central elites connected with the society. The war and the resulting Treaty of Nanjing significantly increased the Qing government's external defense costs, and it lost the ability to control domestic rebellions.[60] Cold weather plus droughts triggered the Taiping Rebellion. Qing emperors delegated local defense to gentry leaders in an attempt to ensure their personal survival. The delegation reshaped elite social terrain one last time and tipped the balance of power between the state and the gentry.[61]

The gentry were now formally involved in both local defense and administration. Thus, political power shifted from central officials to local elites, which according to Philip Kuhn led to the "breakdown of the traditional state."[62] Prasenjit Duara terms this phenomenon "state involution," in which the central government increasingly depended on local elites—via lineage organizations—to perform local governance functions, but was no longer able to control them, thereby making them an unaccountable force in local society.[63]

An important indication of state involution is the rapid growth of clan collective action. Gentry clans maintained their coherence and delineated clan membership by compiling genealogical records. Not all clans kept such records; those that did were almost always the most powerful.[64] In a recently published genealogy register, a research team at the Shanghai Library cataloged more than fifty thousand genealogies (compiled between 1005 and 2007 CE).[65] An entry in the registry reports a record of a clan's genealogy, so a clan

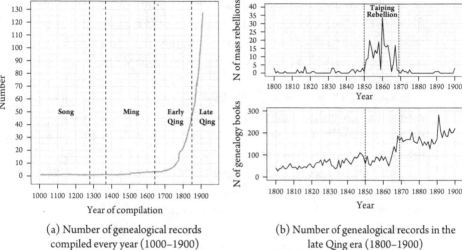

(a) Number of genealogical records
compiled every year (1000–1900)

(b) Number of genealogical records in the
late Qing era (1800–1900)

FIGURE 2.7: Growth of Clan Collective Action

can have multiple entries. For example, the Li clan could have compiled its first genealogy in 1701 and then updated it in 1754 and 1802. Each entry includes information on the clan's surname and current location as well as the year the genealogy was compiled and the number of volumes in the book.[66] I digitalized the whole genealogy register and geocoded every record based on the location of the clan.[67]

Figure 2.7 (panel (a)) shows the (100-year moving average) number of genealogical records compiled every year since the early eleventh century. There was an obvious "elbow" in the mid-eighteenth century, indicating a weakening of state control of these social forces. After the mid-nineteenth century, the number of genealogy records soared from dozens to over a hundred per year.

Most of the growth in the number of genealogical records happened during and after the Taiping Rebellion. Figure 2.7 (panel (b)) indicates there was a sizable increase in genealogical records in the aftermath of the Taiping Rebellion. The number of genealogy books rose from less than 100 before 1850 to nearly 200 by 1870. This increase was not transient; the high level of clan collective action was sustained for decades after the rebellion.

After its defeat in the First Sino-Japanese War (1894–1895), the Qing state established the New Army in an attempt to produce a modern military force that was fully trained and equipped according to Western standards.

Gradually, however, New Army officers and weaponry were absorbed into the framework of the regionally based armies that dated back to the time of the rebellions.[68] Gentry leaders, many of whom were elected to the new provincial legislatures, became local strongmen and gained control over both taxation and military matters.[69]

In 1905, the Qing government abolished the millennium-old civil service examinations, which cut the ties between local elite families and the central government.[70] Declarations of independence from local military forces throughout China prompted the fall of the Qing state in 1911. Frederic Wakeman attributes the "deep" roots of Qing state failure to the longer-term shift in the power balance toward the local gentry and away from the central government that had begun more than a half-century before.[71]

The Taiping Rebellion therefore triggered the proliferation of local social forces that escaped the state's control. The abolishment of the civil service examinations further disconnected these increasingly autonomous social forces from the central state. The elite social terrain during the late Qing period resembled a ring network. Social forces, concentrated in different regions, became a centrifugal force from the dynastic state, leading to its ultimate collapse.

2.4   State Strength

The historical evolution of China's elite social terrain is linked to the ups and downs of state strength, which can be measured as its ability to collect revenue[72]—which in China's case varied a great deal.

We can analyze state strength from two perspectives: (1) fiscal policies (were they designed to strengthen or weaken state strength?) or (2) the actual tax amounts (the most popular measure of state capacity).[73] To levy taxes, the state needs accurate information (e.g., on land, economic production, and population), a bureaucracy to collect the taxes, and an infrastructure to transport the tax payments, all of which require a certain level of capacity.[74]

Figure 2.8 depicts China's fiscal development from 0 to 1900. The upper panel presents the evolution of major fiscal policies.[75] I code each policy according to whether historians consider it to be state strengthening (+1), neutral (0), or state weakening (−1).[76] The graph plots the moving average of these policies. The lower panel presents per capita taxation, based on estimates from a variety of archival and documentary materials.[77] Both

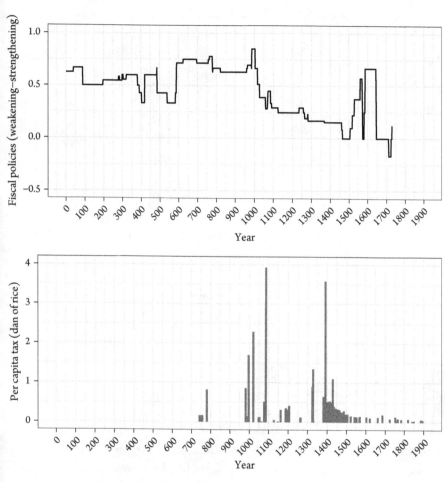

FIGURE 2.8: Fiscal Policies and Per Capita Taxation (0–1900)

graphs demonstrate that China's fiscal capacity peaked in the eleventh century, started to decline afterwards (with transitory increases), and diminished toward the end of the period.

A popular argument that can be traced back to Adam Smith and was more explicitly stated by Thomas Malthus is that China's development failure in the late imperial era had demographic roots: its population was too large for its economy to support.[78] Indeed, the population tripled from 150 million in 1700 to 450 million in 1900.[79] This Malthusian narrative, however, cannot fully explain the low taxation in the late imperial era because while the population growth mainly occurred after 1700,[80] China's per capita taxation started to

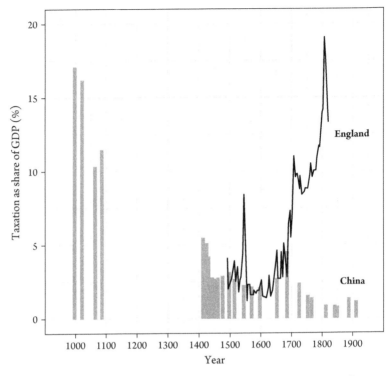

FIGURE 2.9: Taxation as a Share of GDP: China vs. England (1000–1900)

decline much earlier—in the Song and Ming times. Nor can this demographic theory explain why the imperial state failed to adjust its tax policies accordingly. Recent estimates show that Chinese real personal incomes between the mid-eighteenth and mid-nineteenth centuries remained relatively stable, despite a dramatic increase in population.[81] This suggests that there were more people from whom the Chinese state could have extracted taxes, if it had been able to adjust its fiscal policies. But the state stuck to a tax quota, which did not change for centuries.

We see a similar pattern using tax revenue as a share of gross domestic product (GDP), which measures the extent to which the state can extract from total economic output. Figure 2.9 compares taxation as a share of GDP from 1000 to 1900 in China versus England.[82] Again, the share peaked in the eleventh century, and then started to decline. By the start of the nineteenth century, while England taxed 15–20 percent of its GDP, China taxed only 1 percent.

2.4.1   State Strengthening in the Tang Era

Before the tenth century, most of China's fiscal policies were designed to increase central taxation, and taxation continuously increased during this period. A star network of central elites dominated this era of state strengthening. A key fiscal reform during this period was the Two-Tax Reform in the Tang era.

This reform, introduced in 779 to address the fiscal shortfall after the An Lushan Rebellion,[83] aimed to change a flat tax based on public land tenure to a progressive tax that recognized private property. The central state imposed a new land tax, collected based on the amount of land under cultivation, levied in two installments (in summer and autumn).[84]

The tax was costly for the political elites expected to implement it, but only three of 141 major officials publicly expressed opposition to the reform.[85] Why did the overwhelming majority of political elites, big estate owners themselves, support (or at least acquiesce to) a reform that increased their tax burden?

The answer lies in the social terrain of the Tang elites, who formed aristocratic clans. Their dispersed kinship network allowed them to internalize the gains of state strengthening to others from regions far from their own. The central state could dramatically reduce the marginal costs of servicing larger areas by exploiting economies of scale. The dispersed network therefore transcended elites' personal interests and aligned the incentives of a broad coalition in favor of the fiscal reform.

2.4.2   State Maintaining under Song and Ming

Starting in the eleventh century, most fiscal policies started to weaken the state's capacity to extract revenue. This is puzzling, given the growing external threats. The Northern Song Dynasty faced existential threats from the Khitan and Tangut nomadic tribes in the north. Faced with a situation in which a war could break out at any moment, why did the elites not "make the state?"

They tried to, but failed. In 1069 the Song ruler introduced the New Policies, which were the brainchild of one of his cabinet members, Wang Anshi. These policies, which became known as the Wang Anshi Reform, had the goal of "enriching the nation and strengthening its military power."[86] The philosophy of the New Policies was to expand the scope of state power to intensify its participation in the market economy, which would generate a surplus that the state could use to meet its fiscal and military needs.[87]

In the first decade of the New Policies, the Song state's revenues dramatically increased. This explains the brief peak in China's fiscal revenue around the year 1086, as shown in figure 2.8. The bowtie network, which was gradually formed during the early Song era, created a strong anti-reform sentiment.

The state-building coalition was not strong enough to sway a significant number of the Song central elites who were embedded in local vested interests. Many politicians opposed the reform. They viewed local elite families as competing with the state to provide various services. They considered kinship institutions to be the most efficient way to protect their family interests. Politicians also feared that a stronger state threatened their family interests because state strengthening increased the personal costs to them, through taxation.[88]

After Wang Anshi's retirement and the death of the emperor, the opposition leaders completely abolished the reform. Before long, the Northern Song state was significantly weakened and defeated by the Jurchen in 1127.

The state remained relatively weak after the Song era. As the central elites became more locally oriented, centralized state-strengthening reforms became politically impossible. The government, however, still made periodic attempts to improve its tax collection methods. In the mid-Ming period, a powerful grand secretary (首辅) advocated a new method called the Single Whip, which simplified taxation by combining the labor levy and land tax. But the Single Whip was implemented in a decentralized manner, delayed by a coalition of local elites and their representatives in the national government. The policy took more than one hundred years to roll out throughout the country, and was still incomplete when the Ming Dynasty collapsed.

2.4.3   State Weakening under Qing

The Manchu conquest in the mid-seventeenth century brought in a new class of elites—the Manchu Eight Banners. The Eight Banners was a unique Manchu military organization that emerged during military campaigns; it was sustained by a close-knit elite network.[89] Early Qing rulers achieved a level of centralization that was unusual in late imperial China. They enforced policies to diminish the gentry's power and privileges, simplified tax collection by merging land and labor taxes, and delineated central and local revenues. This explains the brief surge in state revenues in the late seventeenth century.

The state-strengthening momentum, however, did not last. With the deterioration of the Eight Banners and the increasing corruption and ineptitude of the Manchus, later Qing rulers increasingly relied on the civil bureaucracy, which was staffed by members of the narrowly interested gentry. Due to political opposition from the bureaucracy, the Qing government did not carry out any cadastral surveys during its 267-year rule; it relied on the late Ming records with infrequent and minor revisions carried out by officials at the provincial and local levels.[90] As a result, the Qing revenues could not keep up with the rapid population growth and the increasing external and internal threats after the First Opium War. When local military groups declared independence in 1911, the Qing government was too broke to hold the country together.

2.5   State Form

The elite social terrain also shaped the two relationships that characterized the state form. The first concerned the relationship between the ruler and the central elite; the second involved the relationship between the state and society. State-society relations in various historical periods represented patterns of different equilibria in China's state development.

2.5.1   Ruler-Elite Relations

Contrary to the popular view that a despotic monarchy dominated China for thousands of years, for a long time the Chinese ruler was weak vis-à-vis the central elite. The medieval aristocracy effectively checked the monarchy's power. From the fall of the Han Dynasty to the founding of the Tang, Chinese emperors shared power with the dominant aristocratic families: the rulers exploited aristocratic social capital to govern society.[91]

During the Tang times, the aristocracy institutionalized its power. Official genealogies identified the empire's most prominent clans, guided the nobility's marriage choices, and provided the emperors with a list of families from which bureaucrats were chosen. These genealogies, compiled by state officials, consistently ranked the imperial clan lower than the most prominent aristocratic families.[92] Infuriated, Tang emperors banned the most prominent clans from intermarrying, which only made them more sought after.[93]

The coherence of the Tang aristocracy checked the ruler's power. For example, the office of the chief councilor was elevated during this period. It started as an informal body of advisors to the emperor; chief councilors were drawn from the central ministers. In the early eighth century, the office became a formal government organ that competed with monarchical power.[94]

The Tang aristocrats' interconnectedness and geographical concentration facilitated collective action and coordination against the throne.[95] Official histories recorded multiple coup attempts, some of which succeeded.[96] In my dataset of Chinese emperors, five of the twelve Tang emperors who ascended after the An Lushan Rebellion were toppled by a coup.[97]

The demise of the medieval aristocracy changed the relationship between the ruler and the central elites. If the Tang emperors were first among equals, rulers after the Song started to dominate the central elite. The rise of absolute monarchy marked a watershed moment in Chinese history.[98]

Song emperors filled the post-Tang power vacuum by relying on expanded civil service examinations to select bureaucrats. Landowning elite families enjoyed a human capital advantage, but there were so many participants in the examinations that the process was competitive and the outcome uncertain. Even the most powerful families struggled to ensure one member per generation obtained office.[99] The establishment of palace examinations, in which the emperor ranked top candidates after a face-to-face interview, further strengthened the monarch's personal authority to select bureaucrats.[100]

The transition from a star network to a bowtie network marked the fragmentation of the central elite during the Song era. Robert Hartwell observed "the diminished cohesiveness among the elite lineages" in Song times.[101] With a fragmented elite, the emperor used a "divide-and-conquer" strategy to dominate the bureaucracy. For example, the Song emperors fragmented military control by separating the Military Affairs Commission (枢密院), which maintained monarchical control over military matters, from the Ministry of War (兵部), which was a civilian-controlled organ in charge of military policy making.[102] The Song rulers also reorganized the top echelon of the bureaucracy by dividing the authority of the office of the chief councilor, which centralized executive power during the Tang times, into three executive branches.[103]

Ming emperors further consolidated their absolute power. In 1380, the Ming founding emperor abolished the entire upper echelon of the central government, including the chief councilor, and concentrated power securely in his own hands.[104] He then brought the ministries under his direct supervision.[105]

China's autocratization was completed during the Qing era. The Grand Council (军机处), which was established in the late seventeenth century and evolved into a permanent privy council, expanded its sphere of authority to all arenas of imperial policy. The council remained a personal "star chamber"

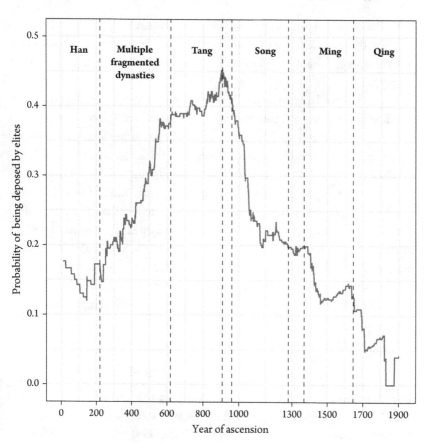

FIGURE 2.10: Probability of Ruler Deposal by Elites (0–1900)

or "kitchen cabinet" granting private advice to the throne. Its members were overwhelmingly Manchu and were often drawn from the emperor's closest circle of relatives and friends.[106]

How rulers ended their reigns is an informative indicator of ruler-elite relations.[107] Here, I rely on an original dataset I collected on all Chinese emperors from 221 BCE to 1912.[108]

Of all 282 Chinese emperors, half died peacefully, while the other half exited office unnaturally. Of these unnatural exits, about half were deposed by the elite (murdered, overthrown, forced to abdicate, or forced to commit suicide).[109]

Figure 2.10 displays the moving average of the probability of being deposed by elites. Emperors from the Song era onward were significantly less likely to be deposed—an indication that the rulers had strengthened their power vis-à-vis the elite. The trend of ruler duration is in stark contrast with that of state strength (figure 2.8) in which fiscal capacity started to decline in the Song era.

China achieved a remarkable level of political durability in the post-Song era. The upper panel of figure 2.11 plots the moving average of ruler duration in China, Europe, and the Islamic world.[110] Chinese rulers were just as secure as European rulers, and both outperformed their Islamic counterparts.

The lower panel of the figure depicts the moving average of the probability of being deposed for rulers in China, Europe, and the Islamic world. For Chinese emperors, this probability declined to less than 30 percent after the seventeenth century; for European kings and queens, it remained around 30 percent until the nineteenth century. Islamic rulers' probability of being deposed reached almost 60 percent in the eighteenth century.

This phase of China's state development can be interpreted as a history of rulers single-mindedly chasing personal power and survival at the expense of state strength.

2.5.2   State-Society Relations

The elite social terrain is also correlated with the ebb and flow of state-society relations. The Tang approach represented direct state rule over society. Thanks to centuries of division and chaos, the Tang state inherited a large amount of public land. The government used what it called the equal field system (均田制) to divide state-owned land into family-sized plots, which it allocated to peasants in exchange for taxes, labor services, and military services.[111] The tenants returned the land to the state when they reached retirement age.[112]

As private landholding replaced the equal field system in the mid-Tang period, the state adjusted its fiscal system to maintain control over society. The Two-Tax Reform established a clear vertical division of fiscal revenues and expenditures between levels of government. The central government granted local authorities a great deal of freedom to manage their own fiscal matters, but required them to submit a tax quota according to prior arrangement based on mutual consultation. This arrangement recognized provincial governors' right to allocate a fixed proportion of the local tax revenue to meet local needs, and assured the central government of a fixed income from each province. The central government thus secured a regular income from direct taxation.[113]

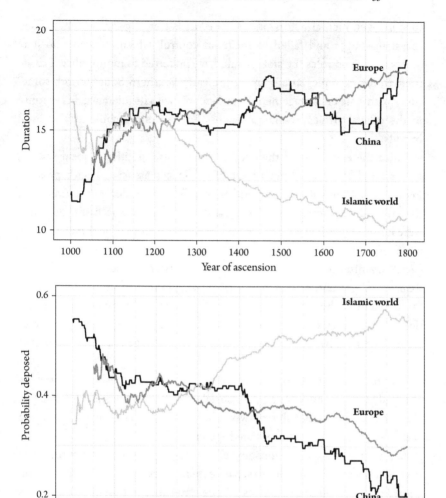

FIGURE 2.11: Ruler Survival in China, Europe, and the Islamic World (1000–1800)

Fiscal control was further reinforced by personnel control, in which capital-based elites rotated between national and local positions every three to four years.[114]

After the Tang-Song transition, however, we observe what Robert Hymes calls the "retreat of the state" or the "shrinkage of state power."[115] The locus of political action and negotiation shifted from the central state to local society. In some cases, the central government deliberately shifted responsibility to nongovernmental actors and/or the market at large.[116] In other cases, the state sought and failed to maintain control, which allowed non-state actors to take on roles the state would have preferred to monopolize. Private militias, for example, sprang up in the early Southern Song period, sometimes with state encouragement but often only with its tolerance, in response to the official armies' weakness against Jurchen encroachments and local bandits.[117]

Once the elites shifted their focus from central politics to local society, they started to face a different set of challenges associated with preserving or expanding their wealth and power. From the eleventh century on, they turned to private-order organizations—the most successful of which were kinship institutions. Trust-based kinship institutions, in which wealthy members donated a plot of land to the lineage trust, became the dominant social organization. The trust held a small portion of each member's total wealth, and generated an income that provided those in need with funding for food and clothing, funerals and weddings, and, most importantly, education. Every branch of the lineage was expected to donate a small portion of arable land held by a deceased member, so the lineage land expanded over time.[118]

The reorientation of the central elites into "local elites" fundamentally changed how they interpreted their social role vis-à-vis the state. Sukhee Lee characterizes the relationship between the state and elites during the Song era and onward as "a tacit yet negotiated agreement."[119]

In this negotiated relationship, elite families partnered with the state because they could not afford to separate themselves from it. This connection helped protect their local interests.[120] The state's recognition of a household's office-holding status was strategically important to help safeguard its economic interests and local prominence.[121] During the Song and Ming times, the state viewed itself as a participant in (and caretaker of) local society, not simply as its ruler.[122]

State-society relations shifted again during the Taiping Rebellion. The rapid growth of private militias soon tipped the balance of power between the state and society.[123] Increasingly autonomous social organizations began to threaten the state's monopoly over violence[124] and took over local administrative functions, such as taxation.[125] The infiltration of local gentry elites into the newly created Qing army was the final straw that broke the empire. Warlordism dominated Chinese politics for the next half-century until the Communist Party unified the country again.

2.5.3   Durability of Equilibria

China's three phases of state development represent three equilibria. They varied in their durability and reflect a fundamental trade-off Chinese rulers faced between personal survival and state strength.

In the first equilibrium—State Strengthening under Oligarchy (618–907)—the ruler enjoyed high state capacity at the expense of personal power. The central elites benefited from a strong centralized state that provided national-level protection. This equilibrium lasted for almost three centuries. Climate shocks in the late ninth century triggered the Huang Chao Rebellion, which eliminated the aristocracy and destroyed the star network.

The second equilibrium—State Maintaining under Partnership (960–1840)—started with a power vacuum in the center. It provided an opportunity for the Song emperors to reshape the elite social terrain through an institutional change—the civil service examinations. The emperors in this second phase exploited the fragmented and localized elite to establish an absolute monarchy at the expense of a much weakened state. The state outsourced local public goods provision to local lineage organizations. A state-society partnership contributed to the exceptional durability of this equilibrium, which lasted for almost one thousand years.

The third equilibrium—State Weakening under Warlordism (1840–1911)—started with the Western intrusion during the Opium Wars. The central state lost its ability to protect its citizens from violence. During the Taiping Rebellion, the central state tolerated and then lost control of private militias. The abolishment of the civil service examinations severed the ties between the central elites and the increasingly independent social forces. Dynastic rule fell in 1911 as local military forces, infiltrated by gentry elites, declared independence. This last equilibrium lasted for decades.

2.6   Concluding Remarks

The paths of state development in China and Europe were diametrically opposed from the seventh to the twentieth century. In Europe, the fall of the Roman Empire created a large number of small kingdoms. Local elites controlled elements of local society, and rulers were unable to exert direct rule over their entire territory.[126] The rulers therefore granted local elites feudal titles in exchange for their cooperation in taxation and war.[127] They also created assemblies to collect information from local societies where the central state was too weak to exert control.[128] This partnership lasted throughout the medieval period until war became more expensive due to advances in military technology.[129] States then centralized their power from the feudal lords and established a professional bureaucracy and standing army.[130] States also institutionalized citizen assemblies and granted more power to the representatives, who were increasingly drawn from the commercial class.[131] European states gained durability and strength simultaneously and became modern democratic nation-states.

China, by contrast, started as a centralized state. Violence, rather than making the Chinese state, destroyed its centralized social network. Chinese rulers reshaped the elite social terrain by recruiting local elites into the bureaucracy. The rulers were able to dominate these local elites, but China's fiscal strength started to decline. Even during the eleventh century when the Chinese state faced existential threats from the north, because of the localized elite social terrain, the elites chose not to strengthen the state. They instead turned to their lineage organizations. These social organizations negotiated with the state to create a partnership that characterized China's state-society relations for almost a millennium.

Social scientists who write about China's state-building process have not paid enough attention to this long period of state-society partnership. This partnership generated a high level of political durability and good governance, despite weakened state fiscal strength. Only during the second half of the nineteenth century did China's central state begin to lose control over society; nation-states in Western Europe steamed ahead, exacerbating the East-West political divergence.

PART II

State Strengthening under Oligarchy

3

State Strengthening in the Tang Dynasty

3.1   A Star Was Born

When Yang Yan was born in 727 CE, China was in one of its golden ages of imperial rule. The Tang Dynasty, founded in 618, reached a peak of political and cultural achievements that were almost unparalleled in Chinese history. Occupying a vast territory and almost one-fourth of the world's economy,[1] the Tang empire was the center of an Asian world linked by economic, political, and cultural ties. Tang merchants structured trade relations with the outside world on the ancient "silk roads." The numerous natural harbors of the fertile south facilitated overseas trade. Much trade still went eastward to Korea and Japan, but substantial new commerce developed with maritime Southeast Asia, India, and the Persian Gulf.[2] Japan was most deeply influenced by Chinese culture and institutions during this period, which shaped the fabric of the former's state structure, laws and institutions, art, literature, and written language.[3] Moreover, Tang writers produced the finest poetry in China's great lyric tradition, which has remained the country's most prestigious literary genre.[4]

But as Yang Yan was growing up, the empire started to display signs of crisis. Under the system of state-controlled land tenure that the Tang rulers inherited from previous dynasties, each married couple was entitled to a grant of land from the state for the duration of their working lives.[5] The amount of land the state controlled, however, gradually lagged behind population growth. Many ended up with no land and became tenant farmers or laborers, while others accumulated holdings and established great estates.

The movement toward private land ownership threatened the fiscal and military systems that were built on this system of public land tenure. Based on the assumption that every household owned the same amount of land, the state collected a fixed amount of agricultural products and labor service from each household. With rising land inequality, however, the landless and the owners of great estates were still expected to pay the same amount. In addition, due to large-scale migration, many inhabitants were not counted in the locality where they were granted land. The tax base therefore shrank.

The collapse of the public land tenure system caused the self-sufficient "regimental army" to deteriorate. In the early days of the dynasty, hereditary regimental soldiers were allocated a plot of land, expected to supply their own basic arms, and were largely exempt from taxation and labor service. After a few generations, soldiers sold their land and left. The state had to rely on mercenaries, which further exacerbated its financial strain.

Yang Yan became chief councilor—the highest-ranking administrator in the empire—in 779. Soon after taking office, he proposed the "Two-Tax" fiscal reform to the emperor, which involved changing the flat tax system to a progressive tax based on property holdings that was collected twice a year, in summer and autumn (which is where it got its name, "two taxes"). This reform shaped China's fiscal system for the next seven centuries until the sixteenth-century Single Whip Reform (discussed in chapter 6).

The greatest puzzle about the Two-Tax Reform was how little opposition it received despite the increased tax burden on the wealthy and powerful— the very group that implemented it. Only 3 of the 141 major officials expressed opposition. Emperor Dezong (779–805) was so keen on the reform, which could substantially increase his total tax revenue, that he immediately adopted Yang Yan's proposal. By February the following year, the Two-Tax measures were implemented throughout the empire.[6] Compared to fiscal reforms in later eras that were debated, delayed, and obstructed, the Two-Tax Reform succeeded like magic.

———

In this chapter, I examine Tang politics and probe the social foundations of state strengthening during this period. Applying the theory elaborated in chapter 1, I argue that the Tang elite, which formed a star network, were an encompassing interest group willing to pay for the costs of state strengthening because their private interests were aligned with those of the state. The stronger state strength, however, came at the expense of the emperor's power and survival. Tang monarchs suffered the highest risk of elite coups throughout the imperial period.

The rest of the chapter is structured as follows. Section 3.2 briefly discusses the two earlier dynasties that influenced Tang politics and society—the Qin and Han. Section 3.3 provides a general introduction of Tang politics, with a focus on the medieval aristocracy and Tang fiscal and military institutions. Section 3.4 examines the mid-Tang crisis, especially the An Lushan Rebellion and how it weakened state control. Section 3.5 examines the details of the Two-Tax Reform in the late Tang era, which helped the dynasty recover from the crisis and regain state control. Section 3.6 discusses the end of the Tang and how it changed the trajectory of China's state development.

3.2 Tang Precursors

The Tang inherited important legacies from its predecessors, the Qin (221–206 BCE) and the Han (202 BCE–220 CE). The Qin unified China and reshaped Chinese politics and society. The Han consolidated imperial rule and left several institutional footprints that influenced China's later development.

3.2.1 Qin Unification

The Qin unified China after prolonged wars. In the latter half of the Zhou Dynasty (1046–221 BCE), the monarchy's control over its territories weakened. Families of the Zhou nobility established independent kingdoms and engaged in internecine wars during the Warring States period (475–221 BCE). The wars pressured the kingdoms to increase the size of their armies. Gradually, these kingdoms extended military service from the nobility to broader segments of the population.

Shang Yang (390–338 BCE), a reformer serving in the Qin government, carried out a series of reforms that helped the Qin defeat other kingdoms and unify the country.[7] To build a centralized army, Shang Yang rewarded Qin peasants who served in the army with land, which their households could hold and work. City-states—the dominant political unit prior to the Warring States—became obsolete in the face of these enormous armies. Defeated city-states were absorbed by their conquerors, who redistributed the land to their own population in exchange for military service and taxes.[8] As city-states disappeared, the old city-based nobility lost its central place in the state order, just as it lost its prominence in the army. In place of the nobility, the state was increasingly dominated by a single autocratic ruler, whose agents registered the peasants and mobilized them into state service and collected taxes to support the ruler's military ambitions.[9]

Under Shang Yang the Qin state transformed military districts, called "counties" (县), into the basis for local civil government. The ruler would directly appoint officials to counties. Eventually, the entire Qin state was divided into counties, thus making universal military service the foundation of the state's administrative apparatus.[10]

The transformation from nobility-governed city-states to centrally managed counties marked China's transition from a feudal state to a bureaucratic state. In a feudal state, such as medieval Europe and China before the Qin, the ruler delegates limited sovereignty over portions of his domain to vassals in exchange for military service and taxation.[11] In a bureaucratic state, such as in premodern Europe and China after the Qin, the ruler directly governs his realm through a system of administration, staffed by appointed professional officials.[12]

Qin's unification of China started an enduring pattern. Between the years 1 and 1900, a single political authority ruled China for more than 1,000 years.[13] In contrast, political fragmentation dominated Europe.[14]

Researchers have proposed a couple of mechanisms to explain the divergence in political fragmentation across the two extremes of the Eurasia landmass. One school emphasizes the importance of population diversity. Quamrul Ashraf and Oded Galor, for example, examine how the greater genetic diversity in Europe than in China may drive political fragmentation.[15] Conversely, the standardization of the Chinese characters under the Qin has been a steady, unifying force throughout China's history.[16] Others focus on geography. Jared Diamond seminally argued that "fractured land" such as mountain barriers, dense forests, and rugged terrain impeded the development of large empires in Europe in comparison to other parts of Eurasia.[17] Peter Turchin and his collaborators argue that proximity to the Eurasian steppe favored the evolution of ultrasocial traits and the rise of large-scale states in Asia as a defensive response.[18] Recently, Fernández-Villaverde and his collaborators have developed Diamond's "fractured land" hypothesis and argued that the location of Europe's mountain ranges ensured that there were several distinct geographical cores of equal size that could provide the nuclei for future European states, whereas China was dominated by a single vast plain between the Yangtze and the Yellow River. In addition, they argue that the presence of a dominant core region of high land productivity in China—in the form of the North China Plain—and the lack thereof in Europe can also explain political unification in China and division in Europe.[19]

3.2.2 Han Institutions

The subsequent Han Dynasty kept China unified and left several important institutional legacies.

First, as external threats abated, Han abolished universal military service in 31 CE. In place of a mobilized peasantry, military service was provided by non-Chinese tribesmen, who were particularly skilled in the forms of warfare used at the frontier, and by convicts or other violent elements of the population, who were transported from the interior to the major zones of military action at the outskirts of the empire. This demilitarization of the interior blocked the establishment of local powers that could challenge the empire, but also led to a recurrent pattern in which nomadic peoples conquered and ruled China.[20] Later dynasties used either a mercenary or hereditary garrisons; universal conscription did not reappear until after the end of the last empire in 1911.

Second, Han further justified imperial authority originally established by the Qin. The emperor was not merely the supreme ruler, chief judge, and high priest but the very embodiment of the political realm—the Mandate of Heaven. The state radiated out from his person: everyone in state service was his servant and held office entirely at his behest. All lands were considered his property, a claim that justified public land ownership and the state monopolies of iron and salt.[21]

Lastly, the "triumph of Confucianism"—a phrase often used to describe intellectual developments in Han times and Emperor Wu's (157–87 BCE) policy of recruiting Confucian scholars into the bureaucracy—created a class of scholar-bureaucrats. These scholar-bureaucrats then accumulated political and economic power, becoming China's medieval aristocracy.[22]

After the fall of the Han, China disintegrated into nearly three hundred years of political fragmentation—the longest period of disunion in Chinese history.[23] Several nomadic kingdoms occupied the north, while ethnically Han regimes divided the south, until the Sui (581–618) unified China again in the late sixth century.

3.3   Early Tang Setup

The Tang Dynasty (618–907), and its short-lived predecessor, the Sui Dynasty, reestablished national unity. Both dynasties inherited their governance structures from the sinicized nomadic kingdoms that divided the North China Plain in the fifth and sixth centuries. But the dominant elites exhibited the highest level of continuity in medieval China. The small group of aristocratic clans that emerged in northern China during the Han times had established powerful regional bases connected by dense intermarriage ties.[24] From the third to the tenth century, the emperors alternated between these powerful families.

The Sui Dynasty succeeded the Northern Zhou (557–581). Like the ruling house of the Northern Zhou, the Sui's founder, Yang Jian, was from the northwestern aristocracy. This small group of powerful families also included the Dugu (the family of Yang Jian's wife) and the Li, the future royal house of the Tang. All were connected with one another and with the Northern Zhou imperial house through complex marriage ties. The succession to the Tang simply transferred the throne to another of this close-knit group of families.[25]

No analysis of medieval Chinese politics is complete without a thorough understanding of the aristocracy; its dense marriage ties and near monopoly of power constituted a strong check on monarchical power. Many of the Tang emperors are famous for their open-mindedness and deference to their subjects for a good reason. While the core male members of the aristocracy congregated in the capitals, their home bases were spreading across the empire. Status endogamy thus created a nationally dispersed marriage network. National, rather than local, politics became the center of contention for the aristocrats. They competed with each other for power in the center, and had a strong incentive to strengthen the central state in order to protect their family interests: this was the key to Tang state making.

3.3.1   The Aristocracy and the Monarchy

The upper class in medieval China occupied the highest echelons of the country's social, intellectual, and economic life, and staffed the government's offices.[26] The third- through seventh-century nine-rank arbiter system, which relied on local recommendations for bureaucratic recruitment, helped perpetuate the powerful families.[27] Office holding soon became a marker of high status. As a result, only the sons of high-ranking men who had held office had much of a chance of receiving high ranks themselves. By the beginning of the fourth century, bureaucratic recruitment had become a system of appointment to office according to family rank.[28] A contemporary famously stated, "the higher ranks have no lowly families, the lower ranks no powerful ones."[29]

By the Tang times, the aristocratic families had formed a restricted marriage circle, into which entry was difficult to obtain except by birth.[30] This close-knit network of families presented an imminent threat to the royal family's predominance.[31] In 632, Emperor Taizong (626–649) ordered a survey of the genealogies of the empire's most prominent clans. He was infuriated to see that the lineage of Cui of Boling (a prefecture in current Hebei Province) had been ranked first in the first tier, while his own clan was ranked in only the third tier.[32] Taizong's son Gaozong (649–683) further forbade a group of the most prominent families from intermarrying (the so-called marriage-ban clans) in an attempt to weaken their coalition and prestige. The ban, however, only served to elevate their status.[33]

The coherence of the aristocracy also constrained monarchical power. During the early years of the Tang Dynasty, Emperor Taizong established an informal body of advisors known as chief councilors, drawn largely from the heads of the three central departments—the Secretariat (中书省), Chancellery (门下省), and Department of State Affairs (尚书省). In 723, Zhang Yue, an aristocratic chief councilor whose pedigree can be traced back to the Han times, convinced Emperor Xuanzong to make the chief councilors' office a formal government organ in its own right, with a separate budget and seal. Gradually, executive power became centralized in the office of the chief councilors.[34]

The Tang emperors have the reputation of being benevolent rulers. Even the brutal Taizong, who murdered two of his brothers and forced his father to abdicate, is remembered as an open-minded ruler who caved in to his advisors. This reputation might be because, as Denis Twitchett points out, the Tang emperors were "constrained by the entrenched interests of the powerful aristocratic group which still provided almost the entire upper echelon of the administration."[35]

3.3.2   The Bureaucracy

The Tang Dynasty inherited the Sui's central government structure. Three central departments dominated the government: the Chancellery and the Secretariat, which acted as policy formulating and advisory organs, respectively, and the Department of State Affairs, which was the chief organ of the executive.[36] Under the Department of State Affairs were six ministries (or boards): the Civil Office (吏部), Finance (民部), Rites (礼部), Army (兵部), Justice (刑部), and Public Works (工部).[37] The three departments shared bureaucratic power, which served the interests of a strong monarch often seen at the beginning of a dynasty. In the mid-Tang period, the Chancellery and Secretariat were merged to form a single organization—the Secretariat-Chancellery (中书门下省)—that formulated policy and drafted legislation. The Department of State Affairs simply became the executive arm of government. This reorganization, pushed by the consolidated aristocracy, opened the way for chief councilors to exercise almost dictatorial powers.[38]

The early Tang government was simple and economical. In 657 it employed 13,465 ranking officials to control roughly 50 million people. Many routine government tasks were entrusted to selected taxpayers, who completed them as a form of labor service.[39] During the first half of the dynasty, the provinces (道) were simply convenient divisions of the empire, which were used as units for periodic inspection. They had no permanent governor or administration, and played no part as intermediaries in the central offices' dealings with the prefectures (州) and counties (县) below them.[40]

Beneath the county level there was no administrative system staffed by members of the bureaucracy. The magistrate depended on the subordinate staff (吏), most of whom were local people, and on the sub-bureaucratic rural administration of the villages. The most important rural administrators were the village elders (里正), who were responsible for providing the data for the registers, allocating land, supervising agricultural methods, and paying taxes.[41]

The civil service examination—arguably imperial China's greatest bureaucratic innovation—started in the Sui era and developed under the Tang Dynasty. The first mention of a degree and a written examination occurred in 595.[42] During the Tang period the examinations never produced more than an elite stream of officials, probably little more than 10 percent of the total bureaucracy, with an average of just over ten graduates a year.[43] Until the end of the Tang era, the great majority of these officials came from the old aristocratic families.[44]

The famous Chinese historian Chen Yinke argued that Empress Wu (690–705)—the only female sovereign in Chinese history—expanded the examinations to cultivate support for her new regime by introducing a new social element into the ruling class.[45] But there is little evidence to support this view. No examinations were held for ten years during the pinnacle of her reign, and afterwards only eighteen advanced scholar (进士) degrees were awarded on average each year.[46] Throughout the Tang era, the vast majority of officials obtained their positions through hereditary privilege, which allowed the aristocracy to successfully preserve its political status. The introduction of the examination system, rudimentary as it was, marked the beginning of an institution for selecting bureaucrats on the basis of merit that was to have far-reaching effects on the subsequent evolution of imperial China.[47]

3.3.3   Public Land Tenure and Flat Tax

During the three centuries of division, the northern nomadic kingdoms controlled a large amount of land due to war and massive southward migration.[48] In 486 the Northern Wei regime (386–534) instituted an equal field system in which state-owned lands were divided into family-sized plots and given to peasants in exchange for taxes and labor service on imperial construction projects.[49]

The Tang Dynasty inherited the equal field system. Each married couple was entitled to a grant of land from the state for the duration of their working, or rather taxpaying, lives.[50]

Households were obligated to pay taxes and perform labor service in exchange for these land grants. The basic unit of taxation was the individual adult male, generally the head of a household.[51] Historical texts commonly referred to the early Tang tax system by the names of its three principal components, combined as zu-yong-diao: land tax (租), labor service (庸), and household tax (调); land tax was paid in grain, labor services in corvée, and household tax in cloth.[52] These liabilities were fixed and did not take into account actual wealth or income, since in theory all landholdings were proportional to the size of the household and therefore should be proportionately taxed.[53]

3.3.4   The Regimental Army

The Tang Dynasty also inherited its military system from the Northern Wei. The Northern Wei military units along the northern frontier were drawn from respected tribes, headed by officers from the nobility. These elite units of hereditary soldiers were linked to their commanders by tribal or pseudo-tribal bonds.[54]

The Tang Dynasty founded its own regimental-type army (府兵) based on the Northern Wei idea that each military unit was locally based. The Tang army comprised about 600 regimental headquarters, each of which controlled 800–1,200 men. These units were spread throughout the country; about two-thirds were within 170 miles of the capital.[55] To ensure central control, each local military governor served no more than four years to prevent them from developing strong personal ties to their officers and men.[56] The local units regularly rotated soldiers into the capital for military service. The central government could rely on these local, self-sufficient units, individually too small to pose any threat to the dynasty, as a ready and reliable source of manpower.[57]

These men were initially chosen from large, well-to-do landed families that could afford to allow one adult male to devote himself exclusively to military training. In the early days of the dynasty, regimental members were listed on special military registers and were largely exempt from taxation and labor service. Each soldier was allocated a plot of land that he or his family and serfs could work.[58] The soldiers provided and maintained their own weapons and equipment, and their own rations.[59] The troops attained nearly professional quality without draining the state's budget. Regimental units also provided manpower for the local police force. Armies at the frontier were also drawn from regimental soldiers, who served alongside non-Chinese mercenaries.[60]

Yet members of well-to-do landed families eventually began to avoid military service, which forced the regimental army to meet its quotas by recruiting men from poor and peasant families. As the prestige of military service declined, the elite central army in the capital and the foreign mercenary forces at the frontiers gradually supplanted the regimental army. By 749, regimental soldiers were no longer called up to serve in the capital or frontier.[61]

3.4   Mid-Tang Crisis

After more than a century of internal stability, the rebellion of An Lushan in 755 nearly brought the dynasty to its knees.[62] It transformed a centralized, rich, stable, and far-flung empire into a struggling, insecure, and divided one.[63] During the rebellion, the state abandoned its early efforts to regulate land ownership; the system of population registration fell into complete chaos; and the central government was cut off from its main revenue sources, which were now controlled by the independent military governors.

The An Lushan Rebellion, however, was a regional rebellion that did not harm the core of Tang politics—the aristocracy. After the Tang government suppressed the rebellion, the central aristocracy re-centralized control. The Tang star network remained intact, which paved the way for the late-Tang fiscal reform.

3.4.1 The An Lushan Rebellion

An Lushan (705–757) was a career military general of partly Turkish and partly Soghdian blood. In the 740s, he rose through the ranks to become the military governor of the Fanyang defense region on the Manchurian frontier.[64] In 755, he rebelled. Within two months, with a seasoned force of roughly two hundred thousand men, An Lushan's troops moved southward through Hebei, took the Tang eastern capital of Luoyang, and advanced to the vicinity of the capital Changan.[65] Emperor Xuanzong (713–756) slipped out of the capital by night with a few of his confidants and his favorite concubine Yang and fled southwest through precipitous mountains into Sichuan. The flight of the emperor and Yang's mysterious death are still among the best-known episodes of Chinese history. The rebellion continued after An Lushan's death and was not suppressed until 763.

Historians have offered three types of explanations for the rebellion. First, some focus on the non-Chinese origins of An and many of his followers, and argue that these minority groups were only superficially influenced by Chinese culture and were moved solely by a lust for conquest and loot. Adherents of this view characterize the An Lushan rebellion as an "external invasion carried out from within."[66] Chen Yinke developed a sophisticated variation on the ethnic conflict theme: an influx of non-Chinese into Hebei from the early eighth century had initiated a process that "barbarized" society in the northeast. This process had gone so far by the 740s that the Tang court installed a "barbarian," An Lushan, as the only way to retain its hold over Hebei and the northeast. Chen Yinke's interpretation therefore extended the ethnic factor beyond An Lushan and the men under his command to involve the population of an entire region.[67]

A second explanation focuses on the center-periphery tension between the Tang center (in the northwest) and Hebei (in the northeast). According to E. G. Pulleyblank, the Tang court's discriminatory policy towards Hebei alienated the region and eventually led to the rebellion. According to this theory, An Lushan emerged as a representative of regional sentiment and interests.[68]

Lastly, an elite conflict view explains the rebellion as a marginalized group's challenge to the dominant ruling class. C. A. Peterson, for example, argues that the gradual domination of the military command structure by men who could hardly be considered members of the Tang ruling elite was the underlying cause. "Soldiers by profession, provincial in outlook, and frequently of humble social origins," Peterson contends, "formed a group quite distinct from the regular bureaucracy." And the social and cultural gap between the court and its frontier commanders permitted a powerful commander to collect support from his fellow officers and declare war on a court with which they felt little affinity.[69]

These three factors—ethnicity, region, and elite—overlapped. It is probably because the divisions between the Tang central government and the northeast military governors reinforced each other that their conflicts were uncompromising. A non-Chinese, marginalized military elite happened to control the northeast frontier, which was far from the empire's political and cultural center.

Consistent with my broader argument, the northeastern military governors as an elite group were a regionally embedded interest coalition, which was not part of the capital aristocracy—a nationally encompassing interest coalition. The An Lushan rebellion does not represent an attempt of this regional group to seize central power, but rather a sign that it was able to garner local autonomy.

The most important long-term damage caused by the rebellion was the loss of central control. The Tang state extended its system of provincial command throughout the empire in an effort to suppress the rebels, which produced a new level of local administration. Unlike the old prefectures, these provinces were often independent units, capable of threatening central power. In the north, some were heavily armed. Surrendered rebel commanders controlled a group of provinces in Hebei and remained semi-autonomous: they paid no revenues to the capital, appointed their own officials, and claimed the right of hereditary succession. These were extreme cases, but the forces of local autonomy and particularism had grown everywhere. The central government, which barely survived the rebellion, delegated significant autonomy to the provinces in order to preserve the integrity of the empire.[70]

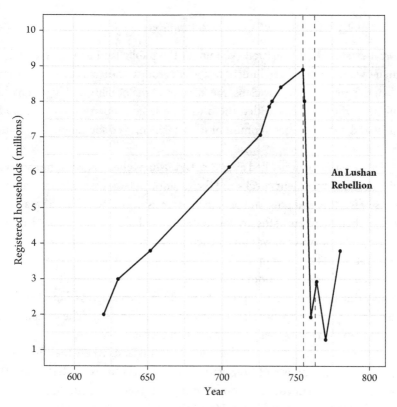

FIGURE 3.1: Number of Registered Households (620–780)
Source: Li (2002, 37, 153).

3.4.2   Decline in Registered Households

The An Lushan rebellion marks the beginning of a new phase of the land problem. It led to the breakdown of the registration system on which the whole
complex arrangement of land tenure and taxation had depended. As figure 3.1
shows, the number of recorded households dropped from nearly nine million
in 755 to fewer than two million in 760. This astonishing decrease was not
indicative of a fall in population, but of a decrease in the area controlled by the
central administration. But the rebellion did lead to the depopulation of large
areas, and further accelerated the population movements from the north.[71]
The registration system and the land allotment ceased to be effective, while
the extensive depopulation and migration destroyed the entire basis of the
zu-yong-diao taxes.[72]

3.4.3   *Great Estates and Declining Revenue from Direct Tax*

Great estates (庄园) existed even under the public land tenure system, but their ownership had been limited to certain groups: the state and the imperial clan; the great aristocratic clans, the families of the nobility and high-ranking officials whose status entitled them to have large properties; and the Buddhist and Taoist religious communities, which enjoyed special privileges and entitlements.[73]

Estate building flourished after the An Lushan rebellion, with the removal of effective government checks and the vacation of large areas of farmland. All sorts of wealthy and powerful people became estate owners, but the majority were either members of the aristocracy or career bureaucrats.[74] Yan Li, a governor in the northwest, was impeached in 809 and found to possess at least 122 estates.[75] They built up estates by taking the land left vacant by farmers who had fled from their homes for various reasons. Sometimes, the powerful simply drove out the small landholders.[76] They then employed dispossessed farmers as tenant farmers or laborers to work their estates.[77] The great landed estate became a widespread feature of the rural economy.

Farmers fled their homes and settled on vacant lands where they no longer appeared on the household registers. Local tax records were destroyed. By 763 the government could no longer re-impose its highly centralized system. It had lost effective control over Hebei and major portions of Henan which, in the hands of former rebel provincial governors, became a bloc of semi-autonomous provinces. More than 25–30 percent of the empire's population escaped central control, which entailed a massive loss of revenue.[78]

The provinces of the Yangtze and Huai valleys in the south, especially Jiangnan, acquired a new and critical importance. Because of the limited central control elsewhere, this region, with its increasing population and great productivity, became the dynasty's chief source of revenue.[79] The government also started to desperately look for new sources of revenue. In 758, it imposed a monopoly tax on the sale of salt following the Han tradition. The merchants, who bought their stock from the government and paid the monopoly tax on it, passed this tax onto the consumer as part of a greatly increased retail price. The government collected such taxes indirectly.[80] From 770 to 780, the salt monopoly, which bypassed the provincial governors without challenging their collection of direct taxes, supplied about half of the regime's central revenues.[81] But the total revenue was available only at sharply reduced levels at a time when administrative action was needed more than ever.[82]

3.5 The Two-Tax Reform

Emperor Dezong ascended to the throne in mid-779 amid high expectations of a resurgence of Tang glory. The new emperor, who was in his late thirties, ambitiously promoted stronger policies to address the state's uncertain financial situation and reassert its control over the empire.[83] Later that year, he appointed Yang Yan, a local official well known for financial innovations, as chief councilor.[84]

3.5.1 Reform Policies

Yang Yan's Two-Tax Reform transformed the flat tax regime based on public land tenure into a progressive tax regime that recognized private property. The government introduced a household levy (户税), based on an assessment of the size and property of every household, without distinguishing whether household members were natives of the locality or settlers from elsewhere. The government also imposed a land levy (地税), collected in summer and autumn on the basis of all land under cultivation in 779. The reform abolished all the miscellaneous taxes that had been levied during earlier reigns.[85]

The summer tax was levied on land growing wheat, and the autumn tax on land cultivating millet. Thus each plot of land was taxed only once per annum.[86] Individuals now had only two basic taxes to pay—the household and land levies; both were assessed on their property and productive capacity, and were collected together at the times when they were most likely to be able to pay.[87]

The reform also established fiscal divisions between levels of government. The central government abandoned any further pretense of direct central control over local financial administration in return for a fixed and regular revenue. There was to be a threefold allotment of revenue at the prefectural level: specific portions were retained for local expenditures (留州), sent to the provincial administration (送使), and dispatched to the central treasury (上供).[88] This arrangement institutionalized the sharing of revenues between the central and local levels, and transferred a portion of direct taxation, which provincial governors were previously able to monopolize, to the center.[89]

The reform was an immediate success. In 780, more tax revenue was collected through the new system alone than from all sources in the previous year.[90] It revitalized the central government's regular financial offices. State revenue was directed to the government treasury rather than the eunuch-controlled palace treasury.

3.5.2   Structural Reasons for the Reform's Success

Historians have attributed the great success of the Two-Tax Reform to two structural changes that had already been underway. First, as Denis Twitchett points out, the reform was "more in the nature of a nationalization and unification of existing methods of taxation than a revolutionary new scheme."[91] The household and land levies had been in use since Empress Wu's time (690–705), and had begun to provide sizable supplementary revenues in addition to the *zu-yong-diao*.[92] The household categories were assigned from the earliest years of the dynasty, and represented officials' rough assessments of a district's wealth, property, and the size of individual households. The rate of collection of the household levy varied depending on the household category, with a higher rate for the richer households.[93]

In a second structural change, commercialization, the monetization of the economy, and increased agricultural productivity provided the socio-economic preconditions for the Two-Tax Reform. The commercial economy developed significantly during the mid-Tang era after the country recovered from the An Lushan rebellion. Thanks to a higher supply of metal and progress in minting technologies, people started to prefer to use coins in market towns. Tang coins were used as far away from the center as Xinjiang. While taxes were still collected in kind in inland areas, they were paid largely in money in the Yangtze and Huai valleys. The shift of the economic center from the north to the Yangtze area made the reform's cash payment easier.[94] Agricultural productivity also increased during the Tang times. The north and south both started practicing crop rotation: the Yellow River region cultivated millet and wheat, which could ripen three times every two years or even twice a year; the Yangtze River region cultivated rice, which ripened two or three times a year. Crops could be harvested in different lands during summer and autumn, making it possible to collect taxes twice per year.[95]

3.5.3   Elite Interest and Reform Success

Socio-economic changes, however, cannot explain why the reform process was so smooth. The reform's success can more importantly be attributed to broad support from elites. Only 3 major officials out of 141 during the whole Dezong reign publicly expressed opposition to the reform.[96] One of them—Liu Yan (刘晏)—opposed it out of his personal rivalry with Yang Yan rather than his policy preference. Liu Yan himself was a reformer who had earlier pioneered some elements of the Two-Tax Reform.[97] The other two opponents—Lu Zhi (陆贽) and Qi Kang (齐抗)—did not lodge a dissent until at least fourteen years after the reform was implemented, and their opposition related primarily to the way in which the reform was implemented.[98]

Why did the overwhelming majority of political elites, who themselves owned large estates, support (or at least acquiesce to) a reform that imposed a heavier tax burden on them? It was not because the reform legitimized private land ownership; political elites could already hold private estates before the reform.[99]

A classic explanation of the underlying motives for enacting redistributive policy states that as a society's level of inequality increases, the median voter—the individual who sits squarely in the middle of the left-right policy spectrum—is more likely to be poor and prefer a higher tax rate on the rich.[100] But this theory hinges on a democratic, majoritarian system in which the poor are able to influence policy decisions, whereas in eighth-century China only the powerful and wealthy could decide on the tax rate. A recent theoretical innovation instead emphasizes the effects of large-scale external war. Kenneth Scheve and David Stasavage argue that, during and after external war, countries start taxing the rich, which compensates the poor for the sacrifices they have made (e.g., by serving in the military). They argue that if existing state policies put the rich in a privileged position, then progressive taxes should be levied to correct this imbalance.[101] This theory also depends on a democratic system in which people believe the state has privileged the wealthy, and a demand for fair compensation is translated into public policy. It is unclear how such demand, if it existed, could have been translated into public policy in an aristocracy-dominated China.

To understand the reform's success, we therefore need to focus on the political elites who made it possible—the Tang aristocrats. The An Lushan Rebellion, as destructive as it was, remained a regional rebellion. It did not threaten the core of the Tang star network. David Johnson analyzes the family background of chief councilors during this period, and finds that the proportion of those from aristocratic clans rose from 56.4 percent in the first half of the Tang Dynasty (618–755) to 62.3 percent in the second half (756–906).[102]

Throughout the Tang era, the core male members of the aristocratic clans congregated in the capital cities of Changan and Luoyang as well as the corridor between the two cities—a region that could be traversed in a few days. Mao Hanguang termed this trend the "centralization of the Tang civil bureaucratic clans."[103] Nicolas Tackett argues that office holding was probably the most common reason a family would relocate far from its hometown.[104] These capital elites were much more likely to hold office generation after generation. Three-quarters of capital elites and over half of elites in the capital corridor demonstrated office-holding traditions: at least three of the five most recent generations had held office. Among officeholders, those from the capital were far more likely to hold offices of national prominence, whereas provincial elites generally served near their homes.[105]

The capital elites formed a close-knit and highly exclusive marriage network. Tang bureaucratic recruitment and promotion depended heavily on patronage and pedigree. The aristocratic marriage network created social capital that facilitated the exchange of patronage between families. The network also served as a double insurance policy: a marriage between two aristocratic clans would enable the next generation to claim a noble pedigree from both sides. The aristocratic clans then used their social connections to recruit and promote their sons and grandsons. In the late Tang era, the aristocracy monopolized nearly all top central government posts.[106] These capital elites also rotated throughout the empire to take all of the top provincial-, prefectural-, and county-level positions. They would return to the capital after three or four years, which helped build connections between the center and the periphery.[107]

The marriage network that was facilitated by capital interactions and regional rotations therefore produced a colony-like relationship. Central families located in the capital connected through marriage ties with multiple families that had home bases in the provinces (recall figure 2.5 in chapter 2). The kinship network of Tang aristocrats exhibited a high dispersion, resembling a star network.[108]

The dispersed geographic span of their kinship networks incentivized officials to strengthen the central state even though they had to pay more taxes. This was because the central state, by exploiting economies of scale, could dramatically reduce the marginal costs of servicing larger areas. The large efficiency gains associated with state strengthening caused elites to prefer paying higher taxes in order to take advantage of the national coverage the state could provide. The star network, therefore, aligned the incentives of the self-interested aristocrats to foster a broad coalition in favor of the fiscal reform.

3.5.4 The Sovereign's Dilemma

The late-Tang emperors' success in gaining state strength, however, came at the expense of their own personal power and survival. The close-knit aristocracy gradually threatened the monarch. Recall from figure 2.10 in chapter 2 that Tang rulers suffered the highest probability of being overthrown by the elite. The interconnectedness of the Tang aristocrats and their geographical concentration facilitated collective action and coordination against the throne. Official histories recorded multiple coup attempts; some succeeded, some failed.[109] In my dataset of Chinese emperors, of the twelve Tang emperors who ascended after the An Lushan Rebellion, five were toppled by a coup.[110]

Eunuchs who acquired much military power in late Tang times were at the forefront of these coups. The collapse of the regimental army propelled Tang emperors to rely on the Shence Army, or "Army of Divine Strategy," commanded by eunuchs and stationed just to the west of Changan to protect the palace.[111] The eunuchs, however, soon co-opted the Shence Army and used it in coups against the emperors.[112]

3.6 The Star Fell

The star network of the Tang elites, however, made them vulnerable to one particular type of threat. The centralization of politics also centralized contentious politics. In the mid-870s, mass rebellions boiled over due to a prolonged period of cold and dry weather.[113] Huang Chao united rebel forces to capture the capital city of Changan in 880 and occupied it for two years.[114]

The occupation had a devastating effect on the Tang capital and the political order it represented. Descendants of the dominant aristocracy who remained members of the national bureaucratic elite resided overwhelmingly in the two capital cities and the adjoining capital corridor. During the 880s, this region was devastated, its population all but annihilated, invariably decimating most of the great elites who lived there.[115] Although the total number of people killed during the occupation will never be known, it is clear that many of Changan's elite residents were unable to escape the city before it fell suddenly to Huang Chao's armies. The rebel troops killed everybody in the capital who could compose poetry.[116] Several current and former chief councilors were trapped and killed before they could flee. Large numbers of other elites who managed to survive the decade—often because they were serving in the provinces when the capital region was overwhelmed—lost their lives in the political purges of the subsequent two decades.[117]

The tragic destruction is most vividly described in the famous ballad written by Wei Zhuang, one of the foremost poets of the day who was in the capital taking the examinations when the bandit army took over. The ballad is called the "Lament of the Lady of Qin," and has been characterized as "a tale of arson, pillage, rape and cannibalism, of rustics masquerading as ministers, of aristocratic bodies sunk in mud and blood."[118]

The Huang Chao Rebellion brought an end to China's medieval aristocracy and the star network. Former-rebel-turned-military governor Zhu Wen established his own Liang state (907–923) during this time, the first of a series of short-lived dynasties that dominated northern China between the overthrow of the Tang Dynasty in 907 and the founding of the Song in 960.[119] Chinese history entered a new era.

4

The Turning Point: Tang-Song Transition

4.1   From Star to Bowtie

Around the turn of the first millennium, the Chinese social landscape changed dramatically: the medieval ruling class vanished from the scene. Starting in the mid-tenth century, a new bureaucratic class began to eclipse the aristocratic ethos of earlier times. Unlike the medieval aristocrats who monopolized the high offices, the new bureaucrats were drawn from a broadly based gentry who viewed a government career as only one of a variety of occupational choices.

The demise of the medieval aristocracy marks the crossing of one of the most important watersheds in Chinese history. A multitude of local elite gentry families emerged to replace the former ruling class. These new gentry families concentrated on consolidating their local power base and sought only occasional office as one element of perpetuating their local status. They preferred to marry locally and no longer congregated in the capital areas. Their interests lay more in local affairs, and they turned more often to their lineage organizations for protection and justice than to the state. They negotiated directly and openly with local or central governments to protect the welfare of their localities. However, they still depended on the state to legitimize their prestige and status.

The transformation of Chinese elites from a national aristocracy to a loose network of local gentry fundamentally altered the country's state-society relations. The constellation of values, institutions, and social structures created as a result of this elite transformation assumed much of the shape it was to have throughout the late imperial period. The gentry elites' partnership with the state undergirded China's long-lasting imperial rule in the second millennium.

Monarchical power rose in this era. While the medieval emperors were from one family among many aristocratic families and were constrained by aristocratic interests, emperors from the Song era onward exercised absolute power over their officials.

In addition to this elite transformation, the "Tang-Song transition" was characterized by a number of other changes, including the rise of absolute monarchy, a commercial revolution that brought about monetization and urbanization, a demographic transformation that shifted the population to the south, an increased level of agricultural productivity, the expanded use of the printing press, and the emergence of Neo-Confucianism.[1] This transition was so significant that historians usually divide China's imperial period into two eras: the early imperial era from Han (202 BCE–220 CE) to Tang (618–906) and the late imperial era from Song (960–1216) to Qing (1644–1911).[2]

––––––

Since Naito Konan first coined the term "Tang-Song transition" in the 1920s, debates have centered around two aspects. The first dispute is over *when* it occurred: historians have proposed arguments that range from the mid-Tang to the Southern Song eras. The second debate is about *why* it happened: the most popular answers focus on specific rulers, events, institutions, and geopolitical factors.

In this chapter, I systematically examine *what* took place in the Tang-Song transition as well as *when* and *why* it occurred. I collected an original dataset that includes biographical information on more than four thousand major officials and over forty thousand of their kin in the Tang and Song eras. My findings shed new light on these debates, using the most comprehensive data to date.

In a nutshell, I characterize the transition as a transformation of the elite social terrain from a star network to a bowtie network. Before the transition, central elites connected a number of overlapping peripheral localities through kinship ties. They also linked to each other in the capital, constituting a coherent national coalition that resembled a star. After the transition, each central elite connected a separate set of peripheral localities through kinship ties, but they were not connected with each other. Thus the central elites fragmented into a bowtie-shaped network.

I show that the transition happened in the late Tang to early Song period. A particularly cold period in the ninth century triggered mass violence, which destroyed the medieval aristocracy. The early Song emperors then filled the power void by expanding the civil service examinations. The competitive examinations prevented the emergence of a new aristocracy. These findings have significant implications, because the Tang-Song transition set a new path of state development.

The rest of the chapter is structured as follows. Section 4.2 introduces the data I have collected for this chapter. Section 4.3 discusses what happened during the Tang-Song transition. Section 4.4 examines when and why the transition occurred. Section 4.5 then discusses how a new model of state-society relations started after the transition.

4.2   A Note on Tang-Song Elite Data

David Johnson and Robert Hartwell pioneered the use of biographical data to explore macro-social changes in the Tang-Song era.[3] More recently, Robert Hymes, Beverly Bossler, Peter Bol, and Nicolas Tackett have continued this tradition and expanded both the geographic scope and time coverage of the data collection.[4]

I build on this tradition and make one crucial improvement. One of the reasons for the disagreements between previous studies is that they are based on different samples of elites. For example, Hymes studies the elites in Fuzhou (Jiangxi Province), which included a mix of national-level officials and locally based elites, and concludes that elite marriage networks became localized between the Northern and Southern Song.[5] By contrast, Bossler studies the families of chief councilors and finds that they maintained their focus on central government posts and had cross-regional marriage networks in both Northern and Southern Song.[6]

I collect my data using a consistent criterion throughout the Tang-Song period. My sample includes all major officials who held positions in the central government at the vice-ministerial level or above. Using this criterion, I identify 2,286 officials in the Tang Dynasty and 1,904 from the Song.[7] They were all male. On average, they started their bureaucratic careers at the age of 27 and lived until the age of 65.

Using the same approach elaborated in chapter 2, I also collected information on these officials' kinship networks.[8] For the Tang era, I collected information on 5,367 individuals who belonged to 246 officials' kinship networks. For the Song period, I gathered information on 36,790 individuals who belonged to 542 officials' kinship networks. Missing data is a serious problem, especially during the Tang Dynasty. The more prominent kin of more prominent individuals were more likely to be documented. We should therefore consider the sample networks to be indicative, rather than representative, of the true networks. Caution is warranted in interpreting the results.

4.3   The Tang-Song Transition: What Happened?

There is considerably greater consensus among historians regarding what the transition involved than when (or why) it happened. In summary, the transition involved: a socio-economic transformation that brought about a higher level of urbanization and monetization; a demographic population shift from the north to the south; an institutional change in political selection from patronage to relative merit; an elite transformation from a nationally oriented aristocracy to a locally based gentry; the scattering of elites from the center to the periphery; the fragmentation of central political elites; and the rise of absolute monarchy.

4.3.1   Structural Changes

During the Tang times, international trade through the silk road and maritime routes greatly expanded. The need for financial transactions accompanied the rise in trade, which brought about a revolution in currency. By 755, the Tang government had built eleven mints with ninety-nine furnaces producing coins.[9] The Song era also experienced a revolution in paper money, promissory notes, and other forms of paper credit to supplement the bulky, heavy strings of copper coins.[10]

The emergence of private estates promoted new agricultural technologies and long-distance trade. The south, especially the Yangtze River valley, was far more fertile and productive than the north, and the transplanting method of rice cultivation that was widely used in southern agriculture enabled it to produce considerable surpluses.[11] Specialization for the market reached its highest level of development in the second half of the Tang period: the production of non-grain crops such as fruits, tea, and sugar became substantial economic activities.[12] This commercial revolution brought about a significant expansion in certain regions of marketing networks deep into the countryside as well as the development and spread of urban centers.[13] By the late eleventh century in the Song Dynasty, two-thirds of state revenues came from taxing non-agricultural sectors, especially from the collection of excise.[14] According to some recent estimates, Song China was probably the

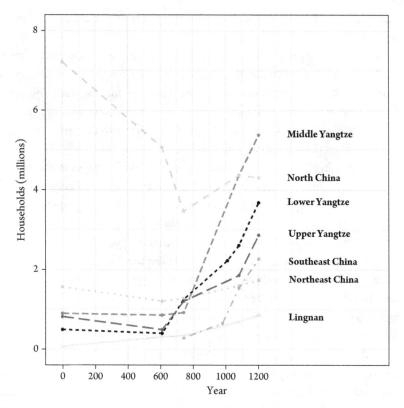

FIGURE 4.1: Number of Households by Region (0–1200)
Source: Hartwell (1982, 369).

richest country in the world with a per capita GDP 20 percent higher than England's.[15]

Between 800 and 1200, Chinese demographics also shifted. In the mid-eighth century, fewer than half of Chinese households lived in the south. By 1200, over 70 percent of households were located in the south.[16] Figure 4.1 shows the number of households from 0 CE to 1200. Dividing China using G. William Skinner's "macroregions"[17] shows that while the number of households in North China continuously declined, those in Middle and Lower Yangtze more than doubled from 800 to 1200.[18]

4.3.2   Political Selection

The Sui emperors introduced the civil service examination system in the early seventh century. But before the Song era, exam graduates accounted for only 6–16 percent of the civil service.[19] And most of these graduates came from either great clans or locally prominent clans with traditions of office holding.[20]

Beginning in 977, the Song government began conferring examination degrees in the hundreds rather than the dozens; the average number of degrees awarded each year increased from approximately 30 for the preceding three centuries to 192 for the years 997–1272. Several hundred thousand typically took the prefectural examinations in the early thirteenth century, compared to a few tens of thousands two centuries before.[21]

The founding Song emperors undertook a series of changes to the examination system that made them a central feature of the political culture. These included increasing the number of degrees given; creating prefectural and palace examinations so that, together with the examination given by the Ministry of Rites, the system had three levels; articulating procedures to ensure the anonymity of the written examinations and therefore the utmost impartiality in their grading; and developing a quota system for the prefectural examinations to regulate the flow of prefectural graduates to the capital. Candidate numbers grew dramatically as a result of these modifications, as did the examinations' competitiveness. A system of government schools emerged in the eleventh century to educate the country's future bureaucrats. With two further eleventh century changes—establishing a triennial schedule for the examinations and selecting the "advanced scholar" (进士) degree as the single degree for examination graduates—the examinations assumed the institutional form that was to characterize them for the next millennium.[22]

E. A. Kracke and Ping-ti Ho argue that the examinations increased social mobility.[23] For example, Kracke finds that in 1149 and 1256, well over half of the men who attained the advanced scholar degree had had no officeholder in their paternal line for the three preceding generations.[24] Scholars who focus on local histories rather than the national lists have revised this view. Robert Hymes, for instance, argues that because the exam lists only provide information on the candidates' three immediate paternal ascendants, offices held by members of collateral lines (uncles, great-uncles, cousins of a higher generation) would not be recorded. By examining a local sample in Fuzhou (Jiangxi), Hymes identifies a small number of families that persistently dominated the exams and paints a less fluid picture of Song society.[25]

While this debate is important, the bigger picture described by Kracke and Ho is still accurate. From the Tang to the Song eras, China experienced a fundamental change in its political selection mechanism. While the Tang aristocrats could obtain office by having the right surname, the Song gentry needed to compete to get into the bureaucracy. John Chaffee shows that the number of exam candidates remained relatively stable in the Northern Song era: 20,000–30,000 took the prefectural-level qualifying examinations in the early eleventh century and 29,000 did so a century later. But by the mid-thirteenth century, during the Southern Song era, he estimates there were at least 400,000 candidates.[26]

The examinations also introduced a meritocratic ethos into Chinese society. Beverly Bossler studies the eulogies written by Song writers, and notes a declining interest in ancestry and an increasing emphasis on examination success during this period. She suggests that whereas once the right family name had been sufficient to assure a young man a political career and a young woman a desirable marriage, by the Song era this was no longer the case. Family connections certainly continued to be an important social and political asset in the Song Dynasty, but ancient pedigrees were no longer required to access political influence; they gradually even lost their social cachet. They were replaced by a new sense of an individual's potential impact on the fortunes of his family: he could "raise up the family by means of the advanced scholar degree."[27]

4.3.3   Elite Strategy

At the social level, the Tang-Song transition involved the transformation of the nature and composition of the Chinese sociopolitical elite. The twelfth-century scholar Zheng Qiao (1104–1162) succinctly described its essence: "Up until the Sui and Tang dynasties, officials had dossiers [identifying the offices of their ancestors], and families had genealogies. The appointment of officials relied upon the dossiers; marriages between families relied upon genealogies. . . . Ever since the Five Dynasties [907–960], one no longer asks about family background when selecting officials, and one no longer asks about family prestige when arranging marriages."[28]

I borrow Robert Hymes' analogy and use two hypothetical families to illustrate what had changed from the Tang to the Song periods.[29] The first, living under a system of patronage, aimed to place as many of its sons as possible in office and to help them achieve offices of the highest possible rank. For these goals, connecting with powerful elites who were already in the bureaucracy, and who could provide patronage, seemed to be the most effective strategy.

The second hypothetical family did not aim to gain office or to advance its members to the highest possible rank. Because the outcome of the examinations was uncertain, this family sought only to guarantee that some members would obtain office from time to time so it could maintain its various legal privileges and social prestige. The best foundation for this family would be to maintain a large family property and to establish close social relationships with other wealthy, powerful families in the area. A solid property base and firm involvement in local elite social networks would help preserve the family's local position when it was out of office, and maintain a foundation from which later generations could again reach office. Since office holding, while still important, was not guaranteed for every son, and because there were many other (and some better) sources of wealth, it would make sense to diversify the family's commitments, sending some sons into the exams, some into trade, some perhaps into military service or militia leadership, and training some as managers of the family property. For the second family, it would therefore be advantageous to use marriage to bind local connections. There would be no special value in marriage ties to more prominent families farther away, since their support might be of little use in a local context.

The first family is representative of the aristocratic families in the Tang era. Because office holding was the single most important determinant of family status, building a marriage coalition with other central elites safeguarded the family's power and status. The second family represents the gentry families of the Song Dynasty. Due to uncertainties about gaining office due to the competitive examinations and the growth in alternative occupations generated by commercialization, building a local power base with solid properties and supportive networks with powerful neighbors became the dominant strategy.

4.3.4   Elite Spatial Distribution

As part of the changing strategies from the Tang to the Song era, elites altered their residence patterns. Beginning in the late fifth century, the northern aristocratic families had begun to become more involved in office holding and the social life of the capital. This process accelerated in the sixth century. By the early Tang period, many men from aristocratic families had moved permanently to areas closer to the two capitals, Changan and Luoyang.[30] Patricia Ebrey provides an economic explanation: the public land tenure (equal-field) system introduced in 485 may have made it harder to maintain or extend

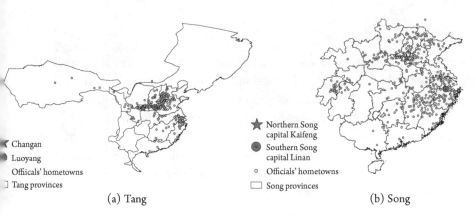

Changan
Luoyang
Offiicals' hometowns
Tang provinces

Northern Song
capital Kaifeng
Southern Song
capital Linan
Officials' hometowns
Song provinces

(a) Tang   (b) Song

FIGURE 4.2: Locations of Major Officials' Hometowns in Tang and Song
Source: *Author's data collection.*

concentrated landholdings, which weakened the families' local bases.[31] As public tenure deteriorated, access to the capitals' patronage networks became the main reason to move to the center. Nearly all ninth-century chief councilors and ministers of personnel were from capital families. Powerful politicians often intervened to promote individuals from their kinship networks, such as a clansman, son-in-law, or nephew.[32]

The residence patterns of Song elites changed dramatically. High-ranking families that were once concentrated in the capital corridor were dispersed across the country for three main reasons. First, as discussed previously, once a family no longer single-mindedly pursued a bureaucratic career for its sons, living in the capital lost its appeal. Second, even if the family still wanted to advance its sons to the bureaucracy from time to time, the establishment of local government schools and the unprecedented expansion of private schools and academies during the Song era made it unnecessary to relocate to the capital for educational purposes.[33] Lastly, the growth of urban towns and market networks beyond the capital areas gave these families an attractive alternative to office holding. The abolition of the public land tenure system in the late eighth century (see chapter 3) made it possible to transfer their economic wealth into landholding and long-term family growth.

Figure 4.2 illustrates this trend of elite scattering by juxtaposing elite residence patterns in the Tang and Song dynasties. While most of the major Tang-era officials congregated around the two capitals in Changan and Luoyang, those of the Song Dynasty were dispersed across the country.

4.3.5   Elite Social Terrain

As the political elites scattered across the country, and chose to marry locally rather than cross-regionally, their social terrain changed from a star network (in which a single center connected different corners) to a bowtie network (in which each central node connected only its own community).

Robert Hymes' study of the Song-era town of Fuzhou found that marriages took place largely within a single county. The residences of intermarried families were clustered around or near the residence of a prominent elite family. These clusterings strongly confirm the short-distance Song marriage pattern.[34]

As discussed above, the expansion of markets and cities, the changing occupational choices of the elite, and the establishment of local schools and academies contributed to the localization of elite social networks in the Song period. Another institutional reason was the civil service examinations. To screen out men with a bad reputation, Song emperors asked prominent local elites to vouch for prospective candidates before they could sit the initial exam.[35] The examination system therefore reinforced the gentry's strategy to contract marriage alliances with notable local neighbors. Studying a sample of successful candidates, Robert Hartwell shows that those who passed the exam were likely to be linked through marriage with an established elite gentry lineage.[36] Robert Hymes provides proof that the need to secure a guarantee from a prominent local man indeed served as a filter that excluded, or at least hindered, men without established connections with the local elite.[37]

By way of comparison, I reproduce two graphs from chapter 2: Figure 2.5 illustrates the kinship network of major late-Tang officials (779–805), and figure 2.6 the network of early-Song officials (997–1022). I add a third graph, which shows the major officials' kinship network in the mid-Song era during Emperor Shenzong's reign (1067–1085). In all three graphs, the larger nodes denote major officials, the smaller nodes indicate their kin, and the edges represent kinship ties. Juxtaposing the three graphs in figure 4.3 to span three centuries displays a dispersion of the central nodes as the major officials scattered across the country. From the Tang to the Song eras, there is an observable change from a star-like network in which one center connected with the periphery to a bowtie-like network, where multiple centers connected with multiple communities. Using the metric I introduced in chapter 2, the average localization score of the Song officials is more than twice (more localized) than that of Tang officials.[38]

(a) Elite social terrain in the late Tang era (779–805)

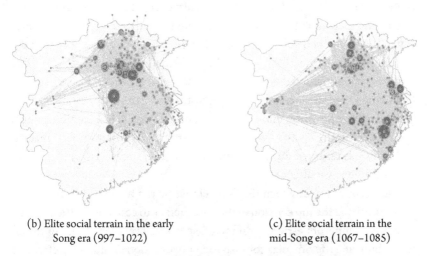

(b) Elite social terrain in the early
Song era (997–1022)

(c) Elite social terrain in the
mid-Song era (1067–1085)

FIGURE 4.3: Major Officials' Kinship Networks in Tang and Song
Source: *Author's data collection.*

4.3.6   Elite Fractionalization and Monarchical Power

As the political elites increasingly chose to intermarry only with their neighbors, they became less likely to be in each other's kinship network unless they lived near each other. This changed the marriage network *among* the political elites. While the Tang central elites were embedded in a close-knit marriage network in which everyone was connected with almost everyone else, the Song central elite network fragmented.

Figure 4.4 depicts the marriage networks among the major officials under the Tang and Song dynasties. Panel (a), reproducing figure 2.5 from chapter 2, shows the marriage network among aristocratic Tang families. Panels (b) and (c) are the marriage networks in the Northern Song, and panels (d) and (e) illustrate the same for the Southern Song. In each graph, a node (circle) indicates a major official, and a link (line) represents a marriage tie.[39] The more marriage ties an official has, the bigger the node. The comparison of these networks yields two main conclusions. First, all of the Song networks are more fractionalized than the Tang marriage network. The density of every Song network is less than half that of the Tang network.[40] I relegate the technical details of calculating fractionalization to the appendix,[41] but the graphs clearly show multiple "communities" in the Song networks and many officials with no connections. Second, the fractionalization remained constant throughout the Song era. From the early eleventh century (panel (b)) to the mid-thirteenth century (panel (e)), the degree of fractionalization did not noticeably change.

The fragmented elite structure contributed to the rise of absolute monarchy in the Song era. Paul Smith notes that the Northern Song witnessed the strengthening of "the authority of the emperor over his ministers."[42] The emperors strengthened their power in two ways during this period. First, they fragmented the bureaucracy. For example, the Song emperors created a Military Affairs Commission under their personal control. While routine matters were routed to the civilian-controlled Ministry of War, major policy-making authority was reserved for the commission in order to reassert imperial control over military matters.[43]

The second way in which the Song emperors tightened their control was by reorganizing the top echelon of the bureaucracy to consolidate their power. The Song emperors assigned different aspects of every policy issue to different bureaucratic organizations, so each organization could not dictate any policy areas. As Paul Smith points out, the three departments—State, the Chancellery, and the Secretariat—had stood as the collective pinnacle of government since the post-Han period. By the eighth century, however, the functional distinctions among them had become blurred. This led to the formation of a combined Secretariat-Chancellery, which was normally headed by a chief councilor, supported by a structure of staff offices that duplicated and supplanted the six ministries of the Department of State Affairs. By the early Song era, the Secretariat-Chancellery controlled all civilian affairs except remonstrance, and together with the Military Affairs Commission comprised the two main government administrations—civil and military. Early emperors

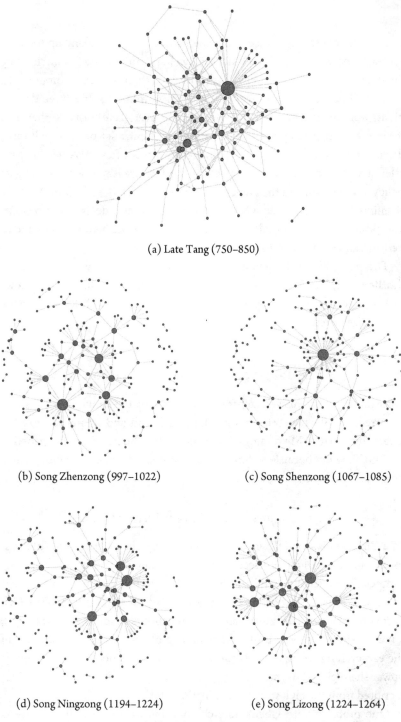

(a) Late Tang (750–850)

(b) Song Zhenzong (997–1022)

(c) Song Shenzong (1067–1085)

(d) Song Ningzong (1194–1224)

(e) Song Lizong (1224–1264)

FIGURE 4.4: Major Officials' Marriage Networks in Tang and Song
Source: Author's data collection.

in the Song era saw the three departments as a way of breaking up the concentrated power of the Secretariat-Chancellery and its chief councilors by dividing the single unified civil authority into three separate components. In new administrative protocols announced in mid-1082, the three departments were revived in a way that diluted their overall authority. Rather than making each department responsible for a particular set of issues, all three departments were made to share different aspects of every issue: the Secretariat was to consider and deliberate, the Chancellery was to investigate policy alternatives, and the Department of State Affairs—the pinnacle of the six ministries—was tasked with putting the final policy decisions into effect. Except in the most unusual circumstances, each department was required to perform and memorialize about its own function alone.[44]

The political elites, fragmented since the Song times, were less able to threaten the rulers. This is consistent with figure 2.10 in chapter 2, which shows that emperors from the Song period onward were significantly less likely to be deposed by elites.

4.4   The Tang-Song Transition: When and Why?

Historians have extensively debated when and why the Tang-Song transition occurred. I briefly review their competing arguments and use my data to adjudicate the debates. My findings demonstrate that the transition happened in the late Tang era because a climate shock prompted a mass rebellion, which destroyed the medieval aristocracy.

4.4.1   Empress Wu in the Late Seventh Century

The Chinese historian Chen Yinke contends that the shift from the old aristocracy to a new ruling class recruited from the examinations happened during Empress Wu's reign around the turn of the seventh century. Chen argues that the founding Tang ruling class was the northwestern aristocracy, which later combined with the great clans of the northeast. Empress Wu (624–705), a female sovereign who broke the male line of succession, was not part of the earlier Tang ruling class. According to Chen's account, after she came to power she replaced the aristocracy with a group of "newly risen bureaucrats" recruited from the civil service examinations.[45]

One problem with Chen's elite competition argument is that he treats the aristocrats and the exam-recruited bureaucrats as two separate groups of elites. The aristocrats, however, had largely co-opted the exam system. Before the expansion of printing in the eleventh century, only wealthy and well-connected individuals could access the books needed to study for the examinations.[46] The majority of successful exam candidates were thus from the great clans.

4.4.2   An Lushan Rebellion in the Mid-eighth Century

Denis Twitchett's explanation of the Tang-Song transition instead emphasizes the institutional and political innovations implemented in the aftermath of the An Lushan Rebellion in the mid-eighth century. He contends that the breakdown of public land tenure (i.e., the equal-field system) and the deregulation of commerce created an environment favorable to the development of new landed and commercial elites. The central government also established provincial financial commissions after the rebellion to tap into these commercial profits. These commissions preferred men of talent to scions of the aristocracy and began recruiting the sons of merchants. This gave "newly risen" elites unprecedented opportunities to enter officialdom and, over time, to acquire political influence.[47]

Yet Twitchett's argument underestimates the old elite's ability to withstand changes in institutional and societal structures. According to David Johnson, in the post–An Lushan period, the majority of Tang chief councilors still came from aristocratic families.[48]

4.4.3   Huang Chao Rebellion in the Late Ninth Century

In Naito Konan's seminal work, he maintains that the Tang marked the end of the period of aristocratic government, and the Song the beginning of the period of autocratic rule, with the late Tang and Five Dynasties (907–960) as the transitional period.[49] Naito, however, is ambiguous about *why* the transition occurred at this time.

David Johnson analyzes the family backgrounds of chief councilors in the Tang and Song eras, and shows that more than half of the Tang chief councilors were from the great clans, compared to one out of forty in the first century of the Song Dynasty.[50] From this observation he concludes, "The old oligarchy suffered a tremendous setback after the fall of the Tang."[51]

What was the "tremendous setback?" The ninth century had some of the coldest years in Chinese history (recall figure 2.2). The cold weather, exacerbated by a prolonged drought, created famine conditions in central China.[52]

In 875, Huang Chao, a failed exam candidate and salt smuggler, collected a group of several thousand followers and joined the numerous rebellions then sweeping the country. Huang's troops captured the capitals of Luoyang and Changan in 881. By studying the tomb epitaphs of the great clans, Nicolas Tackett shows that the Huang Chao Rebellion was catastrophic for the great families, which were concentrated in the capital area. During the two years of occupation, Huang Chao's troops nearly annihilated the local population, including most of the aristocratic families.[53]

4.4.4   From Northern to Southern Song in the Early Twelfth Century

Lastly, some scholars argue that the transition occurred between the Northern and Southern Song in the early twelfth century. In a pioneering article, Robert Hartwell gives less weight to changes between the Tang and Song eras than between the two halves of the Song Dynasty. He argues that a "professional elite" specialized in government service and perpetuated itself in high offices over multiple generations in the Northern Song, while in the Southern Song a "local elite" based its power in local society and "viewed a bureaucratic career as only one of a variety of occupational choices."[54]

Robert Hymes, studying a local sample in Fuzhou (Jiangxi Province), notes that the social behaviors associated with Hartwell's Northern Song "professional elite"—capital residence, intermarriage regardless of regional origin, and self-perpetuation in government—disappeared during the Southern Song period. Hymes concludes that whereas elite families in the Northern Song pursued a "national" or "bureaucratic" strategy centered on attaining high office and building cross-regional marriage networks, elite families in the Southern Song followed a "localist" strategy that concentrated on marrying locally and consolidating their local power base.[55]

Some follow-up studies have questioned Hymes' argument. Beverly Bossler, focusing on the 133 Northern and Southern Song chief councilors, reveals more continuity than change between the two halves of the Song era, which leads her to argue that the geography of marriage was primarily a function of political status: higher-ranking officials in both periods were more likely to have in-laws from outside their hometowns than their lower-ranking contemporaries. She asserts that the higher incidence of local marriage in the Southern Song era can be attributed to the fact that more marriages of commoners were documented in this period.[56]

Sukhee Lee's study of Mingzhou (Zhejiang Province) also reveals remarkable continuity, rather than change, in the patterns of elite marriage between the two halves of the Song period. He contends that elite families in both the Northern and Southern Song arranged a mix of local and non-local marriages. In both periods, Lee shows, approximately half of the elite marriages were between families from the same county while a third were across prefectural borders.[57]

4.4.5   Turning to Data

I use comprehensive data to examine when the Tang-Song transition happened. The timing will also help us understand *why* it happened. Prior studies have shown that we need to use a consistent sample of elites throughout the Tang and Song eras in order to make accurate comparisons. My data include all major national officials from both dynasties. By focusing on the upper echelons of Chinese elites over six centuries, I am able to explore changes and continuities over a long period of time.

I examine three indicators that are emphasized in the literature. First, I calculate the proportion of major officials who entered the bureaucracy through the civil service examinations. This percentage reflects the importance of the examination system in bureaucratic recruitment. Second, I calculate the proportion of major officials who entered the bureaucracy through the civil service examinations *and* were from aristocratic families to determine the extent to which the aristocrats co-opted the exams to perpetuate their power, as prior studies have found. Lastly, I examine the major officials' marriage patterns. I use the standardized localization score (introduced in chapter 2) to measure how local these elites' kinship networks were. I use this measure to explore what Hymes calls the "localist" turn in marriage strategies.

Figure 4.5 shows the proportion of officials who entered the bureaucracy through the civil service examinations (lightly shaded), and the proportion of officials who entered through the examinations *and* were of aristocratic descent (darkly shaded). I divide the officials into cohorts by the year they entered positions at the vice-ministerial level or above.

The figure shows that the percentage of major officials recruited through the examinations never surpassed 50 percent during the entire Tang period. Most of these exam-recruited bureaucrats were from aristocratic families, suggesting that the aristocrats did indeed exploit the exam system. By contrast,

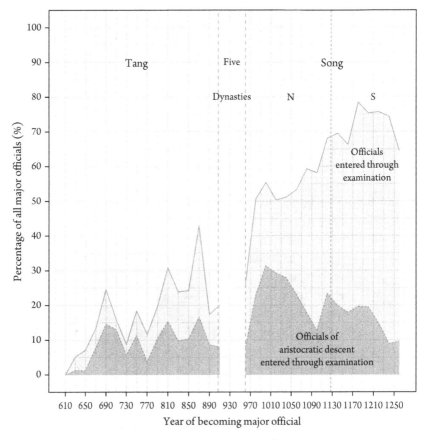

FIGURE 4.5: Bureaucratic Recruitment of Major Officials from Tang to Song
Source: Author's data collection.

during the Song era, the percentage of exam-recruited key officials was almost always over 50 percent and reached almost 80 percent toward the end of the dynasty. Most of these exam-recruited bureaucrats were not of aristocratic descent. Although there were changes in the late seventh and mid-eighth centuries, suggesting a link to Empress Wu's reign and the aftermath of the An Lushan Rebellion, the true structural break occurred in the late Tang era. The most significant increase in the use of examinations and the rise of the gentry occurred between the late Tang and early Song periods.

Next, I examine the elites' marriage patterns. Figure 4.6 shows the major officials' kinship network localization scores (with 95 percent confidence intervals) from the Tang to the Song eras. Recall that the higher the score, the more localized the kinship network is. During the Tang period, the scores were

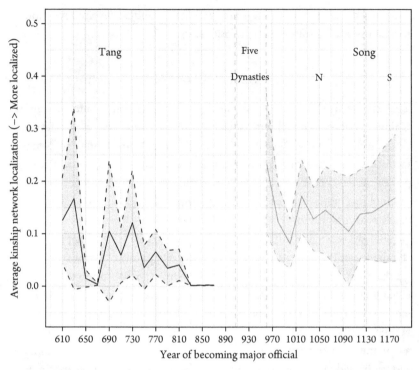

FIGURE 4.6: Major Officials' Kinship Networks from Tang to Song
Source: Author's data collection.

less than 0.1 and became smaller toward the end of the dynasty. By contrast, the scores increased during the Song Dynasty and remained above 0.1 throughout the Song era. This figure reaffirms the pattern that a structural break occurred between the Tang and Song dynasties.

In sum, my findings indicate that an elite transformation in Chinese history occurred in the tenth century that involved the decline of the medieval aristocracy, the rise of meritocracy, and the localization of elite kinship networks. The timing supports the arguments put forward by Naito Konan, David Johnson, and Nicolas Tackett. The climate shock triggered the mass violence during the late Tang period, which destroyed the national aristocracy and created a power vacuum. The early Song emperors seized the opportunity and expanded the civil service examinations to recruit local gentry elites. This strategy served the interests of the monarch because, as E. A. Kracke and Ping-ti Ho show, the civil service examinations increased social mobility and prevented the emergence of a new aristocracy. The elite transformation between the Tang and Song dynasties marks a new era of Chinese political development and led to a new model of state-society relations.

4.5   A New Model of State-Society Relations

The demise of the aristocracy and the rise of the gentry altered how the Chinese state connected with society. If we characterize state-society relations under the Tang Dynasty as a state-dominant direct rule, the Song era facilitated a state-society partnership in which entrenched local elites bargained, but also collaborated, with the state. This partnership became a self-reinforcing equilibrium, contributing to imperial rule's exceptional durability in the next millennium.

The civil service examinations played a crucial role in shaping this partnership between the state and society. As Peter Bol points out, during the Song era the examination system was transformed from an institution for recruiting civil officials into one that allowed local elites to claim the privilege of belonging to a relatively homogenous social elite. When most sons of existing gentry families neither passed the examinations nor gained official rank, they needed a new mechanism to prove they were still part of the elite. The examination system provided the gentry throughout the empire with a universal mechanism for educating the next generation in what it meant to be a member of the literati, perpetuating their families in the local elite, and controlling the membership therein.[58] The examinations, therefore, created a channel of state legitimation and a myth of meritocracy that kept the bowtie together.

To maintain their positions as part of the elite over generations, local gentry families invented a new form of organization. In 1050, Fan Zhongyan—a Northern Song politician—created the first trust-based lineage. Wealthy members of the Fan lineage donated 1,000 or so *mu* (approximately 90 soccer fields) of paddy fields. The annual rents provided Fan's relatives and their descendants with regular support: equal daily grants of grain and annual winter clothing, housing, an education for the boys, financial support for examination candidates, and marriage and funeral expenses. A designated clan member served as the manager of the landed trust endowment, its revenue, and its grant distribution. The trust was intended to be permanent, and its property inalienable.[59]

Fan's lineage proved to be extremely successful. Its numbers rose from approximately 90 in 1050 to over 200 in 1139 and "several hundreds and tens" by 1210. Yet the trust needed little additional land in the rest of the Northern

Song.[60] The trust-based lineage increasingly crowded the countryside of southern China and became the model large kinship organization from the late twelfth century onward.[61]

Such lineage organizations helped secure the long-term survival of gentry families as a unified kinship group. With their entrenched local power base and local interests at heart, the gentry elite from the Song era onward became what Robert Hymes calls "local advocates." They intervened directly and openly with local and central officials to influence the course of local events and government actions.[62]

Nevertheless, the gentry also depended on the state and could not afford to separate from it. Sukhee Lee shows that connectedness to—rather than independence from—the state granted the gentry prestige and safeguarded their local prominence. Some families occasionally obtained offices, which brought privileges, including exemption from taxes and services.[63] This partnership with the state emerged under the Song Dynasty and was reinforced in the Yuan era, when the gentry elite had to collaborate and bargain with an ethnically alien regime.[64] The partnership, when it finally consolidated during the Ming and Qing eras, was key to imperial China's durable rule.

PART III

State Maintaining under Partnership

5

The Rise of the Bowtie in the Song Dynasty

5.1   A Dynasty Full of Paradoxes

When Zhao Kuangyin, a palace guard commander in the service of the Later Zhou Dynasty (951–960), usurped power from a seven-year-old child emperor in 960, there was little indication that his new Song Dynasty would last longer than any of the short-lived dynasties that had ruled China after the Tang.[1] The collapse of Tang power in the final decades of the ninth century unleashed immense forces of rebellion, warlordism, and territorial fragmentation, giving way to a half-century of political division and social turmoil during the Five Dynasties and Ten Kingdoms period (907–960).[2] Zhao Kuangyin and his successors unified the empire, put the military generals under civilian control, expanded the civil service examination system, and created what Mark Elvin has called an "economic revolution."[3] Naito Konan seminally argues that the Song era marks the beginning of China's "modern age," which was significantly different from the medieval period.[4] Today's Chinese are still awed by the Song capital's vibrant economic and social life as depicted in the handscroll painting "Going Up the River During the Spring Festival."

The Song state, society, and economy were rapidly changing; a new equilibrium was established only after a long process of adaptation and adjustment. This process featured at least three paradoxes. The first was the coexistence of a strong monarch and an entrenched local elite. On the one hand, Song rulers gained considerable power over the bureaucracy. While the Tang rulers were constrained by aristocratic interests, the Song rulers exercised almost absolute control over their handpicked officials. On the other hand, it was during the

Song era that a local elite emerged, became entrenched, and sought to prevent state intrusion. This local elite negotiated and collaborated with the central state via its newly invented lineage organizations and governed local affairs on behalf of the ruler. Using Michael Mann's terminology, the Song had strong despotic power but weak infrastructural power.[5]

The second paradox was the coexistence of patronage and merit within the bureaucracy. The early Song emperors expanded the civil service examinations and started conferring hundreds of degrees in every exam cycle. These examinations were competitive and anonymous: only the brightest (and not necessarily those with the best connections) passed. The Song emperors, however, also granted certain high officials the right to "protect" their families by directly appointing designated sons, nephews, or grandsons to office. At any given time in the early Song period, these "princelings" staffed half of the bureaucracy; scholar-officials who were awarded degrees through the exam system filled the rest of the bureaucratic positions.

The last paradox of the transformation that took place during the Song Dynasty was the fusion of successes and failures. During the Song era, government revenues (both in per capita terms and as a share of national income) reached their highest level of the entire imperial period (recall figures 2.8 and 2.9 in chapter 2). For the only time in pre-nineteenth-century Chinese history, revenue from nonagricultural sources equaled—and even surpassed—agricultural revenue in the central government's budget.[6] Nevertheless, the Song period was famous for its military weakness. While the Northern Song could maintain a minimal peace with Tangut Xixia and Khitan Liao by paying an annual tribute, it was finally defeated by Jurchen Jin and fled to the south. The Southern Song was then swallowed up by the Mongol Empire. Song elites tried to strengthen the military by introducing national conscription—in a process parallel to European state building.[7] This effort failed due to opposition from powerful politicians.

———

We can explain these paradoxes using a state-in-society perspective. Following the theoretical framework laid out in chapter 1, I argue that the key to understanding Song politics is the newly risen scholar-officials who became more powerful throughout the Song era. Their social terrain, coalition strategies, and political incentives help us identify the essential conflict that characterizes this period.

After the demise of the Tang aristocracy, a group of merit-based elites rose to power through the civil service examination system. These scholar-officials maintained localized social networks and represented local interests—and competed with patronage-based elites who had obtained their positions through family connections. The patronage-based elites perpetuated their influence through their ancestors' privileges and handed down their power to successive generations. Their behavior resembled that of the Tang aristocrats: they built cross-regional marriage alliances and represented the national interest. While the patronage elites supported a proactive state with higher rates of taxation and a national army, the scholar-officials strived to protect their local interests by keeping the state weak.

The patronage elites formed a coalition supporting an important state-strengthening reform—the Wang Anshi Reform—during the Northern Song era. The initial implementation of the reform successfully increased Song government revenues, which were unparalleled in Chinese history. But the dominance of local interests in the central government led to the reform's eventual failure. The scholar-officials turned instead to rely on private-order organizations. During the Song Dynasty, trust-based lineage organizations emerged to replace other social organizations, and dominated China's social arena for the next millennium.

The sovereign's dilemma manifested itself in a striking way during the Song Dynasty. While localized scholar-officials undermined the emperor's effort to strengthen the state, their fragmentation enabled the emperor to divide and conquer. The Song era witnessed the end of state strengthening and the beginning of an absolute monarchy.

The rest of the chapter is structured as follows. Section 5.2 provides an overview of the early Song state, focusing on the relationship between the ruler and his bureaucracy, the fiscal system, and the military system. Section 5.3 discusses the two types of Song elites: patronage-based professional elites and newly risen scholar-officials. Section 5.4 uses the Wang Anshi Reform as a case study to examine how these two types of elites differed in their preferences regarding the ideal strength of the state. Using information from an original dataset I compiled on the major officials from this period, I show that the nationally marrying professional elites were more likely to support the state-strengthening reform than the locally marrying scholar-officials. Sections 5.5 and 5.6 then explore how the Song state and society, respectively, changed after the Wang Anshi Reform. Section 5.7 concludes by summarizing the main trends in the Song times and afterwards.

5.2   The Early Song State

The Song state was founded on two legacies. The first was the half-century of division, fragmentation, and chaos after the fall of the Tang Dynasty. A chief challenge facing the Song founders was to recentralize power from the military governors and regional warlords while rebuilding the apparatus of the centralized, bureaucratic state.[8] The second was the distant memory of the glorious Tang era. Its basic ideas of governing helped the Song founders, who exploited the Tang legacy and aspired to replicate its success.

5.2.1   The Emperor

The Song era began more as a whimper than a grand event.[9] Zhao Kuangyin, the Song founder, established his dynasty not with a great conquest or an epic struggle but with a furtive palace coup.[10] Subsequent Song emperors took pains to ensure they were not the victim of a similar plot.[11]

Within a year of assuming the throne, Zhao Kuangyin famously employed the occasion of a private drinking party to persuade his generals to exchange their posts for comfortable sinecures as military governors.[12] He then subjected the command hierarchy to more centralized surveillance and control by creating a civilian office, the Military Affairs Commission, and giving it paramount responsibility for military administration. Zhao's description of his fierce determination in this area has been preserved; he asserted: "I am sending more than a hundred scholarly officials with administrative skill to take over the various regional government offices. Even if all of them should turn out to be corrupt, their corruption would hardly be as bad as that of a single corrupt military man."[13] This process took decades to complete. Zhao's brother, who succeeded him, finally finished dismantling the territorial jurisdictions of the remaining military governors and replaced them with civilian officials under the capital's direct control.[14]

The Song founders' choice of centralized control over military autonomy—often described using the phrase "emphasizing the civil and de-emphasizing the military"—is sometimes cited as a source of the dynasty's putative military weakness.[15] But its tightened grip over the military secured the position of the Song emperors for generations and created a new pattern for Chinese politics.[16]

Song monarchs were young or middle-aged adults who occupied their thrones for relatively long periods of time. Unlike in preceding dynasties, there were no baby emperors, no emperors poisoned by eunuchs, no emperors assassinated by military generals, and none deposed by their brothers-in-law. In addition to establishing civilian control of the military, Song monarchs also secured their position by fragmenting the bureaucracy.

Two headquarters occupied the top of the Song bureaucracy: the Military Affairs Commission and the Secretariat-Chancellery. After 1082, Emperor Shenzong (1067–1085) divided and reorganized the Secretariat-Chancellery into three departments: the Department of the Secretariat, the Department of the Chancellery, and the Department of State Affairs.[17] Li Qingchen, a key contemporary politician, remarked, "in his late years Shenzong set up the three departments so he could divide the authority of the councilors and have them watch and check on each other. These were farsighted plans."[18] The Military Affairs Commission, in charge of military policy making, answered directly to the emperor, who guarded this authority and was reluctant to share it, even with chief councilors.[19]

In the second decade of the eleventh century, the Song emperor revived the Censorate (御史台) as a "watchdog" for the bureaucracy.[20] Its purpose was twofold. First, the Censorate independently gathered information and kept the emperor informed about conditions in the state. Second, it kept watch over the bureaucracy and enforced the rules and standards of official conduct. The censors were the sovereign's "eyes and ears."[21] The emperor used the Censorate to keep the power of his chief councilors in check. In 1055, the censor Zhao Bian warned Emperor Renzong (997–1022) that the Censorate was the only effective check on the power of the chief councilors: if the Censorate does not function, "you will not be informed, you will hear no sentiments from below, and ultimately your own position will be endangered."[22]

These institutional configurations placed the emperor far above his officials. Not only were his power and security enhanced; the social distance between the emperor and his ministers increased.[23] As Naito Konan seminally argues, the Song introduced the "monarchical dictatorship" characteristic of late imperial China.[24]

5.2.2   The Bureaucracy

The Song Dynasty marked China's transition from the rule of oligarchs to the rule of bureaucrats. Taizong (976–997), the second Song emperor, dramatically increased the number of degrees conferred through the civil service examinations in 977. From then until the end of the Song era, an average of 192 degrees were awarded each year; an elaborate institutional structure developed to accommodate the expanded system.[25]

John Chaffee lists three motivations behind Taizong's decision to expand the exam system. First, with the conquest of southern China virtually complete, the Song Dynasty faced the challenge of staffing a growing bureaucracy. Second, the great aristocratic families had largely disappeared, so there was no elite group ready to inherit the mantle of government. Third, faced with a recent history of military domination of the government and his own military misfortunes in the war against Khitan Liao that had alienated him from his generals, Taizong used the examinations to curb the power of the generals and the predominantly military elite.[26]

In the long run, the exam system proved to be a brilliant success. By making learning a primary path to power, the Song emperors channeled the energies and secured the allegiance of the landholding elites, and thus provided an enduring foundation of support for the dynasty. John Chaffee estimates that the schools and examinations collectively involved some 200,000 literati in the late Northern Song period. By the mid-Southern Song era, an estimated 400,000 candidates sat the triennial examinations in a much smaller empire. In the most developed and cultured prefectures of the southeast, 2–7 percent of the adult male population typically took the exam.[27]

But the Chinese bureaucracy was not staffed only by these educated men. The Jesuit missionaries used the Latin term *literati* to refer generally to the educated ruling elite of imperial China. This term stressed the common literate culture these officials acquired by preparing for the civil service examinations, in contrast to the often semi-literate aristocracy of the Jesuits' native Europe. In the Song era, however, many of these officials—especially those in the lower ranks of the military bureaucracy—never sat examinations and were barely literate. According to one estimate from the Southern Song, about 3,000 of all government officials were civilians. Merely 40 percent of this group, or 1,200, had passed the examinations and were highly literate.[28] These officials staffed the upper levels of the civilian court administration and served in top provincial posts.[29]

According to the same estimate, 57 percent of officials had entered the service through the *yin* (荫) privilege. *Yin* means "to shelter, cover, or protect." The Song system of protection privilege granted officials above a certain rank the right to designate sons, grandsons, brothers, nephews—or, in some cases, even unrelated persons—for "protection." The recipients bypassed the exams and received an immediate rank, which then qualified them to compete for a functional position.[30]

Corruption and cheating were undoubtedly prevalent in the examinations. Song rulers invented the practice of "blind grading" to prevent powerful officials from influencing the process. Beginning in 992, slips of paper were placed and sealed over the candidates' names in the palace examination papers. Concerns that examiners might recognize a candidate's calligraphy and be partial in their grading led to the further measure of having clerks copy out all examinations before they went to the examiners.[31]

Once recruited into the bureaucracy, each official obtained a rank. The rank determined, for example, where he stood at formal court ceremonies, the color of his official uniform, and the size of his funeral. It also determined the extent of his *yin* privilege.[32]

We do not have sufficient information to assess how promotions worked in the hierarchy. Charles Hartman argues that Song officials' careers were determined by sponsored endorsements and performance evaluations. Every few years, officials submitted documentation to the Bureau of Personnel Evaluation. This documentation included patents of appointment for their present and past functional positions and promotions, a biography, annual evaluations, and, when required, recommendations.[33] Most scholars, however, question how effectively any of the evaluation systems were implemented.[34] Endorsements from powerful officials became crucial. Hartman concludes that any official who rose above the level of prefect (the level below province) in Song China was either extraordinarily gifted or extraordinarily well connected.[35]

5.2.3 The Fiscal System

If the monarchy and bureaucracy reflected the Song Dynasty's response to the previous half-century's militarization and dislocation, the fiscal system was built on another legacy. The Song emperors inherited the basic financial structure from their Tang predecessors and continued the trend of expanding the commercial tax that started in the late Tang era.

The Song's taxation system was based on the Tang-era Two-Tax Reform introduced in 780 (see chapter 3). The autumn tax, which produced about three-quarters of the annual agrarian tax revenues, was collected sometime between the ninth and second months, depending on the area; it assessed a certain amount of grain, or grain and cash, on the expected production of each *mu* (0.15 acres) cultivated in grain or, in the southeast, rice. The summer tax was a money assessment on the expected production of all cultivated fields, including vegetable gardens and orchards, but it too was often commuted to silk or wheat; it was collected between the fifth and ninth months. Together, the summer and autumn taxes were the chief source of government revenues in kind.[36]

The Song Dynasty continued the trend of land privatization that started in the Tang era. The once-prevalent idea that all land in the empire belonged to the emperor had been quietly buried. In the Song period, even tenants who worked government land acquired legal claims to it—claims that could be bought and sold. By the time of the Song era, land had become primarily a basis for assessing taxes and labor services.[37]

To collect the two land taxes, the government divided cultivated land according to its productive capacity into three or four categories, which had different tax rates. The general principle was that no more than one-tenth or one-fifteenth of the total harvest should be paid as the biannual tax described above. Though the tax rates varied enormously across localities, this principle was generally observed; taxes in some areas were as low as one-twentieth or one-thirtieth of the harvest.[38] On top of the two land taxes, the government levied a wide variety of supplementary and miscellaneous taxes and surcharges, such as a transport fee to cover the cost of shipping tax money and goods.[39]

In addition to the land tax, the Song Dynasty also levied a head tax, proportional to the number of adult males aged 20–59 in each household. The head tax was usually paid either in cash or in rice but occasionally in other items such as wheat, spun silk, or salt. In line with a long-term trend moving away from such taxes, the government collected the head tax only in southeast and south China.[40]

The traditional land and head taxes, however, could not keep up with the government's ever-increasing financial needs. The need to pay, outfit, and provision troops stationed along the resource-poor northern frontier forced the Song state to dig deeper into the commercial and agrarian economies, transforming China during this period into what Paul Smith calls a "perpetual wartime economy"[41] or what Guanglin Liu terms a "fiscal state."[42] The number of imperial troops grew from 193,000 around 970 to over 350,000 at the turn of the century, and 432,000 around 1020. In the late 1030s and early 1040s, war with Tangut Xixia in the northwest and uneasy relations with Khitan Liao almost doubled this figure, to 826,000. The enormous cost of supplying armies of this size forced some reductions over the next two decades but, in the mid-1060s, the total still stood at 663,000.[43]

The government therefore needed to increase its revenues. This entailed efforts to collect more revenue from nonagricultural sources of taxation such as its monopolies and the commercial tax. The result was one of the most striking developments of the Song period: for the only time in pre-nineteenth-century Chinese history, revenue from nonagricultural sources equaled and even surpassed agricultural revenues in the central government's budget.[44]

The rapid expansion of the population into south China, technological innovations in agriculture, and the growth of a nationwide trade network made taxing commerce more feasible than it had been. The coastal cities of the east and southeast also became major centers of shipbuilding and international trade. The rapid urbanization and growth of commercial enterprises provided many opportunities for the Song state to exercise its entrepreneurial ingenuity.[45]

The two basic components of the commercial tax were: (1) a transit tax on commodities being transported and (2) a sales tax collected when goods were retailed and, sometimes, when traders purchased them from the producers. These taxes were paid at commercial tax offices.[46] Early in the dynasty (mid-tenth century), over two thousand tax collection centers were established in rural market towns and fairs to collect a sales tax of 3 percent and a transport tax of 2 percent on the retail price of merchandise. Revenues from this source increased fivefold by the middle of the eleventh century.[47]

Song government revenue reached its peak in the mid to late eleventh century at what might have been the highest level in Chinese history. Comparing government revenue for 1064 and 1578 reveals that, although its income from agricultural sources was virtually identical, revenue from nonagricultural sectors under the Song Dynasty was an astounding nine times greater than in the Ming era (1368–1644). During the Ming–Qing period, the Chinese government collected 2–5 percent of national income as taxes;[48] nineteenth-century European states collected 4–6 percent. Estimates for the Song era rely on more tenuous data, but range from 13 percent to an impressive 24 percent.[49]

5.2.4   The Military

The Song Dynasty firmly established the principle of civilian control of the military. The Military Affairs Commission, the highest military organ, employed a greater proportion of civil officials as time went on. During the founding emperor's reign, four of the senior officials on the commission were civil officials and six were military officers. During the second emperor's reign, there were twenty-one civilians and fourteen military officials. And during the reign of the third emperor, the balance shifted to twenty-nine civil officials and fourteen military officers.[50]

The regular armies of the Northern Song were the imperial armies (禁军), originally the personal army of the emperor. The commanding generals and the various units of the imperial armies were thrown together at a moment's notice and were unfamiliar with each other. This reduced the threat to the emperor by preventing generals from developing close relationships with the forces they commanded, but seriously weakened the fighting ability of the imperial armies. The imperial armies were initially central armies that were stationed in the capital, Kaifeng, and rotated to fortify the provinces and the frontier. Later, more and more provincially recruited imperial armies were deployed locally, especially in districts along the northern frontier. These provincial imperial armies did not serve in the capital, but were rotated to fortify the provinces.[51]

In addition to the imperial armies, the Northern Song permanently maintained prefectural armies, local militias, frontier tribal troops, local troops, and bowmen as reserve forces.[52]

Military conscription had never been fully enforced in China after the Han Dynasty abolished universal military service (see chapter 3). The Song Dynasty used volunteers and recruits. It recruited troops particularly during calamitous years when natural disasters made it impossible for peasants to make a living, and military service could be an effective safety valve to prevent rebellions or uprisings by destitute and unemployed people. The government also encouraged the children of military families to follow in the footsteps of their fathers and elder brothers.[53] After soldiers were recruited, they were required to have their faces or arms tattooed with the designation of their military unit in order to prevent desertion. There were many salaried ranks for officers and enlisted men as well as several specific types of allowances. Most military personnel, however, received small allowances, making it difficult for them to live off of their salaries.[54] Military careers were much less prestigious than civil careers. While most civil officials were recruited through the examinations and occupied positions of power, most military officials inherited their rank and occupied more peripheral positions. There was an enormous social distance between the two groups.[55]

Song state building occurred alongside a parallel process of state formation on the steppe. The rapid evolution of Inner Asian statecraft in the tenth to thirteenth centuries allowed states on the northern frontier to support formidable armies. This advantage offset agrarian China's greater wealth and numbers, which prevented the Song Dynasty from assuming a position of supremacy at the center of a China-dominated world order. It was relegated to the position of equal participant in a multi-state East Asian system.[56]

An enduring weakness of the Song military vis-à-vis the nomadic regimes was its shortage of military horses and the backwardness of its cavalry. In the mid-Tang times, the Chinese regime lost the horse-producing areas of the northwest. Thus soldiers had to trade with the minority peoples of the northwest to obtain horses during the Song era. Many of these horses were unsuitable for service as military mounts. Often during the Northern Song, 30–40 percent of cavalrymen were without mounts; by the Southern Song times the proportion of cavalrymen was even smaller. This was an important reason for the Song Dynasty's military failures.[57]

In 1005, the Song government signed the Chanyuan Treaty with Khitan Liao, which involved agreeing to make annual payments and acknowledging Khitan control over the "16 prefectures," a large swath of territory south of the Great Wall that extended from Datong in modern Shanxi in the east through modern Beijing to the coast. Furthermore, the Tangut state of Xixia in the northwest controlled the Ordos region within the bend of the Yellow River and the modern Gansu corridor. After 1127, the Jurchen Jin Dynasty took control of all territory north of the Huai River. The Song Dynasty's failure to re-exert Chinese control over these areas was a constant source of wounded pride and a driving force in domestic politics.[58]

The north and northwest borders were always insecure and required the presence of large standing armies for defense. Unlike other dynasties, which relied on civilian militias conscripted from the peasant population, the Song maintained paid professional armies. For most of the Northern Song era, the state financed a standing army of one million soldiers from a general population of sixty million people. Military expenses for pay, supply, and armaments regularly consumed the vast majority of the state budget.[59] Periods of open hostility, such as the Tangut wars in the 1040s, produced large government deficits and economic instability, and unleashed domestic pressures that roiled the political establishment.[60]

5.3   Elite Social Terrain before the Wang Anshi Reform

The high-ranking elites in the Song bureaucracy were by no means homogeneous. As discussed above, the early Song period was a transitional phase; many elites secured their jobs through patronage, and rising numbers were recruited through the examinations. The patronage system provided a "legacy" track to grant privileges to men from prestigious families, such as the offspring of the founding emperor's core supporters. These "legacy" elites resembled the Tang aristocrats. They considered office holding to be the only career option and aggressively built cross-regional marriage coalitions with other prestigious families.

Yet an increasing number of officials entered the bureaucracy through the examinations. As I show in chapter 4, these families understood the uncertainties of bureaucratic careers and considered office holding as only one career option among several for their sons. Rather than intermarrying with powerful families from afar, they consolidated their local power bases by building local marriage networks.

I constructed an original dataset that includes biographical and network information for all of the major officials (vice-ministerial level or above) during Emperor Shenzong's reign (1067–1085). I use this dataset to investigate the social relations of a generation of Song elites, and to analyze the politics during the Wang Anshi Reform, which happened during Shenzong's reign.

The Northern Song bureaucracy had thirty levels, ranging from the chief councilor to the county clerk.[61] Song emperors designated officials at the vice-ministerial level or above as "major advisory officials" who could wear purple (a symbol of prestige) and appear in court to discuss policy issues with the emperor.[62]

I identify 137 major officials from Li Zhiliang's list of Shenzong officials.[63] They included chief councilors, central secretariats, leaders of major ministries, and the emperor's main advisors.[64] They were all male, Han Chinese, and from landowning elite families. They were, on average, fifty-one years old in 1067. More than two-thirds (70 percent) obtained their jobs by passing the civil service exam; the rest inherited their positions.[65] On average, they started their political careers in 1047: twenty years before Shenzong came to power. Their average bureaucratic rank was ministerial. Using the same approach elaborated in chapter 2, I mapped these officials' kinship networks and geocoded every kin member's location.

Analyzing this dataset reveals a simple pattern that is consistent with the broader narrative. If an official's father obtained his position by passing the civil service examinations (rather than by inheriting it), the official was more likely to have a localized kinship network.[66] This does not mean that every official whose father passed the exams had a localized kinship network. Wang Anshi's father entered officialdom through the exams, but Wang Anshi had a geographically dispersed kinship network (as I will show later). The relationship is probabilistic.

5.4   The Wang Anshi Reform

Constant threats from the border and exhaustive preparations for war strained the Song Dynasty's fiscal situation. In 1065, defense expenditures consumed over 80 percent of the state's income, which caused the government to register the dynasty's first financial deficit.[67] Aged and inexperienced soldiers were hired from the flotsam of the marketplace and were unfit for combat.

In 1069 Emperor Shenzong launched the New Policies, adopting the ideas of the cabinet member Wang Anshi. Later known as the Wang Anshi Reform, these policies established the goal of "enriching the nation and strengthening its military power."[68] The philosophy of the New Policies was to expand the scope of state power to intensify its participation in the market economy, in order to generate a surplus that the state then extracted to meet its fiscal and military needs.[69]

5.4.1   The New Policies

The major reform policies included:[70]

- *Cadastral Surveys and Equitable Tax* (方田均税法). This measure sought to equalize the tax burden across localities and landowners by instituting a series of cadastral surveys. Many localities and powerful families had underreported their landholdings in the past to avoid taxes.[71] The surveys revealed 34.7 million additional acres of land—54 percent of the national total.[72] The discovery of these previously untaxed lands shifted some of the tax burden away from politically powerless landowners to official families with large landholdings.
- *Military Conscription* (保甲法). Before the reform, the state relied on an inefficient and ineffective mercenary army. At the local level, villages formed a variety of voluntary defense organizations to foster security. Over time, some of these private associations became private armies controlled by local elites. The reform created a formal military organization (*baojia*) in which every ten households were organized into a small guard, every five small guard units formed a large guard, and every five large guard units formed a superior guard. Participation

in this security apparatus was compulsory, close to a conscription system; the emperor intended to eventually rotate *baojia* troops into the national army.[73] In 1075, a central bureaucratic agency started to exert control over the *baojia*. As of 1076, there were 6.9 million men on the *baojia* rosters, which represented almost half of the empire's households.[74]

- *Rural Credit* (青苗法). This policy created a state-run rural credit system that was intended to break the private credit monopoly. Previously, rural landlords had a monopoly over agricultural credit and charged high interest rates.[75] The reformers used state-run granaries to buy grains when prices were low and to resell when prices rose, or in times of natural disaster. They also converted the reserves into a liquid loan fund that was to be made in the spring and repaid in the summer and fall. The government also established rules to protect borrowers from unfair official manipulation. By supplanting landlords and private moneylenders as the principal source of rural credit, the state extracted the interest that previously enriched local elites and gave peasants access to low-interest loans.[76]

- *Labor Service* (募役法). This policy imposed a tax, called a "service assistance fee," on all households with property that wanted to avoid government labor service.[77] Before the policy, every household was obliged to undertake government service, for example as office messengers, bookkeepers, granary laborers, or local police officers. Many families were exempt by law, such as officials and town dwellers, or by practice, such as powerful local families whose influence over government clerks gave them *de facto* immunity.[78] The reform required all households eligible for drafted service to pay a tax, graduated according to their assessed wealth.

These policies successfully increased the revenues of the Song government. This income was the lifeblood of Shenzong's campaign against the Tanguts. And though the Tangut War of 1081–1083 exacted an enormous toll in money and men, the New Policies generated sufficient revenues to keep the imperial treasuries full into the next emperor's reign.[79] Meanwhile, the entire population had been organized into *baojia* security units, which gave the state a relatively cheap system of conscription. The *baojia* system also reversed the trend toward putting village-level security in the hands of local elites.[80]

Emperor Shenzong and Wang Anshi were state builders: when faced with external threats, they responded by strengthening the state. For Wang Anshi, this aligned with his family interests. He declared in a letter written in 1056 that: "My objective in entering upon official life was to provide the care for my kin."[81] In another letter written to his friend Wang Fengyuan, he said, "The really great man trains himself for the service of the state . . . I believe that Providence is operative not only in my own personal affairs, but also in the wider matters of empire."[82] Wang's notion that state and family interests were congruent was best reflected in a letter he wrote to the transportation officer Ma: "It is necessary that an individual who is desirous of increasing his family resources, should be dependent for so doing upon the particular state in which he resides. It is necessary also that he who wishes to increase the financial resources of his state should depend upon the empire in order to achieve his object."[83]

5.4.2   The Opposition

Many politicians, however, opposed the reform. They viewed the state as competing with local elite families to provide various services. For example, Sima Guang, Su Xun, Su Zhe, and Zheng Xia insisted that the wealthy served as the pillars of local society and the providers of capital (land and credit) and security to the people, and that the society and economy functioned best when they were least burdened by the state.[84] As for who should provide security, the censor Wang Yansou argued that the pre-reform system was built on a solid communal foundation, in which "households on duty with propertied roots in the community" were kept afloat during their period of service by local elites who came to their aid with labor and material assistance. Under the new reform measure, however, state employees replaced "well-established local families."[85] For Wang Yansou, as for Sima Guang, Zhang Fangping, Liu Zhi, and Yang Hui, only local men with property in the region could be trusted.[86] In the same vein, the censor Deng Runpu memorialized: "under the old system . . . the rural compatriots and relatives all acted as the eyes and ears," and charged that replacing private militias with baojia guardsmen had shattered a natural defense and surveillance network built on personal relationships, leaving local communities powerless.[87] Feng Jing, a scholar at the Institute for the Extension of Literary Arts, questioned Wang Anshi's state army: "Under the old regulations governing the private militias, the officers had all been drawn from the residential families of position and influence. In your baojia system, who will be the leaders?"[88]

Those opposed to the reform considered kinship institutions to be the most efficient way to protect their family interests. They felt that state strengthening threatened their family interests by adding extra costs through taxation. One of the opposition leaders, Sima Guang, made this point force-fully in a debate with Wang Anshi before the emperor: "The output of the world in money and goods is of a fixed and definite amount. If it is in the hands of the state then it is not in the hands of the people."[89] Fan Zhen argued in a memorial to the emperor: "The policy of creating and maintaining a standing army . . . involves the people in heavier taxation and an increase of the burden of public services. . . . On the contrary, the policy of raising Private Militia or People's Corps . . . tends to eliminate these evils . . . Taxation is lighter, and the loyalty of the people remains staunch and true."[90]

Wang Anshi called the elite families that controlled local militias and usury "engrossers"—coercive and predatory magnates who preyed on the people and usurped the fiscal prerogatives of the state.[91] The reformer Lü Huiqing asserted that the policy was so slow to take shape because of this alliance between "the baronial families of officials and engrossers who can easily get others to speak for them."[92]

Historians concur that the core conflict during the Wang Anshi Reform era was a power struggle between nationally oriented elites and informal associa-tions based on alliances between local interest groups that shared common concerns.[93] As Miyazaki Ichisada argued, many Song scholar-officials were torn between their institutional loyalty to the state and their economic loyalty to their families. Ultimately, they tended to follow their economic interests; they became corrupt and self-interested.[94]

5.4.3   Reform Failure

In an absolute monarchy, such as the Song, the ruler had the power to set the agenda, which in turn influenced policy outcomes. Leadership transitions, however, could generate significant shifts in policies and policy outcomes.[95] While the emergence of a state-building leader helps form a state-building coalition among the elites, the death of such a leader will make it difficult for the elites to continue to commit to the state-building project.

In 1074 a prolonged drought in northern China caused thousands of refugees to descend on the capital for relief. The reform's critics convinced Emperor Shenzong that the disaster was Heaven's punishment for the New Policies. Wang Anshi had no choice but to resign.[96] After the emperor's death

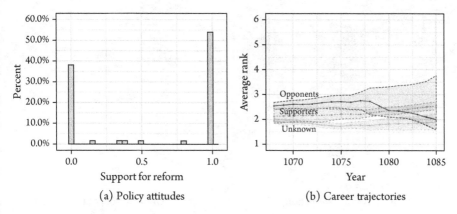

FIGURE 5.1: Major Politicians during the Wang Anshi Reform
Notes: Panel (a) shows the histogram of politicians' policy attitudes toward the state-strengthening reform; 1 indicates support and 0 denotes opposition. Panel (b) shows politicians' average bureaucratic ranks (with 95 percent confidence intervals), grouped according to their attitudes, during the whole reform period. The Y-axis runs from 1 (vice-ministerial level) to 6 (chief councilor).

in 1085, the opposition leaders completely abolished the reform, with support from the dowager empress.[97]

5.4.4   Quantitative Analysis

I now turn to my new datasets to systematically examine why some politicians supported the reform while others opposed it.[98] I probe whether each politician's support for state strengthening is an increasing function of the geographic size of his kinship network.

The politicians were polarized. As panel (a) in figure 5.1 shows, of the sixty-three politicians who expressed an attitude, thirty-four (54 percent) consistently supported the reform, while twenty-four (38 percent) consistently opposed it. Five politicians supported some of the reform policies but opposed others.[99]

Politicians' career trajectories indicate that Emperor Shenzong tried to balance the two camps. Panel (b) in figure 5.1 shows that for most of his reign, the average bureaucratic ranks of supporters and opponents were not significantly different. This suggests that the emperor promoted supporters and opponents roughly equally. As the personnel minister Zeng Gongliang advised the emperor, "it is important to have people of different opinions stirring each other up, so that no one will dare to do wrong."[100]

(a) Wang Anshi (reform leader)   (b) Lü Gongzhu (opposition leader)

FIGURE 5.2: Two Politicians' Kinship Networks

Notes: The large circles represent the locations of the officials (Wang Anshi and Lü Gongzhu), the small dots denote the locations of their kin, and lines depict kinship ties. Wang Anshi's standardized localization score is 0.003, while Lü Gongzhu's is 0.333—ten times more localized than Wang Anshi's.

I also mapped these politicians' kinship networks. Figure 5.2 illustrates with two examples. Panel (a) shows the locations of Wang Anshi's kin, and panel (b) the locations of Lü Gongzhu's kin. The kinship network of Wang Anshi (the reform leader) was scattered all over the country, while that of Lü Gongzhu (an opposition leader) was relatively local.[101]

Using regressions, I can then quantitatively evaluate the relationship between a politician's support for state strengthening and the geographic size of his kinship networks. My hypothesis is that the politicians who had more dispersed kinship networks were more likely to support the reform. My statistical analysis finds strong support for this hypothesis. Reform supporters tended to have geographically dispersed kinship networks, while opponents generally had geographically concentrated kinship networks. This relationship holds even after controlling for a wide range of alternative factors, including hometown characteristics, network centrality, size of the kinship group, number of children, factional ties, philosophical schools, external and internal threats, terrain ruggedness, family civil service exam history, and family migration.[102]

5.5   The Song Emperor's Dilemma

The Wang Anshi Reform was a watershed event in Song history. After its failure, Song central politics became increasingly factionalized. Song emperors traded state strength for personal power and were the biggest beneficiaries of

elite fractionalization. As James Liu argues, "The more bitter the power struggle among the bureaucrats became, the greater was the probability of their
depending upon the support of the emperor, of their playing into the hands
of those around the emperor and in the palace, and of their helping, by design
or by force of circumstances, the growth of absolutism."[103]

During the Wang Anshi Reform, Emperor Shenzong kept both the reformers and opponents in court in order to play them against each other. "Although
the Emperor did not seriously doubt Wang [Anshi]'s loyalty," James Liu speculates, "he was probably afraid that by giving Wang too much power he might
arouse the disloyalty of other leading officials."[104] For many years during the
New Policy era the emperor retained Wen Yanbo, Wang's firm opponent,
as head of the Military Affairs Commission, and ignored Wang's complaints
about him.[105]

Shenzong used the same strategy for other major opposition leaders, such
as Fu Bi and Sima Guang. The emperor kept Fu Bi in the capital until 1072
despite the old man's opposition to change, for example, because he felt that
Fu Bi's "prominence helped to hold together all under Heaven."[106] And Sima
Guang remained Shenzong's closest confidant—perhaps even closer intellectually than Wang Anshi—despite his intransigent opposition to every facet
of the reform agenda. For as Shenzong told Lü Gongzhu in the tenth month
of 1067, "I want Sima Guang by my side not for his opinions on affairs of
state [for as they both agreed Sima, like Wang Anshi, was rather impractical]
but because of his moral power and learning."[107] The emperor believed that
keeping the critics and dissenters by his side would "broaden what he hears
and sees."[108]

As a result, political factions were a prominent feature of Song political
life. Although earlier dynasties also had political factions, they were more
persistent in the Song era and more closely integrated into the dynasty's
political structures.[109]

Elite fragmentation helped the monarch consolidate his power. While the
Northern Song emperors still consulted their chief councilors on important
decisions, the Southern Song emperors had fully established personalist rule.
The second Southern Song emperor, Xiaozong (1162–1189), bypassed the
bureaucracy as well as his chief councilors to personally assume decision-
making authority over an increasingly wide range of affairs. He took personal
control of his government as early as 1163, after court vacillation over war
policy induced him to brush aside his two chief councilors, his Department
of State Affairs, and his Military Affairs Commission to secretly order his
commanding general to attack the Jin.[110]

5.6   Social Development after the Reform

The failure of the state-strengthening reform and the Northern Song's subsequent defeat by the Jurchen Jin reinforced the post-Tang state-society relations in China. With the large-scale flight of Song subjects and officials to the south, the bureaucratic elite of the twelfth and thirteenth centuries were absorbed into a much wider stratum of local lineages. These local lineages viewed government service as just one of an array of mobility strategies. The family and local community became a more appropriate focal point than the centralized bureaucratic state. Elites started to focus their energy and assets on investing in lineage organizations, which they used to resist pressures of downward mobility. Chinese local societies became increasingly exclusive, organized by blood lines. Local elites embedded in these ascriptive associations advocated their local interests and negotiated with the central state, which reinforced existing social cleavages. In line with this change in orientation, a new ideology—Neo-Confucianism—articulated a new conception of the link between individuals and the state that gradually emerged as the ideological underpinning of an increasingly self-conscious local gentry well into the late imperial era.

5.6.1   Shift of Power from State to Society

Robert Hymes characterized the changes from the Northern to the Southern Song as the "retreat of the state" or "shrinkage of state power."[111] He has more recently described them as a "net shift of power downward."[112] At any rate, after the failure of the Wang Anshi Reform, the locus of much political action and negotiation shifted from the central state to local society. This shift manifested in three ways.

First, the central government deliberately transferred responsibility to nongovernmental actors or the market at large. For example, the long-held salt and tea monopolies were stripped away from direct state production and marketing, and toward merchant-mediated systems that introduced licenses.[113]

Second, the state's failure to maintain control over various aspects of society allowed non-state actors to take on roles it would have preferred to monopolize or forbid. For example, the state viewed the private newspaper printers of the late Northern and Southern Song era as illegitimate, but they thrived by supplementing or substituting for the state's own capital gazettes and other channels of information to officials and the populace.[114] Another—and, for the state, more threatening—example was the private militias that sprang up in the early Southern Song, sometimes with state encouragement but often only with its tolerance, in response to the weakness of official armies against Jurchen encroachments and to maintain local order.[115]

Lastly, the state—for lack of interest, will, or funds—simply got out of the way: it stopped doing what it had long done, and let private parties and the market fill the gap. The failure of government relief strategies in the Southern Song period stimulated the development of private substitutes, such as the community granary (社倉) or private charitable granaries (义仓).[116]

As Hymes argues, these three new state tendencies—delegation of responsibility, ineffective attempts at control, and deliberate withdrawal—attracted private stand-ins, from the commercial market, local strongmen, and gentry elites.[117]

The local projects proposed by intellectual leaders of the Southern Song era, such as Zhu Xi, directly replicated the state-led institutions of the Wang Anshi Reform. While Wang envisioned a universal state school system across the empire, Zhu instead proposed local private academies.[118] While Wang created the *baojia* system controlled by the state, Zhu offered the community compact, a voluntary community-based organization that similarly aimed to maintain local order through mutual monitoring and admonition.[119] While Wang introduced a state-run rural credit system, Zhu countered with private, voluntary loans from the community granary.[120]

The local gentry elites early in the Northern Song period defined themselves through their relation to the state, particularly in the pursuit of examinations and office. By the middle Southern Song era, however, they were ensconced in the counties and prefectures of southern China as a locally rooted and largely self-ratifying elite. They defined themselves not through degrees or office, but through education and examination participation, as well as through new horizontal social networks, mostly in a certain area.[121]

5.6.2   Keep It in the Family

Once the elites shifted their focus from central politics to local society, they started to face three new challenges in their attempts to preserve and expand their wealth and power. First, land had fallen out of government control into the hands of countless private parties. By the eleventh century, families owned most of this principal form of wealth. Since sons tended to break up their family's estate upon their father's death, few families survived as a single unit for more than two or three generations. Second, whereas in the previous millennium the political elite had enjoyed privileged hereditary access to official positions, from the tenth century their sons, as well as the sons of other rich and locally eminent families, faced far greater competition for government appointments.[122] The third challenge was that the Song state became increasingly unwilling and unable to fund local public projects and defend against violence from external forces and domestic bandits. The failure of Wang Anshi's state-strengthening reform signaled to the elites that seeking help from the state was no longer a feasible option. In the eleventh century Chinese elites began turning to private-order organizations to deal with these challenges.

Kinship institutions were the most successful private-order organizations. Although kinship organizations developed and matured in the Ming-Qing era, which I discuss in more detail in chapter 7, their basic institutional form—the trust-based lineage—originated in the Song period.

Trust-based lineages did not become the dominant form of private-order institutions right away. Village worship associations, Buddhist establishments, and popular religious shrines were far more common for most of the Song era; these groups performed ritual and economic duties that lineages later took over, such as maintaining ancestral graves, ancestral worship, moneylending, and property holding.[123]

These village-level institutions and religious organizations were more inclusive than lineage organizations. For example, a village worship association was an inclusive territorial institution that actively guided a village's communal affairs. Such associations frequently serviced a whole village, but sometimes encompassed two or more smaller natural villages or a portion of a larger one. Village associations generated a shared sense of community that was based on common worship, residence, work, and defense in a particular place; this sentiment was then nurtured by long-term and multi-sided relationships among its residents, who took turns helping to manage it. Shaped by shared territorial concerns of well-being and security, the members of these communities—hamlets, villages, and even urban neighborhoods—engaged in collective public worship of a deity and formed reciprocal obligations of support.[124]

But trust-based lineages based on common descent proved to be more efficient than these rival organizations because lineage members, connected by blood, were better at solving their collective action and coordination problems. Lineages, however, were exclusive because they did not welcome members from other kin groups. Lineage organizations achieved predominance in Chinese society after the Song times as private ownership of land consolidated, and gentry elites were able to accumulate large amounts of capital over generations. With a much higher income offered by civil service jobs than by other professions,[125] the gentry elites engaged in a lucrative cycle of capital reproduction from human capital (education) to physical capital (land). This cycle sustained the lineage organizations and enabled them to dominate local societies for centuries.

5.6.3   A Negotiated Rule

A new form of state-society relations that emerged after the fall of the Tang Dynasty was consolidated in the wake of the ultimate failure of state activism during the Northern Song era and the expansion of local literati elites. The fall of the Northern Song Dynasty and the subsequent abandonment of its activist policies created not a vacuum of power in local society, but a relatively open field of negotiation. Gradually, a principle called "the mutual convenience of the public and the private" (公私两便) emerged during the Southern Song period that strikes a balance between public and private interests and treats them as moral equals. This concept implies a process of negotiation between the two.[126] In local affairs, the Southern Song government asked for, listened to, and reflected on the opinions of local leaders. It was flexible enough to exploit the work of private entrepreneurs for official purposes, as seen in Sukhee Lee's case study of Mingzhou, where local families were granted permission to run state-owned breweries in exchange for a share of the profits. The mutual convenience of the public and the private was considered a prerequisite for any good policy.[127]

5.6.4   A New Ideology

A new ideology emerged to justify the new order. As Peter Bol describes, during the Song period there was a "reconceptualization of the order of things—of the relations between past and present, cosmos and human affairs, state and society, culture and morality—that would not be fundamentally challenged until the 17th century."[128]

This intellectual movement was termed "Neo-Confucianism." Its leaders included Cheng Yi (1033–1107) and Zhu Xi (1130–1200). Neo-Confucianism transformed traditional Confucianism by asserting that individuals' social worth should be a function of their cultivation of human morality. This new moral philosophy shifted the focus of inquiry away from the problem of *how to make political power function morally* and toward the question of *how individuals can cultivate moral judgment in themselves*. Neo-Confucianism thus had a particular appeal for the masses of literati who aspired to leadership positions and wished to act responsibly but could not reasonably expect an examination degree or office.[129]

5.7 Concluding Remarks

In this chapter, I examine how social changes led to political changes during the Song Dynasty. The transition from the Tang aristocracy to the Song gentry created new dynamics in state-society relations. In the Northern Song era, the localized scholar-officials coexisted with the semi-hereditary "legacy" elites. The localized elites' opposition was an important reason for the failure of Wang Anshi's effort to invigorate the state. After the failure of state activism, the Northern Song state was defeated by the Jurchen Jin, and the model of state-society interaction based on partnership was consolidated. While Chinese elites still depended on the state for recognition and legitimation, they increasingly played a leading role in local affairs and publicly negotiated with the state to protect and advance local interests. Rather than turning to the state, Chinese elites created lineage organizations to protect their property, organize defense, and fund the education of their children. A new ideology, Neo-Confucianism, provided a moral justification of these movements that facilitated their development over the next seven centuries.

Historians often use a "Song-Yuan-Ming transition paradigm" to understand the Song Dynasty's position in China's imperial history.[130] The Song era was different from its predecessor: it featured an elite with more locally based strategies, a monarch whose power was less constrained by his officials, and a society that was more autonomous from the state. From the Song onward, Chinese emperors became single-minded pursuers of personal power and survival at the expense of state strength.

The short-lived alien rule during the Yuan period further reinforced the trend of elite localization. During the Song era, state officials and local elites were basically drawn from the same class, read a similar set of books, belonged to overlapping academic networks, and participated in the same examinations. During the Yuan Dynasty, however, almost all high-ranking officials were ethnic minorities. Officials were different from elites in kind: they were from different ethnic groups. In addition, the virtual breakdown of the examinations as a tool for recruiting officials during most of the Yuan era had a far-reaching impact on the nature of elites. On a practical level, literati elites were deprived of an important means by which to control their own fortunes. On a more symbolic level, they lost an officially recognized mechanism through which to define their group identity.[131] The next chapter describes how the development of social transformations that had germinated during the Song Dynasty were reinforced during the Yuan era and passed on to the Ming Dynasty.

6

State Maintaining in the
Ming Dynasty

6.1   The Twilight of the Ming Dynasty

In 1572, Zhang Juzheng became China's senior grand secretary—the "chief assistant" to the emperor. One of Zhang's ancestors joined the rebellion against the Yuan Dynasty (1279–1368) and fought as a soldier under Zhu Yuanzhang—the founding emperor of the Ming Dynasty (1368–1644).[1] As a result, the Zhang family was designated a military household; it was required to provide one male from each generation for military service.[2]

By Zhang Juzheng's time, the Ming military had deteriorated due to poor pay and heavy service. In the early 1500s, 80–90 percent of the troops had deserted their garrisons and fled.[3] Army officers' prestige plummeted during this period; officials who passed the competitive civil service exam considered themselves superior.[4] Since Zhang belonged to a military household, only one male in each generation could take the civil service exam.[5] His family had put forward candidates in the two previous generations, with no success.[6]

At the age of eleven, Zhang Juzheng was the youngest in his province to pass the first level of the exam. By age twenty-two, he was already an advanced scholar—the highest degree in the civil service exam. He became a scholar-official in the Hanlin Academy, the most prestigious academic institution in the empire, which served as a training ground for future grand secretaries.[7]

The Ming state Zhang was about to begin administering was in terrible shape—particularly the military and economy. The memory of the Ming's defeat by the Mongols and the capture of Emperor Yingzong at Tumu in 1449 still haunted the elites. During the late 1500s, the Ming Dynasty was harassed by Japan-based coastal marauders in the southeast and raiders under Altan and other Mongol chiefs in the north.[8] The Ming troops "were not only unable to destroy enemies, they were incapable of defending themselves."[9] To make matters worse, the founding Ming emperor repudiated the market economy that had developed during the Song times and prohibited private merchants from engaging in overseas trade.[10] The early Ming fiscal system reverted to a heavy reliance on agrarian sources of state income. By Zhang's time, the fiscal system was "on the verge of bankruptcy"; "every treasury was empty."[11]

After he became senior grand secretary, Zhang carried out a series of reforms, which included introducing a performance-based evaluation system for officials, conducting a nationwide land survey, and introducing fiscal reforms. Similar to Wang Anshi's reforms in the eleventh century (see chapter 5), Zhang's reforms sought to "enrich the country and strengthen the military."[12] The most far-reaching measure he advocated was a new tax collection method called the Single Whip (一条鞭法), which combined the service levy and land taxes into a single, consolidated payment in silver.[13] The idea of the Single Whip dates back to 1531, but substantive implementation did not begin until Zhang's administration.

The period from Zhang's inauguration in 1572 until his death in 1582 marked the "last radiant glow" of the Ming Dynasty.[14] At the time of his death, Beijing's granaries held enough grain to feed the capital for nine years. The vaults in Nanjing—the southern capital—likewise contained reserves of 2.5 million taels of silver. The treasuries of Guangxi, Zhejiang, and Sichuan provinces held average deposits of 150,000 to 800,000 taels.[15] None of the military campaigns in the two decades after Zhang could have been conducted without these reserves.[16] His reforms are credited with "prolong[ing] the life of the dynasty by half a century."[17]

Six months after Zhang's funeral, however, all of his policies were reviewed and rejected, and his associates dismissed or impeached. The aversion to his approach was so intense that in the 1580s the local officials who had been negligent about carrying out his land survey were praised as righteous men.[18] The Wanli Emperor revoked the civil service ranks of Zhang's three sons, and two years later he authorized the confiscation of Zhang's properties.[19] Zhang's eldest son, beaten and interrogated, hanged himself.[20] Zhang's most significant reform—the Single Whip—"was never brought to final fulfillment" even in the final years of the dynasty.[21]

If China's state development can be interpreted as a history of the ruler chasing personal power at the expense of state strength, the trade-off could not be starker than it was in the Ming Dynasty. The Ming Dynasty marks the consolidation of a new state-society equilibrium that started in the Song era. In this equilibrium, what I call State Maintaining under Partnership, the ruler established absolute rule over a fragmented elite. The elites accepted the autocrat, because resisting a power-hungry emperor would require costly collective action. But they did not want the state to exert tight control over society; they opposed any attempts to strengthen it. They built lineage organizations to consolidate their local power bases and negotiated with the state to protect their local interests.

Zhang Juzheng's reforms, especially the Single Whip, provide a useful lens through which to analyze the behavior of the Ming elites. I apply the theory elaborated in chapter 1, and argue that political elites with localized kinship networks—the majority of Ming-era politicians—served as representatives of local interests and influenced central policy making to protect their kin's economic interests and autonomy. It is therefore not surprising that it took more than one hundred years for the Single Whip to be adopted across the empire. I show that the localities that had more political representation in the central government were more likely to block its implementation.

The rest of the chapter is structured as follows. Section 6.2 provides a general introduction of the Ming government. Section 6.3 examines Zhang Juzheng's reforms. Section 6.4 presents my empirical analysis. Finally, section 6.5 summarizes the main conclusions and raises a question for the next chapter.

6.2   Political Institutions under the Ming Dynasty

Most Ming government institutions inherited certain features from previous dynasties—including the Tang, Song, and Yuan—but developed distinctive characteristics of their own.[22] The Ming-era bureaucracy represented the culmination of trends that dated back to the Song times, when the emperor was the supreme autocrat, who entrusted the administration of his empire to scholars selected through competitive exams.[23] The civil service dominated government to such an unprecedented degree during the Song and Ming times that neither hereditary nobles nor military officers could challenge its status, although eunuchs sometimes managed to do so via their close personal links to the emperor.[24]

6.2.1   *Absolute Monarchy*

The year 1380 was a major turning point in the evolution of the Ming governance structure. Earlier that year, the founding emperor, Zhu Yuanzhang (the Hongwu Emperor), abolished the entire upper echelon of his central government and concentrated power securely in his own hands.[25] He believed the government centralized too much power in the hands of the chief councilors, so he dismantled the Secretariat (中书省) and the cabinet, and dismissed, tried, or executed their senior members, including the two chief councilors and all other executive officials.[26] The emperor brought the six ministries—Personnel, Revenue, Rites, War, Justice, and Works—under his direct supervision.[27] In later years he repeatedly called on his descendants to impose the death penalty on anyone who dared to propose reappointing chief councilors.[28]

This autocratization of the monarchy had far-reaching ramifications for Ming governance. To start, all matters, no matter how trivial, needed to be submitted to the emperor for final approval. In one eight-day period, the founding emperor received 1,660 memorials discussing 3,391 issues.[29] After Zhu Yuanzhang's death, the empire was unable to function effectively without a strong ruler. Since emperors' abilities and inclinations fluctuated, it was left to others to wield imperial authority when the autocrats were too young, too innocent, or too inattentive to do so themselves.[30] Most later emperors indulged in personal pleasures; Wanli, for instance, refused to attend any meetings for decades.[31]

Ming emperors employed a personal staff of grand secretaries housed in the inner pavilion of the Forbidden City to handle the routine daily flow of memorials.[32] Grand secretaries were accomplished literates who had placed high on the civil service exam and studied at the elite Hanlin Academy.[33] Their duties were confined to putting the emperor's declarations and edicts into an elegant prose style; they were never considered policy makers.[34]

Because grand secretaries normally spent their early careers at Hanlin Academy rather than in active administrative posts, and since they often worked in close cooperation with influential palace eunuchs, their relations with the rest of officialdom were usually uneasy.[35] Ministers and vice ministers almost always had considerable administrative experience in the capital as well as the provinces. To them, grand secretaries lacked roots in the outer court.[36] The Grand Secretariat was considered a symbol and instrument of imperial authority, rather than ministerial or bureaucratic interests. Grand secretaries thus often found themselves in the role of mediators trusted by neither the emperors (who were closer to the eunuchs) nor the bureaucrats. What little influence they were able to wield, in either direction, derived not from their institutional roles, but solely from the force of their personalities.[37] Even Zhang Juzheng—the most powerful grand secretary of Ming times—had limited institutional power to promote his reforms.

6.2.2   The Bureaucracy

The Ming bureaucracy as a whole constituted "the largest such societal superstructure existing in the world at the time."[38] The number of civil officials, persons who received stipends from state revenues, increased from about 5,000 to 24,000 during this era.[39] Every official's status was indicated by his rank, numbered from 1 (highest) to 9 (lowest); each rank was further divided into two degrees: upper (a) and lower (b). A minister was ranked 2a, for example, and a county magistrate 7a.[40]

Despite being a world leader in bureaucratization, due to its large population, Ming China had only four civil servants for every ten thousand people.[41] Civil servants were also spread over 1,138 county offices—each of which governed an average of ninety thousand people in a jurisdiction of 1,300 square miles. Thus even the largest county had no more than thirty salaried bureaucrats.[42] The civil service corps was small mainly due to the low level of taxation (discussed in the next subsection). The low tax revenues also meant that Ming officials were not paid well. The dynasty began by paying officials in rice, but the proportion of their salaries that was paid in rice declined steadily thereafter. The remainder of their salaries was paid in other commodities such as paper money (the real value of which declined to virtually nothing), silk, cotton, and silver. Officials consistently complained that they could not live on their salaries, and the official history of the Ming Dynasty exclaims: "From antiquity, official salaries have never been as meager as this!" Official salaries were reduced to an estimated 4 percent of their nominal values as early as 1434.[43] Capital officials went virtually unpaid; they received no travel allowances when they were transferred to provincial posts, and had no way to reach their new posts other than taking out loans.[44] All local government offices were understaffed; their personnel were also underpaid, and their administrative functions were inadequately carried out.[45] Rampant official corruption ensued.[46]

Men could become civil servants via one of two regular paths: (1) promotion through the ranks of lesser functionaries and (2) recruitment through examination. After the early 1440s, success in the examinations was the only means of ensuring a first-class civil service career.[47] Until 1467, all civil officials of ranks 1–7 were entitled to "protect" one son or grandson, who became automatically eligible either for direct appointment to office or for enrollment as a university student. In 1467, this privilege was restricted to nobles and the highest-ranking central government officials (ranks 1–3).[48] As in the Song times, the nobility as a group was never an influential element in government during the Ming era. The successive Ming emperors appointed a total of 21 dukes, 102 marquises, and 138 earls, almost all of which were awarded in recognition of military achievements. Less than half of these titles were hereditary, and only a few of the rest were perpetuated for more than three generations.[49]

Despite their low salaries, officials enjoyed a variety of privileges and exemptions. For instance, men with civil service exam degrees and their immediate families did not have to pay taxes and were not called on to perform labor service for the state. Depending on their rank, they were permitted to ride on horseback or even in sedan chairs, which commoners were not allowed to do. If officials of ranks 1–3 committed any legal offenses, they were virtually immune to prosecution; no action could be taken against them without specific orders from the emperor. No trial of any capital official, or provincial officials of ranks 5 or higher, could be undertaken without the express permission of the emperor; lesser officials could not be sentenced without imperial approval. Many high-level officials suffered only mild rebukes for offenses that commoners would have been severely punished for.[50]

6.2.3   The Fiscal System

Mark Elvin noticed a decline in China's economy in the fourteenth century. The medieval "economic revolution" that boomed during the Song Dynasty did not continue.[51] Scholars have attributed China's economic decline to Ming rulers' anti-commercial policies. The founding emperor minimized (if not eliminated) the market economy that had developed during the Tang-Song transition and restored the autarkic village economy of the idealized past. In pursuit of this agenda the emperor formulated fiscal policies predicated on a return to unilateral in-kind payments to the state, conscripted labor service, self-sufficient military farms, and payments to officials and soldiers in goods rather than money. In 1374, the emperor banned overseas trade and allowed only highly regulated trade with foreign rulers who had tributary relations with China.[52]

It is still a mystery why the Ming rulers reversed course. Some cited ideological reasons that the founding emperor was determined to eradicate what he regarded as the pernicious influence of Mongol customs and to restore the institutions and values of the agrarian society enshrined in the Confucian Classics.[53] A more plausible reason was probably that the Ming rulers employed anti-market measures to contain the growing economic and political power of the southern commercial elites.

The lower Yangtze River region (Jiangnan) emerged from the late Yuan civil wars relatively unscathed, while the northern and western provinces suffered serious population loss.[54] The destruction borne by the rest of the country only enhanced Jiangnan's preeminent position in the national economy. The founding emperor's decision to establish his capital at Nanjing reflected the economic reality that the resources needed to consolidate his rule and establish military and political control could only come from the Jiangnan region.[55]

Initially the emperor sought the cooperation of the local elite of Jiangnan in his imperial project. The revenue system he enacted in 1371 designated the wealthiest landowners in each county as tax captains (粮长) with responsibility for collecting and delivering tax grain to the capital. By the 1390s, however, the emperor became convinced that the Jiangnan elite, both as government officials and private citizens, were too strong and threatened his rule.

A key event occurred in 1397 when the Jiangnan elites took all of the metropolitan graduate degrees in the civil service examinations.[56] The founding emperor was infuriated by the southerners' dominance; he sentenced the chief examiners to death, ordered a new examination, and added an all-northerner supplementary slate of graduates.[57] Later, a regional quota system was established to further limit the number of exam candidates from the Jiangnan region.[58]

Worrying about southern elites' growing economic and political power, the emperor then purged thousands of officials and confiscated the property of many of Jiangnan's great landowners. By the end of the first emperor's reign more than half of Jiangnan's arable land had been seized by the state.[59]

The anti-commercial policies of the early Ming state, coupled with its expropriation of the wealth of the Jiangnan elite, wreaked havoc on the flourishing market economy of the Jiangnan region and arrested the commercial and urban growth that had continued with little disruption since the Song times.[60]

The Ming state income returned to agrarian sources—primarily the in-kind land tax.[61] The land tax followed the Tang Dynasty's Two-Tax system that was assessed based on productivity (see chapter 3). The "summer tax" and "autumn grain" were collected after each season's harvest.[62]

The Ming Dynasty introduced fixed tax quotas, which represented an average of no more than 6.12 percent of farm output.[63] In 1377 the founding emperor dispatched officials to tour the local business tax stations and set their tax quotas. In 1385 he ordered that stone tablets inscribed with the tax quotas of each province and prefecture be erected in the Ministry of Revenue's office. In 1393 the land tax income reached 32,789,900 piculs (roughly 4 billion pounds) of husked grain. The emperor subsequently declared that taxation by regional quota was an unwritten law. Later, the Xuande Emperor (1425–1435) reduced the total national quota by 3 million piculs to 27 million (roughly 3.6 billion pounds), where it remained for the next two hundred years.[64]

The low levels of taxation seemed to be consistent with Confucian officials' ideal of "minimal governing," but the income generated failed to keep pace with the Ming empire's ever-increasing expenditures in three main areas. First, the imperial kinsmen and kinswomen—the emperors' offspring—all received stipends from state funds.[65] In 1562, one-fifth of state revenue was diverted to the imperial princes.[66] After many generations their number naturally swelled. The Jesuit missionary Alvaro Semedo estimated that by the 1620s they totaled approximately sixty thousand, and modern scholars have estimated that in the last years of the Ming era there were one hundred thousand imperial kinsmen on the state payroll.[67]

Second, in line with the notion that everything under heaven belonged to the emperor, the Ming system made no distinction between state income and the emperor's personal income, or between government expenditures and the emperor's personal expenditures.[68] Exorbitant palace expenses, excessive procurement programs, and land grants to the emperor's favorites and relatives, exacerbated by the misconduct of eunuch commissioners, always incurred immense costs.[69] In addition, the number of palace eunuchs—who lived on state revenue—grew more than a hundred times: from sixty in 1369 to seventy thousand by the end of the dynasty.[70] There were also roughly nine thousand palace women, including concubines and servants, in the last decades of the Ming.[71]

The third area of spiraling expenditures was the army—the largest recipient of Ming government funds. The founding emperor, an impoverished orphan, insisted that his armies must not be a burden to the civilian taxpayers. He fulfilled this promise by adopting the Yuan practice of establishing state farms (屯田) on land that had been abandoned in the turmoil of the late

Yuan years, along with land confiscated from the Mongol nobility and large landlords in the southeast.[72] The government turned these farms over to the military in what was commonly called the *wei-suo* (卫所) system. Each company (*suo*) of guards (*wei*) had its own farm, and each soldier was allocated 50 *mu* (roughly the size of two tennis courts).[73] These troops were expected to serve as part-time farmers and part-time soldiers and to produce enough grain to supply the entire military.[74] During the 1500s, however, state farms steadily fell into disuse, or reverted to *de facto* private ownership, as officers and soldiers deserted their garrisons and large landlords took them over as private holdings.[75] The central government began issuing annual military subsidies instead. Throughout the 1500s, Beijing regularly paid out more than three-fourths of annual state revenues to the army.[76]

Each county was responsible for assessing and collecting taxes from its citizens.[77] According to the law of avoidance, however, county magistrates could not serve in their hometowns and were often sent to districts where "the native dialect was unintelligible and local customs foreign to them."[78] By the time a magistrate became acquainted with the local situation, he was often posted elsewhere. Local officials were also prohibited by law from entering rural areas in order to minimize disturbances to the rural order.[79] County magistrates therefore had to rely on local communities—the *li-jia* (里甲) system—to collect their own taxes. A *li* (community) consisted of 110 households. Responsible men from the ten most affluent households were designated as community heads. The remaining one hundred households were divided into ten *jia* (neighborhoods) containing ten households each. Each community head served for one year, along with ten neighborhood heads whose positions also rotated.[80]

After the community heads collected land taxes, they delivered them to the tax captains, who were selected from the prosperous households. Each tax captain represented several communities and was responsible for delivering approximately ten thousand bushels (roughly 350,000 liters) of tax grain annually to the county magistrate, directly to the capital, or to specified state granaries that were scattered throughout the empire.[81]

6.2.4 *The Military*

The military represented the largest component of Ming government personnel. It grew from 16,489 officers (guards) and 1,198,442 soldiers on regular, permanent duty in 1392 to one hundred thousand officers and four million soldiers in the last decades of the dynasty.[82]

When the founding emperor abolished the chief councilors in 1380, he also reorganized the military to prevent any single general or commissioner from gaining control over more than a small segment of the country's fighting capacity.[83] He divided the Military Affairs Commission into five coequal Chief Military Commissions, each of which was given administrative control over a group of Regional Military Commissions in the provinces and a proportion of the guards who were stationed around the capital.

The new system of guards and companies—wei-suo—constituted the basic military units across the empire. Men could become officers either by inheriting their post[84] or passing military examinations that paralleled the far more influential civil service examinations.[85]

Most of the wei-suo were created as self-sufficient organizations that relied on food supplies from state farms. But the land surrounding troops who were stationed along the Great Wall line of defense was less suitable for farming. So the Ming government revived and adapted an ingenious Song Dynasty plan to exploit the state's monopoly on salt distribution.[86]

The wei-suo system gradually declined in the mid-1400s as the government began recruiting paid volunteer soldiers from civilian and artisan families. By the end of the fifteenth century, recruitment had become standard practice in all situations requiring more than passive defense, such as defending the country against the Japan-based coastal marauders and northern Mongol raiders in the late 1500s.[87]

6.3 Zhang Juzheng's Reforms

Zhang Juzheng came to power in 1572 at an opportune time.[88] The peace settlement with the Mongol chief Altan and the gradual decline in the number of pirate raids enabled the Ming government to finally focus on domestic problems.[89] With the eunuch director Feng Bao and the Empress Dowager Li, the emperor's biological mother, on his side, Zhang had no difficulty influencing his former pupil, the nine-year-old Wanli Emperor.[90] From 1572 to 1582, Zhang attempted to improve the Ming governance structure that had been unchanged since the founding era.

6.3.1 Performance-Based Evaluations

The starting point of Zhang's reforms was to try to make the bureaucracy work for the state. The administrative centerpiece of his regime was the Regulation for Evaluating Achievements (考成法), which assigned time limits for implementing government directives, held officials responsible for failing to do so, and "prioritized performance over seniority in promotion decisions.[91] "In the affairs of the Empire," Zhang wrote in his request for the reform, "it is not difficult to erect laws, but it is difficult to see they are enforced."[92] This new measure allowed Zhang to monitor bureaucratic efficiency and direct a more centralized administration.[93]

Ray Huang concluded that during Zhang's first decade in office, "the efficiency of the imperial bureaucracy reached its zenith," and his administration was able to "match the kind of material splendor usually known only immediately after the establishment of a new dynasty."[94]

6.3.2   Land Survey

After taking office during a time of "fiscal chaos,"[95] Zhang's reforms sought to shore up the public finances. Since the first land survey in the founding era, the total reported acreage of cultivated land in the empire had steadily declined as powerful people became more adept at concealing their holdings.[96] As a result, the government had difficulty collecting taxes, and the unequal distribution of the tax burden caused grievances and even local revolts. Zhang identified the tax exemption (优免) for degree holders as the key issue: non-eligible individuals sought "tax protection" (投靠) from their association with an exempted scholar-gentry.[97] Zhang described this as a practice in which "the rich had land but paid no taxes and the poor paid taxes but had no land."[98]

Zhang sought to uncover concealed holdings and thus equalize the tax burden by conducting a general cadastral survey.[99] Toward the end of 1577, Beijing ordered local officials to "measure the lands of the whole empire." Landowners were required to announce the survey and to measure their holdings together with their tenants, if any, and to apply to the state to have new deeds issued. Tenants would then pay rent according to the amount of land officially entered in the owner's name on the tax register—a procedure that ensured mutual surveillance. Many specialist clerks were employed to conduct the survey; they were paid out of taxes ordered a few years earlier to be retained locally.[100] But the survey was never finished. Two months after Zhang's death, the survey was criticized and later discontinued.[101]

Historians still debate the effectiveness of Zhang's land survey. Martin Heijdra has asserted that it was remarkably successful at generating detailed landholding maps, including the famous "fish-scale registers" (鱼鳞册); local administrators used these maps, which set a new standard for accuracy, for generations to come.[102] The available local evidence corroborates Heijdra's assessment. According to the official record of the Shanxi survey, investigators found that a group of men led by Zheng Jingfang concealed holdings totaling 518,200 *mu* ($\approx$ 74, 131 acres), which the government reclaimed as taxable land. Furthermore, the newly registered lands in a particular county were taxed at the full rate, much to the relief of the honest taxpayers who had been paying extra to make up the shortfall in the regional quota.[103]

Ray Huang, by contrast, is dismissive of the survey because it was never completed. Citing evidence from various localities in Henan, Shandong, and Zhejiang, he argues that it reported old or fabricated data.[104]

Nevertheless, most historians agree that the land survey achieved some degree of local success. Even Ray Huang admitted that "all things considered, [Zhang Juzheng's] land survey was not a total failure. In some counties the returns of 1581 were used as the new basis of taxation. . . . The failure was mainly at the national level."[105] Martin Heijdra further argued that the new land figures, although not reported to the central government, could still be found at the provincial level, and served as the basis for all Qing data.[106]

6.3.3   *Single Whip*

To understand the Single Whip reform, we first need to know what problems it was trying to address. In addition to paying land taxes, the Ming population also needed to provide services to the state. These services ranged from heavy obligations, such as providing office attendants for the government or servicing postal stations, to more ordinary ones, such as doormen, guards, messengers, sedan-chair bearers, cooks, buglers, boatmen, patrolmen, jailers, grooms at government stables, receiving men in the warehouses, operators of canal watergates, and clerical assistants.[107] These obligations were often more than labor services, however, for they also included the contribution and handling of materials and always some small cash payments, which made them a form of taxation referred to as a "service levy" (役).[108]

While the land taxes were applied to each *mu* of land, the service levy was imposed on each able-bodied male (丁). Each household, based on the number of male adults and property holdings, was called upon by the local community (*li*) to provide these services. At the beginning of the dynasty all households were classified into upper, middle, and lower categories, so that service obligations could be distributed accordingly.[109] Each year a particular *jia*—ten households—was called to service.[110]

During the early years of the dynasty, the service levy was light and narrow in scope. In the fifteenth century, however, the demand for raw materials and labor services expanded significantly, and since the land tax quota was not raised, extra government expenses at all levels had to be defrayed by service levies. For example, when the government could not pay official salaries, it permitted its officials to conscript personal attendants from the general population, and payments in silver could substitute for the service of these attendants. In the fifteenth century, tax increases were generally enacted in this way.[111] At a time when the government was becoming more sophisticated and wealthy families were increasingly able to evade their fair share of the financial burden, a system in which ten families in a village, under the direction of a community chief, decided among themselves who should pay what share of the state's operating expenses could not survive.[112]

COMBINING THE SERVICE LEVY AND LAND TAX

The Single Whip was a package of fiscal reforms designed to equalize the tax burden. As Ray Huang contends, "universality and uniformity" was "the spirit of the Single Whip Reform."[113] It represented multiple government efforts to absorb various kinds of payments for the service levy into land taxes, which would be assessed based on landholdings and collected directly by the state in the form of a single, consolidated silver payment.[114] In other words, the Single Whip combined the previously separated service levy (imposed on households) and land taxes (imposed on land) into a single progressive tax, which was based solely on landholdings and paid in silver.[115]

PROGRESSIVE AND UNIVERSAL TAXATION

The Single Whip reform sought to achieve three main goals.

The first was to simplify the tax collection process by "quantifying." Before the reform, land taxes were primarily paid in kind, and local community chiefs and tax captains were responsible for assessing, collecting, and transporting the payments to the government. Different localities used different conversion rates among a variety of commodities including grain, hay, and cotton, as well as indigo, hemp, and sesame seeds, which made it impossible to combine accounts.[116] Likewise, the service levy included so many categories that it was impossible to allocate evenly and keep track of each household's contribution. The influx of silver from overseas in the early fifteenth century made it more popular to settle tax payments in silver, which helped the Single Whip reform simplify tax collection and made accounting possible.[117]

The second goal was to impose a uniform tax rate across the nation. Before the reform, local community chiefs were responsible for assessing and allocating the land tax and service levy, often using different formulas. The Single Whip distributed the tax burden evenly throughout the population, using landholdings as the sole basis. "The intention," Ray Huang argues, "was that the allocation of the service levy to the entire population should result in a set of uniform rates so low that the wealthy households would find it hardly worthwhile to evade them, and the really poor would not be greatly harmed by them."[118]

The third objective of the Single Whip reform was to make taxation fairer in two ways. First, it was essentially a progressive tax based on landholdings, so people with less land paid a lower percentage of tax than those with more land.[119] Second, the Single Whip centralized the power of tax assessment, collection, and transportation away from community chiefs and tax captains—the wealthiest landowners in the community—to the state. According to Liang Fangzhong, these big landowners often bribed community leaders or directly manipulated the tax allocation to shirk their responsibilities.[120] The reform aimed to detach powerful landowners from the process.

DRAWN-OUT LOCAL ADOPTION

The term Single Whip first appeared in an official memorandum brought to the Jiajing Emperor in 1531.[121] But Beijing generally sought to preserve the status quo; the bureaucrats regarded any major innovation as unorthodox.[122] The Single Whip was not adopted until 1568—37 years after it was proposed, mostly at the local level relying exclusively on local officials who were frustrated with the taxation process.[123]

Liang Fangzhong's seminal work, *Chronicle of the Single Whip*, used over one thousand sources, ranging from official histories to local gazetteers, to document 335 events involving the Single Whip reform.[124] These events include policy proposals, pilots, implementation announcements, policy revisions, and commentaries that occurred at the provincial (6.27 percent of the events), prefectural (18.81 percent), or county (74.93 percent) level from 1531 to 1637. Table 6.1 summarizes Liang's data, focusing on implementation in every

TABLE 6.1: Single Whip Implementation Timeline at the Provincial Level

1531	•	Censor Fu Hanchen proposed the Single Whip to Emperor Yingzong
1568–1631	•	Jiangxi Province implemented the Single Whip in most prefectures
1569–1628	•	Southern Zhili Province implemented the Single Whip in most prefectures
1570–1615	•	Shandong Province implemented the Single Whip in most prefectures
1570–1622	•	Zhejiang Province implemented the Single Whip in most prefectures
1571–1616	•	Northern Zhili Province implemented the Single Whip in most prefectures
1572–1630	•	Henan Province implemented the Single Whip in most prefectures
1573–1622	•	Guangxi Province implemented the Single Whip in some prefectures
1575–1580	•	Fujian Province implemented the Single Whip in most prefectures
1576–1605	•	Huguang Province started implementing the Single Whip in most prefectures
1577–1636	•	Guangdong Province implemented the Single Whip in most prefectures
1581–1598	•	Shanxi Province implemented the Single Whip in most prefectures
1584–1610	•	Guizhou Province implemented the Single Whip in some prefectures
1587	•	Sichuan Province implemented the Single Whip in some prefectures
1587	•	Yunnan Province implemented the Single Whip in some prefectures
1589	•	Gansu Province implemented the Single Whip in some prefectures
1589–1599	•	Shaanxi Province implemented the Single Whip in most prefectures

province. More than one hundred years elapsed from the first proposal to its implementation throughout the country.

Figure 6.1 uses Liang's data to graph the number of local Single Whip reforms (at any level). It shows that substantial progress was made under Zhang Juzheng's government during 1572–1582: almost half of the local implementations occurred during this time.

Although Zhang did not initiate the Single Whip, his other reforms, such as the evaluation system and the land survey, provided the incentive structure and data to facilitate the Single Whip reform. He also centralized the reform's implementation, which had been carried out in an "uncoordinated" fashion at the local level.[125]

Zhang never proposed creating or abolishing an office.[126] As grand secretary, he had no power to do so.[127] He circumvented the institutional constraints to implementing the proposed reforms by manipulating personal relationships. Through the eunuch Feng Bao he maintained cordial relations with the empress dowager, and he used her influence to control the emperor.[128] He wrote long letters to his lieutenants, who occupied key positions in the

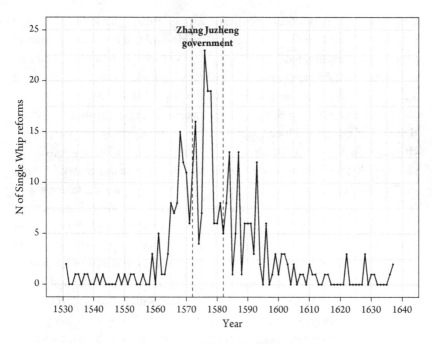

FIGURE 6.1: Number of Local Single Whip Reforms (1531–1637)
Source: Liang (1989, 485–555).

imperial administration, urging them to back his favored proposals. Then, as chief counsellor to the throne, he drafted edicts on the emperor's behalf approving his proposed policies. In his letters he used cajolery, exhortation, complaints, and mild reprimands to effect his will. At times he gave advance notice of the recipient's next assignment or promotion to make it clear that he was responsible for their advancement.[129]

6.3.4   Zhang Juzheng's Widespread Unpopularity

At the peak of his power, Zhang Juzheng was "the enemy of the entire empire."[130] Officials feared and hated his evaluation system, which required them to fulfill certain targets in a timely manner. Landlords were displeased with his land survey and Single Whip reform, which closed the tax loopholes they had enjoyed. Attacks on Zhang culminated in 1577 when Zhang's father died. Dynastic laws and ritual norms required him to relinquish his office and observe a period of mourning at home for twenty-seven months.[131] But either at Zhang's own suggestion or with his connivance, the fourteen-year-old Wanli

Emperor responded to Zhang's request for mourning leave with an imperial edict stating that his service was indispensable, and that he was to be exempt from the full requirement. This decision caused an uproar at court, and officials demanded Zhang's removal.[132] The growing opposition to him triggered a psychological change, which accelerated many of his reforms.[133]

Historians tend to agree that the opposition to Zhang constituted a coalition of local gentry and their representatives in the government. Harry Miller characterizes the tension during the Ming era as a question of sovereignty: should policy-making authority come from the state or the gentry?[134] After the "localist turn" during the Song Dynasty,[135] Miller argues, the Chinese gentry "continued to compete for academic degrees but now viewed them chiefly as a component of local importance, rather than as the basis for a lifetime of service to the state."[136] The gentry also developed a repertoire of community leadership and service, designing improvements to irrigation, providing famine relief, organizing local militias, overseeing religious life, and so on. In some of these projects, the gentry cooperated with the local government, but in most cases they remained the prime movers.[137] Zhang Juzheng, however, "was the man to make sure the gentry worked for the state and not vice versa."[138]

Ray Huang also blames the local gentry for obstructing Zhang's reforms.[139] He points out that colluding with their representatives in the government was the most effective way to block the reforms: "When dissatisfied they could deliberately keep their payments in arrears, or else apply pressure on the local administrator via influential persons."[140]

In 1574, Bai Dong (白栋), the county magistrate of Dong-e County in Shandong Province, applied the Single Whip in his district, collecting the regular land tax at 0.011 taels ($\approx$ \$1 in 2019) per *mu* (6,000 square feet), plus a service levy charge of 0.0092 taels per *mu*. Every adult male in the county was also assessed with an annual payment of 0.13 taels. These rates were not exceedingly low for north China, but the formula was simple. After the first year of application, eleven thousand households that had previously absconded returned to their home areas. Zhang Juzheng praised Bai's achievement, but due to "local dissatisfaction" Bai was impeached by a supervising secretary; the case was suspended after Zhang intervened.[141]

In the Ming era, most local officials were careful to secure some degree of consensus from elites in their district before implementing any new policies. This practice—what Sukhee Lee calls "the mutual convenience of the public and the private"[142]—involved a process of negotiation between the state and society. In circa 1609 the magistrate of Wenshang County, Shandong, explained the irrationality of the district's tax schedule with the following observations in the local gazetteer: "But our silk-robed gentlemen all insisted on their own views; none was willing to compromise. Their quarrelsome arguments almost ended in lawsuits."[143] There were, of course, conscientious local officials who did not yield to gentry power, and indeed fought it tenaciously. Yet such heroism was rarely rewarded, and all too often demanded considerable self-sacrifice from such conscientious magistrates.[144]

Liang Fangzhong, examining the delay in implementing the Single Whip in Jiangxi Province, also identified the coalition between local interest groups and government officials as the main culprit. Governor Cai Kelian (蔡克廉) proposed the idea of the Single Whip in 1556. But his proposal was blocked by "officials and landowners." The province did not start to implement the Single Whip until 1568.[145]

More generally, Joseph Levenson and Franz Schurmann theorized about the parasitic nature of the landholders. In their view, private encroachments on the state's interests were inexorable, because China's "landlord-officials" could hardly be expected to support bureaucratic crackdowns on their own interests. "And so," they wrote, "the concentration of land ensued, the growth of ominous private interests, threatening the state that sought ideally to fragmentize private interest, but whose bureaucracy was staffed by the very people who had to be most controlled."[146]

In a private letter, Zhang Juzheng described the problem using two of his favorite words, the public and the private, to contrast the public spirit he embodied with the treasonable selfishness of all who were against him. "They think only of the injury to their private families and forget the benefit to the public," he said. "In wanting to let slip this opportunity, they are not thinking of their country. In my view, they are not only disloyal but also unintelligent in the extreme."[147]

6.4   Where the Status Quo Survived

Contrary to Zhang Juzheng's reprimand, however, the officials were highly intelligent: their opposition to his reforms was a calculated behavior. The best way to protect their families' interests was to block any reforms that centralized state power and imposed universal taxation. The landowning gentry and their representatives in the government sought to veto Zhang's state-strengthening reforms.

In this section I turn to data to probe the politics of Zhang's reforms. Exploiting the temporal and regional variations in Single Whip implementation, I show that more representation—measured as the number of major central politicians a prefecture produced—is associated with the prefecture's slower adoption of the Single Whip. Consistent with the qualitative evidence presented above, my analysis indicates that politicians, who represented the interests of their local networks, had a strong incentive to maintain the status quo.

6.4.1　Timeline of Local Single Whip Adoption

The outcome variable is the number of years it took for a prefecture to adopt the Single Whip. The data for this analysis comes from Liang Fangzhong's *Chronicle of the Single Whip*.[148] This source lists the year of the reform, the locality, and some short notes on the sources, content, and persons involved. Ming historians have long regarded Liang's work on the Single Whip as authoritative.[149] To the best of my knowledge, the *Chronicle* provides the most detailed and comprehensive timeline of Single Whip implementation at the local level.[150]

I use Liang's data to identify the year in which each prefecture implemented the Single Whip reform. The dependent variable is then the difference between this year and 1531—the year the reform was proposed. Figure 6.2 (panel (a)) shows the number of years it took for each prefecture to implement the Single Whip.[151]

6.4.2　National Representation of Local Interest

The independent variable is the number of major politicians in the central government that a prefecture produced under the Wanli Emperor (1573–1620). I focus on the Wanli reign because the Single Whip was rolled out nationwide during this period. Of the 259 implementation events recorded by Liang Fangzhong, 200 (77.2 percent) happened under Wanli.

Using the definition introduced in chapter 2, major officials were those with a rank of vice minister (3b) or above. Similar to the Song Dynasty, ranks 1a–3b were considered high in the Ming Dynasty.[152] I obtain a list of such positions and the 503 officials who occupied them during 1573–1620 from a variety of archival and contemporary sources.[153] I collected personal information on these 503 officials, such as their hometowns, from the *China Biographical*

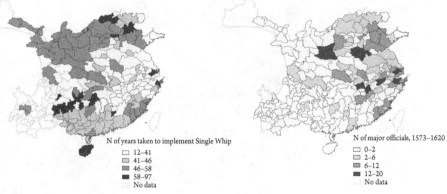

(a) Number of years taken to implement the Single Whip

(b) Number of major central officials from each prefecture (1573–1620)

FIGURE 6.2: Single Whip Implementation and Prefectural Representation in National Politics

Source: Liang (1989, 485–555) and author's data collection.

Database.[154] Figure 6.2 (panel (b)) presents the spatial distribution of their hometowns.

I also collect data on these officials' kinship networks. Consistent with the criteria in chapter 2, an individual's kinship network includes kin established through blood or marriage ties within three generations. Unlike the Song era, for which tomb epitaphs are well documented in the *Complete Prose of Song*, information on marriages in the Ming period is less systematically recorded. I consulted a wide range of materials, from genealogical records to local gazetteers, and managed to obtain information on 1,500 individuals who were kin to sixty-five Ming officials.[155] Since missing data is a serious problem, I exercise caution in interpreting the results.

Simple descriptive statistics indicate that major officials' kinship networks significantly localized from the Song to the Ming eras. The average standardized localization score for Ming officials is four times the score for Song officials.[156] While elite localization had just started in Song times, it consolidated during the Ming era.

As a consequence, Ming officials were also a more fragmented group. Figure 6.3 illustrates the social network of major Ming officials. The central, larger node in each "community" is a major official, and the surrounding smaller nodes are kin members. An edge represents a kinship tie, either by blood or marriage. With a few exceptions, most major officials were not

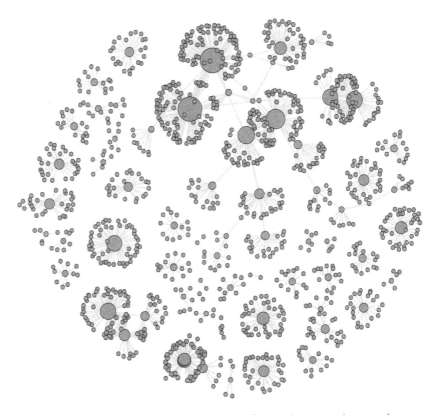

FIGURE 6.3: Social Network of Major Ming Officials and Their Kin (1573–1620)

connected with other officials through kinship ties. The density of the marriage network of Ming officials is only one-thirtieth of that of Song officials.[157]

6.4.3   Where the Reform was Delayed

My statistical analysis shows that prefectures with one additional major official represented in the central government had a 7.7–11.6 percent lower probability of adopting the Single Whip. My findings are consistent when I control for provincial fixed effects, which account for provincial leadership and policy, geography, climate, soil quality, culture, and history.[158] The results indicate that representation in the central government helped localities delay their adoption of the new Single Whip policy.

Why were some prefectures able to send several representatives to the central government, while others were not? As I discussed earlier, in the Ming era, a quota determined how many residents of each region could take the civil service examinations. And since passing the civil service exam was virtually the only way to guarantee a path to elite government positions, the geographic representation in the central bureaucracy largely reflected the performance of different localities in the exam. Statistical analysis of Ming officials' and exam candidates' data suggests that for every 100 advanced scholars from a particular prefecture, 3.4 of them became major officials.[159]

In sum, my statistical analyses suggest that a quota established in the early Ming period determined how many people could take the civil service examinations, which affected how many candidates could pass the exam and become major officials. The number of major officials from each prefecture then influenced the pace of the Single Whip reform: the more major officials a prefecture produced, the slower the implementation of the reform.

6.5   Conclusion

In this chapter, I use the case of Zhang Juzheng's reforms, especially the Single Whip, to show that politicians in late imperial China represented local interests and were interested in maintaining—but not strengthening—the state. They blocked reforms designed to centralize the fiscal system. Continuing a trend since the Song era, the Chinese governing elites became more entrenched in local social networks during this period, which influenced their decision-making in the central government. The emperor also consolidated control over every branch of government as well as the military to create an absolute monarchy. Autocracy and a fragmented elite developed concurrently, while the state remained weak.

In 1640, almost sixty years after Zhang Juzheng's death, the last Ming ruler—the Chongzhen Emperor—rehabilitated Zhang's reputation as a reform hero.[160] But it was too late. Four years later, Li Zicheng's rebel army entered Beijing and Chongzhen hanged himself.[161] The Ming Dynasty fell.

Despite its fiscal weakness, economic decline, and military fragility, however, the Ming Dynasty lasted for almost three hundred years. What sustained its rule? To know the answer, we must look beyond the bureaucracy, taxation, and the ruler, and examine the social structure that undergirded the imperial state. This will be the focus of the next chapter.

7

The Development of Private-Order Institutions

7.1 Commitment Problems and Lineage Organizations

Chinese elites after the eleventh century started to block state building. They opposed national cadastral surveys, resisted military centralization, and delayed fiscal unification. Late imperial China, as a consequence, suffered from fiscal deficits and military incompetence. Local governments provided only minimal public goods and services. The state army could merely protect itself.

But late imperial China, before the Western intrusion, was a period of exceptional stability. Internal rebellion and external military threats had abated. The two dynasties—Ming (1368–1644) and Qing (1644–1911)—each lasted for almost 300 years. A new social order contributed much to the political and social stability during this era. The emergence of this new social order in turn depended on elite social cooperation.

In this chapter, I examine how Chinese elites in the late imperial era relied on social cooperation to provide security and services. Localized elites could exploit a large efficiency gain by relying on social cooperation, rather than the state, to provide basic protection and services. Commitment problems arose, however, when cooperation required collective action and individuals had a strong incentive to shirk. Commitment problems occurred among individuals in the same generation: to provide defense, repair roads, and fund schools, elite members needed to contribute. There were also commitment problems *across* generations: after the older generation invested in the younger generation's education, the younger cohort was expected to protect the elders. The elites therefore faced an organizational problem: social cooperation led to efficiency gains, but commitment problems prevented the elites from exploiting these gains.

Chinese elites invented private-order institutions—lineage organizations and lineage coalitions—to help them overcome such commitment problems in three ways. First, through worshipping a common ancestor, lineage organizations spiritually bonded people who belonged to the same descent group. Second, by compiling genealogy books, lineage organizations could reward reliable members and exclude free-riding members. Third, through intermarriages, lineage coalitions helped exchange "mutual hostages" between lineages.

The long-term gains from staying in and contributing to one's lineage outweighed the short-term benefits of cheating and shirking. So lineage organizations and lineage coalitions made members credibly commit *ex ante* to their fellow members not to cheat or shirk *ex post*.

———

In discussing the development of private-order institutions, I draw on insights from two other fields. The first is economics. While neoclassical economics assumes that the market is efficient, new institutional economics argues that significant costs can arise when market actors negotiate and enforce contracts—what Ronald Coase calls transaction costs.[1] To reduce these costs, economic actors invent institutions, such as the firm, to internalize transactions.[2] Research in political economy shows that state institutions also arise when social groups incur transaction costs.[3] Avner Greif, for example, demonstrates that the inability of powerful clans to cooperate with each other gave rise to the Genoese state. The Genoese state then helped coordinate social groups and achieved both political order and economic growth.[4] I incorporate this notion that people design institutions to reduce transaction costs. But my account provides an alternative causal story. While state institutions arose from a lack of social solidarity in Europe, I show that social solidarity emerged due to the inability of the state to reduce transaction costs in China.

The second outside field is anthropology—specifically the awareness that families are a dynamic phenomenon. Meyer Fortes, for example, highlights the importance of studying "the stages of the developmental cycle" of families because "[t]he developmental factor is intrinsic to domestic organization."[5] Economists, particularly Paul Samuelson and Peter Diamond, formalize this insight into overlapping generations models.[6] The simplest version of such models considers a discrete-time model of an infinite-horizon economy populated by individuals who live for two periods and then die. A new generation is born in each period, so that in any period, the population consists of only two generations—those born at the beginning of the current period (the current "young") and those born at the beginning of the previous period (the current "old"). Decisions made by the "old" will affect the capital accumulation of the "young."[7] I build on this insight and conceptualize lineage organizations as an institutional mechanism to solve the tension between the old and young generations.

The rest of the chapter is structured as follows. Section 7.2 enumerates the uncertainties Chinese elites faced in the late imperial era, including competitive examinations, division of family property, poor public goods provision, government intrusion, and violence. Section 7.3 discusses the commitment problems they faced that encouraged them to rely on social cooperation to deal with these uncertainties. Section 7.4 examines how lineage organizations and lineage coalitions helped Chinese elites overcome their commitment problems. Section 7.5 provides some empirical evidence using an original dataset I compiled for this study. Section 7.6 then discusses the implications of private-order institutions for China's long-term political and economic development.

7.2   Elites Faced Uncertainties

After the fall of China's aristocracy, a new class of elites—the gentry—emerged. In order to perpetuate their wealth, power, and social status, these new elites had to address a wide range of uncertainties, including a competitive examination system, an inheritance system that divided property among all sons, a lack of public goods and services provided by the state, government intrusion, and violence.

7.2.1   Competitive Examinations

Since the Song times, the new elites had to take the competitive civil service examination to become an official. The exam was open to all males regardless of their social background. Ping-ti Ho calculates that from 1462 to 1892 an average of 42.9 percent of advanced scholars came from commoner families.[8] Even for the country's most prominent families, downward mobility was inevitable, because it was difficult for each subsequent generation to keep succeeding in the exam. As the old Chinese saying goes, "A gentleman's grace becomes extinct in five generations."[9] Obtaining an advanced scholar degree was extremely challenging: 0.016 percent of those who took the county-level exam during the Ming period became advanced scholars, and the probability further decreased in the Qing era due to rapid population growth.[10]

During the entire Ming period, only two families produced advanced scholars for five consecutive generations.[11] During the Qing Dynasty, the Zhang clan in Tongcheng (Anhui Province) produced at least one advanced scholar in each generation for six generations.[12] Zhang Ying (1637–1708), the first Zhang to gain national prominence, was minister of Rites. Zhang Ying's son Zhang Tingyu (1672–1755) was grand secretary under three emperors and the most powerful politician in Qing times.[13] Even in this distinguished family, over the next six generations the percentage of Zhang Ying's direct descendants who held official posts fell from 83.3 percent to 19.4 percent, and the percentage of degree holders plunged from 100 percent to 30 percent.[14]

7.2.2   Absence of Primogeniture

The equal division of property among all male heirs (both legitimate and illegitimate) since the Tang era also contributed to downward mobility.[15] Although a man could marry only one wife, he could take as many concubines as he could afford; Patricia Ebrey estimates that about one-third of the elite families in the Song Dynasty had a concubine at some point.[16]

The lineage genealogy of the Weng family from Jianyang (Fujian Province) records an example of how one family's landholdings were greatly reduced within four generations. The great-grandfather, Weng Wancheng, established a 1,280-*mu* estate of rice land, which he left to his four sons. Each son was given 320 *mu*. One of the sons, Boshou, had two sons, each of whom was allocated 160 *mu*. This 160 *mu* was further divided by Boshou's three grandsons, who each received 53 *mu*.[17]

Due to the highly competitive nature of the examination system and the successive division of wealth by inheritance, it was impossible for any individual family to preserve its place at the top of the government and educational ladder for long.[18] Had the division in the Weng lineage continued at this rate until the fifth generation, the households would have found it difficult to sustain themselves as self-cultivating peasants, let alone live off the property's rental income.[19]

7.2.3   Poor Public Goods and Services

Due to the low rates of taxation, the imperial government maintained a minimum level of administration at the local level and provided few public goods and services. Ray Huang describes county-level government in the Ming era as follows: "Governing an area of some 500 to 1,000 square miles, with a population ranging from 30,000 to 250,000, the magistrate's regular staff included only three members of civil service status: the vice-magistrate, the assistant magistrate, and the docket officer."[20] Minimum local governance became a more serious problem in the Qing era when the population dramatically increased. But the Qing government had fewer county-level administrative units than the Han Dynasty (206 BCE–220 CE), which had a much smaller population and territory.[21] Madeleine Zelin estimates that China had 1,360 counties during the early Qing period. Matching the ratio of population to administrative units that prevailed during the early years of imperial rule would have required increasing that number to around 8,500.[22] And to provide China with enough counties to ensure efficient control over the local population, the Qing Dynasty would have had to allocate more than 25.5 million taels ($\approx$ \$752 million in 2019) to county-level governments alone.[23]

For example, since the Ming times local governments had delegated responsibility for irrigation to local elites. According to Zheng Zhenman's study of Haideng County (Fujian Province), the irrigation system was built in the Song Dynasty, but was poorly maintained. In the early Ming period, the county magistrate ordered the local gentry to raise funds to repair the system after it was destroyed in a flood. A new magistrate ordered gentry members to repair the system again twenty-seven years later.[24] Zheng argues that local governments since the Ming era had no funds for local public works such as irrigation. Before the mid-Ming period, local governments conscripted families for labor. After the Single Whip reform (see chapter 6), local governments could no longer levy labor services; they instead "encouraged" gentry families to donate money or directly delegated the work to local gentry.[25]

7.2.4   Government Intrusion

The elites had to deal with sporadic government policies designed to penetrate local society. These policies were usually introduced at the beginning of each dynasty when the emperors were still ambitious, and when the imperial government controlled more resources (e.g., land) after violence and migration as a result of dynastic change. In the early Ming era, for example, the founding emperor divided the populace into hereditary occupational registrations, including commoner, military, and artisan, and created a labor service system in which all adult males could be called on to perform government service.[26] In the early Qing era, to tackle local government deficits, the third Qing emperor—Yongzheng (1722–1735)—ordered the "return of the meltage fee to the public coffers" (火耗归公).[27] Officials in each province were authorized to collect a fixed percentage surcharge on all regular land and head taxes remitted to the central government. This surcharge was retained in the province of origin to provide officials with substantially increased salaries (养廉).[28]

These policies increased the costs to elites and introduced considerable uncertainty to their intra-family relations. For example, the Ming registration system was hereditary, and the government forbade households from dividing their registration. For a military household, this meant that, regardless of whether its descendants lived as a single household or maintained a number of separate domestic and economic units, they had to collectively ensure there was always a soldier at his post.[29] Formally, state officials accepted monetary payments as a substitute for military service and used the income to hire mercenaries. Informally, military-registered households hired mercenaries themselves to fulfill their obligations.[30] But as the number of descendants swelled over generations, it became harder for the household to collectively decide who should pay for the mercenary, and even more difficult to determine who it should be.

7.2.5   Violence

Elizabeth Perry writes: "No country boasts a more enduring or more colorful history of rebellion and revolution than China." More than 65 percent of the military conflicts fought between 1000 and 1800 in China were internal.[31] China's peasants lived at the subsistence level—a situation Richard Tawney likened to "that of a man standing permanently up to the neck in water, so that even a ripple is sufficient to drown him."[32] Exogenous climate shocks (e.g., cold weather or droughts) were important catalysts for peasant rebellions.[33]

Mass rebellions posed serious threats to the property and lives of traditional landowning local elites. Radical redistributive demands were a prominent theme of peasant uprisings, as a song popular among the Taiping rebels attests:[34]

Those with millions owe us their money,
Those who are half poor–half rich can till their fields.

Those with ambitions but no cash should go with us:
Broke or hungry, Heaven will keep you well.

When nearby peasants took up arms, local elites could rely on the state. But the state prioritized the defense of its cities, "and ceded the countryside to its foes."[35] From the Song Dynasty onward, most central governments placed their military garrisons at or near major urban centers. The imperial Ming state constructed hundreds of military garrisons across its territory. Local elites could flock to these "walled safe havens" for temporary refuge from peasant revolts. But when they returned, their houses in the countryside would usually be burned and plundered.[36]

7.3   Social Cooperation and Commitment Problems

Facing these uncertainties and a minimal state, Chinese elites turned to social cooperation. They created a division of labor within their lineage organizations so that one male member in each generation could focus on learning and take the civil service examination. They set aside lineage property that was collectively owned by all lineage members and expected wealthy members to donate to the collective land in their wills. They organized local society, mobilized their lineages, and paid peasants to build roads, fix dikes, and repair dams. Once a proud son succeeded in the examination and became an official, they expected him to influence government policies to protect local interests. When rebels, bandits, and pirates came, they retreated to the mountains, built fortresses, and established private armies.

While social cooperation had the potential to bring significant efficiency gains to the elites, it required individuals to enter into mutually beneficial exchange relationships. They would have to be able to commit to fulfilling their contractual obligations in order to sustain such cooperation. For example, individuals from different generations must commit to each other that after the older generation invests in the younger generation, the young will take care of the old. This commitment problem arose because the exchange was sequential: a considerable amount of time would elapse between the *quid* and the *quo*.[37] Commitment problems could also arise for simultaneous exchanges. For example, the Lin and Huang families may agree to collaborate to repair the dikes, but the Lin family could decide to free-ride and let the Huang family take up the slack. The Huang family, *ex ante* anticipating this *ex post* behavior, would find it best not to collaborate with the

Lin family to begin with. Collective action problems would therefore prevent social cooperation.[38]

7.3.1 Collective Investment in Human Capital

Studying for the examination required collective efforts, because even wealthy families could not afford for all their sons to devote all their time to learning. Preparation usually began at the tender age of six to seven years old, when children were made to recite Confucian textbooks.[39] On average, it took thirty years of uninterrupted study to succeed at the final stage of the examination to become an advanced scholar.[40]

It often took generations for a family to groom one son for the examination. This generational effort is evident in Hilary Beattie's study of eminent families in Tongcheng County (Anhui Province). The Zhang family's ancestors were immigrants who came to the area at the beginning of the Ming Dynasty. They began in a small way and gradually built up their fortunes through the peasant virtues of thrift and hard work. Zhang Ying's fourth-generation ancestor, Zhang Peng, laid the real foundations of the family fortunes. Zhang Peng had only one son, Zhang Mu (1520–1556), who thus inherited all his property undivided. Zhang Mu built it up further and had only two sons, ensuring a minimal division of his inheritance. The elder son, Zhang Chun (1540–1612), was able to devote himself to uninterrupted study. He was rewarded in 1568 by becoming the first in the family to win an advanced degree. His brother, Zhang Jian, remained in the country looking after the land.[41]

Zhang Chun could only afford to devote himself to his studies because he had inherited a large amount of property from his father, which his brother helped to look after. After he became an official, "A great deal of this wealth (from official posts) was channeled directly back into land."[42]

The Zhang family began a lucrative cycle of investment from physical capital (land) to human capital and back again. By 1747, the Zhang lineage had acquired 290 mu ($\approx$ 44 acres) of ritual land, and in the 1820s up to 588 mu. The bulk of these holdings was acquired in the eighteenth century, when the lineage reached the peak of its success as Zhang Ying and his son Zhang Tingyu became nationally prominent politicians.[43]

The Zhang family's pattern of capital accumulation follows a general overlapping generations model. In figure 7.1, at T_1 the young ancestor starts to accumulate resources. At T_2, the middle-aged ancestor transfers resources to his

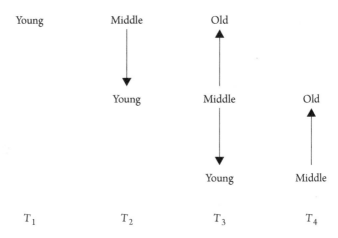

FIGURE 7.1: Overlapping Generations and Capital Accumulation

younger family member. When the young become middle aged (at T_3), they in turn support those who raised them, while also raising a new generation. Transfers between generations continue (T_4 on) as the family reproduces itself over time.[44]

In order to sustain this capital accumulation cycle, every young generation needed to commit to returning home to take care of family affairs. If the older generation anticipates that the young will not return, it will not commit to investing in them, and the cycle will break.

The cycle in the Zhang family broke after Zhang Tingyu—its most successful son. Hilary Beattie noticed that "Zhang Tingyu's sons and grandsons seem to have spent more time at the capital or in office than did those of his brothers and could possibly have been corrupted faster by worldly habits."[45]

7.3.2   Collective Ownership of Property

To avoid the gradual fragmentation of landholdings due to their periodic division through the inheritance process, Chinese elites from the Northern Song onwards instituted a type of lineage property that was held jointly in perpetuity as an inalienable trust.[46] Lineage property consisted mainly of lineage fields, but it could also include houses, capital for usury, and irrigation systems. In commercialized areas, lineages collectively owned industrial and commercial properties, such as shops.

Lineage property developed on a large scale in the Ming and Qing periods. Each generation designated a proportion of its estate as "sacrificial property" to be donated to the collective good of the lineage organization. The lineage used the income from the property to purchase candles and incense, as well as offerings of wine and food, for ancestor worship. In 1392, when Zhou Ziyuan of Jianyang (Fujian Province) divided his estate among his three sons, he told his relatives and friends that he had established sacrificial fields from which his sons would collect the income, in rotation, to meet the expenses of the ancestral temple and ancestral grave.[47]

Branches of the lineage could continue to make collective investments in the joint property. Each branch then had a share in the joint property, similar to a corporate organization.[48] For example, the genealogy of the Zhan clan of Pucheng (Fujian Province) recorded that the clan built its ancestor hall in 1865. Later that year, the eight descendants of the lineage each donated five silver dollars to purchase a garden, which generated an annual rent of 8,000 in cash. The clan then used the income to help meet the expenses incurred by the ancestor hall.[49]

The income from lineage property was mainly used for ancestor worship, the promotion of education, and local public works.[50] By the late Qing era, in some areas the proportion of land held as lineage corporate fields was equal to or greater than privately owned land.[51]

But some branches of the lineage might shirk their responsibility to contribute to the joint estate, especially if there was clear economic inequality within the lineage. A document from the Wang lineage in Pucheng County (Fujian Province) recorded: "when wealth declines, some branches flourish and others are bankrupted. The idle and lazy descendants . . . are still as poor as before, and they even evade or default on the tax they are responsible for paying that year. The sacrifice and cleaning of the graves in the hills is abandoned."[52]

7.3.3   Local Goods and Services

As local financial conditions deteriorated in the Ming and Qing eras, lineage organizations and lineage coalitions played an important role in organizing and managing local public works.[53] These social organizations contributed financial and human resources and collaborated with the imperial state. State officials welcomed the support from social groups because they relieved the state of the fiscal and bureaucratic burden of maintaining the public works. The participation of lineages also helped avoid the inevitable problem of mismanagement whenever large amounts of public funds were involved.[54]

For example, after the Single Whip reform in the mid-Ming Dynasty, local governments often allocated the silver payment collected for public works to other purposes. Local magistrates hence delegated responsibility for projects such as maintaining the irrigation system to lineage organizations. Jinjiang County's gazetteer recorded that in the mid-Ming period, the magistrate asked the Lin, Huang, Su, and Zheng lineages to repair the dikes.[55] Lineages took responsibility for managing the public works after they were finished. Putian County's gazetteer recorded that the government used to manage the local water reserve, but the Zou, Zeng, and Xu lineages had taken over its management in 1602.[56]

Lineages also provided goods and services that benefited the general public in the locality. For instance, the Zhang lineage in Tongcheng took the lead in founding a charitable granary in 1758 to aid the poor during bad harvests.[57] In 1767 the Fang lineage donated land to the county to fund the examination expenses of poor scholars, and in 1797 the Yao lineage made a similar donation.[58]

The collective provision of local goods and services required collective action. After the construction of these infrastructures, elites needed to address another collective action problem: the common pool resource problem. Every family wanted to overuse the resources, because if they did not, other families would[59]—what Garrett Hardin termed the "tragedy of the commons."[60] A lineage document from Zhangzhou (Fujian Province) illustrates this dilemma: "For a long time we have been relying on the ponds for watering our rice paddies and the trees for shading our ancestors' graveyard. Our ancestors devoted their time and energy to build these ponds and plant these trees. . . . Some of their descendants, however, took the ponds as private, and cut the trees."

7.3.4   Resisting the State

Social cooperation could also help elites resist state intrusion. After a lineage member became an official, the lineage—along with the whole area—often expected their proud son to negotiate with the authorities on its behalf. In Tongcheng County, the most frequent local spokesman in the early Qing era was Yao Wenran (1621–1678)—a member of the Yao lineage, a relative by marriage of the Zhang family. Yao was an advanced scholar and rose to the post of junior metropolitan censor in the capital before he retired.[61]

A large part of Yao's ten-year retirement was spent interfering in matters of local administration. Though his family biographer insists that he never acted in his own private interests, he admitted that "whenever there occurred any-thing that would be of benefit or harm to the locality he would send letters back and forth until he got what he requested."[62] For example, he success-fully protested against the increase in his home county's labor service quota; he delayed the enforcement of a new rule that abolished the labor service exemption for degree holders' family members; and he averted the central government's attempt to carry out a new cadastral survey to obtain an accurate register of land and labor.[63] Yao also collaborated with his brother Yao Wenlie (1616–1665), a prefectural judge, to abolish a new policy that imposed a greater financial burden on community (li) leaders.[64]

After Yao Wenran's death in 1678, Zhang Ying took over. As minister of rites, Zhang was the most prestigious of the Tongcheng elite. When he was in the capital, Zhang received complaints and requests from relatives and friends back home about various policies that imposed burdens on the local commu-nity. In 1680 he persuaded his friend, the governor of Anhui, to abolish these policies.[65]

Eminent families intervened for the benefit of the whole locality in order to prevent social unrest and antagonism. As Hilary Beattie observed, after the "social chaos at the end of the Ming," the local elites "had to find more sub-tle and more altruistic-seeming ways of protecting their own interests." "The solution," Beattie argued, "was to return firmly to the earlier tradition of inter-vening directly with the authorities in fiscal matters, ostensibly for the benefit of the whole county. If their action also benefited themselves and their families it was no coincidence."[66]

The successful defense of local vested interests, however, made it virtually impossible for the understaffed authorities to ensure fairness in fiscal admin-istration.[67] The Qing government, for instance, was not able to carry out any nationwide cadastral surveys during its 267-year rule.[68]

In addition to resisting additional burdens, local communities also needed to share the existing taxes and labor services. During the Ming Dynasty, for example, military households were responsible for supplying one male mem-ber in each generation to serve in the military. Often, a single member of the descent group personally fulfilled this military responsibility, and his relatives paid him for this service. Michael Szonyi found that in Fujian, many lineages organized an annual rotation through the branches to administer the respon-sibility for this payment. He noticed, however, that "The arrangement was not a completely stable one. The danger always existed that someone would shirk his responsibility by not making the appropriate payment when it was his turn in the rotation."[69] Shirking was of particular concern to the wealthier members of the group, because they were expected to make up for the shortfall.[70]

7.3.5   Collective Defense

The elites also relied on social cooperation to protect themselves from rebels, bandits, pirates, and, sometimes, their neighbors. They took sanctuary in a relative's home away from conflict-afflicted zones, constructed fortress protections in the mountains, or directly took on the rebels with private militias. During a mass rebellion, for example, local elites could "conscript" their clan to provide temporary shelter, build a fortress, or establish a private militia if the state could not provide sufficient protection.

William Rowe provides a detailed account of how clan militias functioned in Macheng County (Hubei Province). During the Red Turban Rebellion in the late Yuan period, he describes, "Large numbers of Macheng landowners were sufficiently alarmed that they took to the hills and fortified themselves until the rebellions passed over."[71] The lineage was the crucial unit of spatial and social organization that organized the defense. Rowe notes that "Lineage consciousness was probably the most fundamental element in Macheng people's personal identity," as lineages oversaw collective defense through managing the militia.[72] As a result, many fortresses were lineage specific, such as the Yu clan's Cloud Dragon Fort and the Xia clan's Stonewall Fort.[73] Yet not every clan was conscious of its collective identity: some elite members flocked to the cities for refuge during mass rebellions, leaving their poor kin behind.[74]

7.4   Lineage Organizations and Lineage Coalitions

Chinese elites faced an organizational problem in the late imperial era: they needed to design institutions that allowed them to credibly commit to each other so they could exploit the gains from social cooperation. Such institutions needed to enable individuals to commit to each other within their natural groups, such as clans, and facilitate commitments between these groups.

In repeated interactions, individuals might be able to commit to each other based on a reputation mechanism. If people shirked or cheated, the local community would stop cooperating with them. While this mechanism certainly played a role in sustaining collaboration, it could not support an efficient level of cooperation because it was not always possible to enforce the reputation mechanism where there were asymmetries in available information. Information asymmetries could be severe even within the same descent group if a clan was divided into multiple branches and the bond between branches faded over generations.

To some extent, Chinese elites could rely on the legal system to organize social cooperation by punishing bad behavior. But a county government with three civil servants was simply unable to deal with the social problems associated with an increasingly larger population.[75]

Elites therefore turned to private-order institutions.[76] They institutionalized their natural groups by bonding members of the same descent group together using ancestor worship and genealogy records. They also strengthened bonds between these natural groups through intermarriages.

7.4.1   Ancestor Worship

Before the Song era, only the nobility could erect shrines to worship their ancestors. During this period, Neo-Confucians, such as Cheng Yi and Zhu Xi, provided the ideological preconditions for developing lineage organizations. Cheng advocated eliminating the distinctions between aristocrats and commoners for the conduct of ancestor worship and relaxing the restrictions on the number of generations of ancestors that the common people could worship. Zhu suggested setting up an offering hall in the main chamber of the residence to worship four generations of ancestors and instructed that land must be sacrificed to pay for this hall.[77]

This Neo-Confucian ritual, although never formally enshrined in law, became an important ethical justification for the practice of venerating the descent line and uniting the lineage, and stimulated the widespread development of lineage organizations after the Song era. During the Ming Dynasty, it became common to worship ancestors more than four generations distant, although it was officially prohibited. This practice made it possible to expand and maintain lineage organizations over the long term.[78]

Worshipping a common ancestor spiritually bonded individuals from the same descent group. The activities and properties associated with this ritual also linked the group materially. The descendants usually collectively inherited various kinds of sacrificial fields, which ensured that lineage members would continue their communal activities even after private household assets were divided through inheritance.[79] If a branch of the lineage group did not participate in the construction of the ancestral hall, its members would lose their right to inherit the descent line. Only investors and subsequent share-holders were allowed to participate in ancestor worship and the management of sacrificial fields.[80]

Ancestor worship therefore incentivized lineage members to contribute to their collective goods. The ritual also punished free-riders by preventing them from inheriting lineage property. In the Zhang lineage in Tongcheng, Zhang Tingyu's sons and grandsons spent more time in the capital than at home, and did not contribute to worship activities as much as their cousins. Hilary Beat-tie speculates why Zhang Tingyu's descendants had the worst performance in producing degree holders among the branches: "By taking no part in the man-agement of the lineage's joint property they had no opportunity to share in the perquisites and social standing which this may have conferred."[81]

7.4.2   Genealogy

In addition to common ancestor worship, another way to maintain lineage coherence was to compile genealogical records. These books followed a stan-dard template, starting with an account of the clan's origins and history, the growth of its membership over time, and clan settlement and migration pat-terns. They also included descriptions and records of clan property, ancestral halls, and ancestral graveyards; biographies of eminent clansmen, rosters of men and women honored in one way or another; and sometimes scholarly writings by clan members, clan regulations, and imperial favors.[82] Compi-lations and revisions of such records were financed by contributions from lineage members in proportion to the size of their landholdings.[83]

These genealogy books promoted lineage collective action in two ways. First, by documenting the achievements and contributions of individual clan members, they provided "selective incentives"[84] for members to contribute to the clan's collective goods.[85] Second, by collecting and publicizing infor-mation on lineage members, the books helped overcome the information asymmetry problem and facilitated collective enforcement. The Zhang lin-eage in Tongcheng, for example, required all members to keep careful records of births, deaths, marriages, and so on, and to report them to the lineage head on the occasion of the annual ancestor worship. The branch heads were expected to regularly collect all the necessary information on members and send it every three years to those in charge of the ancestral hall, to facilitate a major revision of genealogy records every thirty years; managers of the lineage property likewise provided regular accounts of income and expenditure.[86]

7.4.3   Intermarriage

Chinese elites built ancestral halls and compiled genealogy books to strengthen lineage coherence. But some cooperation required *cross-lineage* collective action. As discussed earlier, the construction and maintenance of irrigation systems demanded large-scale cooperation, which often involved several lineages. Collective defense against severe violent threats, from either foreign enemies or domestic rebellions, likewise required several lineages to collaborate.

Chinese elites used intermarriages—a means of exchanging "mutual hostages"[87]—to form cross-lineage social networks. The two most prominent lineages in Tongcheng, the Yaos and the Zhangs, began to make marriage connections in the early seventeenth century, a practice that persisted late into the nineteenth century.[88] The two lineages became so intermarried in the seventeenth and eighteenth centuries that in 1742 a censor could claim that between them, the two families accounted for almost half of the country's gentry.[89] Three of Zhang Ying's six sons married Yao women; in the next generation Yao marriages rose to 71 percent, though they fell gradually thereafter to 43 percent in the fourth generation and 30 percent in the fifth.[90]

Marriage alliances between prominent local families could also help their representatives in the national government, since these relationships easily translated into alliances in court politics. In the 1620s, a sizable group of Tongcheng officials joined together as Donglin partisans.[91] Zhang Tingyu, who in 1726 became a grand secretary and was soon to be one of the key figures in the newly formed office of the Grand Council, used his privileged position to systematically advance the interests of his own family, and those of his relatives by marriage, particularly by procuring official positions for them. By 1742 their presence in government posts had become so conspicuous that the censor Liu Tongxun wrote a memorial to the emperor in protest, and Zhang Tingyu was warned to be more circumspect.[92]

7.5   Evidence from Quantitative Data

The narrative suggests that elites were motivated to strengthen their lineages in response to the need for: (1) continuous and collective investment in human capital, (2) collective ownership of property, (3) local goods and services, (4) resisting intrusive state power, and (5) defending against violence.

I now evaluate the implications of this narrative by applying these insights to a new dataset created for this study. While I lack the necessary data to test all of these implications, this section provides empirical evidence to support two key implications of the discussion.

First, if lineage organizations allowed Chinese elites to credibly commit to each other, so that lineage members could collectively invest in the younger generation's human capital, there should be a positive correlation between a locality's exam success and the number of lineage organizations, controlling for the level of economic development. Here, the causal arrows go both ways: with more lineage organizations, lineage members were more likely to transfer physical capital into human capital and then back again, which sustained lineage organizations. Second, if lineage organizations developed as a collective defense mechanism against violence, there should be a positive correlation between an area's level of violence and the number of lineage organizations.

The goal of the quantitative analysis is to complement the rich, qualitative evidence provided through case studies by historians. Together, the narrative and the quantitative findings point to important empirical patterns that help us understand how private-order institutions emerged and were sustained in late imperial China.

7.5.1   *Data*

LINEAGE ORGANIZATION

The key outcome variable is *Number of lineage organizations*, which measures the number of unique lineage organizations in a county between 1801 and 1850. I identify lineage organizations in each county using Wang Heming's *Comprehensive Catalog of Chinese Genealogies*.[93] Wang and his team at the Shanghai Library spent eight years cataloging roughly 51,200 genealogy books and records from all known sources—including local and national archives and libraries, private holdings, and overseas collections[94]—from the end of the first millennium to the present day in a print registry.[95] It is the most comprehensive registry of known Chinese clan genealogies to date.[96]

I digitized this entire print registry and geocoded each genealogy book based on its reported location using the *China Historical Geographic Information System* for latitudes and longitudes.[97] To the best of my knowledge, this geocoding is the first such effort of its kind.[98]

Each entry in Wang Heming's registry reports a record of a clan's genealogy book, including the year in which it was compiled. A clan may have had multiple registry entries. For example, the Li clan based in the city of Taiyuan compiled its first genealogy book in 1701 (entry 1), which it then updated in 1754 (entry 2) and 1802 (entry 3), for a total of three genealogy books. Each entry also includes information on the clan's surname and current (at the time) location.

I believe the genealogy book data provide the most systematic and best available proxy—even if imperfect—for documenting lineage organizations in imperial China. Still, data concerns including measurement error remain. The compilation of genealogy books may have been sensitive to the availability of printing materials, changing macro-economic conditions, and migration patterns. My regression analysis ahead will account for such potential confounders by controlling for a wide range of geographic and historical controls and prefectural fixed effects. Furthermore, elites may have found it difficult to compile genealogy books during violent conflicts, and these books may have been less likely to survive and be cataloged. This survival bias, however, will create a downward bias of my estimates and make me less likely to find a positive correlation between violence and the number of lineage organizations.

There were 2,988 genealogy books compiled during 1801–1850. Assuming that a unique surname-latitude-longitude combination identifies a lineage organization, I recognize 2,096 unique lineage organizations that existed throughout China during this period. They certainly did not include all lineage organizations in China during 1801–1850; they were the most powerful lineage organizations at the time. Figure 7.2 shows the spatial distribution of these lineage organizations with their surnames.[99]

I analyze the period 1801–1850 because it was the last half-century before the Western intrusion and the Taiping Rebellion, when lineage organizations increased dramatically. It thus represents the final era of the old regime, and the ultimate product of lineage development during this time. I choose a period of fifty years because it was long enough for a powerful clan to compile a genealogy book if it wanted to since these books were typically revised roughly every half-century, all else constant.[100]

EXAM SUCCESS

To measure exam success, I use the *Number of advanced scholars* in a county during the Qing period before 1801. The data come from the *China Biographical Database*, which provides the name, year of exam, and geocoded

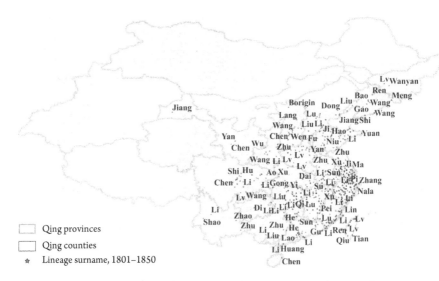

FIGURE 7.2: Spatial Distribution of Lineage Surnames (1801–1850)

hometown location for every advanced scholar in the Ming and Qing eras.[101] The database collects this information from official records. Since advanced scholars obtained the highest degree in the examination, prior studies have used their number to quantify historical human capital in a given locality.[102]

A total of 14,625 individuals became advanced scholars during 1644–1800.[103] I analyze this period so that the exam success variable predates the lineage organization variable. This allows me to examine how past exam success contributed to lineage organization development.

Exam success depended on population size and the government quota for each county's public school, which determined how many pupils could enroll in the local school and take the entry-level exam.[104] Early Qing emperors determined the quota, which remained stable until the Taiping Rebellion.[105] The empirical results reported below control for a county's population density and public school quota.

CONFLICT

I use the *Number of conflicts*—the number of battles in any conflict during 1644–1800—to measure the level of violence in a county. This data comes from the *Catalog of Historical Wars* produced by the Nanjing Military Academy.[106] Between 1644 and 1800, 372 battles linked to 217 wars occurred

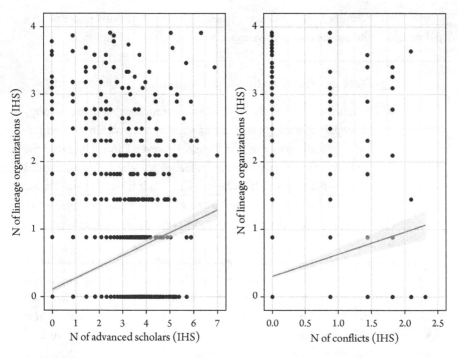

FIGURE 7.3: Exam Success, Violence, and Lineage Organizations: Scatter Plots

within the Qing territory.[107] Over 70 percent of these battles were between domestic rebels and the imperial government.[108]

7.5.2   Findings

Figure 7.3 shows the scatter plots (with fit lines and their 95 percent confidence intervals), which indicate positive correlations between *Number of lineage organizations* and *Number of advanced scholars*, and between *Number of lineage organizations* and *Number of conflicts*.[109]

Using regressions, I find similar patterns.[110] On average, fifty more advanced scholars were associated with one more lineage organization. Similarly, conflict was positively associated with lineage organizations. One additional battle was associated with almost one more lineage organization.

In sum, Qing counties that had more exam success and violence also had more lineage organizations and more lineage activities. The correlational evidence is consistent with the narrative that Chinese elites in the late imperial era institutionalized their lineage organizations to deal with uncertainties brought about by the competitive exam and rising levels of violence.

7.6   State-Society Partnership, Durability, and Prosperity

Max Weber defines the state as "a human community that (successfully) claims the *monopoly of the legitimate use of physical force* within a given territory."[111] The state's monopoly over violence, however, cannot be taken for granted. In late imperial China, private organizations, such as lineages, started to gain control over the means of violence. They built fortresses and walled villages, and established militias. Lineage organizations were also involved in a wide variety of activities in which they collaborated and negotiated with the state.

This state-society partnership helps explain a central paradox in China's imperial rule: its exceptional durability despite declining fiscal strength and military power. Social organizations filled the void left by a weakened state after the Song times. Lineage institutions helped local elites overcome their collective action and coordination problems and provide public goods and services. Meanwhile, local elites still depended on the state for legitimation, which kept them from drifting away and becoming independent. When the state failed to maintain the dikes, local lineages took them on. When rebels arrived, and the government army was defending only the cities, the lineages armed up. Imperial rule stayed resilient facing external and internal challenges *not* because the state was strong, but because social forces stepped in.

This long-run political stability, however, came with economic costs. Robert Bates argues that when coercion is privately provided, poverty is the price of peace, and violence is the price of prosperity. Due to the fear of envy, he explains, "people may seek to increase their welfare by choosing to live in poverty."[112] When making investment decisions, elite Chinese families faced two fundamental dilemmas. First, they had to trade prosperity for peace. If they wanted to get rich, they had to invest in security. Alternatively, if they wanted to maintain peace, they had to remain poor. Second, they could not specialize in economic production, since they had to allocate a significant portion of their resources to defense. Therefore, elite Chinese families could not exploit the benefits of specialization—which Adam Smith considered key to modern economic growth.[113] As a result, the society as a whole could not exploit the division of labor because every family needed to multitask.[114]

In Europe, a different type of social cooperation emerged. Because of religious prohibitions on endogamy, adoption, polygyny, concubinage, divorce, and remarriage,[115] families in Europe never grew as big as those in China.[116] Joseph Henrich contends that the dissolution of the extended family by the Medieval Church laid the foundation for Europe's political and economic modernization.[117] Avner Greif argues that the decline of kinship groups and the rise of nuclear families forced Europeans to look for a new solution to problems of conflict and cooperation, which resulted in people uniting to form corporations. These corporations were voluntary, interest-based, self-governed, and intentionally created permanent associations. They provided safety nets, secured property rights, provided public goods, supported markets, and fostered innovation and training, while the state provided security. Greif credits the emergence of corporations with Europe's "longest post-Roman period of economic growth" and observes that "corporations and nuclear families constituted a distinguishing feature of the particularly European institutional foundations of markets, polities, and knowledge."[118]

In China, however, extended families dominated the society. In the late imperial era before the mid-1800s, there was still a balance between state power and lineage power. Although lineage organizations and coalitions experienced rapid development and became indispensable in local governance and defense, they were not powerful enough to threaten the authority of the state. In this era, the state delegated some of its functions to the lineage organizations and was able to control them. The state-lineage relationship was a partnership. In the next chapter, I discuss how the Western intrusion and the Taiping Rebellion tilted this balance and ended the state's control over social forces.

PART IV

State Weakening under Warlordism

8

State Failure in the Qing Dynasty

8.1   The Long and Winding Dynasty

Qing troops entered Beijing on June 6, 1644, and claimed the throne for their six-year-old emperor. The city's residents were too intimidated by the Manchu soldiers to put up a fight. Only two months previously, rebels led by Li Zicheng had sacked the city and dethroned the last Ming emperor (who then hanged himself). Sitting on the throne for little over a month, Li Zicheng rode with his army to battle the remaining Ming army, not knowing it had recruited help from the Manchus.

In just two generations, the Manchus, an ethnic group living north of the Great Wall, had built a powerful state by conquering and combining a confederation of tribes. Shortly after they founded the Qing Dynasty, they conquered the territories south of the Great Wall and ruled China for almost three hundred years.

Manchu elites were embedded in a close-knit network institutionalized in the Eight Banners—a unique Manchu approach to military mobilization and organization. After their victory, the Manchus imposed their elite structure and Eight Banners system onto the Qing government's administrative structure. The early Qing period experienced a degree of centralization that had rarely been seen in late imperial China since the Song Dynasty. Emperors during the "High Qing" era in the eighteenth century enforced policies to diminish the power and privileges of the gentry, simplified tax collection by merging land and labor taxes, and delineated central and local revenues. Meanwhile, the Qing state extended its reach deep into central Asia and Tibet and achieved a level of territorial control that was rivaled only by the Mongol Empire (1279–1368).

The early Qing emperors were state builders, but they strengthened the central state by circumventing the civil bureaucracy. They relied on a system of secret palace memorials to communicate directly with their bureaucrats, employed officials recruited outside the civil service examination, exhibited extraordinary diligence, and enjoyed exceptional longevity. None of these, however, lasted. With the deterioration of the Eight Banners and the increasing corruption and ineptitude of the Manchus, later Qing rulers increasingly relied on the civil bureaucracy, which was staffed by members of the narrowly interested Han gentry. The Qing Dynasty could not escape the inevitable fate of fiscal and military decline that its predecessors had experienced.

The mid-nineteenth century marked the turning point in Qing—and Chinese—history. After its defeat in the First Opium War (1839–1842), the Qing government was forced to allocate the lion's share of its revenue to military defense, which triggered an unprecedented fiscal crisis. Meanwhile, in the mid-nineteenth century, the "Little Ice Age" reached its peak with particularly cold weather, which created famine conditions in southwest China. The Taiping Rebellion erupted in 1850. It soon occupied the most affluent regions in the country, further cutting off the government's revenue sources. Since the Qing's two standing armies (the Eight Banners and the Green Standards) were more interested in using opium than fighting, the emperor reluctantly allowed local elites to form their own militias. With the help of these militias, the Qing defeated the Taiping and other rebel groups in 1869. But the emperor's survival strategy reshaped China's elite social terrain: local private armies mushroomed during the Taiping Rebellion, lineage organizations experienced the highest levels of growth in the imperial era, and local elites gained the upper hand in local governance.

By granting them a prominent leadership role, the Qing's endorsement of local governance by local elites during the Taiping Rebellion tipped the balance of power. Local elites were now formally involved in both local defense and local administration. After its defeat in the First Sino-Japanese War (1894–1895), the Qing state established the New Army in the hope of creating a modern Westernized military force. Gradually, however, the New Army fell under the control of local elites, and the gentry leaders—many of whom had been elected to the new provincial legislatures—became local strongmen with control over both taxation and military matters. The abolishment of the civil service examinations in 1905 severed the last connection between the central state and local elites. In 1911, military groups controlled by local gentry leaders declared independence. The Qing, along with a thousand years of imperial rule in China, fell.

———

In this chapter, I discuss state decline and failure in China's last dynasty—the Qing (1644–1911). I start with a brief introduction to the High Qing period, examining the origins of the Qing Dynasty and the Manchus, its military institutions, such as the Eight Banners and the Green Standards, and its fiscal institutions. I focus on three centralizing institutions from this period: the Grand Council, the palace memorial, and the Imperial Household Department. Early Qing emperors used these institutions to advocate fiscal innovations, including the incorporation of the labor-service tax into the land tax and the return of the meltage fee to the public coffers. But early successes required the emperor to bypass the civil bureaucracy. This strategy was not sustainable, and later emperors reverted to relying on the bureaucracy. The Qing's fiscal situation started to decline in the late eighteenth century.

I then examine the decline and fall of the Qing state. External threats and internal rebellions further strained the Qing's finances, and local elites gained significant autonomy and power during and after the Taiping Rebellion. The formation and growth of local lineage organizations threatened the central state's monopoly over violence and tipped the balance between state power and gentry power. Whatever was left to connect the state and local elites was further cut off when the Qing government abolished the civil service examination system. China's elite social terrain shifted from a bowtie to a ring.

My empirical analysis focuses on how local elites responded to the Taiping Rebellion. Using genealogy records as a proxy for local elite collective action, I show that counties that experienced more battles during the rebellion experienced a highly significant increase in post-Taiping elite collective action. The renewed emphasis on privately provided security eventually led to state failure. I analyze geocoded data on local military groups that declared independence from the imperial Qing government in 1911, and find a positive and highly significant relationship between post-Taiping elite collective action and declarations of independence.

The rest of the chapter is structured as follows. Section 8.2 introduces the origins of the Qing Dynasty and the politics during the early Qing era. Section 8.3 examines how the state's fiscal and military power stagnated and declined in the mid-Qing era. Section 8.4 discusses how the Qing state lost its monopoly over violence in the aftermath of the Opium Wars and the Taiping Rebellion. Section 8.5 presents an empirical analysis using an original dataset on elite collective action during and after the Taiping Rebellion and its relationship to the Qing's fall. Section 8.6 then concludes by discussing the broader implications of these findings.

8.2   High Qing

The "long eighteenth century" is celebrated in China as the "prosperous age" (盛世) and in the West as the High Qing.[1] This era is famous for its energetic rulers, growing revenues, and expanding territories.

8.2.1   The Origin of the Qing

The Manchus founded the Qing Dynasty in 1636. The name "Manchu" first appeared at this time, and coincided with the creation of a unified state.[2] The Manchus were previously known as the Jurchens (女真), who descended from the founders of the Jin Dynasty in the twelfth century. For centuries, they lived in the forests and along the rivers of what is now the Russian province of Primorsky Krai and the Chinese province of Heilongjiang.[3] The Ming state administered Jurchen lands through local garrisons and granted commanderies to Jurchen tribal leaders to secure their loyalty.[4]

In 1616, Nurhaci (1559–1626) unified all Jurchen tribes and declared himself the "bright khan" of the "Latter Jin country." He issued his "Seven Grievances" against the Ming and openly rejected Ming rule. Nurhaci later moved his capital to the former Ming city of Shenyang, where his eighth son Hong Taiji (1592–1643) founded the Qing Dynasty.[5]

8.2.2   The Eight Banners

The Eight Banners, "the most famous of all Manchu institutions," were the key to Manchu success.[6] Serving as both military and civil administration institutions, the Eight Banners traced their origins to the methods used to conduct large-scale hunts. Manchu leaders used this system as an umbrella organization to oversee the mobilization of military forces and the management of the associated populations, including Manchus, Mongols, acculturated frontier Chinese, and Koreans.[7] For the Manchus, "the army was society,"[8] and membership in the banners was acquired at birth. Thus the banners were the institutional home of a martial caste—an exclusive hereditary social group distinguished by a common occupation, soldiering.[9]

The banners initially included yellow, white, red, and blue, and were later expanded to eight with a red border added to the flags (the flag of the red banner was bordered in white). The banners were further subdivided along ethnic lines: the Mongol Eight Banners, the Chinese Eight Banners, and the original Manchu Eight Banners. The fully formed "Eight Banner" system, achieved in 1642, therefore consisted of twenty-four banners; the Manchu banners outranked those of the Mongols and Chinese.[10]

Military service was obligatory for all males in the banners, and each soldier was assigned a tract of land once he was enrolled. Though he was not required to farm it himself since he did not owe land tax, his family members either farmed it themselves or hired agricultural serfs to do so.[11] The banners were "cradle-to-grave" institutions that administered the Manchu population's births, deaths, marriages, adoptions, changes in residence, and employment.[12] They also served as a crucial power base for the Manchu nobility—the khan, the princes, and the commanders—who held them virtually as private property.[13]

After they conquered China, the Manchus implemented a similar system of banner landholding there.[14] But this system never worked quite as well. Supporting the growing banner population that became steadily impoverished was one of the greatest challenges for Qing finance.

8.2.3   The Green Standards

In addition to the Eight Banners, the Qing state also maintained a second armed force, the Green Standard Army. This army, made up of Han Chinese soldiers, was about three times larger than the banners.[15] Green Standard soldiers were initially defected Ming soldiers; later they were recruited from the general population.[16] Their greater number enabled Green Standard troops to maintain a substantial presence in rural areas, where they functioned more as a police or national guard force, quelling local unrest and supervising grain transport. Banner troops, however, were garrisoned mainly in the cities.[17]

8.2.4   The Fiscal System

The Qing government inherited its entire tax structure from the preceding Ming Dynasty and operated it with few changes for two centuries.[18] Land accounted for over 70 percent of total public revenue.[19] It generally comprised two components: (1) the combined land tax and labor services (地丁) and (2) the grain tax. In 1712 the Kangxi Emperor (1664–1722) froze the labor service quota at the previous year's level.[20] In the second quarter of the eighteenth century it was incorporated into the land tax (摊丁入亩).[21] In addition to the land tax, which was paid in money, landowners in most places had to pay a grain tax to the government, which had also been converted into money payments by the late Qing era.[22]

The traditional taxes also included the salt tax and the native customs, which contributed merely 12 percent and 7 percent, respectively, to the total government revenues.[23] Thus before the mid-nineteenth century, the Qing Dynasty relied heavily on direct taxes (especially the land tax).

Collecting the land tax required accurate records of land registration. After the Manchus gained control of China, the first emperor ordered that the tax quotas of the late Ming era should serve as the basis for assessing the land tax and labor services, and that the records of the cadastral survey carried out by the late Ming reformer Zhang Juzheng (see chapter 6) should be the basis for land registration.[24] For the next two centuries, the Manchu regime did not carry out any cadastral surveys; it relied on the late Ming records with infrequent and minor revisions carried out by officials at the provincial and local levels.[25]

8.2.5 Centralization Efforts

The High Qing era had the good fortune of having three remarkably capable, hard-working, and long-lived rulers—two of whom ruled for 60 years each—reigning under the titles Kangxi (1664–1722), Yongzheng (1722–1735), and Qianlong (1735–1796).[26] Different from their Ming predecessors, early Qing rulers were embedded in a nationally coherent elite network that was forged before and during the conquest and institutionalized in the Eight Banners.

Before they conquered China, the leading clans of Jurchen tribes intermarried extensively, which helped them maintain good relations and form a close-knit social network.[27] The Manchu rulers consolidated this network by granting leadership positions to the head of each clan in the Eight Banners. Together, the clan leaders formed the Qing nobility, which included members of the Aisin Gioro clan, who were descendants of Nurhaci, as well as members of other leading clans. The nobility was entrusted with hereditary titles. The best-known title was Prince of the Iron Cap (铁帽子王), which was awarded to men outside the imperial lineage who had rendered extraordinary service to Nurhaci and Hong Taiji, founder of the Qing Dynasty.[28]

After the Kangxi Emperor took the throne at the age of seven, he married the daughters of his regents, and his sister married the son of another regent. As Jonathan Spence points out, "many of them remained close to the Kangxi Emperor until their deaths, and they gave him a network of supporters that cut across Manchu lineage lines."[29]

The national elite network forged through intermarriages enabled early Qing rulers to enact reforms that enhanced the power of the monarchy and strengthened central government institutions without worrying about the elites revolting. During its first century, the Qing regime introduced three significant innovations to its central administration—the Grand Council, the palace memorial, and the Imperial Household Department. All three institutions operated outside the regular bureaucracy and were staffed by personal clients of the throne rather than by successful civil service examination candidates; each is discussed in turn below.

THE GRAND COUNCIL

The most dramatic of the Qing innovations in central administration was the Grand Council (军机处), which began during the Kangxi reign as an informal advisory commission for military affairs. Under Yongzheng, this informal body evolved into a permanent privy council housed in the palace, and its sphere of authority expanded to all arenas of imperial policy. But it was never regularized into the empire's formal bureaucratic structure; it remained something of a personal "star chamber" or "kitchen cabinet" granting private advice to the throne. Though an especially trusted Han minister might occasionally be included, the council was overwhelmingly Manchu. Its leading members were often drawn from the emperor's closest circle of relatives and friends.[30]

THE PALACE MEMORIAL

The management of communications determined the throne's ability to exercise control over its vast domains. In the early decades of the Qing Dynasty, following Ming precedent, memorials (题本) from individual officials were relayed to the throne via the appropriate ministries and subsequently archived by the corresponding office of the Grand Secretary. With the establishment of the Grand Council, however, a separate special category of communication was created, known as secret or palace memorials (奏折). These memorials were sent directly to the inner court for immediate reading by the emperor in consultation with the council; only then were they recirculated downward to the Grand Secretary and the appropriate ministry for comment or action. These palace memorials did not supersede routine memorials, and were only used for the most urgent items demanding immediate attention. Routine memorials, which still comprised the vast majority of communications, became confined to regular reports, for example on the weather, harvest yields, grain reserves, common criminal cases, and the maintenance of public works. The Grand Council strictly limited the number of officials who were authorized to submit palace memorials to under one hundred individuals, which included ministers and vice ministers of the six ministries, governors, governors-general, high-ranking military officers, and selected others.[31]

Using his vermilion brush—a color used exclusively by the monarch—the emperor could freely exchange ideas in private communications with his officials. Secret palace memorials were the chief means by which the emperor developed bonds of trust between himself and certain officials. In one of Yongzheng's rescripts, he displayed his fondness for one of his most trusted officials, Tian Wenqing:[32]

> You should rest and recuperate in a warm room and you should wait until you are completely normal before you go out and move around. Even if it is the New Year, you need not over exert yourself to participate [in ceremonial activities]. Showing respect for your sovereign and fulfilling your ritual responsibilities does not require that you perform ceremonies, but that you follow my orders. Even if it causes ignorant types to engage in unfavorable criticism, you have me to stand up for you. What is the harm?

The emperors also used the memorials to attack what they interpreted as inefficiency, incompetence, and corruption, among other problems. The following, scribbled by Qianlong on a memorial from a provincial official, was typical:[33]

> When you were serving in the Board [of Punishments] you were an outstanding official. As soon as you are posted to the provinces, however, you take on disgusting habits of indecisiveness and decadence. It is really detestable . . . . You take your sweet time about sending in memorials, and there isn't a word of truth in them! You have really disappointed my trust in you, you ingrate of a thing!

The Yongzheng Emperor used this communication channel to push for his fiscal reform, "return of the meltage fee to the public coffers" (火耗归公). The reform allowed officials in each province to collect a fixed-percentage surcharge—the meltage fee—on all regular land and head taxes remitted to the central government. This surcharge was then retained in the province of origin to provide officials with substantially increased salaries as well as "public expense funds" with which to carry out certain administrative responsibilities and projects to benefit the local area. Madeleine Zelin argues that the palace memorials were the key to Yongzheng's success in implementing this reform because the secret channel enabled the emperor to give orders directly to local officials and circumvent the civil bureaucracy.[34]

THE IMPERIAL HOUSEHOLD DEPARTMENT

The Qing Dynasty also established the Imperial Household Department (内务府), which was dedicated to the emperor's personal service and to managing his various private financial interests throughout the realm. The department was staffed by bondservants, following a model of personal servitude that had deep roots in Jurchen culture.[35] Its establishment had the significant consequence of clearly distinguishing between the inner and outer courts by separating the imperial purse from the state treasury.[36]

8.3   Qing's Fiscal and Military Decline

Even during the High Qing era, the Qing government's per capita fiscal capacity started to decline. From the mid-seventeenth to the mid-nineteenth century, the Chinese population tripled, from 100–150 million to 410 million.[37] Traditional accounts, relying on a Malthusian logic, blame the population growth as a culprit for Qing's economic and fiscal decline.[38] Recent estimates, however, show that Chinese real personal incomes between the mid-eighteenth and the mid-nineteenth centuries remained relatively stable, despite a dramatic increase in population.[39] This suggests that there were more people from whom the Chinese state could extract taxes, if the state was able to adjust its fiscal policies. But the Qing tax structure, which was based on land, was not able to take advantage of the growing population. According to Tuan-Hwee Sng's estimates, in 1685 the Qing state's tax revenue was sufficient to feed and clothe 9.6 percent of the Chinese population. This fell to 7.7 percent in 1724, 5.4 percent in 1753, and 2.3 percent in 1848.[40] Meanwhile, the Qing military also started to deteriorate. While the Bannermen, with swords at their sides and daggers in their belts, were feared in the early Qing period like their Japanese samurai contemporaries, they acquired an almost comic image of sloth and ineptitude in the nineteenth century.[41]

8.3.1   Stagnant Revenues

The main reason for the Qing's fiscal decline, despite its dramatic population growth and territorial expansion, was that it failed to update the land records and land registration devices it had inherited from the Ming Dynasty. These devices included three documents. First, the "fish-scale registers" (鱼鳞图册) described the size, boundary, grade, and owner of each plot of land surveyed in the early Ming period. Second, the "yellow registers" (黃册) contained information on the number of persons in each household, as well as their age, sex, and occupation. They also detailed the land owned, the land tax, and labor services borne by each household. The third document was the complete book on taxes and labor services (赋役全书), which was based on Zhang Juzheng's nationwide cadastral survey (see chapter 6).[42]

Figure 8.1 illustrates the amount of registered land in the Ming and Qing periods, based on Yeh-chien Wang's estimates.[43] Although the Qing Dynasty had a much larger territory and population, its registered land did not surpass the 1600 Ming level until the nineteenth century.

The stagnant land registration resulted in stagnant tax collection. Qing land tax assessment used the following formula: *land tax quota = registered land area × tax rate*, where the tax rate was classified according to the land's fertility or topographical condition.[44] The total amount of taxes an administrative area (district, prefecture, or province) could collect was therefore a function of its registered land area and tax rate. This total amount constituted the area's tax quota. There was little revision of the tax quota throughout the Qing period.[45]

Since the land tax constituted the lion's share of the Qing government revenue, a fixed land tax quota meant a fixed revenue and a fixed budget for the government.

8.3.2   Conservative Bureaucracy

Why had there not been an appreciable increase in the land tax for more than two hundred years? Scholars have offered several explanations. Tuan-Hwee Sng, for example, focuses on geography. He argues that the Chinese ruler's

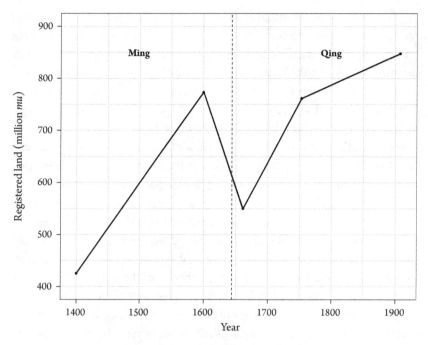

FIGURE 8.1: Registered Land during Ming and Qing

inability to closely monitor bureaucrats in a large domain created opportunities for the bureaucrats to exploit taxpayers. To prevent overexploitation,
the Qing state had to keep taxes low.[46] Taisu Zhang, by contrast, emphasizes ideology. He argues that witnessing the fall of the Ming Dynasty in the
hands of mass rebels, the Qing elites developed and justified an ideology of
minimal state intrusion, especially low land tax, to avoid suffering the same
fate.[47] Lastly, Debin Ma and Jared Rubin turn to political institutions. Using
a principal-agent model, they argue that Chinese rulers, unconstrained by
the rule of law and unable to commit to not predating on their tax-collecting
agents (and the masses), may find it optimal to settle for a low tax equilibrium,
while permitting bureaucrats to keep extra, unmonitored taxes.[48]

   These explanations all indicate that the Qing state chose not to raise taxes.
Historical evidence, however, shows that it tried, but failed. For example,
in the early Kangxi period, the Qing government announced that it would
increase the labor service quota. But the initiative was opposed by powerful
officials and subsequently aborted. Around the same period, the Qing state
tried to carry out a new cadastral survey to obtain an accurate register of land;
the idea was averted by officials as well.[49]

The evidence is consistent with my overall argument that political elites in the late imperial era were localized and not interested in strengthening the central state. Like all of its imperial predecessors, the Qing bureaucracy wanted to maintain the status quo. Although they were blessed with a centralized elite structure that was composed of the Manchu nobility, the Qing emperors also needed to rely on the Han civil bureaucracy to govern an empire with a Han majority. Soon after the conquest, the Qing reorganized its government institutions according to the Ming model, with grand secretary positions and the Hanlin Academy staffed by Han civil servants. The Qing rulers tried to maintain ethnic "fairness" by having double posts at nearly every level of the central bureaucracy: for every ministry there was a Manchu minister and a Han minister, two Manchu vice ministers and two Han vice ministers, and so on.[50] But the Han Chinese held a clear advantage in mastering the classics and writing the elegant essays the civil service examinations required. According to Mark Elliot's calculation, only one of the 108 first-place palace examination honors awarded during the Qing era ever went to a bannerman (a Mongol); no bannerman ever finished second.[51] Gradually, the Han officials became the "power elite" within the bureaucracy; the Manchu elites were relegated to symbolic "prestige elite" positions.[52] During times of crisis (such as internal rebellions), Qing rulers were more likely to appoint Han elites as governors.[53]

The Chinese civil bureaucracy had always upheld light taxation as a panacea. Local communities praised officials who succeeded in reducing the local tax quota. To win the respect and support of the locals, especially the local gentry, officials at all levels were highly motivated not to increase the registered land within their jurisdiction.[54] Officials throughout the empire interpreted Kangxi's 1712 decree of "never raising labor service taxes" as "never raising taxes" and applied it to the land tax, especially after it absorbed the labor service tax in the second quarter of the eighteenth century.[55] Although a cadastral survey was discussed from time to time, bureaucratic opposition made it "politically undesirable."[56]

Without an increase in land registration, the only way to boost tax revenue was to raise the tax rate. To avoid provoking popular revolts, emperors generally ordered that the rate should be determined to be satisfactory to both the government and the people: local magistrates were instructed to first consult with the local community about imposing a land tax surcharge to ensure the general public would accept the additional fees.[57] Given the gentry's influence in society, their advice and cooperation were necessary for the fulfillment of the magistrate's official duties; their connections with officialdom allowed them to appeal to higher authorities to overrule a magistrate's decision or even to impeach him (see chapter 7).[58] Yet the local gentry often enjoyed a preferential collection rate, and their representatives in the bureaucracy had no incentives to go beyond what was required by the quota.

8.3.3   Increasing Expenditures

With stagnant revenues, the Qing government nevertheless needed to care for a growing banner population. The arrangement between the dynasty and the banners was that in exchange for their willingness to risk their lives, the state saw to the material needs of all banner soldiers and their families. Soon after the conquest, each banner household received a tract of land, which was intended to provide a permanent source of income. The banner soldiers also received a monthly salary paid in silver and grain.[59] The Eight Banner economic order began to fall apart after only twenty years. Because of cruel treatment, Chinese peasant-serfs fled their Manchu masters, who had neither the time nor energy to closely manage their estates. Banner land was soon abandoned and found its way back into Chinese hands. Because bannermen were prohibited from seeking employment outside the banner system or the state bureaucracy, by the middle of the eighteenth century they had a reputation for leading an idle, parasitic existence.[60]

From the beginning of the dynasty, military spending remained the state's largest outlay, consuming 50–60 percent (or even 70 percent) of the budget. Most of this went to the Eight Banners and the Green Standards. Service in the Eight Banners was a hereditary privilege, and the number of people relying on it for their livelihood inevitably swelled over time. The failure of the banner land system meant that the welfare of the ever-increasing banner population was a financial burden that fell wholly upon the state. By the mid-eighteenth century, funding the Eight Banners was crippling the dynasty's finances.[61] The Qing spent an estimated 28–30 million taels ($\approx$ \$2.5 billion in 2019) every year to support the military establishment.[62] Of the money spent on the two armies, roughly 40 percent went to the Eight Banners and 60 percent to the Green Standards.[63] Another set of estimates by Chen Feng shows that combined capital and provincial military expenditures rose from 20 million taels before 1730 to 27 million taels after 1735.[64] This suggests that approximately 14 million taels, 21–25 percent of the annual budget, were spent annually to maintain the entire Eight Banner population.[65] The banner population became one of the poorest classes in the nineteenth century after losing their land, which caused the group's morale to rapidly deteriorate.[66]

The Qing Dynasty's finances never fully recovered after it spent three-quarters of its fiscal reserves putting down the White Lotus Rebellion that began in 1796.[67]

8.4   Late Qing

State-society relations in China prior to the mid-1800s were best character-ized as an *ancien régime* equilibrium, or what I call "State Maintaining under Partnership," in which the imperial government and gentry partnered in gov-ernance, providing public goods and protecting local communities. Although the gentry took an increasingly leading role in local governance, they still had to depend, albeit to varying degrees, on the centralized monarchical state to back up their class positions and prerogatives. This state-society partnership was key to imperial rule's durability.

The mid-nineteenth century was a turning point in China's state-society relations. Britain's victory over China in the First Opium War (1839–1842), along with the resulting Treaty of Nanjing (1842), significantly increased the Qing government's costs of external defense, which made it unable to control the development of local lineage organizations. During the Taiping Rebel-lion (1850–1864), the government reluctantly delegated local defense to local elites, which tipped the balance of power between the state and society. Local elites started to gain the upper hand in local governance and defense, which created centrifugal forces that brought down the Qing Dynasty.

8.4.1   The First Opium War

The Treaty of Nanjing forced the Qing government to pay 21 million silver dollars to Britain and concede control of five treaty ports (e.g., Shanghai).[68] This large reparation payment triggered an "unprecedented financial crisis."[69]

The Qing government enacted new taxes, the burden of which fell mainly on local elites.[70] The new commercial tax derived much of its revenue from the salt trade, which the landowning elites dominated.[71] Although the new rural tax was exacted on entire villages rather than individuals, local elites were typically called on to pay the provisional levy upfront, and villagers did not always reimburse them.[72]

More importantly, the military defeat greatly undermined the imperial gov-ernment's viability in the eyes of the elites, to the extent that "China's sheer existence as a sovereign country was profoundly threatened."[73] Gentry leaders began to vocally criticize the government's political, economic, and military weaknesses and advocate a "self-strengthening" movement.[74]

8.4.2 The Taiping Rebellion

To make things worse, the northern hemisphere in the mid-nineteenth century experienced some of the coldest years in recorded history (recall figure 2.2 from chapter 2). Famine conditions arose in southwest China.[75]

Led by Hong Xiuquan, a schoolteacher who had failed the imperial civil service exam, and who believed himself to be the younger brother of Jesus, the Taiping rebels banded together in 1850. In 1853, they captured the city of Nanjing in Jiangsu Province, declaring it the capital of the Taiping Heavenly Kingdom. At the height of its power, the Taiping controlled nearly 200 counties across five provinces along the lower Yangtze River. Ping-ti Ho called the Taiping Rebellion the "greatest civil war in world history."[76]

The property and lives of the landowning elites were severely threatened by the Taiping rebels, many of whom were peasants who had lost their land when they could no longer afford to farm or maintain it. When the Taiping rebels captured the city of Yongan in Guangxi Province in 1851, for example, they "sent out sizable groups of troops to raid the fugitives' homes and seize their grain stores, livestock, salt and cooking oil, and even their clothing."[77] During one raid, approximately 2,000 rebels expropriated the belongings of two wealthy families, taking "five days and nights to list and carry away the families' accumulated stores."[78] The Taiping leadership attempted to implement radical land redistribution.[79] Although this land reform ultimately failed, peasants within Taiping-controlled zones refused to pay rents to their landlords, burned their tenancy contracts, and sometimes beat their landlords to death.[80] Outside of Taiping-controlled territory, waves of refugees generated fear among the inhabitants of surrounding counties: "Rumors of every kind about the atrocities committed in Nanjing swirl through the countryside . . . the mere appearance of four long-haired rebels in one neighboring market town sets off a stampede of fear in which twenty-seven Chinese are trampled to death."[81]

8.4.3 Local Militarization

The imperial Qing state was "fiscally broken" by the mid-nineteenth century due to a combination of external and internal turmoil.[82] Qing military forces—the Eight Banners and the Green Standards—were typically paid late and were in poor fighting shape.[83] Furthermore, corruption was rampant in the military.[84]

In despair, the Xianfeng Emperor (1850–1861) reluctantly agreed to allow local elites to raise private local militias for protection. Traditional lineage organizations played a key role in organizing, funding, and leading such militias (see chapter 7). For instance, in one Hunan county, local contributions made up nearly 90 percent of militia expenditures.[85] Local elites also managed the militias' finances without Qing oversight. Moreover, clan leaders almost always led these militias.[86] To mobilize clan members to join a militia, the clan leader would rely on his lineage ties; militias were often named after the leading clan that formed it.[87]

With help from the scholar-official Zeng Guofan and his private militia (called the Hunan Army), the imperial Qing state finally put down the Taiping Rebellion and other mass rebellions by 1869.[88] This victory brought a period of stability and reform to the Qing government.[89]

Indeed, victory over the Taiping rebels enabled the Qing state to survive for another four decades. Between 1849 and 1885, central government revenue grew from 43 to 77 million taels ($1.3 to 2.3 billion in 2019), much of which was raised through maritime customs.[90] While this increase in revenue allowed the Qing state to begin to respond to new foreign and domestic challenges, it was not enough.[91] Furthermore, the state was forced to reduce its traditional provision of non-military public goods.[92] In the mid-eighteenth century, the central government spent more than 11 percent of its annual budget on public works, including the construction of new dams and dikes.[93] By 1891, however, only 3 percent went toward public works.[94]

The emperor's pursuit of personal survival, however, came at the expense of the state's control over society (the sovereign's dilemma). By granting them a prominent leadership role, the Qing's endorsement of local governance by local elites during the Taiping Rebellion eventually tipped the balance of power.[95] Local elites were now formally involved in both local defense and local administration. According to Philip Kuhn, this shift in political power from central officials to local elites led to the "breakdown of the traditional state."[96] Prasenjit Duara terms this phenomenon "state involution," by which the central government increasingly depended on local elites—via lineage organizations—to perform local governance functions, but was no longer able to control them, thereby making them an unaccountable force in local society.[97]

8.4.4   The 1911 Revolution

After its defeat in the First Sino-Japanese War (1894–1895), the Qing state established the New Army in the hope of producing a modern military force that was fully trained and equipped according to Western standards. Gradually, however, New Army officers and weaponry were absorbed into the framework of the regionally based armies that dated back to the time of the rebellions.[98] Local elites, many of whom were elected to the new provincial legislatures, became local strongmen with control over both taxation and military matters.[99]

In 1905, in an effort to modernize China's education system, the Qing government abolished the millennium-old civil service examination system.[100] This severed the last connection between the state and the increasingly centrifugal local elites. The vertical ties in the bowtie network broke; China's social terrain deteriorated into a ring.

The Wuchang Uprising, which was followed by declarations of independence from local military forces throughout China, prompted the fall of the Qing state in 1911. According to Frederic Wakeman, the "Revolution of 1911 can be seen as a series of provincial secessions from the empire, led in every major province but one by officers of the New Army units or by gentry leaders of the new provincial assemblies."[101] Wakeman attributes the "deep" roots of Qing state failure to the longer-term shift in the balance of power toward local elites and away from the central government that had begun more than a half-century before, writing:[102]

> The fall of the old order was thus the culmination of processes which began during the 1850s in response to internal rebellion and external aggression: the development of regional armies, the rise of a rural managerial class, the political entrenchment of the gentry in provincial government, and so forth . . . the extinction of the dynastic state was really the handiwork of the new elites that had emerged during the last half-century of the Qing rule.

8.5   A Quantitative Assessment

The narrative suggests that the violence during the Taiping Rebellion motivated the local elites to protect themselves by relying on lineage organizations rather than the weakened central state. This tipped the balance between state power and social forces: local elites became increasingly independent from the state, leading to state failure in 1911.

In this section, I use original quantitative data collected for this book to perform an in-depth analysis of elite collective action in response to the mid-nineteenth century Taiping Rebellion. I show that mass battles during the rebellion significantly increased post-Taiping elite collective action, proxied by the number of genealogy books. I then provide evidence that the renewed emphasis on private-order institutions may have eventually led to state failure. I analyze the extent to which local decisions to declare independence from the imperial Qing government in 1911 were a function of greater elite collective action during the post-Taiping period. I find a positive and highly significant relationship between post-Taiping elite collective action and declarations of independence, even after considering a wide range of alternative explanations.

8.5.1   Taiping Rebellion and Local Elite Collective Action

I start with an in-depth analysis of the Taiping Rebellion. Figure 8.2 (top panel) indicates that mass rebellions in the nineteenth century peaked during 1850–1869.[103] There were 230 mass rebellion battles during this period, nearly 60 percent of which involved the Taiping (the remainder involved other rebel groups such as the Nian). There was also a sizable increase in elite collective action in the aftermath of the Taiping Rebellion (figure 8.2, bottom panel). Here, I use the number of genealogy books to proxy for local elite collective action. The number of genealogy books rose from less than one hundred before 1850 to nearly two hundred by 1870.

The surge in mass rebellions between 1850 and 1869 offers a novel laboratory in which to compare pre- and post-rebellion elite collective action. I define the counties that did not experience a mass rebellion in 1850–1869 as the "control group" and those that experienced at least one mass rebellion battle during this period as the "treatment group." We should expect that while elite collective action did not change significantly in the "control group," it increased significantly in the "treatment group."[104]

Figure 8.3 plots the average number of genealogy books for the control and treatment groups.[105] While both groups followed relatively similar trend lines prior to the start of the Taiping Rebellion, there was a 25 percent increase in the slope of the trend line for the treatment group (but much less so for the control group) after the rebellion. My regression analysis confirms this

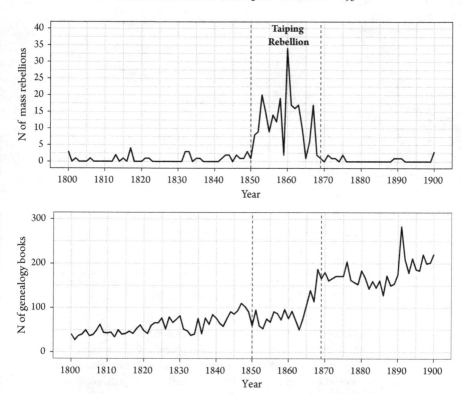

FIGURE 8.2: Mass Rebellion and Elite Collective Action (1800–1900)

finding, showing that counties that had more mass rebellion battles during the Taiping Rebellion experienced a positive and highly significant change in local elite collective action.[106] The coefficient estimate suggests that an additional rebellion was associated with a 20 percent increase in the number of genealogy books.[107]

8.5.2   Local Elite Collective Action and the 1911 Revolution

Another prediction is that the large increase in locals' elite collective action and formation of private militias in the aftermath of the Taiping Rebellion changed the long-standing balance of power between the Qing state and local elites. These elites began to mobilize more local resources and increase local autonomy.

To proxy for local resistance to Qing rule, I geocode the location of each elite group that declared independence from the Qing state in 1911.[108] Figure 8.4 shows the locations of these revolutionary elite groups, which I use

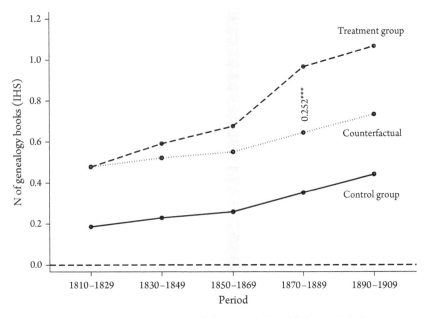

FIGURE 8.3: Lineage Activity Trends Before and After the Taiping Rebellion
Notes: This figure shows the change in average clan activity in China as proxied by
the inverse hyperbolic sine (IHS) of the number of genealogy books, calculated as
ln(Genealogy Books + *(Genealogy Books²* + 1)$^{1/2}$), for counties that experienced at least one
mass rebellion battle during the Taiping Rebellion between 1850–1869 (treatment group) and
those that did not (control group). The dotted line (counterfactual) indicates how average
elite collective action for the treatment group would have followed if the Taiping Rebellion
had never taken place. Shaded vertical line represents start of Taiping Rebellion in 1850.

to create a binary indicator variable, *Declaration of independence*, which equals
1 if at least one local elite group declared independence within the borders of
a county.

My regression analysis suggests that counties that had higher levels of post-
Taiping elite collective action (more genealogy books between 1890 and 1909)
were more likely to declare independence in 1911.[109]

Ying Bai and Ruixue Jia argue that counties that had higher quotas for the
imperial civil service exam were more likely to experience revolutionary uprisings once this system was abolished.[110] This is consistent with my argument
that the abolishment facilitated the formation of the ring network. To account
for this additional factor, I include the *Civil service exam quota* in the regressions.[111] Consistent with Ying Bai and Ruixue Jia's argument, the coefficient
estimate for *Civil service exam quota* is also positive and highly significant.

Qing provinces
Qing counties
Beijing
Declaration of independence, 1911

FIGURE 8.4: Declarations of Independence (1911)

Overall, these results are consistent with the implication of my earlier discussion that a large increase in local elite collective action can eventually lead to state failure.

8.6   Conclusion

What was the fundamental reason for the fall of imperial China? It may be useful to adopt Lawrence Stone's terminology to distinguish preconditions, precipitants, and triggers.[112]

The precondition, the long-term trend that made the breakdown possible, was the gradual weakening of the imperial state. For a long time, from the Song to the High Qing era, the partnership between the state and local elites formed an equilibrium. The ruler, representing the state, was secure and not threatened by the fragmented and localized elites; the elites, entrenched in local social networks, enjoyed their autonomy from the state and used their resources to perpetuate their power and prestige. They also collaborated to control the peasantry and suppress mass revolts when necessary. This equilibrium maintained a minimal level of state strength, but failed to strengthen the state. After the Song Dynasty, China's per capita fiscal revenue decreased. With a larger territory and population and expanding commerce, the imperial state was unable to tax its population and economy, resulting in poor public goods provision and declining military power. Imperial rule endured, but China's fiscal and military capabilities slowly declined.

This *ancien régime* equilibrium would have lasted longer if China existed in isolation. The world, however, was changing. Frequent warfare, high levels of military spending, the heavy use of gunpowder technology, and the ease of adoption co-evolved over hundreds of years and led to the development of superior military technology in Western Europe.[113] In the nineteenth century, the Chinese were no match for Britain's new weapons—steamboats, heavy artillery, rockets, and rapid-fire rifles. Although it was not obvious when an encounter would take place, it was doomed to happen sooner or later.

Two precipitants, the First Opium War and the Taiping Rebellion, made the Chinese elites realize that they could no longer partner with the state, since it was too weak. While some elites still hoped for an imperial restoration by participating in the "self-strengthening" movement, most of them turned to their own private lineage organizations and abandoned the state.

The trigger, however, was Qing emperors' decision to concede the means over violence to local gentry groups in order to survive in domestic crises. For more than one thousand years since the Tang times, Chinese state elites were deeply embedded in society. Regardless of whether it was the star-shaped aristocratic network in the Tang era or the bowtie-shaped gentry network in the Song-Ming era, the state and society were always interlocked through elite networks. During the Taiping Rebellion, however, the Qing rulers reshaped the elite social terrain to maximize their personal survival, which disconnected the state from the society. Social forces broke free from state control and, eventually, overthrew the state. Previous rulers traded state strength for personal survival; late Qing rulers, in exchange for their own survival, gave up long-term state survival. The 1911 Revolution ended the Qing Dynasty, which had ruled China for almost three hundred years. It also ended imperial rule in China, which had lasted for thousands of years.

PART V

Conclusion

9

The Long Shadow of the Empire

9.1   When History Meets Politics

China's state development was shaped by elite network structures that characterized state-society relations, rather than by representative institutions or bellicist competition. For two thousand years, its rulers faced the sovereign's dilemma: strengthening the state and holding onto power required different elite social terrains. When elites were in geographically broad and densely interconnected networks, they preferred a strong state capable of protecting their far-flung interests, and their cohesiveness constituted a threat to the ruler's survival. Yet when elites relied on local bases of power and were not tightly connected, they instead sought to hollow out the central state from within; their internal divisions enabled the ruler to play competing factions against each other to secure his personal survival. Throughout imperial China's state development, rulers were both constrained by and reshaping (when they had the opportunity) the elite social terrain to make a trade-off between state strength and personal survival.

The *social* origins of state development took China down a different, yet long-lasting, path that diverges from the European norm. While European states had increased their capacity to collect taxes and become more durable by the modern era, the Chinese state gained durability at the expense of state strength.

Highlighting the importance of elite social structures broadens our understanding of varieties of state-building models and challenges the received wisdom generated by European experiences. War, for example, rather than making the Chinese state, destroyed its centralized social network and weakened the state.

The primary goal of this book is to take a preliminary step towards creating a framework with which to analyze alternative paths of state development. Drawing on Chinese history, I propose elite social terrain as a new variable to gauge long-term state development. In the short run, the elite social terrain makes the state; in the long run, the state shapes the elite social terrain.

———

What if everything I have said about China's historical state development is valid, but irrelevant to the rest of the world? Can a theory generated from China's past illuminate its present? What does Chinese history tell us about state development in general?

In this last chapter, I take a tour of the developing world in Africa, Latin America, and the Middle East and show how the three ideal types of elite social terrains (star, bowtie, and ring) help us understand state-building experiences in other regions of the world. I conclude by discussing how imperial legacies have created key challenges in China's modern state building as well as aspects of Chinese historical state development that can help us understand state building today.

9.2   Struggles for Centralization in Africa

States in sub-Saharan Africa have encountered many of the same challenges as the Chinese state. But due to differences in geography and population density, African state development followed a different path.

As Jeffrey Herbst argues, the fundamental problem facing state builders in Africa—whether they were pre-colonial kings, colonial governors, or presidents in the independent era—has been to project authority over vast, sparsely populated territories.[1] Most African states started with a structure resembling a ring network—a center that struggled to connect and control its periphery. During the colonial era, European colonizers relied on locally embedded traditional leaders—chiefs—to rule, which created a bowtie network. But the ties between the central administration and the local chiefdoms were much weaker than the family ties in the Chinese case. In the early era of independence, authoritarian regimes (especially those led by the military) emerged in several African countries. Elites in these regimes were disconnected from society and relied on force to stay in power, which returned them to a ring network. Recent democratization has increased the chiefs' power by making them the brokers between national politicians and local societies. A new bowtie network has therefore emerged. Depending on geography and population distribution, however, the strength of the ties in this bowtie network varies across countries in Africa.

9.2.1 Pre-Colonial Era

The anthropologists Meyer Fortes and E. E. Evans-Pritchard distinguish between two types of political systems in early African societies. One type had centralized authority, and a society in which cleavages based on wealth, privilege, and status corresponded to the distribution of power and authority. The Zulu, Ngwato, Bemba, Banyankole, and Kede were examples of such *centralized societies*. The other type lacked centralized authority, and had a society in which there were no sharp divisions of rank, status, or wealth. The Logoli, Tallensi, and Nuer were examples of such *decentralized societies*. In these decentralized societies, even the largest political unit included only a small, homogenous group of people, all of whom were linked to one another through kinship ties. There were no centralized political organizations above the village level, and the political structure and kinship organization were completely fused.[2]

Most pre-colonial African societies were decentralized. George Murdock ranked every society in the world according to its political hierarchy, and categorized only 10 percent of pre-colonial sub-Saharan societies as centralized.[3] In decentralized societies, traditional leaders, often called chiefs, had power by virtue of their association with the customary mode of governing a place-based community. Villages were often named after these leaders. The position of chief was hereditary, and monopolized by the community's "royal family" or "ruling lineage."[4]

Even in centralized systems in sub-Saharan Africa, the center struggled to control its periphery. Igor Kopytoff describes the pattern of pre-colonial political authority as a core with disconnected outlying territories: "The core, usually the area of earliest political consolidation, continued to be ruled directly by the central authority. Then came an inner area of closely assimilated and politically integrated dependencies. Beyond it was the circle of relatively secure vassal polities . . . This circle merged with the next circle of tribute-paying polities, straining at the center's political leash. Beyond, the center's control became increasingly symbolic."[5]

These outlying territories could easily escape central control. In Jan Vansina's depiction of central African kingdoms, "provinces could break off from the kingdom whenever circumstances were favorable. This happened in Kongo, in the Kuba kingdom, and in the Lunda empire, where every ruler who was far enough away . . . became independent."[6]

Jeffrey Herbst's characterization of pre-colonial Africa bears a striking resemblance to a ring network: "power was (quite realistically) conceived of as a series of concentric circles radiating out from the core."[7] He contends that African leaders controlled only a political core due to the high cost of extending formal authority in vast territories with low population densities. "As a result," Herbst asserts, "beyond the political core, power tended to diminish over distance."[8]

9.2.2   Colonial Era

European countries began colonizing Africa in 1880. The colonizers' main objective was to extract the continent's natural resources at the lowest possible cost. They relied on (or created) mid-level intermediaries with the traditional right to rule in order to govern on the cheap. Sir Frederick Lugard—the codifier of indirect rule and the most important practitioner of colonialism in Africa—justified retaining the traditional African system of rule as a practical response to the problems he faced: "so vast a country, inhabited by many millions, must always be inadequate for complete British administration . . . it was, therefore, imperative to utilise and improve the existing machinery."[9]

European colonizers split up previously centralized kingdoms into chiefdoms and imposed a hierarchy of chiefs; the highest-level chiefs reported directly to the colonial authorities.[10] They standardized the chiefs' powers in an attempt to raise revenue and maintain order.[11] They also increased the chiefs' control over land to empower colonial control at the local level.[12]

Previous studies have exhaustively compared the policies associated with the "direct rule" of the French, in which French officials filled even fairly low-level administrative offices; the "indirect rule" of the British, in which the indigenous chiefs fulfilled these roles; and the Belgians' hybrid "quasi-indirect rule."[13] The reality, however, was less straightforward. Catherine Boone demonstrates that the autonomy accorded to local elites often varied more within empires than it did across them. She argues that colonial administrators varied their governance strategies depending on how hierarchical the traditional governance structures were in particular regions, and whether the chiefs were considered willing allies.[14]

By building up the chiefdoms as the principal units of native administration, European colonizers created a bowtie network in which the colonial authorities ruled in partnership with the chiefs, who in turn controlled specific territories through social organizations. As Christopher Clapham notes, the Europeans ensured the chiefs were "representatives of specified families within each chiefdom" and "created a group of local patrons with their own clienteles within the chiefdom."[15] Joel Migdal writes that the colonizers created "new bonds by regarding the population as members of social organizations led by chiefs," who, by relying on the tribal organization, "controlled key resources, including material goods, jobs, violence, and defense."[16]

The ties that connected the colonial administration and the local chiefs, however, were weak. Unlike the Chinese state, which used the civil service examinations to hold the bowtie network together, colonial powers primarily relied on patronage and coercion to maintain unity. The colonial period, therefore, set the stage for continued conflicts. The power and number of chiefs rapidly expanded, which exacerbated tensions between rival tribes and factions. Europeans committed resources to the creation, or in some cases the resurrection, of the chiefs' powerful roles in a framework of fragmented administrative entities, which shaped the distribution of indigenous social control in Africa through independence and beyond.[17]

9.2.3   Post-Colonial Era

The wave of decolonization began with Ghana's independence in 1957. The bowtie network that was loosely held together by European colonizers collapsed into a ring network throughout the continent for two reasons. First, as Herbst argues, the peace in post-colonial Africa, partly thanks to the Charter of the Organization of African Unity, did not provide the necessary pressure for African states to mobilize revenue through efficient administration and state penetration into society. The reliance on indirect taxation and non-tax revenues attenuated, if not eliminated, the link between the state and society. The new states were too weak to control the chiefs, who retained much of their power and resources, particularly land, from the colonial era.[18]

The second reason for the change in network type was that a significant portion of Africa's newly independent states were ruled by their military, as Robert Bates shows. From the beginning of the 1970s to the end of the 1980s, in more than 30 percent of the observations, Africa's heads of state came from the armed forces.[19] These military elites had few ties to the civilian population and were seldom ethnically representative of their populations. Further, African militaries did not try to develop their own means of mobilizing the population, especially in rural areas.[20]

Although nationalist leaders across Africa have called to remove chiefs and transfer their power to efficient new bureaucracies overseen by elected politicians, Kate Baldwin finds that most efforts to replace chiefs have failed. Across Africa, traditional leaders run court systems, allocate land, and organize local labor gangs.[21] Societies across the continent became more autonomous from state control in the 1960s to 1980s than during the colonial era.

In the late 1980s, the post-Cold War "third wave" of democratization swept across Africa.[22] As Bates shows, whereas from the early 1970s to the mid-1980s more than 80 percent of the country-year observations contained no- or one-party systems, by the mid-1990s more than 50 percent of countries in sub-Saharan Africa had multiparty systems.[23]

Kate Baldwin argues that democratization has increased the power of chiefs. Democratic elections incentivize national politicians to maintain good relationships with the chiefs in their constituencies. Chiefs, with their traditional authority and social networks in local communities and their long time horizons, can help national politicians implement development projects, which in turn helps politicians stay in touch with the voters and win re-election.[24] But Baldwin also reminds us that these development projects are geographically targeted programs, commonly known as "pork," rather than national public goods. The benefits of such programs are thus often disproportionately skewed towards chiefs' villages or homesteads.[25]

Democratization has forged a new bowtie network in Africa that differs from the one in its colonial past. Democratically elected politicians now connect to chiefs, who represent their local interests, rather than colonizers. But as Baldwin shows, these connections are still localized: politicians only connect to chiefs in their own constituencies.

The center's ability to connect different localities varies significantly throughout Africa. Country borders arbitrarily drawn by the Europeans during what has come to be known as the "Scramble for Africa" have remained largely unchanged since independence. African countries are therefore different sizes and shapes, with an imbalanced distribution of population between the center and the periphery.

Herbst distinguishes between three general categories of countries based on their political geographies and population distributions.[26] The first set of countries are large and have densely populated areas. But these areas are not contiguous; they are often far apart. Applying Herbst's classification to the African continent, the Democratic Republic of the Congo is an example of this first category. It has pockets of densely populated areas around Kinshasa and scattered throughout its vast landmass. For countries in this category, the center finds it physically challenging to connect the periphery. A large number of outlying groups, which are spatially distinct and can be mobilized around ethnic and cultural symbols, can compete with the state.[27] The relationship between the center and these groups almost resembles a ring network.

Herbst labels the second category "hinterland" countries. For example, Chad, Mali, Mauritania, and Niger are exceptionally large, but have relatively small areas of high and medium population density and then vast hinterlands where few people live. The capital struggles to control the vast territory in hinterland countries. Yet since the population of these countries is concentrated near the capital, the government is in close proximity to a large percentage of the population. The extreme example is Mauritania: despite its vast territory, 54 percent of its population lives in urban areas.[28]

Countries in the third category have the highest concentration of power in one area, usually around the capital, where it is easiest for the state to rule them; population densities decrease as the distance from the capital increases. The small countries of Benin, Botswana, Burkina Faso, Central African Republic, Eritrea, Gabon, Guinea, Sierra Leone, and Zimbabwe are all in this category.[29] These cases are closer to a star network in which the center connects all social groups (which are also in the center). Similar to the Chinese case, this star structure is vulnerable to centralized violence. Herbst notices that in these countries, the capitals become battlegrounds: Bissau, Brazzaville, Freetown, and Maseru were all destroyed between 1997 and 1999 because it was so easy for combatants to target the center of power.[30]

In sum, ring and bowtie networks dominated African state development. A constant challenge for African state building has been the centers' attempts to connect and control the peripheries. The African case also adds nuances to my China-generated theory. Unlike China, which has a high population density, the scattered population distribution in sub-Saharan Africa makes it costly for the central state to connect local social groups. Even when a bowtie network emerged during the colonial and post-democratization eras in Africa, the connections between the center and localities were much weaker than those in China.

9.3   Despotic and Infrastructurally Weak States in Latin America

States in Latin America are also perceived to be weak. To paraphrase Miguel Centeno, they do not dominate society. He classifies most Latin American states, even well into the twentieth century, as highly *despotic*, yet *infrastructurally weak*. Centeno argues that they are despotic because state elites can make decisions without negotiating with civil society. They are weak due to the state's inability to implement decisions.[31]

Centeno traces Latin American state building to the colonial era and demonstrates that, like imperial China, war occurred largely *within* rather than *between* states in the region.[32] He argues that these internal conflicts were the "wrong kind of wars": they reinforced, rather than challenged, existing social divisions.[33] He also contends that the availability of foreign loans prevented Latin America from embarking on the "coercion-extraction" cycle that strengthened European states; instead of producing states built on "blood and iron," wars constructed Latin American states made of "blood and debt."[34]

The colonial and post-independence eras in the region have both been characterized by tension between the core and the periphery. This tension often manifests itself in elite-society or center-local relations, which constrains the ability of Latin American states to extend their reach into what Guillermo O'Donnell calls "brown spots"—areas with a low degree of state presence.[35]

9.3.1   *Bowtie Network under Colonial Rule*

Latin America has a long tradition of fragmented sovereignty. Early on in the colonial project, Spain recognized considerable regional diversity and autonomy, and even floated a plan to divide the continent into three kingdoms— Mexico, Peru, and Nueva Granada. The conflicts over sovereignty were not simply between the provinces and the capital, but also *within* the provinces, between regional and municipal governments. The colonial state barely controlled large parts of the empire. Most of northern Mexico was beyond its control, as was the southern area of the continent.[36]

The Bourbon reforms initiated by Charles III of Spain in the mid-eighteenth century attempted to recentralize authority and increase revenue.

Spain's Bourbon army was created and granted greater institutional autonomy in response to a heightened foreign threat from the British. But the result was a military separate from society and above the state.[37] By shifting resources to the state, these reforms also exacerbated elite divisions between the state and the church. They also triggered an intra-elite struggle between the American-born *criollos* and the Spanish-born *peninsulares*. The latter had the most to gain from attempts to delocalize administration and associated efforts to increase immigration from Spain.[38]

Despite the efforts of Charles III, Latin America entered the nineteenth century more divided than ever. The Americas as a whole resented the imposition of an order dictated in Madrid. The various subunits of the Bourbon domains wished to protect and expand their autonomy vis-à-vis the central power. Centeno's description of colonial-era Latin America as a bowtie network largely resembles late imperial China (but with weaker ties) and colonial Africa: "Each part of the empire was connected to the center, but the separate regions were not linked with one another."[39]

9.3.2   Divergent Paths in the Post-Colonial Era

Napoleon's invasions of Spain in 1808 provided the spark as well as the opportunity for Latin American independence. Independence movements erupted all over the continent by 1810.[40] Wars of independence exacerbated conflicts over sovereignty because both rebel and loyal administrations sought to acquire resources in order to establish control over particular areas. The discrepancy in resources available to the provinces actually abetted regionalism, since it often made the richer regions (which were generally associated with the capital) reluctant to enter into political contracts that required them to share their wealth.[41] The Mexican case demonstrates this pattern found across the continent: it essentially dissolved into a "series of satrapies dominated by caudillos."[42] As happened in China under warlordism, the continent collapsed into a ring network.

Marcus Kurtz argues that the central state's ability to incorporate local elites at the time of independence critically determined whether later state-building efforts were successful. If elites beyond the governing faction achieved meaningful incorporation and a share of political power, as they did in Uruguay after 1876 and in Chile, institutional development and expanded state capacity were likely. Yet where the central authorities were at odds with powerful regional or local elites, or where the central state was dependent on the tax-collecting power of provincial strongmen or holders of venal office, as in Uruguay before 1876 and in Peru, political centralization would be blocked. In other words, a star network at the time of independence facilitated state building, while a bowtie or ring network blocked it. Kurtz's logic runs parallel to mine when he argues that where elites were incorporated—either through cooperation in the form of an "oligarchic democracy" or through imposition in more absolutist bureaucratic settings—their "collective interests can be organized within the state," and even difficult choices that have principally longer-term payoffs can be made.[43]

Hillel Soifer's argument about post-independence state building also emphasizes the relationship between the core and periphery. He points out that the nature of "political geography" matters: in countries with a single dominant urban core, an elite consensus on the importance of extending central authority for development could take hold. Yet where multiple regional centers each commanded a distinct regional political economy, constructing a central state authority would be unlikely to promote development. Similar to my argument about local elites' reliance on local services, Soifer argues that when there were multiple urban centers, elites clashed because each region had distinct public goods preferences, and regions had self-contained economies and could generate sufficient economic production on their own to maintain (and even increase) local standards of living without the need for national integration.[44]

While Soifer maintains that political geography determines whether state-building projects will emerge, he further contends that whether elites connect with multiple localities will determine whether such projects *succeed*. He shows that "outsiders"—bureaucrats who are deployed from other places— are generally more responsive than local elites to the central state's policy preferences. Outsiders' greater reliance on state institutions for legitimacy and power motivates them to help facilitate an increased state presence in their communities. The interests of state agents deployed from outside the community align more closely with state builders than those of local elites appointed to administrative posts. Thus outsiders are more likely to collaborate with—and even promote—state-building efforts. This was the case in Mexico and Chile, and to a lesser extent in Peru after 1895.[45] In other words, elites embedded in a star network have a strong incentive to strengthen the state.

Sebastian Mazzuca discusses countries in Latin America that are closer to a bowtie. These cases, he argues, often display a "distinct combination of territorial stability and capacity failure."[46] In these countries, the obstacles to developing state capacities were the result of mutually convenient bargains struck by central state makers and peripheral potentates, who, far from being eliminated during state formation, obtained institutional power to reinforce local bastions. Mazzuca compares Uruguay and a counterfactual independent state of Buenos Aires. He shows that, over the course of the nineteenth century, Buenos Aires enjoyed greater economic prosperity and fiscal strength than Uruguay. In the early 1860s, however, Buenos Aires merged with a large periphery subdivided into an array of political bastions dominated by patrimonial lords. Argentina was the territorial outcome of the merger. In Argentina, patrimonial rule in the peripheries not only survived but also propagated, via power-sharing arrangements, throughout the political arena. As a result, Argentina became what I would call a bowtie state with patronage ties connecting the central state and the periphery. Although its territorial arrangement has been stable, as in late imperial China, the Argentine state is much weaker than that of Uruguay, which suggests the kind of state Buenos Aires could have become if it had not unified with the Andean mini-states in the 1860s.[47]

In summary, Latin America's state development evolved from a bowtie network in the colonial era to a diverse set of post-independence scenarios. The paths varied depending on whether the central state established connections with local societies at the time of independence as well as the types of bargains struck between the core and the periphery. If the central state assigned bureaucrats from the capital to administer local areas, thus forming a star network, state building was likely to succeed; if it delegated control to local elites or relied on patronage networks, forming a bowtie, state territories would be stable, but state capacity would remain low.

9.4 Tribe and State in the Middle East

The Middle East was the cradle of human societies' "pristine" states. The first states in the Mesopotamian alluvium emerged about six thousand years ago.[48] The physical environment, however, created daunting challenges for effective rule. Patricia Crone argues that, except for the Fertile Crescent, land in the Middle East was partially or wholly useless to agriculturalists and suitable for stock breeding only with seasonal migration; such land had limited carrying capacity, and the proceeds of stock breeding fluctuated wildly.[49]

It was therefore difficult to develop sedentary agricultural communities beyond the fertile Tigris-Euphrates River system. Hugh Kennedy writes that the defining feature of human geography for what has become the Muslim world is "the presence of large numbers of nomadic or transhumant peoples" in deserts near settled agricultural areas.[50] Crone, in the same vein, notes that "nomadic populations are necessarily small, widely dispersed, poor and incapable of accumulating the stable surpluses required for the maintenance of states."[51]

The key to understanding Middle Eastern state development is its tribal nature. Tribal societies, by making "systematic use of kinship for their sociopolitical organization," provide an alternative form of organization to the state.[52] When these tribes acquired a sense of common purpose, for example during external conquest, their primitivity gave them a huge advantage over the state.[53] Without a common mission, however, the tribal states soon disintegrated into countless societal groups.[54]

9.4.1 Maintaining a Bowtie Network during the Classical Period

Tribal conflict gave Muhammad the opportunity to unify the Arab world and found Islam. In 620, the fighting between two pagan tribes in Yathrib (now Medina) had grown so bad that they could no longer protect themselves against the three Jewish tribes with which they shared an oasis. They invited Muhammad to arbitrate their quarrels; in return, the pagan tribes agreed to give sanctuary to the Meccan Muslims. The emigration of Muslims from Mecca to Yathrib, called the *hijra* in Arabic, enabled Muhammad to unite his followers as a community—an *umma*. This event solidified Muhammad's reputation as both a prophet and a lawgiver—a religious *and* political leader.[55]

Muhammad's successors continued his tradition by creating a bowtie network. Muawiyah I, the founder of the Umayyad Caliphate, relied on the Arab tribes to stay in power and kept them loyal by requiring tribal representatives to reside at his court in Damascus.[56] The caliphs ruled indirectly through tribal chiefs at the local level. In 670, all settlements were divided into quarters or fifths, in the nature of a large semi-artificial tribe, which could organize an army or city. The leaders of these units were tribal chiefs, who formed the tribal aristocracy (*ashraf*) of the Umayyad period. The chiefs linked the governor and the governed in the system of indirect rule; they commanded their units in times of war and were responsible for them in times of peace.

Their positions rested on the dual basis of influence within the tribe and acceptability to the authorities.[57]

But tribalism in Arabic societies created great obstacles to state centralization during the High Caliphate. For instance, Sunni Muslims acknowledged the Umayyad and Abbasid caliphs as the legitimate leaders of the *umma*. Shi'a Muslims, by contrast, regarded Muhammad's son-in-law Ali as his true successor, and rejected all the Umayyad and Abbasid caliphs.[58] As political unity broke down during the ninth and tenth centuries, different sects founded various dynastic states.[59]

The High Caliphate also introduced a uniquely Islamic institution— military slaves, called *mamluks*. According to Crone, slave armies began to appear between 800 and 820, first in North Africa, and then in Spain and Egypt. They became common throughout the Abbasid Caliphate in the mid-ninth century. The *mamluks* were largely Turks captured by the tribes beyond the Muslim border in Central Asia. They were almost always forced to convert to Islam. The *mamluks* were "culturally dissociated" because they were aliens unconnected to the local society. They were also "personally dependent" because they were essentially bodyguards tied to a specific commander.[60] *Mamluks* were responsible for collecting taxes, maintaining order, and controlling important resources.[61] In return for their military service, the state granted them a temporary, nonhereditary deed to land called an *iqta*.[62]

Lisa Blaydes and Eric Chaney argue that *mamluks* directly influenced Islamic state-society relations. While European rulers needed to negotiate with feudal lords to raise armies to defend their territory, Islamic rulers bypassed local elites by creating highly skilled armies of foreigners who had no ties to the society and swore allegiance directly to the sultan.[63] The lack of state-society linkages weakened Islamic elites' incentives to strengthen the state.

9.4.2 Divide and Conquer under the Ottoman Empire

Turkic and Mongol invasions during the twelfth and thirteenth centuries largely weakened Arab rule. The traditional ties built by Arab rulers between the central state and local society broke down; the bowtie network collapsed into a ring network with Turks or Mongols at the top and Arabs at the bottom.[64]

It was not until the fourteenth century that the Middle East was unified under the Ottoman Empire. Founded by Turkish tribes, the empire ruled much of southeastern Europe, western Asia, and northern Africa between the fourteenth and early twentieth centuries. The Ottoman sultans faced a similar set of challenges as their Arab predecessors: conquest brought them previously autonomous and powerful local power holders, who had to be integrated into the system and convinced to relinquish at least some of their revenue to the new state. With the conquest of the Balkans and then the Arab lands, new cultural and religious groups had to be incorporated, settled, and respected to induce them to contribute to the empire's welfare.[65]

Karen Barkey contends that the Ottoman Empire pursued a state development path that was different from Europe's but similar to China's, which she calls "bargained incorporation."[66] According to her account, the Ottoman state started with a centralized pattern of direct control through appointed officials, then experienced an interim period of mixed center-periphery control, and ended up developing a system of indirect control through local notables.[67] The Ottoman rulers gradually unified the fragmented ring network by creating a bowtie network.

During Ottoman state development, a complex compact between the state and society gradually incorporated all potentially autonomous elites and organizations into the state. From the fourteenth to the sixteenth century, the Ottoman ruling house managed to shape a variety of internal forces to its own will by offering deals, forcing migration, and through sheer coercion. Regardless of the means employed, the end result was to tie all potential regional elites and potential corporate entities to the state without giving them the freedom to autonomously organize. The core of the empire, the Balkans and Anatolia, had more or less uniform administrative arrangements for land tenure, taxation, and other fiscal policies, whereas the rest of the empire—the periphery—experienced indirect rule. State control was exerted through ties from the periphery to the center, which separated the elites from the common people, all of whom were responsive to the center but not to each other. Similar to a bowtie network, relations with the center were strong, while those among groups and communities were weak; this weakness was maintained by practices such as rotating regional offices. Sociopolitical and economic links generated by patronage and trade all extended from the periphery to the central state. Because links within the periphery were weak, social disorganization became the norm in Ottoman provinces.[68]

Ottoman rulers, according to Barkey, were state builders who tried to centralize the state. Their attempts at centralization inevitably provoked local opposition. Rather than quelling the opposition, Barkey argues that the

Ottoman state consolidated its control with a "brokerage style" of centraliza-tion, which helped the state tighten its grip on the periphery. For example, it rotated state-appointed officials to discourage strong patron-client ties. Once banditry developed, the state both used the brigands to suppress the peasantry and was drawn into negotiations with their leaders. Banditry hence became a potential agent in the hands of many regional officials. All the while, state interest in extracting rents and tributes continued.[69]

Similar to the Chinese emperors, who relied on a "divide-and-conquer" strategy to manage the elites, Ottoman sultans "pit different groups against each other in competition for state rewards, that is, to maintain a state-controlled contest in society."[70] The Ottoman state managed to divide the elites in such a way as to set landholder against landholder, governor against governor, and governor-general against governor-general. In this competi-tive atmosphere, elites were unable to organize to engage in concerted action against the state.[71]

There were many parallels between the Ottoman and Chinese empires. Both were governed in a bowtie network, and both were able to maintain merely an acceptable level of state strength. And both were exceptionally durable. The Ottoman Empire lasted for over six hundred years. The legiti-mating role of Islam was important,[72] but the state's ability to divide and con-quer elites and maintain a bowtie network played a crucial role in sustaining the large empire.

The rise of Western Europe put the Ottoman state—like China—on the defensive. In 1699 the Ottomans signed the Treaty of Karlowitz, which ceded control of Hungary to the Habsburg Empire—a significant sign of decline. Economic conditions also deteriorated. Europe's discovery of the New World and of sea routes around Africa to Asia's riches weakened the Muslim coun-tries' control over the main trade routes.[73] The Ottoman Empire sided with Germany during World War I. With support from the British, the Arab Revolt broke out in 1916. Late in October 1918, the Ottoman Empire signed an armistice with the Allies. Europeans soon divided the Ottoman territories, and the Arabs gained their independence from the Turks only to be colonized by the Europeans.[74]

9.4.3   Varieties of Post-Colonial States

The style of European colonization largely determined the path of state devel-opment in the former Ottoman regions. In colonies where Europeans relied on local elites, a bowtie network was created to connect the colonial state and local elites. Where the colonizers relied on their own administrators, local elites were not incorporated and became autonomous from the state, producing a ring network.

This difference is best described by Lisa Anderson's comparison of Tunisia and Libya, both of which were quasi-independent Ottoman provinces. The critical difference between the two countries' state formation was the impact of French and Italian colonial rule in sustaining or destroying the local bureaucratic administrations that developed during the nineteenth century. These different approaches generated different post-independence political organizations and social structures.[75]

As Anderson demonstrates, in Tunisia, the French (under the guise of a protectorate) retained, strengthened, and extended the bureaucratic administration of the local state and incorporated local elites into it. In Libya, the Italians replaced the local administration with an Italian system that the local population was prohibited from participating in. The increased bureaucratization of local administration in Tunisia during the seventy-five years of the Protectorate, Anderson argues, furthered the shift away from kinship organizations. The broad-based nationalist movement and the increasing importance of professional rather than personal attributes in the local leadership highlight the extent of the social structural changes made during this period, as personalistic clientelism gave way to policy brokerage. In Libya, the destruction of the pre-colonial administration also demolished the clientele networks that had grown up around it. The absence of the stable administration that had sustained the patrons of these networks eventually led to the demise of the networks themselves—and a return to relying on kinship as the primary organizational principle in the hinterlands.[76]

Political crises illustrate the significance of these changes in post-independence Tunisia and Libya. Both events illuminate the social structural implications of the preceding decades of bureaucratic development and disintegration. In Tunisia, the model of personalistic representation of clienteles, which had characterized the initial reaction to the French occupation, was supplemented (and increasingly supplanted) by policy brokerage, as local elites began to represent constituencies with more universal common interests. The obligations of responsible government imposed by independence encouraged state elites to sustain themselves and their allies through patronage, but the interest-based constituencies fostered by state policy soon demanded representation in decision-making.

In Libya, the absence of a stable local administration, the revival of kinship groups, and the widespread distrust of bureaucracy that dated back to the Italian period left the country to be ruled at independence by individuals whose claims rested on little more than European patronage or military power. Their stance toward the bureaucracy was uninterested or even hostile, and they profoundly distrusted broad-based political organization.[77]

Anderson concludes that the social structures imposed during colonial rule significantly affect the development of newly independent states. In this case, Tunisia (which had what resembles a bowtie network) has enjoyed a long record of stable, independent, civilian rule, while Libya (which had a ring-type network) has been rocked during its thirty years of independence by administrative corruption, military takeover, and revolutionary upheaval.[78]

9.5   Let History Rhyme

Can a theory generated from China's past shed light on its present? Its state building in the modern era certainly differs from its imperial past. Modern states are embedded in a more globalized international community, which generates pressure to learn from (and compete with) other nation states. Modern rulers also need to construct a political system to connect with the masses, whose opinions and actions are far more important in politics now than they were in the past. Formal institutions, such as political parties, emerge and play an important role in regulating elite behaviors. Communication and transportation technologies make geographic barriers, which in the past constituted an insurmountable obstacle, less daunting. Properly analyzing China's state building after 1911 would thus require another monograph.[79] But if we believe that the past is a good guide to the future, China's imperial past provides important clues for us to understand some of the challenges of building a centralized state in the modern era.

In the late 1920s, after Mao Zedong emerged as the leader of the Chinese Communist Party (CCP), he faced some of the same challenges as his imperial predecessors in imposing a new political order. A gentry class dominated the traditional rural society. Peasants usually belonged to lineage organizations led by the landowning elites. These lineage organizations were based on a common ancestor and cross-cut class divisions. Landless peasants were in the same clan as their landowning relatives. The clans used their charity land to support peasants by paying for their weddings and funerals, which considerably lessened class tensions.[80]

When Mao tried to use land reforms to mobilize the peasants against the landowning elites, he soon realized that the major cleavage in rural China was between clans rather than between classes *within* clans. As Elizabeth Perry shows in her investigation of communist mobilization in northern China, traditional social organizations "cut across class lines" to produce community bonds that inhibited "horizontal class identity."[81] Lower-class families were more scared of losing their kinship protection than of being exploited by their wealthier relatives.[82] Rich peasants, often in collusion with their poor relatives, concealed their actual landholdings and slowed the land revolution.[83] For instance, when the communists mobilized peasants to carry out the "rent and interest reduction policy" in northern China in 1942, Yao Hei-tzu, a tenant, convinced other tenants in the area to refrain from participating in the campaign because the largest landlord in the village was his uncle.[84] When communist leaders attempted to organize the peasants in Hailufeng for a land revolution, lineage and community heads took the opportunity to settle old scores with rival neighboring clans. Peasants there took up arms not against their landlords, to whom they were often related, but to defend strictly local and family interests.[85]

In 1928 Mao expressed his frustration with the difficulties of mobilizing the peasants in a now-famous essay, *Struggle in the Jinggang Mountains*. He lamented: "But as the feudal family system prevails in every county, and as all the families in a village or group of villages belong to a single clan, it will be quite a long time before people become conscious of their class and clan sentiment is overcome in the villages."[86]

Given the social terrain that was the legacy of China's imperial past, any revolution to build a new regime would have to be what Theda Skocpol calls a "social revolution," which involves basic transformations of a society's state and class structures.[87] A mere top-down reform that imposes political changes but preserves the traditional social structure (what the Kuomintang's policies tried to achieve) would repeat the millennium-old dilemma with which imperial rulers struggled.

Indeed, as Perry argues, one key to the party's success was its program to "restructure local society."[88] Although land reforms met strong local opposition in the south in the 1920s, they started to make headway in the 1930s after the party marched to the north, where lineage power was weak.[89] Mark

Selden argues that the communist policies, especially land reforms, were key to the CCP's success.[90] The CCP's land reforms, which began in the 1930s and lasted until the 1950s, transformed the traditional social order that had dominated Chinese state-society relations since the Song Dynasty. After the reforms, the landowning elites nearly vanished, and the communist state nationalized all land in the country—for the first time since the Tang Dynasty's equal-field system—and set up cooperatives based on existing village organizations.[91] The new regime also created a new level of government—township—between the county and village. Thus unlike the imperial dynasties, the communist state was able to extend its power below the county level.[92]

State building in modern China therefore transformed the fundamental fabric of society and paved the way for the country's economic modernization. Industrialization grouped people based on employment and area of residence rather than lineage networks, which helped the party-state control the smallest units of economic production.[93] Marketization further altered what Vivienne Shue calls China's traditional honeycomb-like rural structure, promoted migration, and extended the "reach of the state" deep within society.[94] The Chinese state has finally overcome the sovereign's dilemma by embarking on a new path of state development that fosters strength *and* durability.

What real-world lessons can we draw from China's historical state development? After World War II, many countries declared independence from their colonial powers and established their own states. Almost all of these newly independent states emerged in what is now known as the developing world. It is no coincidence that many of the world's most serious problems, from poverty to AIDS to civil wars to terrorism, are disproportionately concentrated in these new states. While these problems have geographic and social roots, their political cause is theorized to be *state weakness*.[95] State building has thus become the top priority facing the developing world.[96]

These developing nations now face the same state-building dilemma that China did in the past: a coherent elite that can take collective action to strengthen the state can also revolt against the ruler. Many of the policy interventions carried out by the international community, such as the World Bank and the International Monetary Fund, focus on strengthening bureaucracies.[97] But the Chinese experience demonstrates that *state weakness is a social problem that cannot be resolved with a bureaucratic solution.* Leaders in developing countries may need *incentives* to build state capacity, as doing so may compromise their personal survival. Lessons from China's past and present indicate that state building should go beyond a narrow focus on strengthening bureaucracies to make elite social structures more compatible with a strong state *and* a durable regime.

If history rhymes, as it frequently does, we need a better understanding of how society works before we can grasp how politics works.

Appendices

Appendix for Chapter 2

A.1   Climate Change and Violence

TABLE A.1: Temperature Anomalies and Conflict: OLS Estimates

	Number of external wars		Number of mass rebellions	
Dependent variable	(1)	(2)	(3)	(4)
Temperature anomaly (degrees Celsius)	18.987***	13.931***	−17.749**	−11.541*
	(4.102)	(3.946)	(7.131)	(6.263)
Number of external wars (lag)		0.366***		
		(0.064)		
Number of mass rebellions (lag)				0.311**
				(0.125)
Outcome mean	11.597	11.632	8.304	8.326
Outcome std dev	14.183	14.212	18.454	18.500
Observations	191	190	191	190
R^2	0.095	0.224	0.049	0.139

Notes: Estimation method is ordinary least squares (OLS). Unit of analysis is decade. Dependent variable in columns (1) and (2) is the number of external war battles. Dependent variable in columns (3) and (4) is the number of mass rebellion battles. Variable of interest is temperature anomaly, defined as the temperature departure from the 1851–1950 average. Columns (2) and (4) include the lagged dependent variable. Robust standard errors in parentheses. ***, **, and * indicate statistical significance at 1%, 5%, and 10% level, respectively.

A.2   Calculating Social Fractionalization

One approach to uncovering community structures in social networks is based on edge removal. The intuition is as follows: if two groups of nodes are only loosely connected with each other, then removing the edges between those two groups will generate components in the restricted network. Communities correspond to those components in the restricted network.

Approaches based on edge removal differ in terms of the selection rule regarding which edges to remove. I follow an algorithm proposed by Girvan and Newman (2002) that consists of the sequential removal of edges with high betweenness centrality. This centrality measure captures the extent to which the edge serves as a link between different groups. It is calculated using the number of shortest paths between nodes in the network.

The Girvan-Newman algorithm proceeds as follows:

1. Calculate betweenness for all edges in the network. Remove the edge with the highest betweenness.
2. Recalculate betweenness for all edges affected by the removal.
3. Repeat from step 2 until no edges remain.
4. From the resulting dendrogram (the hierarchical mapping produced by gradually removing these edges), select the partition that maximizes network modularity (characterized by dense connections within clusters and sparse connections between them).

The algorithm delivers a partition of C communities (indexed by $c = 1, \ldots, C$), each containing a share s_c of distinct nodes (officials). I then use this to compute the measure of social fractionalization (SF), using the standard Herfindahl-Hirschman index:

$$SF = 1 - \sum_{c=1}^{C} s_c^2.$$

The measure can be interpreted as the probability that two randomly selected officials are from different communities.

A.3   Tables and Figures

TABLE A.2: Major Fiscal Policies in China (221 BCE–1911 CE)

Year	Dynasty	Policy Name (English)	Policy Name (Chinese)	Coding
216 BCE	Qin	Self-Report of Cultivated Land	黔首自实田	1
202 BCE	Western Han	Separation of Royal and Government Treasuries	财政皇室与政府分开	0
196 BCE	Western Han	Local Government Reporting of Fiscal Account	上记制度	1
120 BCE	Western Han	State Monopoly of Salt and Iron	盐铁官营	1
119 BCE	Western Han	Merchants' Property Tax	算缗	1
110 BCE	Western Han	Price Adjustment and Stabilization	均输	1
110 BCE	Western Han	Price Equalization and Standardization	平准	1

Year	Dynasty	Policy Name (English)	Policy Name (Chinese)	Coding
98 BCE	Western Han	State Monopoly of Alcohol	酒专卖	1
81 BCE	Western Han	Abolishment of State Monopoly of Alcohol	废除酒专卖	1
39	Eastern Han	Cadastral Survey	度田令	1
88	Eastern Han	Abolishment of State Monopoly of Salt and Iron	废除盐铁官营	−1
196	Eastern Han	Military Agro-Colonies	屯田制	1
280	Western Jin	State Allocation of Land	占田法	1
280	Western Jin	Household Tax	户调制	1
321	Eastern Jin	Commercial Tax	估税	1
485	Northern Wei	Public Land Tenure (Equal-Field System)	均田令	1
486	Northern Wei	(Lower) Household Tax	租调制	−1
584	Sui	Public Land Tenure (Equal-Field System)	均田制	1
590	Sui	Military Agro-Colonies	兵农合一	1
624	Tang	Public Land Tenure (Equal-Field System)	均田令	1
624	Tang	Land and Household Tax	租庸调	1
758	Tang	State Monopoly of Salt	盐专卖	1
764	Tang	State Monopoly of Alcohol	酒专卖	1
780	Tang	Abolishment of Public Land Tenure (Equal-Field System)	废除均田制	−1
780	Tang	Abolishment of State Monopoly of Salt	废盐专卖	−1
780	Tang	Two-Tax Reform	两税法	1
782	Tang	State Monopoly of Tea	茶专卖	1
960	Northern Song	Two-Tax	两税	1
960	Northern Song	State Monopoly of Salt	盐专卖	1
960	Northern Song	State Monopoly of Tea	茶专卖	1
960	Northern Song	State Monopoly of Alcohol	酒专卖	1
960	Northern Song	State Monopoly of Alum	矾专卖	1
964	Northern Song	Centralization of Fiscal Revenue	集中财权	1
1005	Northern Song	Alteration of State Monopoly of Tea	改变茶专卖	−1
1017	Northern Song	Abolishment of State Monopoly of Salt	取消盐专卖	−1
1028	Northern Song	Abolishment of State Monopoly of Alum	取消矾专卖	−1
1059	Northern Song	Abolishment of State Monopoly of Tea	废止茶专卖	−1
1069	Northern Song	Rural Credit (Green Sprout)	青苗法	1
1069	Northern Song	Price Adjustment and Stabilization	均输法	1
1070	Northern Song	Labor Service Fee	免役法	1
1071	Northern Song	Cadastral Surveys and Equitable Tax	方田均税法	1
1072	Northern Song	State Trade	市易法	1
1085	Northern Song	Abolishment of Rural Credit (Green Sprout)	废除青苗法	−1
1085	Northern Song	Abolishment of Price Adjustment and Stabilization	废除均输法	−1
1085	Northern Song	Abolishment of Labor Service Fee	废除免役法	−1
1085	Northern Song	Abolishment of State Trade	废除市易法	−1
1085	Northern Song	Abolishment of Cadastral Surveys and Equitable Tax	废除方田均税法	−1

Continued on next page

Year	Dynasty	Policy Name (English)	Policy Name (Chinese)	Coding
1236	Yuan	State Monopoly of Salt	盐专卖	1
1368	Ming	Military Agro-Colonies	屯田	1
1368	Ming	Salt Tax (Abolishing Salt Monopoly)	盐税	−1
1581	Ming	Single Whip (Absorbing Household Tax in Land Tax)	一条鞭法	1
1644	Qing	Returning to Ming Tax Quota	正赋	−1
1644	Qing	Salt Tax (Returning to Ming Tax Rate)	盐课	−1
1645	Qing	Allocation of Land to Eight-Banner and Manchu Nobility	圈地令	−1
1711	Qing	Freezing Labor Service Quota	永不加赋	−1
1724	Qing	Melting Fee	耗羡归公	1
1729	Qing	Absorbing Household Tax in Land Tax	摊丁入亩	1

TABLE A.3: Exit of Chinese Emperors (221 BCE–1911 CE)

Cause	Method of Exit	Frequency	Percent
Health	Natural Death	152	53.90%
Elites	Murdered by Elites	34	12.09%
	Deposed by Elites	24	8.51%
	Forced by Elites to Abdicate	17	6.03%
	Committed Suicide under Pressure from Elites	1	0.35%
	Subtotal	76	26.95%
Civil War	Deposed in Civil War	20	7.09%
	Died in Civil War	10	3.55%
	Committed Suicide during Civil War	1	0.35%
	Forced to Abdicate facing Internal Threats	1	0.35%
	Subtotal	32	11.34%
External War	Committed Suicide during External War	4	1.42%
	Forced to Abdicate facing External Threats	3	1.06%
	Subtotal	7	2.48%
Family	Murdered by Son	5	1.77%
	Murdered by Concubine	1	0.35%
	Subtotal	6	2.12%
Other	Elixir Poison	4	1.42%
	Volunteered to Abdicate	4	1.42%
	Accidental Death	1	0.35%
	Subtotal	9	3.19%
	Total	282	100%

約、讕據、分鬮等,卷二至四世系。

上圖 美國猶他

014-2032 [湖南平江] 王氏第十次續修族譜三卷首一卷 王國賓纂修。1915 年三槐堂木活字本,七冊。書名據版心、目錄、書衣題。書名頁題儲文閣梓。

先祖同上。卷首序、凡例、源流、誥軸、祭禮、家訓、家誡、遷徙、傳贊、墓誌銘、墓圖、契據等,卷一至三世系。

上圖 尋源姓氏 美國猶他

014-2033 [湖南平江] 王氏族譜 王甲春纂修。1921 年三槐堂木活字本,三冊。存卷首上、下。書名據書衣、書名頁、版心題。六欄本。

先祖同上。存卷爲序、誥敕、源流考、祠圖墓記、傳記、契約等。

上圖 美國猶他

014-2034 [湖南平江] 王氏族譜 王德丞纂修。1934 年三槐堂石印本,一冊。存卷首一至二。書名據書衣、書名頁、版心題。目錄題王氏十一修族譜。書名頁題平江儲文閣美東承印。十一修本。

先祖同上。存卷爲序、源流表、誥敕、各縣族別表、垂絲總表、祠圖、規訓、契據等。

上圖 美國猶他

014-2035 [湖南醴陵] 醴陵南城王氏族譜 (清) 王添煥纂修。清道光元年(1821)植三堂木活字本,一冊。存卷四至六。書名據版心題。

始遷祖安仲,字培厚,號植嘉,明初自江西安福縣金田移居湖南醴陵縣。存卷爲齒錄。

上圖 美國猶他

014-2036 [湖南醴陵] 醴陵南城王氏續修族譜二十一卷首二卷 (清) 王紫春等纂修。清咸豐十年(1860)植三堂木活字本,十四冊。書名據版心、書簽、卷端題。書名頁題王氏族譜。

先祖同上。卷首序、誥敕、家訓、族約、祭祀規戒、祀產等,卷一至二十一齒錄。

上圖

014-2037 [湖南醴陵] 醴陵南城王氏三修族譜 纂修者不詳。清光緒間植三堂木活字本,二十二冊。存卷首(殘)、卷一至三十、三十二至四十四。書名據版心、卷端題。

先祖同上。卷首序、誥敕、家訓、族約、祭祀規戒、祀產等,餘卷爲齒錄、世系圖等。

上圖 美國猶他

014-2038 [湖南醴陵] 醴陵南城王氏五修族譜 王昌柱纂修。1995 年植三堂鉛印本,八冊。書名據封面題。

先祖同上。

湖南圖

014-2039 [湖南醴陵] 醴南三都王氏族譜 纂修者不詳。清光緒間興仁堂木活字本,二冊。存卷二、五。書名據版心題。卷端題三都王氏族譜。佚名增補至民國初年。

始遷祖貴霖。卷二世系、卷五齒錄。

上圖 美國猶他

014-2040 [湖南醴陵] 醴西攸塢王氏五修族譜十二卷首一卷 王業錞纂修。1943 年三槐堂木活字本,十三冊。書名據版心、書衣、卷端題。書名頁題王氏族譜。

始祖祐,字景淑,宋名相王旦之父。始遷祖夢熊,字見功,祐十七世孫,明天啟四年自湖南湘陰移居醴陵治西攸塢。卷首序、制制、祭禮,卷一至二祠圖、墓圖,卷三傳贊、志銘,卷四至五垂絲,卷六至十二齒錄。

上圖

014-2041 [湖南攸縣] 陂下市王氏重修族譜四卷 (清) 王寶三等纂修。清乾隆十六年(1751)三槐堂刻本,一冊。書名據版心題。

始遷祖文卿,明初自江西安福縣移居攸縣北鄉陂下市。卷一序、村祠圖、詩文、傳記、家訓,卷二至四世系。

FIGURE A.1: A Sample from the Comprehensive Catalogue of Chinese Genealogies

Appendix for Chapter 4

B.1 Social Fractionalization in the Song Dynasty

I first show an example of how community detection works, using the major officials under Emperor's Zhenzong (997–1022). In Appendix figure B.1, panel (a) shows the marriage network among major officials. Each node is a major official, and each edge a marriage tie. Panel (b) shows the communities uncovered using the Girvan-Newman algorithm. I can then calculate a social fractionalization index for groups of major officials for the whole Song period.

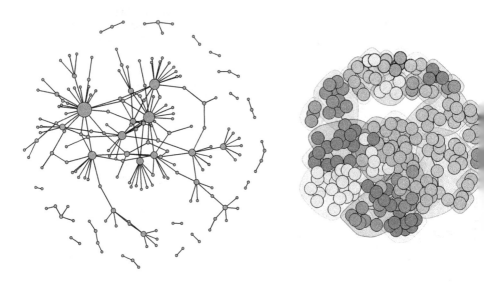

(a) Major officials' marriage network   (b) Communities in the marriage network

FIGURE B.1: Major Officials' Marriage Network and Communities
under Emperor Zhenzong (997–1022)
Source: Author's data collection.

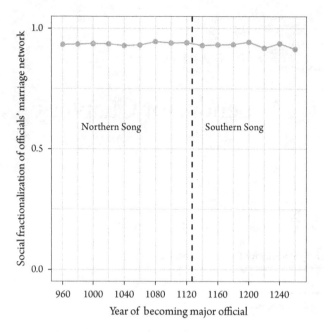

FIGURE B.2: Social Fractionalization of Major Officials' Marriage Networks
in Song (960–1279)

Appendix figure B.2 shows the social fractionalization of major officials' marriage networks for the whole Song period. I first divide all the officials into cohorts, by the year they entered into vice-ministerial level or above positions. I then use the Girvan-Newman algorithm to detect communities in each cohort of officials and calculate the social fractionalization score for that cohort.

Recall that the social fractionalization score is the probability that two randomly selected officials are from different communities (appendix section A.2). The higher the score is, the more fractionalized the network is. As appendix figure B.2 shows, the social fractionalization in the Song era remained at a very high level (around 0.9). This indicates that the high-ranking central elites in Song times were highly fractionalized, and this fractionalization stayed very stable throughout the Song period.

Appendix for Chapter 5

C.1 Background of the Wang Anshi Reform

TABLE C.1: Summary Statistics for Dataset in Chapter 5

	N	Mean	Std Dev	Min	Max
Support for reform (continuous)	63	0.574	0.482	0.000	1.000
Reform party	74	0.527	0.503	0.000	1.000
Local concentration of kin	68	3.336	6.686	0.001	38.334
Betweenness centrality	137	25.664	55.796	0.000	443.731
N of kin	70	101.957	110.517	1.000	566.000
N of children	70	2.014	1.378	1.000	8.000
Factional tie with reform leader	137	0.204	0.405	0.000	1.000
Kin centroid exposure to external wars	68	0.026	0.008	0.013	0.061
Kin centroid exposure to mass rebellions	68	0.062	0.015	0.033	0.112
Ruggedness Index	117	77268.661	65227.410	6938.060	320378.719
Father passing exam	137	0.190	0.394	0.000	1.000
Any uncle passing exam	137	0.131	0.339	0.000	1.000
Grandfather official status	137	0.496	0.502	0.000	1.000
Father migration	137	17.371	84.333	0.000	767.121

C.2 Analysis of the Wang Anshi Reform

I systematically test the hypothesis that politicians' support for state strengthening is positively correlated with the geographic span of their kinship networks.

I estimate the following benchmark ordinary least squares (OLS) specification:

$$\textit{Support for reform}_i = \alpha + \beta \textit{Local concentration of kin}_i + \mu_j + \mathbf{XB} + \epsilon_j. \tag{C.1}$$

TABLE C.2: Political Selection and Geography of Kinship Network: OLS Estimates

Dependent variable	Local concentration of kin		
	(1)	(2)	(3)
Father passing exam	4.855*	4.798*	5.118*
	(2.621)	(2.711)	(2.864)
Any uncle passing exam		−0.268	−0.231
		(3.474)	(3.386)
Grandfather official status			−2.332
			(1.665)
Prefectural FE	Yes	Yes	Yes
Outcome mean	3.336	3.336	3.336
Outcome std dev	6.686	6.686	6.686
Observations	68	68	68
R^2	0.341	0.341	0.356

Notes: Estimation method is OLS. The unit of analysis is an individual politician. Dependent variable is an index on local concentration of kin. Variable of interest is whether the politician's father passed the civil service exam. Robust standard errors clustered at the prefectural level in parentheses. ***, **, and * indicate statistical significance at 1%, 5%, and 10% level, respectively.

The dependent variable *Support for reform$_i$* is a continuous variable that measures politician i's degree of support for the reform. The variable of interest, *Local concentration of kin$_i$*, is an index measuring how geographically concentrated politician i's kinship network was. My hypothesis predicts that β, the quantity of interest, will be negative. μ_j includes politicians' hometown prefecture fixed effects. All standard errors are robust, clustered at the prefectural level j to account for any within-prefecture correlation in the error term.

I consider the following alternative explanations. First, politicians' individual characteristics, such as family wealth, might influence their calculations. For example, those from wealthier families had more resources to support kinship organizations, and hence were less likely to support the state-building reform. Hometown characteristics such as geography, history, culture, and cropping patterns also affected politicians' attitudes. For example, those from regions that were vulnerable to nomadic invasions or domestic rebellions might have had a stronger incentive to strengthen the state (Tilly 1992; Slater 2010). Moreover, a redistributive logic would predict that politicians from regions with good-quality soil and high agricultural yields would be more likely to oppose state building because they must pay disproportionately more taxes because of higher incomes (Meltzer and Richard 1981). There

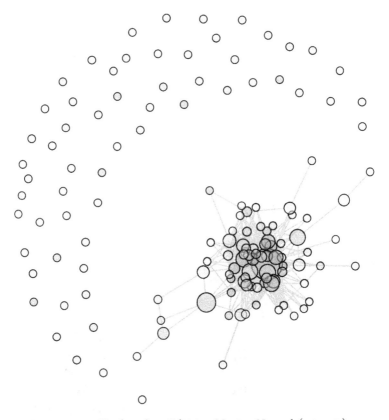

FIGURE C.1: Northern Song Politicians Marriage Network (1167–1185)
Notes: This figure shows the social network among the 137 major politicians in the
Northern Song Dynasty. Each node is a major politician. Each edge measures whether there is
a marriage tie between the two politicians through one's children, as defined in figure 2.4.

is, unfortunately, scarce data on politicians' family wealth. However, there
is a consensus among historians that Song-era high-ranking officials were a
relatively homogenous group from wealthy landowning families (Liu 1959,
16). To control for their hometown characteristics, I include prefecture fixed
effects, which consider features of each politician's hometown at the prefectural level (the level at which Song government institutions (such as taxation
and security) were clustered (Smith 2009*b*, 407)).

Second, recent work using social network analysis shows that the more
central an actor is in a network, the more impact his or her actions have on
the actions of others, and the more likely he or she is to take action (Naidu,
Robinson, and Young 2021). Appendix figure C.1 illustrates the network of

the 137 politicians; edges indicate marriage ties. I then control for each politician's *Betweenness centrality*—a measure of a node's influence over the flow of resources in a network (Padgett and Ansell 1993, 1278).

Third, one might suggest that it is the number of kin members or children, rather than their location, that matters. Holding geographic distribution constant, a coordination logic might predict that having a large number of relatives would increase the transaction costs of coordination at the local level, which could induce politicians to buy services from the state—a "focal point" (Schelling 1960, 57). I hence control for the total number of kin (*N of kin*) and the total number of children (*N of children*). These covariates also deal with the problem that some politicians' networks were better recorded than others'.

Fourth, the Song era was characterized by the rise of factional politics and divergent philosophical schools (Bol 2008). To code each politician's factional ties, I first identified the reform leaders. Reform leaders included Wang Anshi, Lü Huiqing, and Cai Que (Liang 2009 [1908]; Williamson 1935; Liu 1959; Deng 1997; Smith 2009b). I then follow historians' work to define each politician as having a factional tie with a reform leader if at least one of the following conditions is met: 1) he was in an examiner-examinee relationship with a reform leader, 2) he passed the civil service exam in the same year as a reform leader, or 3) he was in the same philosophical school, as defined by Bol (2008, 61–5), as a reform leader. The indicator *Factional tie with reform leaders* measures each politician's relationship with the reform leaders.

Fifth, politicians whose kin were more exposed to nomadic invasions or domestic rebellions might prefer a stronger state. To measure external threats to kin, I constructed an index using the "market potential" approach to measure their relatives' exposure to all external war battles fought in the fifty-year period prior to Shenzong's reign. *Kin centroid exposure to external wars* is thus $\Sigma_{w \in W}(1 + distance_{k_c,w})^{-1}$, where $distance_{k_c,w}$ is the "as the crow flies" distance (in kilometers) from the centroid of the kinship network k_c to an external war battle w. The set W includes all external war battles fought between the Song and a non-Song regime, such as Xixia or Liao, from 1016 to 1065. The locations of external war battles are from the *Catalog of Historical Wars* produced by the Nanjing Military Academy (2003). This index increases as external war battles moved closer to the centroid of the kinship network. Similarly, I construct an index *Kin centroid exposure to mass rebellions*: $\Sigma_{r \in R}(1 + distance_{k_c,r})^{-1}$, where $distance_{k_c,r}$ is the distance from the centroid of the kinship network k_c to a mass rebellion battle r. The set R includes all mass rebellion battles fought between the Song government and a mass rebel group (e.g., peasants, artisans) from

TABLE C.3: Local Concentration of Kin and Support for Reform: OLS Estimates

Dependent variable	Support for reform (continuous)		
	(1)	(2)	(3)
Local concentration of kin	−0.015***	−0.024***	−0.024*
	(0.004)	(0.007)	(0.012)
Betweenness centrality	No	No	Yes
N of kin	No	No	Yes
N of children	No	No	Yes
Factional tie with reform leader	No	No	Yes
Kin centroid exposure to external wars	No	No	Yes
Kin centroid exposure to mass rebellions	No	No	Yes
Ruggedness Index	No	No	Yes
Father passing exam	No	No	Yes
Father migration	No	No	Yes
Prefecture FE	No	Yes	Yes
Outcome mean	0.446	0.446	0.446
Outcome std dev	0.483	0.483	0.483
Observations	40	40	40
R^2	0.062	0.732	0.850

Notes: Estimation method is OLS. The unit of analysis is an individual politician. The variable of interest is an index on the local concentration of kin; higher values indicate more localized networks. Robust standard errors clustered at the prefectural level in parentheses. ***, **, and * indicate statistical significance at 1%, 5%, and 10% levels, respectively.

1016 to 1065. The locations of mass rebellion battles are also from the Nanjing Military Academy (2003). This index increases as mass rebellion battles moved closer to the kinship network's centroid.

Sixth, all my distance measures use "as the crow flies" distances, which do not consider terrain conditions. One might argue that a politician who has kin living in mountainous areas can depend on natural barriers for defense, therefore they rely less on the state. I hence control for *Ruggedness Index*, which uses the grid-cell-level data provided by Nunn and Puga (2012) to calculate the average Terrain Ruggedness Index across all the grid cells covered by the politician's kinship network.

Lastly, the politician's family history is important. I control for *Father passing exam* to measure whether the politician's father entered officialdom by taking the exam (as opposed to inheriting his position). This variable also proxies for the politician's father's political orientation because the Confucian exam should have had an effect on the father's political views, which might have in turn influenced his strategies in shaping his son's (i.e., the politician's) kinship network. I also control for *Father migration* to measure how far the politician's father migrated away from his original hometown. Appendix table C.1 displays the summary statistics for all of the variables.

Appendix table C.3 presents the estimates of the benchmark model. I use listwise deletion so the estimates are based on the forty politicians for whom I have full information on all the variables. Column (1) shows the bivariate relationship between *Local concentration of kin* and *Support for reform*. Column (2) adds politicians' hometown prefecture fixed effects. Column (3) adds additional control variables.

In all specifications, there is a negative correlation between *Local concentration of kin* and *Support for reform*, and the coefficient is statistically significant at the 90 percent level. The magnitude of the coefficients suggests that a one-standard-deviation increase in *Local concentration of kin* is associated with a 25–40 percent decrease in the standard deviation of support for the reform.

In sum, I find strong support that politicians' support for state strengthening is positively correlated with the geographic size of their kinship networks.

Appendix for Chapter 6

D.1 Background

TABLE D.1: Summary Statistics for Dataset in Chapter 6

	N	Mean	Std Dev	Min	Max
N of major officials, 1573–1620	230	2.004	3.750	0.000	20.000
N of advanced scholars, 1368–1572	230	53.748	94.817	0.000	586.000
N of years taken to implement Single Whip	42	49.024	12.687	37.000	97.000
N of years taken to implement Single Whip (provincial or prefectural)	138	51.964	11.271	37.000	97.000
N of years taken to implement Single Whip (provincial or prefectural or county)	175	49.583	12.014	12.000	97.000
Implementation of Single Whip	230	0.183	0.387	0.000	1.000
Implementation of Single Whip (provincial or prefectural)	230	0.600	0.491	0.000	1.000
Implementation of Single Whip (provincial or prefectural or county)	230	0.761	0.427	0.000	1.000

TABLE D.2: Sources for Ming Major Officials' Kinship Networks

Chinese Name	English Name	Secondary Individual Study	Genealogy	Primary Source	Gazetteer
张四维	Zhang Siwei	Xiong (2012) and Guo (2007)	Li (2018)		Zhao (1993)
申时行	Shen Shixing				
张瀚	Zhang Han	张瀚《松窗梦语》研究 Ren (2010), 《王国光评传》			
王国光	Wang Guoguang	Feng (2013), Zhang and Wu			
张居正	Zhang Juzheng	(1987)			
吕调阳	Lv Diaoyang			光禄大夫柱少傅兼太子太傅吏部尚建殿间所吕公墓 in Zhang and Wu (1987) Vol.3	
马自强	Ma Ziqiang	张居正与山西官商家族, 马自强年谱	Liang (2012)	奈麓堂集卷二六·光大夫太子太保尚文大士少保文乾庵公墓 in Ma Clan (1870)	
王锡爵	Wang Xijue	Yuan (2017), Ma (2013)			
赵志皋	Zhao Zhigao	赵志皋集·行状			
张位	Zhang Wei				
于慎行	Yu Shenxing	Feng (2012)		封一品夫人少保公元配曹氏神道碑 in Li (1997) Vol.110	Fang and Zhu (2009)
李廷机	Li Tingji	Li (1970)		于慎行墓志铭 in Li and Xie (2011)	
梁梦龙	Liang Menglong	论梁梦龙		蔡复一集	
杨巍	Yang Wei	Zhang (2018)		Liang (1650)	

Continued on next page

TABLE D.2: *(continued)*

Chinese Name	English Name	Secondary Individual Study	Genealogy	Primary Source	Gazetteer
宋	Song Xun		明清时期商丘宋氏家族研究(未见)	Song (1739)	
陆光祖	Lu Guangzu		Ding and Chen (2016)	政大夫吏部尚五公行 in Chen (1997) Vol.16	Tan (1891)
孙丕扬 赵世卿	Sun Piyang Zhao Shiqing	Peng (2015)		历城文苑采撷·赵世卿墓志铭 in Licheng Cultural and Historical Documents Research Commission (2010)Vol.19	
张守直 万士和 徐学谟 谭纶	Zhang Shouzhi Wan Shihe Xu Xuemo Tan Lun	Zunhua (2013) Ye (2010) Hu (2007)		部尚文恭履公行 in Xu (1964)	
王崇古 方逢时	Wang Chonggu Fang Fengshi	大隐楼集·附录		王公崇古墓志铭 in Jiao (1991) Vol.39 诰封一品夫人方母余氏墓志铭 in Wu (1830)Vol.2	
吴兑	Wu Dui	Kang (2012)	Yu (2015), Yang (2018)	Wu and Wu (1924)	
张佳胤 王之诰 吴百朋 潘季驯	Zhang Jiayin Wang Zhigao Wu Baipeng Pan Jixun	张佳胤年谱 张居正集·张文忠公行实 Wu (2012) Zhao (2017), Jia (1996), 潘季驯		附行 in Zhang (1997) Vol.65	
黄克	Huang Kezuan	Li (2009)			

姓名	Name	Source	Citations
朱衡	Zhu Heng	太子太保工部尚书正一品食正一品俸安未公墓志 in Hu (1983) vol.92	
衷贞吉	Zhong Zhenji	山房稿卷二.政大夫都察院左都御史太子太保洪溪衷公神道碑	
杨一魁	Yang Yikui	光禄大夫柱太子太保工部尚书后山公配累一品夫人氏合葬墓 in Zhao (1595) vol.16	Zhang (2015) Xu (2015)
胡执礼 魏学曾 耿定向	Hu Zhili Wei Xuezeng Geng Dingxiang	德大夫正治上卿督尚太子少保恭天耿先生行 in Jiao (1997) vol.33	Zhao (2009)
葛守礼	Ge Shouli	先祖考太子少保都察院左都御史川葛公行述 in Ge (1983) vol.5	
刘光济	Liu Guangji	政大夫南京兵部尚致仕合公墓 in Wang (2009) vol.23	Chen (2014)
何维柏 裴应章	He Weibo Pei Yingzhang	大泌山房集卷七八.太子少保南京吏部尚裴公墓志 in Li (1997) vol.78	
王之垣	Wang Zhiyuan	新城王氏家谱	山东新城王氏家族文化研究 / Chang (2017), Wu (2014)
赵用贤 张一桂	Zhao Yongxian Zhang Yigui		Xie (2014)
汪道昆	Wang Daokun	通大夫部左侍郎兼翰林院侍士王公墓志铭 in Tang (1997) vol.8	Zhang (2008), Zhang (2014), Wang (2006), Liu (2008)

Continued on next page

TABLE D.2: (continued)

Chinese Name	English Name	Secondary Individual Study	Genealogy	Primary Source	Gazetteer
萧廪	Xiao Lin			神道碑 in Li (1970) vol.24; 兵部右侍郎尚公墓 in Lu (2009) vol.12	
贾三近	Jia Sanjin	Yin (2014)			
宋应昌	Song Yingchang			略朝保定山等兵部右侍郎蔡院右都御史宋公行 in Huang (2009a) vol.17	
王宗沐	Wang Zongmu	Qiu (2004)	王宗沐年谱，章安王氏族谱		
陶承学	Tao Chengxue		Wang (2016) (Vol. 42)	南京礼部尚书进阶资善大夫赠太子少保泗桥陶公墓 in Sun (1814) vol.11	
刘一儒	Liu Yiru			封中大夫南京光禄寺卿碧泉公墓 in Zhang (2009[1593]) vol.26	
张岳	Zhang Yue			明故政大夫督湖川都察院右都御史太子少保襄峰公墓 in Xu (2009) vol.17	
邵陛	Zhao Bi		Ding and Chen (2016)		
沈思孝	Shen Sixiao			刑部左侍郎部公行 in Chen (1995) vol.8	
庞尚鹏	Pang Shangpeng	Deng (2007)	Chen (2015),		
余懋学	Yu Maoxue	Huang (2009b)	Wang (2007)		
宋仪望	Song Yiwang	Zeng (2012)			

侯东莱	Hou Donglai	白榆集文集卷十八．明故正大夫兵部右侍郎兼都察院右都御史侯公墓 in Xu (1964) vol.16
杨廷相	Yang Tingxiang	文林郎兵科事中慎公暨配庵人合葬墓志 in Xu (1964) vol.16
李植	Li Zhi	福建政司左政使衡李公洎配鄣夫人行 in Feng (1997) vol.18
刘尧海 曹三	Liu Yaohui Cao Sanyang	紫园草卷五．明政大夫南京兵部尚凝公行 in Feng (1997) 明故政大夫南京工部尚太子少保云山曹公暨配吕夫人行状 in Xu (1964) vol.19
海瑞 宋仕	Hai Rui Song Shi — Hai and Chen (1962)	德大夫南京都察院右都御史太子少保可泉宋公行 in Liu (2009) vol.16
习孔教 陈省	Xi Kongjiao Shen Xing — Ye (2011)	通大夫兵部右侍兼都察院右都御史幼溪公墓志 in Ye (1997) vol.11
林景 周邦杰	Lin Jingyang Zhou Bangjie	林母徐孺人墓志 in Li (1997) vol.99 明中大夫通政司左通政念庭周公墓 in Wu (2009) vol.17
唐鹤徵	Tang Hezhi — Zhang (2016)	宗册．明故太常寺少卿凝庵唐翁墓志铭 in Tang Clan (1990)
萧崇业	Xiao Chongye — Zhu (2015)	

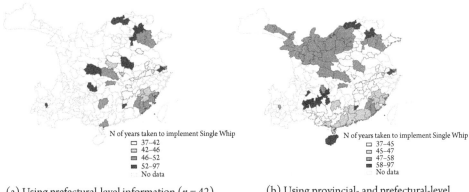

(a) Using prefectural-level information ($n = 42$)

(b) Using provincial- and prefectural-level information ($n=138$)

FIGURE D.1: Number of Years Taken to Implement the Single Whip

Source: Liang (1989, 485–555).

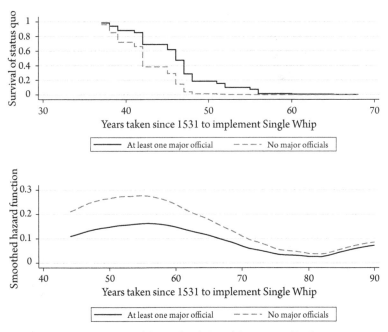

FIGURE D.2: Estimated Survival and Hazard Functions of Prefectures with and without at Least One Major Official

D.2   Analysis of the Single Whip

Appendix figure D.2 displays the estimated survival rates (upper panel) and hazard rates (lower panel) for two types of prefectures: (1) prefectures with no

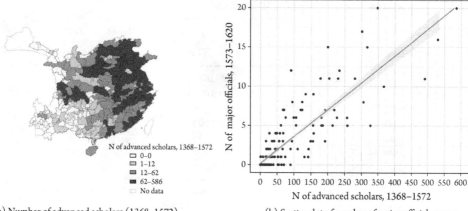

(a) Number of advanced scholars (1368–1572)

(b) Scatterplot of number of major officials versus number of advanced scholars

FIGURE D.3: Number of Advanced Scholars and Its Correlation with the Number of Major Officials

TABLE D.3: National Representation and Delay in Adopting the Single Whip: Survival Analysis

	Failure = Adoption of Single Whip					
	Shared Frailty Cox Models					
	Prefectural		Prefectural + Provincial		Prefectural + Provincial + County	
Level of data collection	(1)	(2)	(3)	(4)	(5)	(6)
N of major officials, 1573–1620	0.923**	0.884***	0.913***	0.908***	0.924***	0.911***
	(0.033)	(0.035)	(0.027)	(0.028)	(0.021)	(0.022)
Provincial FE	No	Yes	No	Yes	No	Yes
Outcome mean	49.024	49.024	51.964	51.964	49.583	49.583
Outcome std dev	12.687	12.687	11.271	11.271	12.014	12.014
Observations	42	42	138	138	175	175

Notes: Estimation method is shared frailty Cox model. Unit of analysis is prefecture. Dependent variable is the number of years taken to implement the Single Whip. In columns (1) and (2), the dependent variable uses information only at the prefectural level. In columns (3) and (4), the dependent variable uses information at the provincial level if information at the prefectural level is missing. In columns (5) and (6), the dependent variable uses information at the county level if information at the prefectural or provincial level is missing. Variable of interest is the number of national major officials a prefecture produced during 1573–1620. Exponentiated coefficients (hazard ratios) are reported, with standard errors in parentheses. ***, **, and * indicate statistical significance at 1%, 5%, and 10% level, respectively.

TABLE D.4: Advanced Scholars and Major Officials: OLS Estimates

Dependent variable	N of major officials, 1573–1620	
	(1)	(2)
N of advanced scholars, 1368–1572	0.034***	0.034***
	(0.002)	(0.003)
Provincial FE	No	Yes
Outcome mean	2.004	2.004
Outcome std dev	3.750	3.750
Observations	230	230
R^2	0.751	0.776

Notes: Estimation method is OLS. Unit of analysis is prefecture. Dependent variable is the number of major officials in the national government during 1573–1620. Variable of interest is the number of advanced scholars during 1368–1572. Standard errors clustered at the provincial level in parentheses. ***, **, and * indicate statistical significance at 1%, 5%, and 10% level, respectively.

major officials in the national government (rank 3b or above) and (2) prefectures with at least one major central government official. For prefectures that had at least one major official in the national government (represented by the solid line), the status quo was more likely to survive and had a lower hazard of being replaced by the Single Whip. The opposite is true for prefectures without representation in the national government (dashed line).

Appendix for Chapter 7

E.1   Figures

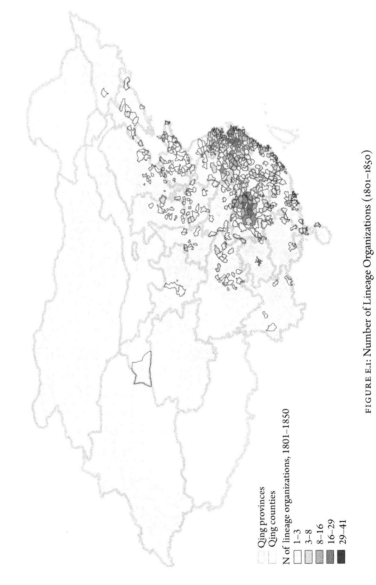

FIGURE E.1: Number of Lineage Organizations (1801–1850)

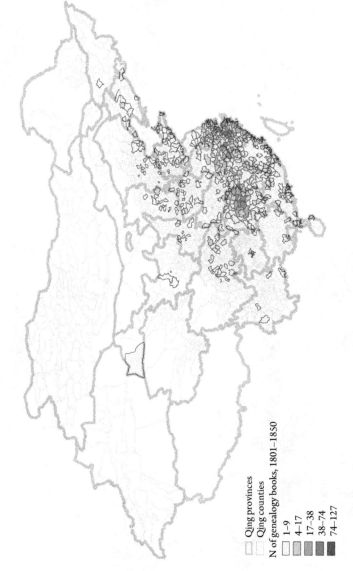

FIGURE E.2: Number of Genealogy Books (1801–1850)

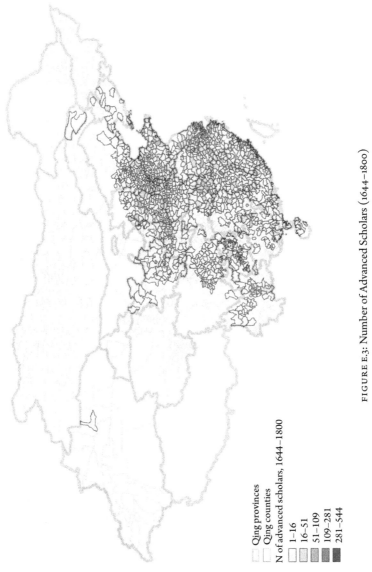

Qing provinces
Qing counties
N of advanced scholars, 1644–1800
1–16
16–51
51–109
109–281
281–544

FIGURE E.3: Number of Advanced Scholars (1644–1800)

Qing provinces
Qing counties
N of conflicts, 1644–1800
1–1
1–2
2–3
3–5

FIGURE E.4: Number of Conflicts (1644–1800)

E.2   Analysis of Lineage Organizations

TABLE E.1: Summary Statistics for Dataset in Chapter 7

	N	Mean	Std Dev	Min	Max
N of lineage organizations	1985	1.029	3.839	0.000	41.000
N of lineage organizations (IHS)	1985	0.368	0.831	0.000	4.407
N of genealogy books	1985	1.474	6.920	0.000	127.000
N of genealogy books (IHS)	1985	0.393	0.906	0.000	5.537
Latitude	1985	33.034	6.981	18.544	52.645
Longitude	1985	110.935	8.163	74.597	134.033
Area (degree)	1985	0.563	2.826	0.000	112.086
Elevation (km)	1728	0.637	0.792	0.001	4.813
Slope	1728	2.425	2.234	0.014	15.661
Distance to major rivers (log)	1728	3.848	2.201	0.000	7.696
Agricultural suitability for rice	1728	0.755	0.430	0.000	1.000
Population density	1699	132.535	141.580	0.000	874.100
N of Ming garrisons	1728	0.166	0.573	0.000	6.000
Public school quota	1985	9.979	7.412	0.000	26.000
N of advanced scholars	1983	7.369	24.066	0.000	544.000
N of conflicts	1983	0.157	0.502	0.000	5.000
N of advanced scholars (IHS)	1983	1.389	1.489	0.000	6.992
N of conflicts (IHS)	1983	0.122	0.357	0.000	2.312

Notes: See text for variable descriptions and data sources.

Appendix table E.2 shows the regression results of the correlates of lineage organizations and genealogy books.

I control for a range of geographic factors, including *Latitude, Longitude, Area, Elevation, Slope,* and *Distance to Major Rivers (log)*.

I also control for *Agricultural suitability for rice,* which is the average z score of each county's environmental suitability for growing wetland rice. The data are based on the United Nations Food and Agriculture Organization's Global Agro-Ecological Zones database (*Food and Agriculture Organization of the United Nations* 2018). An initial condition for the emergence of lineage organizations is that there should be sufficient food to support big families and enough wealth to be disproportionally distributed to certain families. In agrarian societies, grain production was the primary source of wealth, and wheat and rice were the main crops in imperial China. Scholars argue that rice cultivation was more favorable to lineage formation. While wheat only ripens once a year, rice can ripen up to three times a year, which provides food for a larger population. In addition, rice cultivation is labor intensive and requires large-scale cooperation (Bray 1986, 17). Rice growing, therefore, necessitates

TABLE E.2: Exam Success, Violence, and Lineage Organizations: OLS Estimates

| Dependent variable | N of lineage organizations | | | N of genealogy books | | |
| | (Original) | | (IHS) | (Original) | | (IHS) |
	(1)	(2)	(3)	(4)	(5)	(6)
N of advanced	0.031***	0.019**		0.045***	0.026*	
scholars	(0.009)	(0.008)		(0.014)	(0.014)	
N of conflicts	0.959**	0.736**		1.205**	0.933**	
	(0.417)	(0.330)		(0.581)	(0.455)	
N of advanced			0.086***			0.090***
scholars (IHS)			(0.025)			(0.027)
N of conflicts (IHS)			0.159**			0.172**
			(0.074)			(0.080)
Controls	No	Yes	Yes	No	Yes	Yes
Prefecture FE	No	Yes	Yes	No	Yes	Yes
Outcome mean	1.030	1.163	0.415	1.475	1.665	0.443
Outcome std dev	3.841	4.067	0.872	6.923	7.351	0.951
Observations	1983	1699	1699	1983	1699	1699
R^2	0.063	0.604	0.598	0.037	0.548	0.605

Notes: Estimation method is OLS. Unit of analysis is county. Sample includes all counties in the Qing Dynasty. Dependent variable in columns (1) and (2) is the number of lineage organizations during 1801–1850. Dependent variable in column (3) is the number of lineage organizations during 1801–1850 in inverse hyperbolic sine (IHS) transformation. Dependent variable in columns (4) and (5) is the number of genealogy books during 1801–1850. Dependent variable in column (6) is the number of genealogy books during 1801–1850 in inverse hyperbolic sine (IHS) transformation. Variables of interest in columns (1), (2), (4), and (5) are number of conflicts and number of advanced scholars during 1644–1800. Variables of interest in columns (3) and (6) are number of conflicts and number of advanced scholars during 1644–1800 in inverse hyperbolic sine (IHS) transformation. Controls include latitude, longitude, area, elevation, slope, distance to major rivers (log), agricultural suitability for rice, population density in 1820, number of Ming garrisons, and public school quota. Standard errors clustered at the prefectural level in parentheses. ***, **, and * indicate statistical significance at 1%, 5%, and 10% level, respectively.

intensive cooperation among clan members: the mass mobilization of labor is required to construct irrigation and flood control works (Perkins 1969, 8). Geographically, lineage organizations were more developed in the south (where rice was cultivated) than in the north (which grew mainly wheat) (Freedman 1958, 129).

I use *Population density* (persons/km^2) measured in 1820, which is considered the most accurate population estimate in the Qing period (Cao 2000). This variable is potentially post-treatment, but given that population data before 1800 was not reliable, I use this measure with the understanding that it will cause a downward bias in my estimates. *Agricultural suitability for rice* and *Population density* are also good proxies for economic prosperity.

I use the *Number of Ming garrisons* to proxy for state capacity. Upon taking power, the imperial Ming state embarked on an ambitious garrison construction plan, largely to help suppress mass revolts (Downing 1992, 50). I thus geocode data on the location of each military garrison over the whole Ming period according to the *China Historical Geographic Information System* (2018).

To measure the civil service exam quota, I use *Public school quota*, which is the number of seats granted to each county public school in the early Qing period (Aisin Gioro 1899, Volumes 371–380).

Appendix table E.1 shows the summary statistics of these variables.

Appendix for Chapter 8

F.1   Background

TABLE F.1: Summary Statistics for Dataset in Chapter 8

	N	Mean	Std Dev	Min	Max
A: Period, 1790–1809					
Genealogy books	1983	0.337	1.618	0.000	28.000
Genealogy books (IHS)	1983	0.161	0.527	0.000	4.026
B: Period, 1810–1829					
Genealogy books	1983	0.537	2.665	0.000	51.000
Genealogy books (IHS)	1983	0.211	0.630	0.000	4.625
C: Period, 1830–1849					
Genealogy books	1983	0.719	3.441	0.000	61.000
Genealogy books (IHS)	1983	0.261	0.705	0.000	4.804
D: Period, 1870–1889					
Genealogy books	1983	1.611	7.651	0.000	115.000
Genealogy books (IHS)	1983	0.406	0.925	0.000	5.438
Mass rebellion, 1850–1869	1983	0.114	0.445	0.000	8.000
E: Qing Cross-Sectional Analysis, 1890–1911					
Declaration of independence in 1911	1983	0.045	0.208	0.000	1.000
Genealogy books (IHS)	1983	0.497	1.023	0.000	5.513
Civil service exam quota	1983	9.989	7.409	0.000	26.000
Longitude	1983	110.942	8.149	74.597	134.033
Latitude	1983	33.030	6.981	18.544	52.645
Area (degree)	1983	0.506	1.310	0.000	27.322
Distance to Beijing (log)	1983	6.921	0.724	2.537	8.193
Distance to major rivers (log)	1728	3.848	2.201	0.000	7.696
Distance to nearest coast (log)	1728	5.379	1.803	0.000	8.079
Passing Qing courier routes	1728	0.195	0.396	0.000	1.000
Elevation (km)	1728	0.637	0.792	0.001	4.813
Slope	1728	2.425	2.234	0.014	15.661
Population density	1699	132.535	141.580	0.000	874.100
Agricultural suitability for rice	1728	0.755	0.430	0.000	1.000

Notes: See text for variable descriptions and data sources.

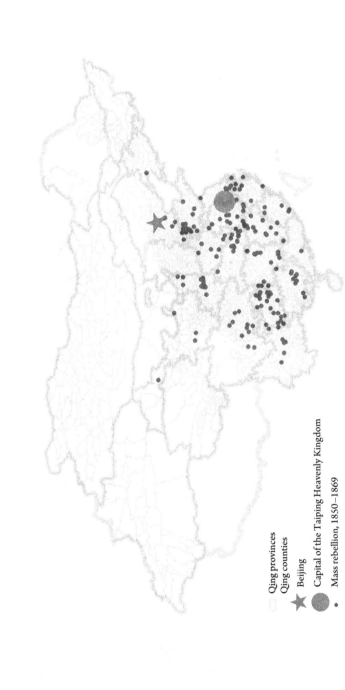

Qing provinces
Qing counties
Beijing
Capital of the Taiping Heavenly Kingdom
Mass rebellion, 1850–1869

FIGURE F.1: Mass Rebellion Locations (1850–1869)

Qing provinces
Qing counties
N of genealogy books, 1890–1909
1–9
9–27
27–54
54–93
93–124

FIGURE F.2: Number of Genealogy Books (1890–1909)

F.2 Analysis of Elite Collective Action and the 1911 Revolution

In column (1) of appendix table F.2, I first test the common trends assumption using the first two twenty-year pre-treatment periods (1790–1809 + 1810–1829). The White Lotus Rebellion took place during this period, which could have increased local elite collective action. The DiD coefficient estimate is relatively small in magnitude and statistically insignificant.

In column (2) of appendix table F.2, I then test the common trends assumption using the next two twenty-year pre-treatment periods (1810–1829 + 1830–1849). The DiD coefficient estimate is relatively small in magnitude and statistically insignificant at the 95 percent level (but statistically significant at the 90 percent level).

Column (3) of this table shows my main DiD coefficient estimate. Counties that experienced more mass rebellion battles during 1850–1869 experienced a positive and highly significant change in local elite collective action (as

TABLE F.2: Mass Rebellion and Lineage Activity: Difference-in-Differences Estimates

Dependent variable	N of genealogy books (IHS)		
	1790–1809 + 1810–1829	1810–1829 + 1830–1849	1830–1849 + 1870–1889
Data time frame	(1)	(2)	(3)
Period (1810–1829)*Mass rebellion (1850–1869)	0.044 (0.057)		
Period (1830–1849)*Mass rebellion (1850–1869)		0.054* (0.032)	
Period (1870–1889)*Mass rebellion (1850–1869)			0.205*** (0.053)
County FE	Yes	Yes	Yes
Period FE	Yes	Yes	Yes
Outcome mean	0.186	0.236	0.334
Outcome std dev	0.581	0.669	0.825
Observations	3966	3966	3966
R^2	0.885	0.911	0.900

Notes: Estimation method is OLS. Unit of analysis is Qing county. Dependent variable is lineage activity as proxied by the inverse hyperbolic sine (IHS) of the number of genealogy books. Variable of interest is the interaction term between period and number of mass rebellions. Robust standard errors clustered at county level in parentheses. ***, **, and * indicate statistical significance at 1%, 5%, and 10% level, respectively.

TABLE F.3: Lineage Activity and Declaration of Independence: OLS Estimates

Dependent variable	Declaration of Independence, 1911			
	(1)	(2)	(3)	(4)
Genealogy books (IHS)	0.036***	0.048***	0.042***	0.037***
	(0.007)	(0.010)	(0.010)	(0.010)
Civil service exam quota				0.006***
				(0.002)
Prefectural FE	No	Yes	Yes	Yes
County-level controls	No	No	Yes	Yes
Outcome mean	0.045	0.045	0.052	0.052
Outcome std dev	0.208	0.208	0.222	0.222
Observations	1983	1983	1699	1699
R^2	0.032	0.193	0.207	0.218

Notes: Estimation method is OLS. Unit of analysis is Qing county. Dependent variable is binary indicator of formal declaration of independence from imperial Qing state in 1911. Variable of interest is lineage activity as proxied by the inverse hyperbolic sine (IHS) of the number of genealogy books, between 1890 and 1909. County-level controls include latitude, longitude, area, distance to Beijing (log), distance to major rivers (log), distance to nearest coast (log), passing Qing courier routes, elevation, slope, population density, and agricultural suitability for rice. Robust standard errors clustered at county level in parentheses. ***, **, and * indicate statistical significance at 1%, 5%, and 10% level, respectively.

proxied by the number of genealogy books written during the period) from 1830–1849 to 1870–1889. The coefficient estimate suggests that an additional rebellion was associated with a 20 percent increase in the number of genealogy books.

NOTES

Chapter 1

1. For more on how the fall of the Roman Empire influenced European political development, see Acemoglu and Robinson (2019), Scheidel (2019), and Stasavage (2020).

2. For a discussion of these two political transformations in Europe, see Dincecco (2011).

3. For a description of the rise of representative institutions and their role in state building in Europe, see North and Weingast (1989), Stasavage (2003), and Cox (2016). For a critique of this literature, see Boucoyannis (2015), who argues that representative institutions emerged when powerful rulers used them to compel nobles to meet in these institutions in order to extract concessions from them.

4. Hintze (1975), Brewer (1989), Tilly (1992), Downing (1992), Spruyt (1994), Besley and Persson (2008), and Blaydes and Paik (2016) discuss how interstate conflicts motivated state building in Europe.

5. Weber (1946 [1918], 78).

6. Evans and Rauch (1999).

7. European countries account for only a small percentage of the world's states, and David Stasavage posits that their experience may simply have been "an accident." See Stasavage (2016, 145). S. E. Finer likewise characterizes European state development as "highly idiosyncratic." See Finer (1997, 5).

8. See Guo (2019) for the estimated share of taxation in GDP.

9. Wittfogel (1959).

10. See Jin and Liu (2011). Zhao (2015, 6) argues that after a Confucian-Legalist state was formed during the Qin era, the country's political-cultural structure was quite resilient until the early twentieth century. Pines (2012) maintains that fundamental ideological principles, such as unity under a single monarch, sustained China's exceptional longevity.

11. Notable exceptions include Ma (2021), who examines ideological changes during the mid-nineteenth century as a response to Western influence, and Zhang (2021), who studies changes in ideology with respect to taxation in the early Qing era due to political elites' reflection on the downfall of the Ming Dynasty.

12. For discussions and critiques of this theory, see Yang (1954), Skinner (1985), and Fairbank (1983).

13. For discussions of early state formation, see Hui (2005) and Zhao (2015).

14. For studies on fiscal weakness in late imperial China and the fall of the dynastic state, see Shue (1988), He (2013), Sng (2014), Sng and Moriguchi (2014), Bai and Jia (2016), Koyama,

Moriguchi, and Sng (2018), Ma and Rubin (2019), and Chen and Mattingly (2021). One notable exception is Huang and Yang (2020), who explain the Chinese system's "longevity mechanisms" by examining the civil service examination system.

15. Why do I use the term "state" when writing about China's history? Most English-language studies to date have referred to Chinese polities as "dynasties" or "empires." I use "state" to invoke the ways in which China's institutions resemble those of states in other times and places. For a similar approach, see Ebrey and Smith (2016). The steps Chinese rulers took to stabilize their control are much like those used by state builders in other places; the need to extract revenue, pay for armies, and control society are key features of states worldwide, past and present, East and West. Focusing on the generic process of state development frees me from asking the Euro-centric question of why China did not build a European-style nation state. Instead, I can explore what China's experience can tell us about state development in general.

16. I use the terms "state strength" and "state capacity" interchangeably.

17. Mann (1984).

18. I got inspiration for the term "social terrain" from Bates (2017), who uses "political terrain" to describe whether a polity is centralized or decentralized.

19. For an introduction to the star and ring (line) networks, see Wasserman and Faust (1994, 171). For an introduction to bowtie networks, see Broder et al. (2000, 318).

20. The number of nodes and ties in the graphs is plotted for aesthetic considerations and is not theoretically significant.

21. This conceptualization is based on Douglass North's seminal idea that the state trades a bundle of services with the population in return for revenue. See North (1981, 23).

22. They also vary along a third dimension—the degree to which local social groups are connected. The lateral ties between social groups play a secondary role in the theory, which I discuss later in the chapter.

23. Searle (1988).

24. Bates (2017).

25. Barraclough (1976).

26. Bates (2017).

27. For more information on pre-colonial African kingdoms, see Fortes and Evans-Pritchard (1950), Vansina (1966), and Kopytoff (1987).

28. I discuss how my framework sheds light on state development in Africa, Latin America, and the Middle East in Wang (2021b) and the concluding chapter.

29. For discussions of the role of private-order institutions in providing protection and justice, see Gambetta (1996), Greif (2006), and Dixit (2011).

30. The state exhibits economies of scale and scope for two reasons. First, there are fixed costs associated with establishing a set of facilities, such as warehouses, arsenals, roads, and communication infrastructures. Up to a point, the costs increase less than proportionally to the geographic span. To the extent that public services are non-rival and non-excludable, scale economies are achieved by exploiting these decreasing marginal costs. Second, establishing central institutions may facilitate the specialization of labor and capital. For example, soldiers working in a smaller, regional arsenal must perform many unrelated tasks, such as producing, maintaining, and fixing weaponry. In a central arsenal, some soldiers may specialize in producing weapons, which increases efficiency. For more theoretical discussions of scale economies

of the state, see Friedman (1977), Alesina and Wacziarg (1998), and Ferejohn and Rosenbluth (2010).

31. For a seminal discussion of cross-cutting versus reinforcing social cleavages, see Lipset and Rokkan (1967).

32. This mechanism is closely related to the argument of Jha (2015), which shows that overseas shareholding aligned the incentives of different elites during England's Civil War (1642–1648) and knitted together a pro-reform coalition in favor of parliamentary supremacy.

33. This dynamic is similar to what political scientists call pork barrel politics, in which the benefits of government-funded programs are concentrated in a particular area but the costs are spread among all taxpayers. See Ferejohn (1974) for a seminal discussion of pork barrel politics.

34. Li (1979 [1177], 279: 6834–5; 364: 8703–6).

35. Olson (1982, 48).

36. Burt (1992).

37. Duara (1988, 74).

38. The popular game-theoretical term "multiple equilibria" refers to the fact that at any point in time, the game can jump from one equilibrium to another. My concept of "multiple *steady-state* equilibria" instead implies that at any point in time, the equilibrium is unique unless it is shocked, but the equilibrium path may lead to different steady states depending on the historical context. For seminal work on the concept of steady state, see Solow (1956). Acemoglu and Robinson (2020) applied the idea to state-society relations.

39. Miguel Centeno characterizes state structure in colonial-era Latin America as a system in which: "Each part of the empire was connected to the center, but the separate regions were not linked with one another." See Centeno (2002, 143). Similarly, Christopher Clapham notes that under colonial rule, African chiefs were confined to serving as "representatives of specified families within each chiefdom" and thus "created a group of local patrons with their own clienteles within the chiefdom." See Clapham (1982, 84–5).

40. For example, in pre-colonial Africa, as Jeffrey Herbst argues, "power was (quite realistically) conceived of as a series of concentric circles radiating out from the core." See Herbst (2000, 45). Lisa Anderson points out that in post-colonial Libya, the destruction of the pre-colonial administration by the Italian colonizers eventually led to a return to relying on kinship as the primary organizational principle in the hinterlands. See Anderson (2014, 9–10).

41. Tilly (1995, 13).

42. Acemoglu and Robinson (2019, 345).

43. Dahl (1959).

44. Truman (1971).

45. For a synthesis of structural-functionalism, see Almond and Powell (1978).

46. Anderson (1979).

47. Wallerstein (1974).

48. Hall (1989).

49. Hall and Soskice (2001) discuss "varieties" of welfare states in advanced democracies.

50. See, for example, Johnson (1982).

51. Evans, Rueschemeyer, and Skocpol (1985, vii).

52. Evans, Rueschemeyer, and Skocpol (1985, vii).

53. Skocpol (1985, 9).

54. Hintze (1975) and Tilly (1992). Besley and Persson (2008), Dincecco, Federico, and Vindigni (2011), and Blaydes and Paik (2016) empirically test the relationship between war making and state making. For critiques, see Queralt (2019), Dincecco and Wang (2018), and Grzymala-Busse (2020). Queralt (2019), for example, argues that the availability of external capital in the nineteenth century weakened the motivation to increase fiscal capacity in order to wage wars.

55. Tilly (1975, 42).

56. For the theory's application in China, see Hui (2005); for a discussion of war and state formation in Japan, see Ferejohn and Rosenbluth (2010); for its relevance in Africa, see Herbst (2000); for Latin America, see Centeno (2002).

57. For a general theoretical discussion, see Mahoney (2000). For examples of historical research, see Ertman (1997) and Ziblatt (2006).

58. Levi (2002, 37).

59. North and Weingast (1989). Also see critiques from Stasavage (2002), Pincus and Robinson (2014), and Abramson and Boix (2019), who argue that parliamentary power dynamics generated by economic changes were the fundamental driving force.

60. Bates and Lien (1985).

61. Levi (1988).

62. Migdal (1988, 269).

63. Shue (1988).

64. Perry (1993).

65. Migdal, Kohli, and Shue (1994).

66. Acemoglu and Robinson (2019).

67. Weber (1946 [1918], 78).

68. E.g., Migdal (1988).

69. Frisby (2002, ix).

70. Levi (1988, 2).

71. Geddes (1996).

72. Tilly (1992), Slater (2010), and North, Wallis, and Weingast (2012).

73. Bates (2010) and Greif (2006).

74. See, for example, Tilly (1992) for external war, and Slater (2010) for internal conflict.

75. Lerner (1958), Lipset (1959), and Deutsch (1961).

76. Anderson (1979) and Moore (1966).

77. Huntington (1968).

78. Pomeranz (2000).

79. Acemoglu, Johnson, and Robinson (2005).

80. Allen (2009).

81. Greif and Tabellini (2017).

82. Mokyr (2016).

83. Scheidel (2019).

84. Rosenthal and Wong (2011).

85. Vries (2015).

86. E.g., Wong (1997) and Pomeranz (2000).

87. E.g., Broadberry, Guan, and Li (2018).

88. Migdal (1988), Shue (1988), Perry (1993), Migdal, Kohli, and Shue (1994), and Acemoglu and Robinson (2019).

89. For pioneering works that examine state-society linkages, see Evans (1995) and Levitsky and Way (2010). For a seminal effort to analyze the blurred boundary between the state and society, see Grzymala-Busse and Luong (2002).

90. Hegel (1991, 23).

91. Bates et al. (1998).

92. Check my Harvard Dataverse at https://dataverse.harvard.edu/dataverse/yuhuawang.

Chapter 2

1. Changes in atmospheric concentrations of carbon dioxide and greenhouse gases, aerosol concentrations, volcanic activity, and solar radiation all cause the Earth's surface temperature to change. Scientists have recently made significant progress using proxy evidence from sources such as tree rings, corals, ocean and lake sediments, cave deposits, ice cores, boreholes, glaciers, and documentary evidence to reconstruct large-scale surface temperature over the past 2,000 years.

2. For a synthesis of these studies, see National Research Council (2006).

3. Ge et al. (2013).

4. Ge et al. (2013, 1156) define a temperature anomaly as a departure in temperature from the 1851–1950 average.

5. The dots represent temperature anomalies at the decade level, while the line represents the locally weighted smoothing.

6. See, for example, Burke, Hsiang and Miguel (2015).

7. Nanjing Military Academy (2003).

8. For examples of using these data in quantitative analysis, see Dincecco and Wang (2018) and Dincecco and Wang (2020).

9. Wilkinson (2000, 501).

10. I believe selection bias is unlikely to be severe, since each official book was written by relatively contemporaneous historians whose main task was to recount the available facts and derive lessons for the incoming dynasty. I am therefore confident that the main historical conflicts in imperial China are well represented in the *Catalog*. The official history books, however, did not record casualty totals, which limits my ability to determine the magnitudes of various conflicts.

11. This coding method is similar in spirit to that of Jia (2014, 96), and yields broadly similar patterns of mass rebellion across time and space.

12. This definition is based on the seminal work by Chen (2007 [1940], 3).

13. Scott (2017, 223).

14. For a discussion of the connection between the ecological environment and mass rebellion in historical China, see Perry (1980), Kung and Ma (2014), Jia (2014), and Dincecco and Wang (2020).

15. For a historical account of the Huang Chao Rebellion, see Tackett (2014).

16. For an empirical analysis of how mass rebellion changed the state and society in China, see Dincecco and Wang (2020).

17. Appendix table A.1 shows the results. My preferred specifications control for the lagged dependent variable.

18. For these alternative explanations, see Gurr (1970), Tilly (1978), Tarrow (1994), Lohmann (1994), Kang (2010), and Horowitz, Stam, and Ellis (2015).

19. The imperial Chinese bureaucracy had thirty levels, ranging from the chief councilor at the top to county clerks at the bottom. See Gong (1990, 15). Emperors in the Tang and Song eras designated officials at the vice-ministerial level or above as *major advisory officials* who could appear in court in front of the emperor to discuss policy issues. See Gong (1990, 20).

20. My research team first used Li (2013, 16–7, 47–8, 62–70) and Zang, Zhu, and Wang (1987) to identify which positions were at the vice-ministerial level or above during the Tang and Song eras. We then collected the names of the officials who occupied these positions using Yan (1986), Yu (2003), Hu (2000), Sun (2009), Yu (2000), and *China Biographical Database* (2018). Next we obtained their biographical information from *China Biographical Database* (2018), a relational database with biographical information on approximately 422,600 individuals, primarily from the seventh through the nineteenth centuries.

21. *The Complete Prose of Song* (全宋文), edited by Zeng and Liu (2006), includes hundreds of epitaphs recorded in the collected works of Song writers. We also consulted *China Biographical Database* (2018) and other biographical sources to construct kinship networks.

22. Bossler (1998, 11).

23. *China Historical Geographic Information System* (2018).

24. The network is undirected, which means that Zhang and Liu are connected if Zhang is in Liu's kinship network *or* if Liu is in Zhang's kinship network.

25. Density is defined as $2L/k \times (k-1)$, where L is the number of observed ties in the network, and k is the number of politicians in the network. Thus, network density is a ratio that ranges from 0 (less connected) to 1 (more connected). See Marsden (1993).

26. In social network analysis, researchers use community structures to measure a network's coherence. One approach that is used to detect community structures is based on edge removal. The intuition is as follows: if two groups of nodes are only loosely connected with each other, then removing the edges between them will generate components in the restricted network. Appendix A provides details of how I use an algorithm proposed by Girvan and Newman (2002) to measure a network's social fractionalization.

27. The standardized localization score for politician i is defined as $\sum_{k \in K}(1 + distance_{i,k})^{-1}/K$, where $distance_{i,k}$ denotes the "as the crow flies" distance (in kilometers) from politician i to his kin k. The set K includes all kin members of i. This index is generic and does not rely on administrative units, which are different sizes and often determined by time-variant, arbitrarily drawn borders. See Harris (1954) and Krugman (1998).

28. See Yu (2003 [1956]).

29. Ebrey (1978, 17).

30. Johnson (1977, 22).

31. Ebrey (1978, 18).

32. These four categories were labelled simply A (甲), B (乙), C (丙), and D (丁), and known collectively as the "Four (categories of) Clans" (四姓). See Johnson (1977, 28). During this time, every great clan was associated with the prefecture in which its ancestral home was

found. Most medieval texts began identifying aristocratic families with greater precision at this time, preceding the surname with the clan's place of origin, a component of clan appellation referred to as the "choronym" (郡望). The Cui clan of Qinghe was thus distinguished from the Cui clan of Boling, for example. See Tackett (2014, 30).

33. Johnson (1977, 55).

34. Ebrey (1978, 2).

35. Goody (1983, 123).

36. Ebrey (1986, 2).

37. The faster reproduction of the wealthiest elites is similar to what Gregory Clark calls the "survival of the richest." See Clark (2008).

38. Tackett (2014, 44).

39. Stone (1965, 79).

40. Tackett (2014, 84).

41. Tackett (2014, 25–6).

42. Tackett (2014, 133–4).

43. Tackett (2014, 182).

44. Chinese elites usually had multiple concubines and hence a large number of sons and daughters. They could intermarry with capital elites *and* local elites.

45. See Freeman (2000).

46. The network draws on data from Tackett (2014).

47. This marriage network included 65 of the 75 patrilines with the largest numbers of known officeholders; 72 of 104 chief councilors (the highest bureaucratic position) serving from 800 to 880 were from clans appearing on this diagram. See Tackett (2014, 122–4).

48. The density of the Tang aristocratic families is 0.028.

49. The average standardized localization score of these officials' kinship networks is 0.044.

50. Daron Acemoglu, James Robinson, and Ragnar Torvik observe that centralization can have a "political agenda effect": state centralization, which involves elites coordinating nationally, induces citizens to organize nationally as well—rather than at the local or "parochial" level. See Acemoglu, Robinson, and Torvik (2020, 749).

51. Tackett (2014, 240).

52. Somers (1979, 745).

53. Tackett (2014, 218).

54. Chaffee (1995, 16).

55. Kracke (1947) and Ho (1964).

56. Naito (1992 [1922]).

57. For a more detailed discussion, see Hymes (1986, 115–7).

58. Beattie (1979).

59. Hymes (1986) and Beattie (1979).

60. For the Treaty of Nanjing, see Wakeman (1975, 137). For more on the Qing government's finances, see Shi and Xu (2008, 55).

61. For a description of the Taiping Rebellion, see Platt (2012).

62. Kuhn (1970, 211).

63. Duara (1988, 73–4).

64. Hsiao (1960, 333).

65. These records were collected from private holdings and public libraries all over the world, including the Genealogical Society of Utah—the largest overseas collection of Chinese genealogies. See Wang (2008). Wang (2008) is considered China's "most comprehensive genealogy register." See Greif and Tabellini (2017, 2).

66. Appendix figure A.1 shows a sample of the register.

67. My research team first used optical character recognition to scan the whole register (ten books) into an Excel file and manually checked every entry to ensure its accuracy. We then consulted *China Historical Geographic Information System* (2018), which provides coordinates of historical localities, for geocoding.

68. Skocpol (1979, 78).

69. Wakeman (1975, 228–32, 235–7).

70. Bai and Jia (2016).

71. Wakeman (1975, 228).

72. Levi (1988, 2).

73. See, for example, Besley and Persson (2009).

74. See Stasavage (2020).

75. I collect data on China's major fiscal policies from the *History of Finance in Imperial China* edited by Wang (1981). Appendix table A.2 lists these major fiscal policies and my codings.

76. I consider a policy that increased (decreased) tax extraction to be state strengthening (state weakening); I coded those that maintained the status quo as neutral.

77. To obtain estimates of historical taxation and population, my research team consulted the following sources: Du (1988), Ho (1959), Peng (1965), Ma (1986), Li (1995), Wang, Liu, and Zhang (2000), Ge (2000), Wu (2000), Cao (2000), Wang (2003), Peng (2006), Ye (2006), Kato (2006), Chen and Shi (2007), Ning (2007), Qi (2007), Li (2007*b*), Liang (2008), Allen (2009), Baten et al. (2010), Allen et al. (2011), and Quan (2012).

78. Malthus (1992 [1806], 41, 183–4).

79. Lavely and Wong (1998, 719).

80. According to Lavely and Wong (1998, 719), China's population grew by 29 percent in the fifteenth century, 40 percent in the sixteenth century, and 0 percent in the seventeenth century.

81. Rosenthal and Wong (2011, 48–49).

82. I obtain the data from Guo (2019).

83. The An Lushan Rebellion was an armed conflict between the Tang government and various regional powers led by the military governor An Lushan. The rebellion and subsequent disorder significantly weakened the Tang's control of northeastern regions. Chapter 3 discusses this rebellion in more detail.

84. Twitchett (1970, 40).

85. Li (2002, 124, 283, 327).

86. Liang (2009 [1908], 165).

87. Deng (1997, 48).

88. Sima (1937 [1086], 42: 543–5) and Li (1979 [1177], 179: 48).

89. Elliott (2001).

90. Wang (1973, 27).

91. See Tian (2015 [1989]) and Johnson (1977).

92. Wechsler (1979, 212–3).

93. Tackett (2014, 35).

94. Dalby (1979, 590–1). It is important to note that the aristocratic effort to increase bureaucratic power did not fully succeed. Dalby (1979, 591) points out that after the An Lushan Rebellion, many central government offices became moribund as their functions were transferred to new ad hoc offices. By the 780s, therefore, the heads of the civilian government faced formidable organizational difficulties in putting policies into action. Another attempt in 786 to centralize all executive power in the office of the chief ministers also failed.

95. The logic is similar to Blaydes and Chaney's (2013) discussion of ruler duration in feudal Europe vs. the Islamic world. Elites were scattered in the former, which made the ruler safer. The *mamluks* (slave soldiers) in the latter were concentrated in the capital, threatening the sultan.

96. Dalby (1979, 601, 634).

97. These five were Xianzong (805–820), Jingzong (824–826), Wuzong (840–846), Zhaozong (888–904), and Aidi (904–907). According to the official histories, eunuchs played an important role, with aristocratic acquiescence, in leading these coups. See Dalby (1979, 635).

98. Naito (1992 [1922]).

99. Kracke (1947) and Ho (1964).

100. Chaffee (1995, xxii).

101. Hartwell (1982, 405).

102. Smith (2009*b*, 461).

103. Smith (2009*b*, 462).

104. Hucker (1998, 75).

105. Hucker (1998, 75).

106. Rowe (2009, 40–1).

107. Blaydes and Chaney (2013) pioneered the use of ruler data to explore political survival.

108. My primary sources are *Chronologies of Chinese Emperors and Their Families* edited by Du (1995) and *The Complete Biographies of Chinese Emperors* edited by Qiao et al. (1996), the most reliable and systematic sources I can find on Chinese emperors.

109. Appendix table A.3 provides a breakdown by type of exit.

110. For European and Islamic monarchs, my main sources are McNaughton (1973), Morby (1989), Blaydes and Chaney (2013), and Kokkonen and Sundell (2014).

111. Lewis (2009, 54).

112. Twitchett (1970, 4–5).

113. Twitchett (1970, 41–2).

114. Tackett (2014, 182).

115. Hymes (1986, 175).

116. Hymes (2015, 538).

117. Hymes (2015, 539).

118. McDermott (2013, 111–22).

119. Lee (2009, 7).

120. Lee (2009, 35).

121. Such households were exempt from village service on a fixed amount of land in accordance with their rank. They also had the right to hire someone else to fulfill their village service

beyond their tax-free land, and enjoyed a 50 percent reduction in their service exemption tax. See Lee (2009, 58–60).

122. Lee (2009, 149).

123. Kuhn (1970, 211–225) and Von Glahn (2016, 380–381).

124. Kuhn (1970, 211).

125. Duara (1988, 73–4).

126. Barraclough (1976).

127. Bloch (2014).

128. Stasavage (2020).

129. Downing (1993).

130. Tilly (1992).

131. North and Weingast (1989).

Chapter 3

1. Maddison (2007, 381).

2. Lewis (2009, 3–4).

3. Twitchett (1979, 1).

4. Lewis (2009, 1).

5. Twitchett (1970, 2).

6. Li (2002, 226).

7. For state-strengthening policies under Qin, see Hui (2005), Fukuyama (2011), and Zhao (2015).

8. This process is similar to the state-making process in medieval Europe described by Tilly (1992).

9. Lewis (2007, 32).

10. Lewis (2007, 33).

11. Bloch (2014).

12. Creel (1964, 163–4).

13. Ko and Sng (2013, 480).

14. The ninth-century fall of the Carolingian Empire resulted in a high level of political fragmentation in Europe. See Strayer (1970, 15). This fragmentation was enduring. In 1500, for example, it is likely that there were at least two hundred independent states in Europe. See Tilly (1992, 45).

15. Ashraf and Galor (2013).

16. Hui (2005), Fukuyama (2011), and Zhao (2015).

17. Diamond (1997). Hoffman (2015), however, points out that China is more mountainous than Europe.

18. Turchin et al. (2013).

19. Fernández-Villaverde et al. (2020).

20. Lewis (2007, 3).

21. Lewis (2007, 63).

22. See Yu (2003 [1956]).

23. Wright (1979, 48).

24. For more on the early development of the aristocratic clans, see Yu (2003 [1956]), Mao (1966), Johnson (1977), and Ebrey (1978).

25. Twitchett (1979, 4) and Wright (1979, 57–63).

26. Ebrey (1978, 1).

27. Ebrey (1978, 17) and Johnson (1977, 22).

28. Ebrey (1978, 18).

29. Johnson (1977, 22).

30. Ebrey (1978, 31).

31. Recall figure 2.5 (panel (a)) in chapter 2 in which the Tang aristocratic families formed a high-density marriage network.

32. Wechsler (1979, 212–3).

33. Tackett (2014, 35).

34. Dalby (1979, 590–1). The aristocratic effort to increase bureaucratic power did not fully succeed. After the An Lushan Rebellion, the functions of many central government offices were transferred to new ad hoc offices. A later attempt in 786 to centralize all executive power in the office of the chief ministers also failed. See Dalby (1979, 591).

35. Twitchett (1979, 13).

36. Wechsler (1979, 169).

37. Wright (1979, 81–2).

38. Twitchett (1979, 15).

39. Twitchett (1979, 13).

40. Twitchett (1970, 104-5).

41. Twitchett (1970, 105–6).

42. Wright (1979, 86).

43. Wechsler (1979, 214).

44. Twitchett (1979, 21).

45. Chen (2001, 202).

46. Twitchett and Wechsler (1979, 275).

47. Wright (1979, 93).

48. Chen (2001, 156).

49. Lewis (2009, 54).

50. See Lewis (2009, 54). According to the Land Statues of Tang, every male aged 18–60 was eligible for 100 *mu* of land (about 13.3 acres). Of this, 80 *mu* was to be "personal share land" and 20 *mu* "land held in perpetuity." Personal share land reverted to the state when the occupier reached the age of 60, while land held in perpetuity was transferred to the legal heirs upon the occupier's death. See Twitchett (1970, 4–5).

51. Li (2002, 89–90).

52. Twitchett (1970, 2).

53. Lewis (2009, 55–6).

54. Chen (2001, 140–1) and Wright (1979, 97).

55. Lewis (2009, 44).

56. Lewis (2009, 48).

57. Wechsler (1979, 175–6).

58. Lewis (2009, 44).

59. Wechsler (1979, 207).
60. Lewis (2009, 45).
61. Lewis (2009, 45–6).
62. Twitchett (1979, 7).
63. Peterson (1979, 464).
64. Dalby (1979, 561).
65. Dalby (1979, 562).
66. See Peterson (1979, 470–1) for a discussion of this view.
67. Chen (2001, 210–8).
68. Pulleyblank (1955, 75–81).
69. Peterson (1979, 472).
70. Twitchett (1979, 17).
71. Twitchett (1970, 17).
72. Twitchett (1970, 34).
73. Twitchett (1970, 26).
74. Twitchett (1970, 21).
75. Twitchett (1970, 18).
76. Twitchett (1970, 12).
77. Twitchett (1970, 26).
78. Peterson (1979, 485).
79. Peterson (1979, 486).
80. Twitchett (1970, 49).
81. Peterson (1979, 495).
82. Peterson (1979, 496).
83. Peterson (1979, 497–8)
84. Li (2002, 76).
85. Twitchett (1970, 40).
86. Twitchett (1970, 36).
87. Twitchett (1970, 40).
88. Peterson (1979, 498–9) and Li (2002, 105).
89. Twitchett (1970, 41–2).
90. Dalby (1979, 581).
91. Twitchett (1970, 39).
92. Twitchett (1979, 355).
93. Twitchett (1970, 29–31).
94. Li (2002, 217–221).
95. Li (2002, 223–4).
96. Li (2002, 124, 283, 327).
97. Li (2002, 116–9).
98. Li (2002, 283, 327).
99. Twitchett (1970, 26).
100. Meltzer and Richard (1981).
101. Scheve and Stasavage (2016).
102. Johnson (1977, 132).

103. Mao (1981, 421).

104. Tackett (2014, 56).

105. Tackett (2014, 84).

106. Tackett (2014, 122–4).

107. Tackett (2014, 182).

108. The average standardized localization score of the Tang officials' kinship networks is 0.044—less than half of the Song average localization score.

109. Dalby (1979, 601, 634).

110. These five late-Tang emperors include Xianzong (805–820), Jingzong (824–826), Wuzong (840–846), Zhaozong (888–904), and Aidi (904–907).

111. Dalby (1979, 573–4).

112. Dalby (1979, 635).

113. Tackett (2014, 240).

114. Somers (1979, 745).

115. Tackett (2014, 218).

116. Somers (1979, 747).

117. Tackett (2014, 218).

118. Somers (1979, 747).

119. Somers (1979, 781).

Chapter 4

1. See Naito (1992 [1922]) for a seminal discussion of the Tang-Song transition and Chen (2017) for a recent review of the literature.

2. See, for example, Ebrey (1978, 1).

3. Johnson (1977) and Hartwell (1982).

4. Hymes (1986), Bol (1994), Bossler (1998), and Tackett (2014).

5. Hymes (1986).

6. Bossler (1998).

7. My research team first used Li (2013, 16–7, 47–8, 62–70) and Zang, Zhu, and Wang (1987) to identify the relevant positions during both dynasties. We then collected the names of the officials who occupied these positions using Yan (1986), Yu (2003), Hu (2000), Sun (2009), Yu (2000), and *China Biographical Database* (2018). We then obtained their biographic information from *China Biographical Database* (2018), a relational database with biographical information on approximately 422,600 individuals, primarily from the seventh to the nineteenth century. I am confident that this is a relatively complete list of all major officials in the Tang and Song times because prominent individuals, especially government officials, were well documented in Chinese official histories.

8. For Tang officials' kinship networks, I rely on *China Biographical Database* (2018) and Tackett (2014). For Song officials' kinship networks, I use *The Complete Prose of Song* (全宋文) edited by Zeng and Liu (2006), which includes hundreds of epitaphs recorded in the collected works of Song writers, and *China Biographical Database* (2018).

9. Lewis (2009, 33).

10. Lewis (2009, 118).

11. Twitchett (1979, 6).

12. Lewis (2009, 137).

13. Tackett (2014, 4).

14. Liu (2015).

15. Broadberry, Guan, and Li (2018, 33).

16. Hartwell (1982, 369).

17. Skinner (1977, 211–20).

18. The household data are from Hartwell (1982, 369).

19. Chaffee (1995, 15).

20. Chaffee (1995, 16).

21. Chaffee (1995, 16).

22. Chaffee (1995, xxii). The other degree that coexisted with the "advanced scholar" degree was the classicist degree (明经). While the "advanced scholar" examinations tested on poetry and essay writing, the classicist examinations focused on memorizing Confucian cannons, which was considered an easier task.

23. Kracke (1947) and Ho (1964).

24. Kracke (1947).

25. Hymes (1986, 35–62). Jiang and Kung (2020) provide empirical support for this revised view showing that family background is a strong predictor of exam success in the Qing era.

26. Chaffee (1995, 16–35).

27. Bossler (1998, 17–23).

28. Cited from Tackett (2014, 5).

29. Hymes (1986, 115–7). Hymes introduces a Northern Song family and a Southern Song family, which I argue resemble an aristocratic family in the Tang and a gentry family in the Song era, respectively.

30. Ebrey (1978, 28).

31. Ebrey (1978, 28).

32. Tackett (2014, 133–4).

33. Bossler (1998, 49).

34. Hymes (1986, 94).

35. Hartwell (1982, 419).

36. Hartwell (1982, 419).

37. Hymes (1986, 45).

38. The average localization score of the Song officials is 0.102—more than twice that of Tang officials (0.044).

39. Figure 4.4 panel (a), drawing on Tackett's (2014) data, uses families as nodes.

40. In figure 4.4, the late Tang network (panel (a)) has a density of 0.028; the Song Zhenzong network (panel (b)) has a density of 0.011; the Song Shenzong network (panel (c)) has a density of 0.010; the Song Ningzong network (panel (d)) has a density of 0.012; The Song Lizong network (panel (e)) has a density of 0.012.

41. Appendix B provides the details and results of calculating the social fractionalization among Song major officials over time using the Girvan-Newman algorithm.

42. Smith (2009b, 461).

43. Smith (2009b, 461).

44. Smith (2009*b*, 462).
45. Chen (2001, 202).
46. Tackett (2014, 138).
47. Twitchett (1979, 20–1).
48. Johnson (1977, 131–41).
49. Naito (1992 [1922], 10–18).
50. Johnson (1977, 132–41).
51. Johnson (1977, 146).
52. Tackett (2014, 240).
53. Tackett (2014, 218).
54. Hartwell (1982, 365–406).
55. Hartwell (1986, 115–7).
56. Bossler (1998, 5,88,204).
57. Lee (2009, 64–5).
58. Bol (1990, 168–171).
59. McDermott (2013, 134).
60. McDermott (2013, 135).
61. McDermott (2013, 115).
62. Hymes (1986, 127–8).
63. Lee (2009, 52).
64. Lee (2009, 207).

Chapter 5

1. Hartman (2015, 27–8) and Chaffee (2015*a*, 7).
2. Smith (2009*a*, 1).
3. Elvin (1973, 112).
4. Naito (1992 [1922]).
5. Mann (1984).
6. Golas (2015, 148).
7. See Tilly (1992).
8. Smith (2009*a*, 4).
9. Hartman (2015, 48).
10. Hartman (2015, 28).
11. Hartman (2015, 85).
12. Smith (2009*a*, 12).
13. Golas (2015, 142).
14. Smith (2009*a*, 13).
15. Smith (2009*a*, 12).
16. Golas (2015, 142).
17. Hartman (2015, 98).
18. Hartman (2015, 128).
19. Hartman (2015, 85).
20. Hartman (2015, 30). This institution can be traced back at least to the Han Dynasty (202 BCE–220 CE).

21. Hartman (2015, 103).

22. Hartman (2015, 111).

23. Hartman (2015, 44).

24. Naito (1992 [1922]).

25. Chaffee (2015*b*, 291).

26. Chaffee (2015*b*, 291).

27. Chaffee (2015*b*, 312).

28. This number is much lower than what is shown in figure 4.5 using the major offi-cials, indicating that exam success was important for placement in the upper echelons of the bureaucracy.

29. Hartman (2015, 33).

30. Hartman (2015, 55).

31. Chaffee (2015*b*, 292).

32. Hartman (2015, 59).

33. Hartman (2015, 63).

34. E.g., Hartman (2015, 74).

35. Hartman (2015, 73).

36. Golas (2015, 158–9).

37. Golas (2015, 165).

38. Golas (2015, 159).

39. Golas (2015, 160).

40. Golas (2015, 161-2).

41. Smith (2009*b*, 348).

42. Liu (2015).

43. Golas (2015, 148).

44. Golas (2015, 148) and Liu (2015, 61).

45. Hartman (2015, 22).

46. Golas (2015, 177).

47. Hartman (2015, 22).

48. Guo (2019).

49. Hartman (2015, 23–4). Figure 2.9 in chapter 2, which is based on Guo's (2019) estimates, shows that the Song state collected 13–17 percent of national income as taxes.

50. Wang (2015, 215–6).

51. Wang (2015, 216–7).

52. Wang (2015, 217).

53. Wang (2015, 218–9).

54. Wang (2015, 219).

55. Hartman (2015, 52).

56. Smith (2009*a*, 14–5).

57. Wang (2015, 235).

58. Hartman (2015, 28).

59. Among the most important Song policies were those that encouraged merchants to buy grain and deliver it to the frontiers in exchange for cash, salt, or tea. See Golas (2015, 198).

60. Hartman (2015, 28–9).

61. Gong (1990, 15).

62. Gong (1990, 20).

63. Li (2003).

64. Li (2013, 16–7, 47–8, 62–70) provides a full list of these positions.

65. I obtained their biographical information from *China Biographical Database* (2018).

66. Recall that I use an index to measure how localized an individual's kinship network is. *Local concentration of kin* for official i is defined as $\sum_{k \in K}(1 + distance_{i,k})^{-1}$, where $distance_{i,k}$ is the "as the crow flies" distance (in kilometers) from politician i to his kin k. The set K includes all kin members of i. The underlying logic is that this index of local concentration increases as all kin move closer to the politician. Appendix table C.2 provides empirical support for this historical observation.

67. Smith (2009*b*, 349).

68. Liang (2009 [1908], 165).

69. Deng (1997, 48).

70. The New Policies also encompassed a state trade policy (市易法) to regulate and tax commercial trade, as well as irrigation and drainage policies (农田水利法) to encourage local governments to build water projects to facilitate agricultural development. See Deng (1997, 88).

71. Liu (1959, 39).

72. Smith (2009*b*, 393).

73. Williamson (1935, 181).

74. Smith (2009*b*, 413–4).

75. Deng (1997, 88).

76. Williamson (1935, 142–3).

77. Deng (1997, 88).

78. Smith (2009*b*, 400).

79. Smith (2009*b*, 434).

80. Williamson (1935, 197) and Smith (2009*b*, 427).

81. Wang (2017 [1086], 74: 14).

82. Wang (2017 [1086], 75: 19).

83. Wang (2017 [1086], 75: 22). The Chinese original is 富其家者资之国，富其国者资之天下，欲富天下，则资之天地.

84. Qi (1987, 1163–8).

85. Li (1979 [1177], 364: 8703–6).

86. Sima (1937 [1086], 49:626–8) and Li (1979 [1177], 224: 5444–6, 6787–91).

87. Li (1979 [1177], 279: 6834–5).

88. Toghtō (1985 [1343], 192(145): 6).

89. Sima (1937 [1086], 42: 543–5).

90. Li (1979 [1177], 179: 48).

91. Wang (2017 [1086], 4: 72).

92. Li (1979 [1177], 215: 5237, 227: 5522).

93. Hartwell (1982, 421).

94. Miyazaki (1992 [1953], 339–75).

95. On how leadership transitions affect authoritarian politics, see Jones and Olken (2005).

96. Deng (1997, 238–9).

97. Deng (1997, 254).

98. I collected information on these politicians' attitudes toward the reform from three primary sources: *The History of Song* (宋史) edited by Toghtō (1985 [1343]), *The Extended Continuation to Comprehensive Mirror in Aid of Governance* (续资治通鉴长编) edited by Li (1979 [1177]), and *The Complete Prose of Song* (全宋文) edited by Zeng and Liu (2006). Toghtō (1985 [1343]) is a biographical history of the Song Dynasty compiled by historians in the Yuan Dynasty (1279–1368), while Li (1979 [1177]) is a chronological history of the Northern Song era compiled by historians in the Southern Song Dynasty (1127–1279). These books are the most authoritative sources of Song history, and both were written by relative contemporaries, based on official court records. See Wilkinson (2000, 501). But contemporaries might have political and personal biases. For example, a Southern Song historian who was descended from a Northern Song politician might have an incentive to reinterpret his ancestor's words, depending on how the reform was perceived at the time of writing. By contrast, *Complete Prose of Song* is a 360-volume, 100-million-word collection of Song writings compiled by Chinese literature researchers using a literary criterion in the twenty-first century. Instead of summarizing and interpreting what the politicians said, as in Toghtō (1985 [1343]) and Li (1979 [1177]), Zeng and Liu (2006) record all the writings, such as memorials to the emperor, in their original form. I am confident that triangulating these three sources brings us as close to historical reality as it is possible to get. My research team read all of these books and identified every mention involving at least one of the 137 major politicians in our sample. We then selected all of their activities related to the Wang Anshi Reform, such as writing to the emperor or participating in public discussion, and manually coded every politician according to his attitude toward the reform. For example, a politician who wrote to the emperor to denounce the reform would be considered an opponent, while we coded one who supported the reform in court discussions as a supporter.

99. Over half of the politicians (seventy-four, or 54 percent) did not explicitly express an attitude toward the reform. Most of them (forty-nine) were in ceremonial positions, such as in the Ministry of Rites, which was in charge of religious rituals and court ceremonies. A simple explanation is that these seventy-four politicians were not in policy-relevant positions and therefore did not have a policy attitude. In the main analysis, I use listwise deletion, without making any assumptions about their implicit attitudes. Elsewhere, I employ three alternative approaches to handle these politicians. First, I code them as neutral and create a trichotomous dependent variable—support (1), neutral (0), and oppose (−1). Second, I restrict my sample to a subset of politicians who held policy-relevant positions. Third, I randomly assign a value to these politicians by flipping a coin (i.e., drawing from the Bernoulli distribution). All three of these approaches produce the same results. See Wang (2021a).

100. Li (1979 [1177], 213: 5169).

101. I choose Lü Gongzhu partly for visualization considerations: although his kinship network was more localized than Wang Anshi's, it was dispersed enough to show the whole network on a national map.

102. I discuss the technical details of the statistical test in appendix C. I provide a more stringent test of this hypothesis and a wide range of robustness checks in Wang (2021a).

103. Liu (1959, 60).

104. Liu (1959, 92).

105. Liu (1959, 92).

106. Smith (2009*b*, 356).
107. Smith (2009*b*, 356-7).
108. Smith (2009*b*, 367).
109. Hartman (2015, 46).
110. Smith (2009*a*, 31).
111. Hymes (1986, 175).
112. Hymes (2015, 536).
113. Hymes (2015, 538).
114. Hymes (2015, 538).
115. Hymes (2015, 539).
116. Hymes (2015, 539-40).
117. Hymes (2015, 540).
118. Hymes (2015, 541).
119. Hymes (2015, 542).
120. Hymes (2015, 542).
121. Hymes (2015, 622).
122. McDermott (2013, 39).
123. McDermott (2013, 7).
124. McDermott (2013, 53).
125. For a classic study on the gentry's income, see Chang (1962).
126. Lee (2009, 142).
127. Lee (2009, 149).
128. Bol (2015, 665).
129. Bol (2015, 668-9).
130. E.g., Smith and Von Glahn (2003).
131. Lee (2009, 207).

Chapter 6

1. Wei (1999, 31).
2. Hucker (1998, 63).
3. Hucker (1998, 65).
4. Huang (1981, 158).
5. Wei (1999, 32).
6. Wei (1999, 33).
7. Wei (1999, 36–45).
8. Hucker (1998, 67).
9. Hucker (1998, 65).
10. Von Glahn (2016, 285–8).
11. Wei (1999, 552).
12. Wei (1999, 653).
13. Huang (1974, 118).
14. Huang (1998, 522).
15. Huang (1998, 522).

16. Huang (1974, 302).

17. Huang (1974, 301).

18. Huang (1974, 301).

19. Huang (1981, 37–8).

20. Huang (1981, 39).

21. Huang (1974, 118).

22. Huang (1974, 1).

23. Hucker (1998, 9).

24. Hucker (1998, 9).

25. Hucker (1998, 75).

26. Hucker (1998, 75).

27. Hucker (1998, 75).

28. Hucker (1998, 75).

29. Huang (1974, 5).

30. Hucker (1998, 104).

31. Huang (1998, 513–4) and Huang (1981, 75–6).

32. Wakeman (1972, 39).

33. Huang (1981, 18).

34. Huang (1981, 18).

35. Hucker (1998, 78).

36. Hucker (1998, 78).

37. Wakeman (1972, 40) and Hucker (1998, 78).

38. Hucker (1998, 16).

39. The latter figure includes some 1,500 members of the central government in Beijing. See Hucker (1998, 29). An additional 51,000 lesser functionaries (吏), who assisted civil officials but were not paid by the state, served the civil government and the army. See Huang (1998, 48).

40. Hucker (1998, 41).

41. Liang (2008, 270) estimates China's population in 1602 at 56,305,050.

42. Huang (1974, 184) and Hucker (1998, 16).

43. Hucker (1998, 51). Moreover, salary rice was converted into these other forms of payment at very unfavorable below-market rates.

44. Huang (1974, 49).

45. Huang (1974, 184).

46. Huang (1974, 48).

47. Hucker (1998, 30).

48. Hucker (1998, 32).

49. Hucker (1998, 29).

50. Hucker (1998, 48–49).

51. Elvin (1973, 203).

52. Von Glahn (2016, 285–8).

53. Von Glahn (2016, 285–6).

54. Demographic historians estimate that China's population fell by at least 15 percent, and perhaps as much as a third, between 1340 and 1370. See Wu (2000, 387–91).

55. Von Glahn (2016, 285–7).

56. The Ming dynasty's examination system did not originally include provisions to ensure that the civil servants selected via this process were geographically balanced. Consequently, southerners and southeasterners, who represented the wealthiest and most cultured areas of the empire, dominated the early examinations. See Hucker (1998, 39).

57. Hucker (1998, 39).

58. A regional quota system was established in 1425 that reserved 40 percent of all metropolitan graduate degrees for northerners and left the remaining 60 percent for all others. Soon thereafter, a minor adjustment reserved 10 percent of the degrees for men from the "central" region, which included the relatively underdeveloped provinces of Sichuan, Yunnan, Guangxi, and Guizhou. The quota for northerners was reduced at this time to 35 percent, with 55 percent of degrees allocated to southerners, including southeasterners. Apart from occasional minor tinkering, these regional quotas remained in effect until the end of the Ming Dynasty. See Hucker (1998, 39).

59. Von Glahn (2016, 285–95).

60. Von Glahn (2016, 295–6).

61. Huang (1974, 39).

62. Huang (1974, 40). Land that yielded double crops paid taxes twice. Under previous dynasties the summer tax also comprised a number of commodities such as cotton, silk, and tea, and the Ming generally retained this practice.

63. Huang (1974, 89).

64. Huang (1974, 47). Fixed tax quotas were basically a Ming policy; they were followed less rigidly by the Tang and Song dynasties.

65. Hucker (1998, 26–7) shows that all male offspring of an emperor other than the heir were assigned a "fief" away from the capital and received state stipends equivalent to 10,000 bushels of grain every year; female offspring received the equivalent of 2,000 bushels annually.

66. Hucker (1998, 25).

67. Hucker (1998, 24–5).

68. Huang (1974, 6–7).

69. Huang (1974, 6–9).

70. Huang (1974, 56–7).

71. Hucker (1998, 20).

72. Hucker (1998, 70).

73. Huang (1974, 40) shows that a standard *mu* was approximately 6,000 square feet. This area of land in south China could be expected to produce 2 piculs of husked grain annually.

74. Hucker (1998, 62–71).

75. Hucker (1998, 72).

76. Hucker (1998, 72).

77. Hucker (1998, 89).

78. Huang (1974, 96). The law of avoidance required that officials avoided serving in their hometowns.

79. Huang (1974, 44).

80. Heijdra (1998, 458).

81. Hucker (1998, 91).

82. Hucker (1998, 54).

83. Hucker (1998, 75).

84. The inheritance system dated from the dynasty's founding era. A large proportion of later Ming officers, like Zhang Juzheng's grandfather and father, were awarded their posts based on their ancestors' actions to help the founding emperor win and consolidate the empire (Hucker 1998, 56). Some served under the Yongle emperor (Emperor Chengzu) in his usurpation of the throne in 1401 and in his subsequent campaigns.

85. Hucker (1998, 57). The Ming *wei-suo* system differed from the early Tang era's regimental army system of professional career soldiers, which is credited with the Tang dynasty's great military achievements (see chapter 3). See Hucker (1998, 62).

86. Salt production was based in the central coastal region of eastern China. There, wholesale merchants traditionally purchased vouchers entitling them to specific quantities of salt that could be claimed in certain sections of the country. The government proclaimed in 1370 that these vouchers could only be issued in return for grain deliveries to the northern frontier garrisons. Given the enormous potential profits of salt distribution, rich merchants soon began to set up merchant farms (商屯) in the north, where tenant farmers produced grain for delivery to nearby garrisons in exchange for the coveted vouchers. For more detail on this system, see Hucker (1998, 71).

87. Hucker (1998, 67–8).

88. Huang (1974, 295).

89. Altan reached a peace agreement with the Ming government in 1570 in exchange for his grandson, who had defected to the Ming and been taken hostage earlier that year. See Wei (1999, 371–85) for more details.

90. Huang (1998, 523).

91. Wei (1999, 502–38).

92. Miller (2009, 32).

93. Miller (2009, 32).

94. Huang (1998, 525–6).

95. Huang (1998, 524).

96. Miller (2009, 44–5).

97. Miller (2009, 38).

98. Miller (2009, 39).

99. Miller (2009, 44–5).

100. Heijdra (1998, 447–8). In the beginning, new surveys were sometimes performed too quickly, and there was good reason to believe that some reported results were false, but heavy punishments were soon imposed to remedy these problems. Measures were also taken to ensure that clerks did not have too much power or discretion; their names were recorded in the registers to hold them responsible for their work. The surveys mostly revealed large increases in cultivated area, although occasionally lower figures resulted from the new surveys, possibly because of the use of new standards of measurement or as a result of correcting what had originally been falsified figures.

101. Huang (1974, 301).

102. Throughout the Ming era, cadastral records were referred to as "fish-scale registers." The maps accompanying the landholding survey records depicted the boundaries of the many small plots, which had the appearance of scales on a fish. The term was used in the Song Dynasty as early as 1190; records compiled then continued to be used, updated or not, throughout the

Yuan and into the Ming era. The owners of registered plots all received certificates of ownership. See Heijdra (1998, 443–9).

103. Miller (2009, 51).

104. Huang (1974, 300–1).

105. Huang (1974, 301).

106. Heijdra (1998, 448–9).

107. Liang (1989, 38–9) and Huang (1974, 34).

108. Huang (1974, 34).

109. Huang (1974, 35–6).

110. Under the direction of the community (*li*) chief of the year, the *jia* performed the local tax collection and delivery, and fulfilled all material and labor needs on behalf of the entire community. The other units paid their regular taxes, but did not have service obligations that year. Thus in a ten-year period all households took a one-year turn at discharging their service obligations. See Huang (1974, 34–6).

111. Huang (1974, 110).

112. Huang (1974, 110).

113. Huang (1974, 132).

114. Huang (1974, 117–8).

115. Huang (1974, 122) shows that localities adopted one of two methods to implement the Single Whip. One approach, employed in Zhejiang, Fujian, and Guangdong, was to use the number of piculs of grain in the regular land tax assessment as the taxable unit and add a surcharge onto it. The second method, widely adopted in the north, was to directly assess the service levy payment on each *mu* of taxable land, in effect creating a general rate increase. Some localities, such as Suzhou and Songjiang, combined both approaches: they collected some portions of the service levy from each *mu* of taxable land, and others from an additional tax on each picul of grain.

116. Huang (1974, 15–6).

117. Huang (1974, 121).

118. Huang (1974, 131).

119. Huang (1974, 131) contests this argument, contending that the tax regime before the Single Whip was also progressive because it took into account property assessment. But as Liang (1989, 40–1) shows, before the reform, taxation was assessed based on both the number of adult males and landholdings, so landless households with several adult males were heavily burdened by the service levy.

120. Liang (1989, 42–3).

121. As Huang (1974, 110–117) shows, attempts to simplify the service levy had been ongoing for a century under different names. For example, starting in 1443, the Ming government introduced the "equally distributed service" (均徭), which split the previous ten-year service cycle into two five-year cycles. In each cycle, the county magistrate published a list of all the regular labor services required from the district and graded each item according to the weight of the burden it imposed. Individual households in the communities (*lijia*) were also graded in three main categories (upper, middle, and lower). Each taxpayer's grade was then matched with the grade of the service assignment. Such lists helped to check some of the abuses perpetuated by the community chiefs and to ensure that households performed their fair share of the

services. Several southern provinces also experimented with the "ten-sectioned tapestry method" (十段锦), in which the officials divided the ten years' payment at uniform rates into ten equal parts, and assessed them on the entire pool of available adult males and the total taxable acreage on an annual basis.

122. Huang (1974, 45).

123. Huang (1974, 96).

124. Liang (1989, 485–555).

125. Miller (2009, 28) and Huang (1974, 96).

126. Huang (1974, 298).

127. Huang (1998, 523).

128. Huang (1974, 297).

129. Huang (1998, 523).

130. Huang (1974, 299).

131. Huang (1998, 526). Miller (2009, 40) maintains that the mourning period during this time would have been three years.

132. Huang (1998, 526).

133. Huang (1974, 300).

134. Miller (2009, 3).

135. The "localist turn" refers to the change of elite strategies from building a national social network through intermarriages in the Tang Dynasty to building local social networks in the Song Dynasty. See chapter 4 for more details.

136. Miller (2009, 10–11).

137. Miller (2009, 11).

138. Miller (2009, 25).

139. Huang (1974, 97).

140. Huang (1974, 97).

141. Huang (1974, 97).

142. Lee (2009, 142).

143. Huang (1974, 97–8).

144. Huang (1974, 98).

145. Liang (1989, 485–555).

146. Levenson and Schurmann (1971, 92–4).

147. Miller (2009, 27).

148. Liang (1989, 485–555).

149. See Heijdra (1998, 492).

150. Of the 335 total events Liang records, I dropped all events that did not involve full-scale implementation, such as proposals, informal pilots, commentaries, endorsements, and revisions. The unit of analysis is prefecture—the lowest level at which a geographic information system (GIS) shapefile is available according to *China Historical Geographic Information System* (2018).

151. Liang's data includes 259 events, 10 of which occurred at the provincial level, 46 at the prefectural level, and 203 at the county level. Appendix figure D.1 (panel (a)) displays the information at the prefectural level. Focusing on prefectures inevitably creates a missing data problem. I therefore utilize the information on Single Whip implementation in provinces and

counties to expand the data in two ways. First, if there is no implementation information for a prefecture, I use the first year of implementation at the provincial level (above the prefecture) to proxy for the start of the reform in the prefecture. Appendix figure D.1 (panel (b)) shows the implementation using information from the provincial or prefectural level. Second, if there is no information at either the provincial or prefectural level, I use the first year a county (under the prefecture) implemented the reform to proxy for the start of the reform in the prefecture. Figure 6.2 uses information on implementation from the provincial, prefectural, and county levels. These two steps expand the sample size to 138 and 175, respectively.

152. Hucker (1998, 41).

153. I start with the *Veritable Records of the Ming Dynasty* (明实录), an official chronological history written by historians in the Ming era, and edited and published by Shanghai Shudian Press (2015). I rely especially on the essay *Rules on Rank, Level, Title, and Pay* (品阶勋禄制), which lists all positions and their ranks in the founding era. For contemporary sources, I consult Liu and Sun's (2014, 404) *Table of Ming Major Civil Ranks* (明代主要文职官员品级表), Zang, Zhu, and Wang's (1987, 121–3) *Government Institutions, Military Institutions, and Civil Service Examinations in Chinese Dynasties* (历代官制、兵制、科举制表释), Zhang's (2009) *Chronicle of Ming Civil Positions* (明代职官年表), and Wang's (2014) *Study on Ming State Organizations* (明代国家机构研究) to identify all the positions of rank 3b and above. I then rely on Zhang (2009) to find the names of the officials who occupied these positions during 1573–1620.

154. *China Biographical Database* (2018).

155. My sources combine primary sources, such as genealogical records, gazetteers, archival documents, and memorials, and secondary sources, such as biographical studies of these individuals. The sources include Chang (2008), Chang (2017), Chen (2015), Deng (2007), Feng (2012), Feng (2013), Guo (2007), Huang (2009b), Liang (2012), Liu (2008), Li (2018), Ma (2013), Peng (2015), Qiu (2004), Ren (2010), Wang (2007), Xie (2014), Xiong (2012), Xu (2015), Yang (2018), Ye (2010), Ye (2011), Yin (2014), Yuan (2017), Zeng (2012), Zhang (2008), Zhang (2018), Zhao (2017), Zhao (2009), Chen (2014), Chen (1997), Hai and Chen (1962), Chen (1995), Ding and Chen (2016), Feng (1997), Ge (1983), Huang (2009a), Hu (2007), Hu (1983), Jiao (1991), Jiao (1997), Jia (1996), Kang (2012), Zunhua (2013), Liang (1650), Li (2009), Li and Xie (2011), Li (1970), Liu (2009), Li (1997), Lu (2009), Song (1739), Sun (1814), Tang (1997), Tan (1891), Wang (2006), Wang (2016), Wang (2009), Wu (2012), Wu and Wu (1924), Wu (2009), Wu (1830), Wu (2014), Tang Clan (1990), Xu (2009), Xu (1964), Ma Clan (1870), Licheng Cultural and Historical Documents Research Commission (2010), Ye (1997), Yu (2015), Zhang (2016), Zhang (2014), Zhang (2015), Zhang (1997), Zhang (2009[1593]), Zhang and Wu (1987), Zhao (1993), Zhu (2015), Fang and Zhu (2009), and Zhao (1595). I match these sources with each major Ming official in appendix table D.2.

156. I employ the same metric as in chapter 2 to calculate Ming officials' localization scores, standardized by the number of kin. Higher scores indicate more localized kinship networks. Because the Northern Song and Ming territories were of roughly equal size, we can compare the standardized localization scores for their officials. The average standardized localization scores for Song and Ming officials are 0.102 and 0.448, respectively.

157. Specifically, I am comparing the marriage network among Ming officials (not shown here) with the Song officials in figure 2.6 panel (a). The Song network has a density of 0.011,

while the density of the Ming network is 0.0003. I interpret the Ming density with caution due to the severe problem of missing data.

158. I employ survival analysis to determine *whether* a prefecture adopted the Single Whip, as well as how long it took to do so. Survival time is calculated as the number of years a prefecture maintained the status quo of not implementing the reform after 1531, and failure is coded as 1 if the prefecture adopted the Single Whip. I use a Cox proportional hazard model to estimate the risk of prefectures adopting the new policy, because such models are more suitable when there are no "strong theoretical reasons to expect one distribution function over another." See Box-Steffensmeier and Jones (2004, 48). I use shared frailty models (based on province) to account for both *between-* and *within*-province variation in national representation and status quo survival. In some specifications, I include provincial fixed effects to control for provincial-level covariates, such as provincial leadership and policy, geography, climate, soil quality, culture, and history. An alternative explanation for why some localities adopted the Single Whip earlier than others is that soil quality and grain productivity were higher in the south, so the land tax represented a relatively heavier burden there, whereas the service levy was heavier in the north. According to this line of reasoning, when the Single Whip absorbed the service levy into the land tax, it changed little in the south, but created a substantial burden in the north. Many politicians of northern origin opposed the Single Whip on this basis. See Liang (1989, 333). The provincial fixed effects hold provincial-level variations constant and examine within-province variation in adoption of the Single Whip. Appendix table D.1 presents the summary statistics. Appendix table D.3 presents the estimates of the hazard ratios. A hazard ratio smaller than 1 indicates a lower probability of policy adoption. To avoid biases introduced by control variables, Model (1) only includes *N of major officials*. The estimates are stable when I employ alternative measures of the dependent variable, which use provincial- and county-level information to proxy for prefectural-level implementation. Appendix figure D.2 presents the survival and hazard rates.

159. Appendix figure D.3 panel (a) shows the regional distribution of advanced scholars—who obtained the highest degree—in the years before Wanli. The data on Ming advanced scholars is from *China Biographical Database* (2018). Panel (b) illustrates the strong positive correlation between the number of advanced scholars (1368–1572) and the number of major officials (1573–1620). Appendix table D.4 presents the regression results with provincial fixed effects, which confirms this correlation, with a statistically significant coefficient of 0.034. I am certainly not arguing that the exam quota and successful candidates were the only determinants of national representation. Wealth, cultural tradition, and past exam success were also important correlates of how many major officials a prefecture produced. The provincial fixed effects can partly control for these confounders, but my ability to rule out these alternative factors is constrained by the limited data available for this period.

160. Wei (1999, 897).

161. Miller (2009, 3).

Chapter 7

1. Coase (1937).

2. Coase (1937) and Williamson (1981).

3. See, e.g., North and Weingast (1989) and Greif (1989).

4. Greif (2006, chapter 8).

5. Fortes (1969, 3).

6. Samuelson (1958) and Diamond (1965).

7. Drazen (2000, 35).

8. Ho (1964, 121).

9. Ho (1964, 166).

10. Chen (2017, 7–8).

11. Ho (1964, 166).

12. Ho (1964, 166).

13. Beattie (1979, 100).

14. Beattie (1979, 103).

15. Schurmann (1956, 512).

16. Ebrey (1986, 2).

17. Zheng (2001, 311).

18. Ho (1964, 126–167).

19. Zheng (2001, 312).

20. Huang (1974, 26).

21. Skinner (1977, 20).

22. Zelin's calculation is based on constant returns to scale. In reality, however, because of scale economies, administrative units exhibit increasing returns to scale and do not need to increase in the same ratio as population does.

23. Zelin (1984, 306).

24. Zheng (2009, 57).

25. Zheng (2009, 57).

26. Szonyi (2002, 58).

27. The meltage fee was a charge added to regular tax remittances to compensate for the inevitable loss of silver that resulted when payments were melted down into large ingots for transporting to the central government. See Zelin (1984, 88).

28. Zelin (1984, xii).

29. Szonyi (2002, 60).

30. Szonyi (2002, 61).

31. Dincecco and Wang (2018, 343).

32. Tawney (1966, 77).

33. Perry (1980, 3). Kung and Ma (2014), Jia (2014), and Dincecco and Wang (2020) show a significant correlation between negative climate shocks and peasant rebellions. Also see chapter 2 for a discussion and empirical analysis of the relationship between climate shock and conflict.

34. Spence (1996, 160).

35. Rowe (2007, 28–9).

36. Beattie (1979, 45).

37. Greif (2000, 254).

38. Olson (1982, 18).

39. Rawski (1979, 183).

40. Chaffee (1989, 344).

41. Beattie (1979, 88–89).

42. Beattie (1979, 37).

43. Beattie (1979, 107).

44. For an application of the overlapping generations model to real-world cases, see Bates (2017, 69).

45. Beattie (1979, 108).

46. For instance, politician and scholar Fan Zhongyan devised a charitable estate (义庄) around 1049 to provide permanent maintenance and education for all branches of his family. See Beattie (1979, 9) and Faure (2007, 68). Recall that this was a time of "the localist turn" when elites renewed their interest in promoting large-scale kinship organizations and activities at the local level (chapter 5).

47. Zheng (2001, 309–310).

48. Zheng (2001, 122).

49. Zheng (2001, 122–3).

50. Zheng (2001, 114).

51. Zheng (2001, 308).

52. Zheng (2001, 99).

53. While a lineage organization was based on a single clan with the same surname, a lineage coalition was built by multiple clans with different surnames.

54. Li (2007a) provides detailed accounts of how social communities, through various kinds of granaries, collaborated with the state in famine relief during the Qing era.

55. Zheng (2009, 58).

56. Zheng (2009, 58).

57. Beattie (1979, 52).

58. Beattie (1979, 52).

59. Ostrom (1990, 24).

60. Hardin (1968, 1243).

61. Beattie (1979, 72).

62. Beattie (1979, 72).

63. Beattie (1979, 72–5).

64. Beattie (1979, 76).

65. Beattie (1979, 77).

66. Beattie (1979, 70–1).

67. Beattie (1979, 79).

68. Wang (1973, 27).

69. Szonyi (2002, 66).

70. Szonyi (2002, 67).

71. Rowe (2007, 54).

72. Rowe (2007, 65–6).

73. Rowe (2007, 205).

74. Rowe (2007, 29).

75. For more on local governments' legal functions, see Ch'u (1962).

76. Organization theory predicts that when cooperation leads to efficiency gains that the market and legal system fail to capture, private-order institutions will emerge. See Williamson (1985, 168) and Greif (1989, 866).

77. Zheng (2001, 269–271).

78. Zheng (2001, 272–273).

79. Zheng (2001, 281).

80. Zheng (2001, 285–286).

81. Beattie (1979, 107–108).

82. Hsiao (1960, 334).

83. Beattie (1979, 94).

84. Olson (1965, 51).

85. Hsiao (1960, 334).

86. Beattie (1979, 95–106).

87. Williamson (1983, 519).

88. Beattie (1979, 41).

89. Beattie (1979, 52).

90. Beattie (1979, 104).

91. Beattie (1979, 41).

92. Beattie (1979, 100–101).

93. Wang (2008).

94. For instance, Wang's registry includes all ten thousand microfilmed genealogy records archived by the Genealogical Society of Utah—the largest overseas collection of Chinese genealogy. See Wang (2008, 8–9).

95. Appendix figure A.1 shows a sample of the *Catalog*.

96. Greif and Tabellini (2017, 2).

97. *China Historical Geographic Information System* (2018).

98. I used optical character recognition software to read the entire registry into a Microsoft Excel file. With the help of research assistants, I manually checked each entry in order to ensure accuracy.

99. Appendix figure E.1 shows the number of lineage organizations in each county. I also use *Number of genealogy books* during 1801–1850 as an alternative dependent variable. Appendix figure E.2 shows the number of genealogy books in each county. While the *Number of lineage organizations* reflects the development of private-order organizations, the *Number of genealogy books* proxies for the activities of these organizations. Both figures are consistent with previous qualitative evidence that lineage organizations and lineage activities were more prevalent along the Yangtze River and in the southeast than in other parts of China. See Freedman (1958, 129).

100. Clans were traditionally expected to update their genealogy book every three generations. See Feng (2006, 67). John Chaffee shows that males typically married and had their first child in their late teens. See Chaffee (1989, 345). Three generations translates into $3 \times 18 = 54$ years, or roughly one-half century.

101. *China Biographical Database* (2018).

102. Chen (2017).

103. Appendix figure E.3 shows the number of advanced scholars in each county. Consistent with the qualitative evidence, exam success was concentrated along the Yangtze River and in the southeast. See Ho (1964, 222–37).

104. These pupils were called *shengyuan* (生员)—entry-level examiners. See Chang (1955, 73–79).

105. Bai and Jia (2016, 685).

106. Nanjing Military Academy (2003). Scholars have widely used the *Catalog* to study historical conflicts in China. For example, see Bai and Kung (2011) and Jia (2014). This catalog contains detailed information including dates, the locations of individual battles, and the leaders of each major internal and external conflict that took place in China from approximately 1000 BCE to the downfall of the Qing Dynasty in 1911. The quality of the conflict data coverage may vary by place and time. A wide range of geographic and historical controls and prefectural fixed effects will help account for these regional differences.

107. Appendix figure E.4 shows the number of conflicts in each county.

108. This is consistent with the pattern identified by Dincecco and Wang (2018) that conflicts in China were mostly internal throughout the imperial period. Some of the largest conflicts included the battles between the new Qing government and the remaining Ming forces, the rebellion of Wu Sangui, the Qing campaign against the Dzungars in Xinjiang, and the White Lotus Rebellion. I do not differentiate between internal and external conflicts in the empirical analysis, because they both represent violence. For a fine-grained analysis examining different types of conflicts, see Dincecco and Wang (2020).

109. Because all three variables are skewed with lots of zeros, I take the inverse hyperbolic sine (IHS) of the raw numbers. For example, N of Lineage Organizations (IHS) $\equiv$ ln $[N\ of\ Lineage\ Organizations + (N\ of\ Lineage\ Organizations^2 + 1)^{1/2}]$. This transformation reduces the range of the mean and variance, and allows me to make use of all observations, since it is defined at zero. See Burbidge, Magee, and Robb (1988) for a justification of using IHS.

110. Appendix table E.2 shows the regression results. Mazumder and Wang (2021) provide a more stringent test of the relationship between exam success and lineage organizations and obtain the same results. Since the measure of conflict combines battles fought in both external and internal conflicts, its coefficient reflects the weighted average effect of all types of conflict. Dincecco and Wang (2020) break down different types of conflicts and provide a more nuanced test.

111. Weber (1946 [1918], 78) (emphasis in original).

112. Bates (2010, 30).

113. Smith (1986 [1776], 109).

114. For discussions of how kinship institutions influenced China's economic development in the late imperial era, also see Zhang (2017), who argues that kinship hierarchies were the primary determinants of sociopolitical status, which allowed many poor but senior individuals to possess status and political authority highly disproportionate to their wealth. For a review of the role of informal institutions in China's long-term economic development, see Ma (2004).

115. By limiting the circumstances under which wealth could be passed on to heirs, the Church could inherit large amounts of property and attain political power. See Goody (1983, 123).

116. Greif (2006, 308–309).

117. Henrich (2020).

118. Greif (2006, 310).

Chapter 8

1. This period spanned from the Kangxi Emperor's final consolidation of Qing rule, in around 1680, to the death of the Qianlong Emperor in 1799. See Wakeman (1970) and Rowe (2009, 63).

2. Elliott (2001, 47).

3. Elliott (2001, 47).

4. Elliott (2001, 48).

5. Elliott (2001, 56).

6. Farquhar (1968, 204).

7. Elliott (2001, 39).

8. Fletcher (1986, 23)

9. Elliott (2001, 39).

10. Elliott (2001, 59).

11. Elliott (2001, 62).

12. Elliott (2001, 40).

13. Elliott (2001, 62).

14. Elliott (2001, 62).

15. Elliott (2001, 128).

16. Editorial Team of the Chinese Military History (2006, 499).

17. Elliott (2001, 129).

18. Wang (1973, 9).

19. Wang (1973, 80).

20. Spence (2002, 178).

21. In Zhili Province, for instance, the labor service tax was apportioned upon the land tax by adding one-fifth to the latter—that is, 0.2 tael more was to be collected for each tael of the land tax proper. See Wang (1973, 10).

22. Wang (1973, 10).

23. Wang (1973, 80). For the former, the Qing government granted certain merchants a monopoly on selling salt in assigned regions of consumption; in return, the merchants paid tax in proportion to the quantity of salt they sold. For the latter, customs stations near commercial or high-traffic areas collected taxes on commodities in transit. A designated station in the Guangdong Delta was also tasked with collecting import and export duties. See Wang (1973, 10).

24. Wang (1973, 21).

25. Wang (1973, 27).

26. Rowe (2009, 63).

27. Elliott (2001, 53).

28. Elliott (2001, 79–80).

29. Spence (2002, 162).

30. Rowe (2009, 40–41).

31. Rowe (2009, 41–42).

32. Zelin (1984, 201)

33. Rowe (2009, 42).

34. Zelin (1984, xii–xiv).

35. Rowe (2009, 40).

36. Zelin (1984, xii).

37. Wang (1973, 6).

38. Malthus (1992 [1806], 183–4).

39. Rosenthal and Wong (2011, 48–49).

40. Sng (2014, 119).

41. Elliott (2001, 129).

42. Wang (1973, 21).

43. Wang (1973, 24).

44. The land classified-rate structure was based on the anticipated productivity of the land and included several categories such as paddy land, dry land, terrace land, and marsh land. Each category was further divided into a number of grades and subgrades, which varied by province and even between districts in the same province. See Wang (1973, 32). Many parts of the country instead fixed a standard rate for land of diverse productivity by converting several *mu* or more of lower-grade land into one *mu* of upper-grade land, or into one fiscal *mu*. This approach sought to streamline multiple tax rates into a single rate and to ensure that a district's registered land and land tax quota conformed with the established quota of acreage and taxes. See Ho (1959, 103–116).

45. Wang (1973, 32).

46. Sng (2014). Also see Koyama, Moriguchi, and Sng (2018) and Sng and Moriguchi (2014).

47. Zhang (2021).

48. Ma and Rubin (2019). Also see Hao and Liu (2020), who argue that the lack of a credible commitment from the emperor to the provincial governors led to the latter's weak incentive to collect revenues.

49. For both cases, see Beattie (1979, 72–5).

50. Elliott (2001, 201).

51. Elliott (2001, 203).

52. Elliott (2001, 40).

53. Xi (2019).

54. Wang (1973, 28).

55. Wang (1973, 29).

56. Wang (1973, 27).

57. Wang (1973, 33).

58. Wang (1973, 34).

59. Elliott (2001, 191–192).

60. Elliott (2001, 193).

61. Elliott (2001, 307).

62. Lee (2000).

63. Lee (2000, table 1.1).

64. Chen (1992, 194–199).

65. Elliott (2001, 310).

66. Elliott (2001, 313–322).

67. Mann and Kuhn (1974, 144). The White Lotus Society was a network of devotional popular religion congregations in the belt of provinces reaching from Sichuan in the west to Shandong in the east. The Qing army put down the rebellion in the early nineteenth century. See Mann and Kuhn (1974, 136–144) and Rowe (2009, 155–157).

68. Wakeman (1975, 137).

69. Shi and Xu (2008, 55).

70. Shi and Xu (2008, 107) and Duara (1988, 3).

71. Chang (1962, 151).

72. Duara (1988, 219).

73. Skocpol (1979, 73).

74. Wakeman (1975, 181–2).

75. Spence (1996, 81).

76. Ho (1959, 238).

77. Spence (1996, 141).

78. Spence (1996, 141).

79. Luo (2009, 753–4).

80. Luo (2009, 787–810).

81. Spence (1996, 193).

82. Platt (2012, 150).

83. Kuhn (1970, 10), Shi and Xu (2008, 58–60), and Platt (2012, 118).

84. Platt (2012, 119).

85. Kuhn (1970, 89–92).

86. Yang (2012, 335).

87. Yang (2012, 335).

88. Other mass rebellions broke out around the same period across Qing territory, including the Nian and Small Swords Society Rebellions. Most such rebellions were put down in 1869. For this reason, in the empirical analysis I code the Taiping Rebellion period as 1850–1869.

89. Wright (1962).

90. Rosenthal and Wong (2011, 201–2).

91. Rosenthal and Wong (2011, 201) and Von Glahn (2016, 380–382).

92. Rosenthal and Wong (2011, 200).

93. Shi and Xu (2008, 50).

94. Shi and Xu (2008, 232).

95. Kuhn (1970, 211–225) and Von Glahn (2016, 380–381).

96. Kuhn (1970, 211).

97. Duara (1988, 73–4).

98. Skocpol (1979, 78).

99. Wakeman (1975, 228–232, 235–237).

100. Bai and Jia (2016).

101. Wakeman (1975, 225).

102. Wakeman (1975, 228).

103. This figure reproduces figure 2.7 from chapter 2.

104. The intuition behind this analysis is based on a difference-in-differences (DiD) approach. In the DiD framework, the "first difference" is temporal—the extent to which elite collective action changed from the pre-Taiping to the post-Taiping period, while the "second difference" is regional—the extent to which elite collective action changed due to exposure to mass rebellion. Formally, I denote elite collective action in the control group before the Taiping Rebellion as Y_1^c and after the rebellion as Y_2^c. Similarly, I denote pre-Taiping clan activity in the treatment group as Y_1^t and post-Taiping activity as Y_2^t. The DiD estimator is therefore $(Y_2^t - Y_2^c) - (Y_1^t - Y_1^c)$.

105. To reduce the skewness of the variable, I take the inverse hyperbolic sine (IHS) of the raw numbers. Here, the identification assumption is that if the Taiping Rebellion had never taken place, then average elite collective action for the control and treatment groups would have followed a common trend. Thus, the control group can be used to infer the counterfactual evolution of average clan activity in the absence of mass rebellion for the treatment group.

106. I estimate the following DiD specification:

$$Number\ of\ Genealogy\ Books(IHS)_{i,t} = \alpha + \beta Period_{i,1870-1889} \times Rebellion_{i,1850-1869}$$
$$+ \mu_i + \lambda_t + \epsilon_{i,t}. \tag{8.1}$$

The outcome variable, *Number of genealogy books (IHS)*, reflects local elite collective action in a county in each twenty-year period between 1790 and 1889 (i.e., 1790–1809, 1810–1829, 1830–1849, 1850–1869, 1870–1889). The treatment variable is *Mass rebellion (1850–1869)*, which measures the number of mass rebellions in a county during the Taiping Rebellion. Appendix figure F.1 shows the locations of all mass rebellions during this time. $Period_{1870-1889}$ is a binary indicator variable for the period 1870–1889 (the pre-Taiping period, 1830–1849, is the reference group). The DiD estimator is $Period_{1870-1889} \times Rebellion_{1850-1869}$. I expect the coefficient estimate on this estimator to be positive in sign and statistically significant. I also control for county and period fixed effects. All standard errors are robust, and clustered at the county level. Appendix table F.1 shows the summary statistics of all the variables used in this section.

107. Appendix table F.2 shows the results. Note that the results do not strongly support the common trend assumption for the DiD analysis because the DiD estimator for the period from 1810–1829 to 1830–1849 is significant at the 10 percent level. I therefore do not interpret the finding as causal.

108. The information on the locations of these groups is from Guo (2015).

109. Appendix figure F.2 shows the number of genealogy books recorded in each county during this period. Given that this test uses cross-sectional data (and thus I can no longer include county fixed effects), I address the possibility of omitted variable bias by including prefectural fixed effects and county-level control variables for local (i.e., agricultural, economic, and geographical) observables. These covariates include latitude, longitude, area, distance to Beijing (log), distance to major rivers (log), distance to nearest coast (log), passing Qing courier routes, elevation, slope, population density, and agricultural suitability for rice. Appendix table F.3 displays the results when I regress *Declaration of independence* on post-Taiping elite activity between 1890 and 1909 (*Genealogy books*). Column (1) shows the raw

bivariate correlation, Column (2) adds prefectural fixed effects, and column (3) adds the county-level control variables. The coefficient estimate is positive in sign and highly significant across all specifications.

110. Bai and Jia (2016).

111. I rely on the same source as Bai and Jia (2016) for Qing exam quota data: the *Imperially Established Institutes and Laws of the Great Qing Dynasty* of Aisin Gioro (1899, vols. 371–80).

112. Stone (2017 [1972], 9).

113. Hoffman (2015, 19–66).

Chapter 9

1. Herbst (2000, 11).

2. Fortes and Evans-Pritchard (1950, 5–7).

3. Murdock's five-point scale differentiates between more and less centralized states. Only three African societies achieved the maximum centralization score. See Murdock (1967).

4. Baldwin (2016, 21–3).

5. Kopytoff (1987, 29).

6. Vansina (1966, 247).

7. Herbst (2000, 45).

8. Herbst (2000, 56).

9. Cited from Herbst (2000, 83).

10. Baldwin (2016, 30).

11. Baldwin (2016, 31).

12. Boone (2014, 28).

13. See, e.g., Migdal (1988, 104).

14. Boone (2003).

15. Clapham (1982, 84–5).

16. Migdal (1988, 116).

17. Migdal (1988, 123).

18. Herbst (2000, 126,131,173).

19. Bates (2015, 21).

20. Herbst (2000, 177).

21. Baldwin (2016, 3–4).

22. Huntington (1993).

23. Bates (2015, 26).

24. Baldwin (2016, 9–10).

25. Baldwin (2016, 11).

26. Herbst (2000, chapter 5).

27. Herbst (2000, 145–7).

28. Herbst (2000, 152).

29. Herbst (2000, 154).

30. Herbst (2000, 157).

31. Centeno (2002, 10).

32. Centeno (2002, 17).

33. Centeno (2002, 127).

34. Centeno (2002, 23).

35. O'Donnell (1993, 1359).

36. Centeno (2002, 143).

37. Centeno (2002, 142).

38. Centeno (2002, 151).

39. Centeno (2002, 143).

40. Centeno (2002, 48).

41. Centeno (2002, 145–6).

42. Centeno (2002, 146).

43. Kurtz (2013, 39–40).

44. Soifer (2015, 4–5).

45. Soifer (2015, 22).

46. Muzzuca (2021, 1).

47. Muzzuca (2021, 9–10).

48. Scott (2017, 3).

49. Crone (1994, 457).

50. Kennedy (2010, 283).

51. Crone (1994, 457).

52. Crone (1994, 447).

53. Crone (1994, 458).

54. Crone (1994, 449).

55. Rubin (2017, 49).

56. Goldschmidt Jr and Boum (2015, 50).

57. Crone (1980, 31).

58. Rubin (2017, 57).

59. For example, two Shi'a dynasties threatened the Sunni Abbasids in Baghdad: the Fatimids, who challenged their legitimacy, and the Buyids, who ended their autonomy. See Goldschmidt Jr and Boum (2015, 73).

60. Crone (1980, 75–84).

61. Lapidus (1973, 39).

62. Blaydes (2017, 494).

63. Blaydes and Chaney (2013, 22).

64. Arjomand (2010, 249).

65. Barkey (1994, 30).

66. Barkey (1994, 9).

67. Barkey (1994, 2).

68. Barkey (1994, 26).

69. Barkey (1994, 11–12).

70. Barkey (1994, 36).

71. Barkey (1994, 56).

72. For an analysis of the role of Islam in the Middle East's political and economic development, see Kuran (2012) and Rubin (2017).

73. Goldschmidt Jr and Boum (2015, 119).

74. Goldschmidt Jr and Boum (2015, 173–4).

75. Anderson (2014, 4–8).

76. Anderson (2014, 9–10).

77. Anderson (2014, 10–1).

78. Anderson (2014, 3).

79. Book-length works on post-1911 state building include Duara (1988), Shue (1988), Pomeranz (1993), Perry (1993), Koss (2018), Strauss (2020), and Ghosh (2020).

80. Rankin, Fairbank, and Feuerwerker (1986, 30).

81. Perry (1980, 224, 231).

82. Rankin, Fairbank, and Feuerwerker (1986, 31).

83. Ch'en (1986, 193).

84. Perry (1980, 241).

85. Bianco (1986, 312–3).

86. Mao (1965, 93).

87. Skocpol (1979).

88. Perry (1980, 239).

89. Koss (2018, chapter 5) discusses the CCP's organizational development in the south vs. north during the war era.

90. Selden (1970).

91. For accounts of land reforms in the 1950s, see Strauss (2020, chapter 4).

92. Schurmann (1966, 405–42).

93. Walder (1988).

94. Shue (1988).

95. E.g., Fearon and Laitin (2003).

96. Fukuyama (2014).

97. Evans and Rauch (1999).

BIBLIOGRAPHY

Abramson, Scott F., and Carles Boix. 2019. "Endogenous Parliaments: The Domestic and International Roots of Long-Term Economic Growth and Executive Constraints in Europe." *International Organization* 73(4):793–837.

Acemoglu, Daron, and James A. Robinson. 2019. *The Narrow Corridor: States, Societies, and the Fate of Liberty*. New York, NY: Penguin Press.

Acemoglu, Daron, and James A. Robinson. 2020. "The Emergence of Weak, Despotic and Inclusive States." *NBER Working Paper No. 23657*.
   URL: *http://www.nber.org/papers/w23657*

Acemoglu, Daron, James A. Robinson, and Ragnar Torvik. 2020. "The Political Agenda Effect and State Centralization." *Journal of Comparative Economics* 48(4):749–778.

Acemoglu, Daron, Simon Johnson, and James Robinson. 2005. "The Rise of Europe: Atlantic Trade, Institutional Change, and Economic Growth." *American Economic Review* 95(3):546–579.

Aisin Gioro, Kungang. 1899. *Imperially Established Institutes and Laws of the Great Qing Dynasty (Qinding daqing huidian shili)*. Beijing, China: Zhonghua Book Company (Zhonghua shuju).

Alesina, Alberto, and Romain Wacziarg. 1998. "Openness, Country Size and Government." *Journal of Public Economics* 69(3):305–321.

Allen, Robert C. 2009. "Agricultural Productivity and Rural Incomes in England and the Yangtze Delta, c. 1620–c. 1820." *The Economic History Review* 62(3):525–550.

Allen, Robert C., Jean-Pascal Bassino, Debin Ma, Chritine Moll-Murata, and Jan Luiten Van Zanden. 2011. "Wages, Prices, and Living Standards in China, 1738–1925: In Comparison with Europe, Japan, and India." *The Economic History Review* 64(1):8–38.

Almond, Gabriel Abraham, and G. Bingham Powell. 1978. *Comparative Politics: System, Process, and Policy*. Boston, MA: Little, Brown and Company.

Anderson, Lisa. 2014. *The State and Social Transformation in Tunisia and Libya, 1830–1980*. Princeton, NJ: Princeton University Press.

Anderson, Perry. 1979. *Lineages of the Absolutist State*. New York, NY: Verso Books.

Arjomand, Saïd Amir. 2010. "Legitimacy and Political Organization: Caliphs, Kings, and Regimes." In *The New Cambridge History of Islam*, ed. Robert Irwin. Vol. 4. New York, NY: Cambridge University Press, chapter 7, pp. 225–273.

Ashraf, Quamrul, and Oded Galor. 2013. "Genetic Diversity and the Origins of Cultural Fragmentation." *American Economic Review* 103(3):528–533.

Bai, Ying, and James Kai-sing Kung. 2011. "Climate Shocks and Sino-Nomadic Conflict." *Review of Economics and Statistics* 93(3):970–981.

Bai, Ying and Ruixue Jia. 2016. "Elite Recruitment and Political Stability: The Impact of the Abolition of China's Civil Service Exam." *Econometrica* 84(2):677–733.

Baldwin, Kate. 2016. *The Paradox of Traditional Chiefs in Democratic Africa.* New York, NY: Cambridge University Press.

Barkey, Karen. 1994. *Bandits and Bureaucrats: The Ottoman Route to State Centralization.* Ithaca, NY: Cornell University Press.

Barraclough, Geoffrey. 1976. *The Crucible of Europe: The Ninth and Tenth Centuries in European History.* Berkeley, CA: University of California Press.

Baten, Joerg, Debin Ma, Stephen Morgan, and Qing Wang. 2010. "Evolution of Living Standards and Human Capital in China in the 18–20th Centuries: Evidences from Real Wages, Age-Heaping, and Anthropometrics." *Explorations in Economic History* 47(3):347–359.

Bates, Robert H. 2010. *Prosperity and Violence: The Political Economy of Development.* New York, NY: W. W. Norton.

Bates, Robert H. 2015. *When Things Fell Apart.* New York, NY: Cambridge University Press.

Bates, Robert H. 2017. *The Development Dilemma: Security, Prosperity, and a Return to History.* Princeton, NJ: Princeton University Press.

Bates, Robert H., Avner Greif, Margaret Levi, Jean-Laurent Rosenthal, and Barry R. Weingast. 1998. *Analytic Narratives.* Princeton, NJ: Princeton University Press.

Bates, Robert H., and Da-Hsiang Donald Lien. 1985. "A Note on Taxation, Development, and Representative Government." *Politics and Society* 14(1):53–70.

Beattie, Hilary J. 1979. *Land and Lineage in China: A Study of T'ung-Ch'eng County, Anhwei, in the Ming and Ch'ing Dynasties.* New York, NY: Cambridge University Press.

Besley, Timothy and Torsten Persson. 2008. "Wars and State Capacity." *Journal of the European Economic Association* 6(2-3):522–530.

Besley, Timothy, and Torsten Persson. 2009. "The Origins of State Capacity: Property Rights, Taxation, and Politics." *American Economic Review* 99(4):1218–1244.

Bianco, Lucien. 1986. "Peasant Movements." In *The Cambridge History of China: Republican China, 1912–1949, Part 2,* ed. John King Fairbank and Albert Feuerwerker. Vol. 13. New York, NY: Cambridge University Press, chapter 6, pp. 270–328.

Blaydes, Lisa. 2017. "State Building in the Middle East." *Annual Review of Political Science* 20:487–504.

Blaydes, Lisa, and Christopher Paik. 2016. "The Impact of Holy Land Crusades on State Formation: War Mobilization, Trade Integration, and Political Development in Medieval Europe." *International Organization* 70(3):551–586.

Blaydes, Lisa, and Eric Chaney. 2013. "The Feudal Revolution and Europe's Rise: Political Divergence of the Christian West and the Muslim World before 1500 CE." *American Political Science Review* 107(1):16–34.

Bloch, Marc. 2014. *Feudal Society.* London, UK: Routledge.

Bol, Peter K. 1990. "The Sung Examination System and the Shih." *Asia Major* 3(2):149–171.

Bol, Peter K. 1994. *"This Culture of Ours": Intellectual Transitions in T'ang and Sung China.* Palo Alto, CA: Stanford University Press.

Bol, Peter K. 2008. *Neo-Confucianism in History.* Cambridge, MA: Harvard University Press.

Bol, Peter K. 2015. "Reconceptualizing the Order of Things in Northern and Southern Sung." In *The Cambridge History of China: Sung China, 960–1279, Part II*, ed. John W. Chaffee and Denis Twitchett. Vol. 5. New York, NY: Cambridge University Press, chapter 9, pp. 665–726.

Boone, Catherine. 2003. *Political Topographies of the African State: Territorial Authority and Institutional Choice*. New York, NY: Cambridge University Press.

Boone, Catherine. 2014. *Property and Political Order in Africa: Land Rights and the Structure of Politics*. New York, NY: Cambridge University Press.

Bossler, Beverly Jo. 1998. *Powerful Relations: Kinship, Status, & the State in Sung China (960–1279)*. Cambridge, MA: Harvard University Asia Center.

Boucoyannis, Deborah. 2015. "No Taxation of Elites, No Representation: State Capacity and the Origins of Representation." *Politics & Society* 43(3):303–332.

Box-Steffensmeier, Janet M., and Bradford S. Jones. 2004. *Event History Modeling: A Guide for Social Scientists*. New York, NY: Cambridge University Press.

Bray, Francesca. 1986. *The Rice Economies: Technology and Development in Asian Societies*. Oxford, UK: Basil Blackwell.

Brewer, John. 1989. *The Sinews of Power: War, Money, and the English State, 1688–1783*. Cambridge, MA: Harvard University Press.

Broadberry, Stephen, Hanhui Guan, and David Daokui Li. 2018. "China, Europe, and the Great Divergence: A Study in Historical National Accounting, 980–1850." *The Journal of Economic History* 78(4):955–1000.

Broder, Andrei, Ravi Kumar, Farzin Maghoul, Prabhakar Raghavan, Sridhar Rajagopalan, Raymie Stata, Andrew Tomkins, and Janet Wiener. 2000. "Graph Structure in the Web." *Computer Networks* 33(1-6):309–320.

Burbidge, John, Lonnie Magee, and Leslie Robb. 1988. "Alternative Transformations to Handle Extreme Values of the Dependent Variable." *Journal of the American Statistical Association* 83(401):123–127.

Burke, Marshall, Solomon Hsiang and Edward Miguel. 2015. "Climate and Conflict." *Annual Review of Economics* 7(1):577–617.

Burt, Ronald S. 1992. *Structural Holes: The Social Structure of Competition*. Cambridge, MA: Harvard University Press.

Cao, Shuji. 2000. *China Demographic History: Qing Dynasty (Zhongguo renkou shi: Qing shiqi)*. Shanghai, China: Fudan University Press (Fudan daxue chubanshe).

Centeno, Miguel Angel. 2002. *Blood and Debt: War and the Nation-State in Latin America*. University Park, PA: The Pennsylvania State University Press.

Chaffee, John W. 1989. "Status, Family and Locale: An Analysis of Examination Lists from Sung China." In *A Collection of Essays on Song History Studies to Celebrate the Birthday of Dr. James Liu (Liu Zijian boshi jinian songshou songshi yanjiu lunji)*, ed. Kinugawa Tsuyoshi. Tokyo, Japan: Dohosha, chapter E1, pp. 341–356.

Chaffee, John W. 1995. *The Thorny Gates of Learning in Sung China: A Social History of Examinations*. Albany, NY: State University of New York Press.

Chaffee, John W. 2015a. "Introduction: Reflections on the Sung." In *The Cambridge History of China: Sung China, 960–1279, Part II*, ed. John W. Chaffee and Denis Twitchett. Vol. 5. New York, NY: Cambridge University Press, Introduction, pp. 1–18.

Chaffee, John W. 2015*b*. "Sung Education: Schools, Academies, and Examinations." In *The Cambridge History of China: Sung China, 960–1279, Part II*, ed. John W. Chaffee and Denis Twitchett. Vol. 5. New York, NY: Cambridge University Press, chapter 5, pp. 286–320.

Chang, Borui. 2017. "A Chronology of Zhao Yongxian (Zhao Yongxian nianpu)." M.A. Thesis, Shanghai Normal University.

Chang, Chung-li. 1955. *The Chinese Gentry*. Seattle, WA: University of Washington Press.

Chang, Chung-li. 1962. *The Income of the Chinese Gentry*. Seattle, WA: University of Washington Press.

Chang, Rui. 2008. "Chronology of Shen Shixing (Shen Shixing nianpu)." M.A. Thesis, Lanzhou University.

Chen, Aizhong. 2015. "The History of Yu Clan in Tuochuan, Wuyuan (Wuyuan tuochuan Yu shi jiazushi tanwei)." *Huizhou Social Sciences (Huizhou shehui kexue)* (5):48–56.

Chen, Feng. 1992. *A Study of Qing's Military Expenses (Qingdai junfei yanjiu)*. Hubei, China: Wuhan University Press (Wuhan daxue chubanshe).

Chen, Gaohua, and Weimin Shi. 2007. *Comprehensive History of Chinese Economy: Yuan (Zhongguo jingji tongshi: Yuandai jingji juan)*. Beijing, China: Economic Daily Press (Jingji ribao chubanshe).

Chen, Gaoyong. 2007 [1940]. *Categorization and Statistics of Natural Disasters and Conflicts in Historical China (Zhongguo lidai tianzai renhuo biao)*. Beijing, China: Beijing Library Press.

Chen, Hongjun. 2014. *A Sketch of the Epitaph for Wife of He Weibo, the Shangshu of the Ming Dynasty Nanjing Ritual Department Unearthed in Guangzhou (Guangzhou chutu mingdai nanjing libu shangsu He Weibo furen laoshi muzhi jilue)*. Guangdong, China: Lingnan Literature and History Publishing House (Lingnan wenshi).

Ch'en, Jerome. 1986. "The Communist Movement 1927–1937." In *The Cambridge History of China: Republican China, 1912–1949, Part 2*, ed. John King Fairbank and Albert Feuerwerker. Vol. 13. New York, NY: Cambridge University Press, chapter 4, pp. 168–229.

Chen, Song. 2017. "The State, the Gentry, and Local Institutions: The Song Dynasty and Long-Term Trends from Tang to Qing." *Journal of Chinese History* 1(1):141–182.

Chen, Ting, and Daniel Mattingly. 2021. "The Missionary Roots of Nationalism: Evidence from China." Forthcoming, *Journal of Politics*.

Chen, Yidian. 1997. *Compilation Draft of Scholar Mr. Chen (Chen xueshi xiansheng chuji)*. Beijing, China: Beijing Press (Beijing chubanshe).

Chen, Yinke. 2001. *Collected Works of Chen Kinke (Chen Yinke ji)*. Beijing, China: Joint Publishing (Sanlian shudian).

Chen, Younian. 1995. *Chen Gongjie Court Document Collection (Chen Gongjie gong wen ji)*. Shanghai, China: Shanghai Ancient Books Publishing House (Shanghai guji chubanshe).

China Biographical Database. 2018.
   URL: *https://projects.iq.harvard.edu/cbdb/home*

China Historical Geographic Information System. 2018.
   URL: *http://sites.fas.harvard.edu/%7Echgis/*

Ch'u, T'ung-tsu. 1962. *Government in China under the Ch'ing*. Cambridge, MA: Harvard University Press.

Clapham, Christopher S. 1982. *Private Patronage and Public Power: Political Clientelism in the Modern State*. London, UK: Burns & Oates.

Clark, Gregory. 2008. *A Farewell to Alms: A Brief Economic History of the World*. Princeton, NJ: Princeton University Press.

Coase, Ronald Harry. 1937. "The Nature of the Firm." *Economica* 4(16):386–405.

Cox, Gary W. 2016. *Marketing Sovereign Promises: Monopoly Brokerage and the Growth of the English State*. New York, NY: Cambridge University Press.

Creel, Herrlee G. 1964. "The Beginnings of Bureaucracy in China: The Origin of the Hsien." *The Journal of Asian Studies* 23(2):155–184.

Crone, Patricia. 1980. *Slaves on Horses: The Evolution of the Islamic Polity*. New York, NY: Cambridge University Press.

Crone, Patricia. 1994. "The Tribe and the State." In *The State: Critical Concepts*, ed. John A. Hall. London, UK: Routledge, chapter 17, pp. 446–473.

Dahl, Robert A. 1959. *Who Governs?: Democracy and Power in an American City*. New Haven, CT: Yale University Press.

Dalby, Michael T. 1979. "Court Politics in Late T'ang Times." In *The Cambridge History of China: Sui and T'ang China, 589–906, Part I*, ed. Denis Twitchett. Vol. 3. New York, NY: Cambridge University Press, chapter 9, pp. 561–681.

Deng, Guangming. 1997. *Northern Song Reformist Wang Anshi (Beisong zhengzhi gaigejia wang anshi)*. Hebei, China: Hebei Education Press (Hebei jiaoyu chubanshe).

Deng, Zhihua. 2007. "The Birth and Family History of the Economic Reformer Pang Shangpeng in the Mid Ming Dynasty (Mingzhongye jingji gaige jia Pang Shangpeng chusheng ji qi jiashi kao)." *History Teaching: College Edition (Lishi jiaoxue: gaoxiao ban)* (1): 73–75.

Deutsch, Karl W. 1961. "Social Mobilization and Political Development." *American Political Science Review* 55(3):493–514.

Diamond, Jared. 1997. *Guns, Germs, and Steel: The Fates of Human Societies*. New York, NY: W. W. Norton.

Diamond, Peter A. 1965. "National Debt in a Neoclassical Growth Model." *The American Economic Review* 55(5):1126–1150.

Dincecco, Mark. 2011. *Political Transformations and Public Finances: Europe, 1650–1913*. New York, NY: Cambridge University Press.

Dincecco, Mark, Giovanni Federico, and Andrea Vindigni. 2011. "Warfare, Taxation, and Political Change: Evidence from the Italian Risorgimento." *The Journal of Economic History* 71(4):887–914.

Dincecco, Mark, and Yuhua Wang. 2018. "Violent Conflict and Political Development over the Long Run: China versus Europe." *Annual Review of Political Science* 21:341–358.

Dincecco, Mark and Yuhua Wang. 2020. "Internal Conflict and State Development: Evidence from Imperial China." Working Paper.
    URL: *http://dx.doi.org/10.2139/ssrn.3209556*

Ding, Hui, and Xinrong Chen. 2016. *Collection and Study of the Family Pedigree of the Imperial Examination Family in Jiaxing in the Ming and Qing Dynasties (Mingqing jiaxing keju jiazu yinqin puxi zhengli yu yanjiu)*. Beijing, China: China Social Sciences Publishing House (Zhongguo shehui kexue chubanshe).

Dixit, Avinash K. 2011. *Lawlessness and Economics: Alternative Modes of Governance*. Princeton, NJ: Princeton University Press.

Downing, Brian M. 1992. *The Military Revolution and Political Change: Origins of Democracy and Autocracy in Early Modern Europe.* Princeton, NJ: Princeton University Press.

Downing, Brian M. 1993. *The Military Revolution and Political Change: Origins of Democracy and Autocracy in Early Modern Europe.* Princeton, NJ: Princeton University Press.

Drazen, Allan. 2000. *Political Economy in Macroeconomics.* Princeton, NJ: Princeton University Press.

Du, Jianmin. 1995. *Chronologies of Chinese Emperors and Their Families (Zhongguo lidai diwang shixi nianbiao).* Shandong, China: Qilu Bookstore Publishing House (Qilu shushe).

Du, You. 1988. *A Comprehensive Encyclopedia (Tong dian).* Beijing, China: Zhonghua Book Company (Zhonghua shuju).

Duara, Prasenjit. 1988. *Culture, Power, and the State: Rural North China, 1900–1942.* Palo Alto, CA: Stanford University Press.

Ebrey, Patricia Buckley. 1978. *The Aristocratic Families in Early Imperial China: A Case Study of the Po-Ling Ts' ui Family.* New York, NY: Cambridge University Press.

Ebrey, Patricia Buckley. 1986. "Concubines in Sung China." *Journal of Family History* 11(1):1–24.

Ebrey, Patricia Buckley, and Paul Jakov Smith. 2016. *State Power in China, 900–1325.* Seattle, WA: University of Washington Press.

Editorial Team of the Chinese Military History. 2006. *Military Institutions in Chinese Dynasties (Zhongguo lidai junshi zhidu).* Beijing, China: People's Liberation Army Press (Jiefangjun chubanshe).

Elliott, Mark C. 2001. *The Manchu Way: The Eight Banners and Ethnic Identity in Late Imperial China.* Palo Alto, CA: Stanford University Press.

Elvin, Mark. 1973. *The Pattern of the Chinese Past: A Social and Economic Interpretation.* Palo Alto, CA: Stanford University Press.

Ertman, Thomas. 1997. *Birth of the Leviathan: Building States and Regimes in Medieval and Early Modern Europe.* New York, NY: Cambridge University Press.

Evans, Peter B. 1995. *Embedded Autonomy: States and Industrial Transformation.* Princeton, NJ: Princeton University Press.

Evans, Peter B., Dietrich Rueschemeyer, and Theda Skocpol. 1985. *Bringing the State Back In.* New York, NY: Cambridge University Press.

Evans, Peter B., and James E. Rauch. 1999. "Bureaucracy and Growth: A Cross-National Analysis of the Effects of "Weberian" State Structures on Economic Growth." *American Sociological Review* 64(5):748–765.

Fairbank, John King. 1983. *The United States and China.* Cambridge, MA: Harvard University Press.

Fang, Ding, and Shengyuan Zhu. 2009. *Jinjiang County Gazetteer (Qianlong jinjiang xianzhi).* Beijing, China: Chinese Classic Ancient Books Database (Zhongguo jiben gujiku).

Farquhar, David M. 1968. "The Origins of the Manchus' Mongolian Policy." In *The Chinese World Order,* ed. John King Fairbank. Cambridge, MA: Harvard University Press, chapter 9, pp. 198–205.

Faure, David. 2007. *Emperor and Ancestor: State and Lineage in South China.* Palo Alto, CA: Stanford University Press.

Fearon, James D., and David D., Laitin. 2003. "Ethnicity, Insurgency, and Civil War." *American Political Science Review* 97(1):75–90.

Feng, Erkang. 2006. "On the 'Self-Governance' Nature of Clans in the Qing Dynasty (Jianlun qingdai zongzu de zizhi xing)." *Journal of Huazhong Normal University (Huazhong shifan daxue xuebao)* 45(1):65–70.

Feng, Mengzhen. 1997. *Kuaixue Hall Collection (Kuai xue tang ji).* Jinan, China: Qilu Bookstore Publishing House (Qilu shushe).

Feng, Ming. 2013. "A Critical Examination of Zhang Juzheng's Family History (Zhang Juzheng jiashi kaobian)." *Journal of Yangtze University (Changjiang daxue xuebao)* 36(1):5–7.

Feng, Shuling. 2012. "A Study on Yu Shenxing (Yu Shenxing yanjiu)." M.A. Thesis, Shandong Normal University.

Ferejohn, John A. 1974. *Pork Barrel Politics: Rivers and Harbors Legislation, 1947–1968.* Palo Alto, CA: Stanford University Press.

Ferejohn, John A., and Frances McCall Rosenbluth. 2010. *War and State Building in Medieval Japan.* Palo Alto, CA: Stanford University Press.

Fernández-Villaverde, Jesús, Mark Koyama, Youhong Lin, and Tuan-Hwee Sng. 2020. "The Fractured-Land Hypothesis." *National Bureau of Economic Research Working Paper 27774.*
 URL: *https://www.nber.org/papers/w27774*

Finer, Samuel Edward. 1997. *The History of Government, Volume II.* New York, NY: Oxford University Press.

Fletcher, Joseph. 1986. "The Mongols: Ecological and Social Perspectives." *Harvard Journal of Asiatic Studies* 46(1):11–50.

Food and Agriculture Organization of the United Nations. 2018.
 URL: *http://www.fao.org/faostat*

Fortes, Meyer. 1969. "Introduction." In *The Developmental Cycle in Domestic Groups,* ed. Jack Goody. New York, NY: Cambridge University Press, chapter 1, pp. 1–14.

Fortes, Meyer, and Edward Evan Evans-Pritchard. 1950. *African Political Systems.* New York, NY: Oxford University Press.

Freedman, Maurice. 1958. *Lineage Organization in Southeastern China.* London, UK: University Athlone Press.

Freeman, Linton C. 2000. "Visualizing Social Networks." *Journal of Social Structure* 1(1):4.

Friedman, David. 1977. "A Theory of the Size and Shape of Nations." *Journal of Political Economy* 85(1):59–77.

Frisby, David. 2002. *Georg Simmel.* London, UK: Psychology Press.

Fukuyama, Francis. 2011. *The Origins of Political Order: From Prehuman Times to the French Revolution.* New York, NY: Farrar, Straus and Giroux.

Fukuyama, Francis. 2014. *State-Building: Governance and World Order in the 21st Century.* Ithaca, NY: Cornell University Press.

Gambetta, Diego. 1996. *The Sicilian Mafia: The Business of Private Protection.* Cambridge, MA: Harvard University Press.

Ge, Jianxiong. 2000. *China Demographic History Vol. 3 (Zhongguo renkou shi).* Shanghai, China: Fudan University Press (Fudan daxue chubanshe).

Ge, Q., Z. Hao, J. Zheng, and X. Shao. 2013. "Temperature Changes Over the Past 2000 yr in China and Comparison with the Northern Hemisphere." *Climate of the Past* 9(3):1153–1160.

Ge, Xin. 1983. *Jiyu Mountain Hut Manuscripts (Ji yu shan fang gao).* Taipei, Taiwan: Taiwan Commercial Press (Taiwan shangwu yinshuguan).

Geddes, Barbara. 1996. *Politician's Dilemma: Building State Capacity in Latin America*. Berkeley, CA: University of California Press.

Ghosh, Arunabh. 2020. *Making It Count: Statistics and Statecraft in the Early People's Republic of China*. Princeton, NJ: Princeton University Press.

Girvan, Michelle, and Mark E. J. Newman. 2002. "Community Structure in Social and Biological Networks." *Proceedings of the National Academy of Sciences* 99(12):7821–7826.

Golas, Peter J. 2015. "The Sung Fiscal Administration." In *The Cambridge History of China: Sung China, 960–1279, Part II*, ed. John W. Chaffee and Denis Twitchett. Vol. 5. New York, NY: Cambridge University Press, chapter 2, pp. 139–213.

Goldschmidt Jr, Arthur, and Aomar Boum. 2015. *A Concise History of the Middle East*. New York, NY: Hachette.

Gong, Yanming. 1990. "On the Bureaucratic System in Song Dynasty and Its Significance (*Lun songdai guanpin zhidu jiqi yiyi*)." *The Journal of Southwestern Normal University (Xinan shifan daxue xuebao)* 1:13–23.

Goody, Jack. 1983. *The Development of the Family and Marriage in Europe*. New York, NY: Cambridge University Press.

Greif, Avner. 1989. "Reputation and Coalitions in Medieval Trade: Evidence on the Maghribi Traders." *Journal of Economic History* 49(4):857–882.

Greif, Avner. 2000. "The Fundamental Problem of Exchange: A Research Agenda in Historical Institutional Analysis." *European Review of Economic History* 4(3):251–284.

Greif, Avner. 2006. "Family Structure, Institutions, and Growth: The Origins and Implications of Western Corporations." *American Economic Review* 96(2):308–312.

Greif, Avner, and Guido Tabellini. 2017. "The Clan and the Corporation: Sustaining Cooperation in China and Europe." *Journal of Comparative Economics* 45(1):1–35.

Grzymala-Busse, Anna. 2020. "Beyond War and Contracts: The Medieval and Religious Roots of the European State." *Annual Review of Political Science* 23:19–36.

Grzymala-Busse, Anna, and Pauline Jones Luong. 2002. "Reconceptualizing the State: Lessons from Post-Communism." *Political & Society* 30(4):529–554.

Guo, Huixia. 2007. "Chronology of Zhang Siwei (Zhang Siwei nianpu)." M.A. Thesis, Lanzhou University.

Guo, Jason Qiang. 2019. "A Quantification of Fiscal Capacity of Chinese Government in the Long Run." New York University Ph.D. Dissertation.

Guo, Limin. 2015. *Atlas of Chinese Modern History (Zhongguo jindaishi ditu ji)*. Beijing, China: StarMap Press (Xingqiu ditu chubanshe).

Gurr, Ted Robert. 1970. *Why Men Rebel*. Princeton, NJ: Princeton University Press.

Hai, Rui, and Yizhong Chen. 1962. *Hai Rui Compilation (Hai Rui ji)*. Beijing, China: Zhonghua Book Company (Zhonghua shuju).

Hall, Peter A. 1989. *The Political Power of Economic Ideas: Keynesianism across Nations*. Princeton, NJ: Princeton University Press.

Hall, Peter A., and David Soskice. 2001. *Varieties of Capitalism: The Institutional Foundations of Comparative Advantage*. New York, NY: Oxford University Press.

Hao, Yu, and Kevin Zhengcheng Liu. 2020. "Taxation, Fiscal Capacity, and Credible Commitment in Eighteenth-Century China: The Effects of the Formalization and Centralization of Informal Surtaxes." *The Economic History Review* 73(4):914–939.

Hardin, Garrett. 1968. "The Tragedy of the Commons." *Science* 162(3859):1243–1248.

Harris, Chauncy D. 1954. "The, Market as a Factor in the Localization of Industry in the United States." *Annals of the Association of American Geographers* 44(4):315–348.

Hartman, Charles. 2015. "Sung Government and Politics." In *The Cambridge History of China: Sung China, 960–1279, Part II*, ed. John W. Chaffee and Denis Twitchett. Vol. 5. New York, NY: Cambridge University Press, chapter 1, pp. 19–138.

Hartwell, Robert M. 1982. "Demographic, Political, and Social Transformations of China, 750–1550." *Harvard Journal of Asiatic Studies* 42(2):365–442.

Hartwell, Robert M. 1986. "New Approaches to the Study of Bureaucratic Factionalism in Sung China: A Hypothesis." *Bulletin of Sung and Yüan Studies* (18):33–40.

He, Wenkai. 2013. *Paths Toward the Modern Fiscal State*. Cambridge, MA: Harvard University Press.

Hegel, Georg Wilhelm Fredrich. 1991. *Elements of the Philosophy of Right*. New York, NY: Cambridge University Press.

Heijdra, Martin. 1998. "The Socio-Economic Development of Rural China during the Ming." In *The Cambridge History of China. Volume 8, The Ming Dynasty, 1368–1644, Part 2*, ed. Denis Twitchett and Frederick W. Mote. New York, NY: Cambridge University Press, chapter 9, pp. 417–578.

Henrich, Joseph. 2020. *The Weirdest People in the World: How the West Became Psychologically Peculiar and Particularly Prosperous*. New York, NY: Farrar, Straus and Giroux.

Herbst, Jeffrey. 2000. *States and Power in Africa: Comparative Lessons in Authority and Control*. Princeton, NJ: Princeton University Press.

Hintze, Otto. 1975. *The Historical Essays of Otto Hintze*. Palo Alto, CA: Stanford University Press.

Ho, Ping-ti. 1959. *Studies on the Population of China, 1368–1953*. Cambridge, MA: Harvard University Press.

Ho, Ping-Ti. 1964. *The Ladder of Success in Imperial China: Aspects of Social Mobility, 1368–1911*. New York, NY: Columbia University Press.

Hoffman, Philip. 2015. *Why Did Europe Conquer the World?* Princeton, NJ: Princeton University Press.

Horowitz, Michael C., Allan C. Stam, and Cali M. Ellis. 2015. *Why Leaders Fight*. New York, NY: Cambridge University Press.

Hsiao, Kung-Chuan. 1960. *Rural China: Imperial Control in the Nineteenth Century*. Seattle, WA: University of Washington Press.

Hu, Cangze. 2000. *A Study of the Censor System in Tang (Tangdai yushi zhidu yanjiu)*. Shanghai, China: Fujian Education Press (Fujian jiaoyu chubanshe).

Hu, Changchun. 2007. *A Biography of Tan Lun (Tan Lun pingzhuan)*. Jiangxi, China: Jiangxi People's Publishing House (Jiangxi renmin chubanshe).

Hu, Yinglin. 1983. *Shao's Mountain Hut Collections (Shao shi shan fang ji)*. Taipei, Taiwan: Taiwan Commercial Publishing House (Taiwan shangwu yinshuguan).

Huang, Ray. 1974. *Taxation and Governmental Finance in Sixteenth-Century Ming China*. New York, NY: Cambridge University Press.

Huang, Ray. 1981. *1587, A Year of No Significance: The Ming Dynasty in Decline*. New Haven, CT: Yale University Press.

Huang, Ray. 1998. "The Lung-ch'ing and Wan-li Reigns, 1567–1620." In *The Cambridge History of China. Volume 7, The Ming Dynasty, 1368–1644, Part 1*, ed. Frederick W. Mote and Denis Twitchett. New York, NY: Cambridge University Press, chapter 5, pp. 511–584.

Huang, Ruheng. 2009a. *Yulin Collection (Yu Lin ji)*. Beijing, China: Chinese Classic Ancient Books Database (Zhongguo jiben gujiku).

Huang, Yan. 2009b. "A Study on Shuo Yi (Shuo Yi yanjiu)." M.A. Thesis, Hunan Normal University.

Huang, Yasheng, and Clair Yang. 2020. "A Longevity Mechanism of Chinese Absolutism." Forthcoming, Journal of Politics.

Hucker, Charles O. 1998. "Ming Government." In *The Cambridge History of China. Volume 8, The Ming Dynasty, 1368–1644, Part 2*, ed. Denis Twitchett and Frederick W. Mote. New York, NY: Cambridge University Press, chapter 1, pp. 9–105.

Hui, Victoria Tin-bor. 2005. *War and State Formation in Ancient China and Early Modern Europe*. New York, NY: Cambridge University Press.

Huntington, Samuel P. 1968. *Political Order in Changing Societies*. New Haven, CT: Yale University Press.

Huntington, Samuel P. 1993. *The Third Wave: Democratization in the Late Twentieth Century*. Norman, OK: University of Oklahoma Press.

Hymes, Robert. 1986. *Statesmen and Gentlemen: The Elite of Fu-Chou Chiang-Hsi, in Northern and Southern Sung*. New York, NY: Cambridge University Press.

Hymes, Robert. 2015. "Sung Society and Social Change." In *The Cambridge History of China: Sung China, 960–1279, Part II*, ed. John W. Chaffee and Denis Twitchett. Vol. 5. New York, NY: Cambridge University Press, chapter 8, pp. 526–664.

Jha, Saumitra. 2015. "Financial Asset Holdings and Political Attitudes: Evidence from Revolutionary England." *Quarterly Journal of Economics* 130(3):1485–1545.

Jia, Ruixue. 2014. "Weather Shocks, Sweet Potatoes and Peasant Revolts in Historical China." *The Economic Journal* 124(575):92–118.

Jia, Zheng. 1996. *Critical Biography of Pan Jixun (Pan Jixun pingzhuan)*. Jiangsu, China: Nanjing University Publishing House (Nanjing daxue chubanshe).

Jiang, Qin, and James Kai-sing Kung. 2020. "Social Mobility in Late Imperial China: Reconsidering the 'Ladder of Success' Hypothesis." Forthcoming, *Modern China*.

Jiao, Hong. 1991. *Contemporary Anecdotes and History Encyclopedia (Guo chao xian zheng lu)*. Taipei, Taiwan: Mingwen Bookstore (Mingwen shuju).

Jiao, Hong. 1997. *Jiao Danyuan Collection (Jiao shi dan yuan ji)*. Beijing, China: Beijing Press (Beijing chubanshe).

Jin, Guantao, and Qingfeng Liu. 2011. *The Cycle of Growth and Decline: On the Ultrastable Structure of Chinese Society (Xingshi yu weiji: lun zhongguo shehui chaowending jiegou)*. Beijing, China: Law Press (Falü chubanshe).

Johnson, Chalmers. 1982. *MITI and the Japanese Miracle: The Growth of Industrial Policy, 1925–1975*. Palo Alto, CA: Stanford University Press.

Johnson, David George. 1977. *The Medieval Chinese Oligarchy*. Boulder, CO: Westview Press.

Jones, Benjamin F., and Benjamin A. Olken. 2005. "Do Leaders Matter? National Leadership and Growth Since World War II." *Quarterly Journal of Economics* 120(3):835–864.

Kang, David C. 2010. *East Asia before the West: Five Centuries of Trade and Tribute*. New York, NY: Columbia University Press.

Kang, Ruifang. 2012. *Wu Dui and Ming Dynasty Border Defense against Mongolia (Wu Dui yu ming meng bianfang)*. Inner Mongolia, China: University of Inner Mongolia Publishing House (Neimenggu daxue chubanshe).

Kato, Shigeshi. 2006. *Research on Gold and Silver in Tang and Song Era: Focusing on Monetary Function of Gold and Silver (Tangsong shidai jinyin zhi yanjiu: yi jinyin zhi huobi jineng wei zhongxin)*. Beijing, China: Zhonghua Book Company (Zhonghua shuju).

Kennedy, Hugh. 2010. "The City and the Nomad." In *The New Cambridge History of Islam*, ed. Robert Irwin. Vol. 4. New York, NY: Cambridge University Press, chapter 8, pp. 274–289.

Ko, Chiu Yu, and Tuan-Hwee Sng. 2013. "Regional Dependence and Political Centralization in Imperial China." *Eurasian Geography and Economics* 54(5-6):470–483.

Kokkonen, Andrej, and Anders Sundell. 2014. "Delivering Stability—Primogeniture and Autocratic Survival in European Monarchies 1000–1800." *American Political Science Review* 108(2):438–453.

Kopytoff, Igor. 1987. "The Internal African Frontier: The Making of African Political Culture." In *The African Frontier: The Reproduction of Traditional African Societies*, ed. Igor Kopytoff. Bloomington, IN: Indiana University Press, chapter 1, pp. 3–85.

Koss, Daniel. 2018. *Where the Party Rules: The Rank and File of China's Communist State*. New York, NY: Cambridge University Press.

Koyama, Mark, Chiaki Moriguchi, and Tuan-Hwee Sng. 2018. "Geopolitics and Asia's Little Divergence: State Building in China and Japan after 1850." *Journal of Economic Behavior & Organization* 155:178–204.

Kracke, Edward A. 1947. "Family vs. Merit in Chinese Civil Service Examinations Under the Empire." *Harvard Journal of Asiatic Studies* 10(2):103–123.

Krugman, Paul. 1998. "What's New About the New Economic Geography?" *Oxford Review of Economic Policy* 14(2):7–17.

Kuhn, Philip A. 1970. *Rebellion and Its Enemies in Late Imperial China: Militarization and Social Structure, 1796–1864*. Cambridge, MA: Harvard University Press.

Kung, James Kai-sing, and Chicheng Ma. 2014. "Can Cultural Norms Reduce Conflicts? Confucianism and Peasant Rebellions in Qing China." *Journal of Development Economics* 111:132–149.

Kuran, Timur. 2012. *The Long Divergence: How Islamic Law Held Back the Middle East*. Princeton, NJ: Princeton University Press.

Kurtz, Marcus J. 2013. *Latin American State Building in Comparative Perspective: Social Foundations of Institutional Order*. New York, NY: Cambridge University Press.

Lapidus, Ira M. 1973. "The Evolution of Muslim Urban Society." *Comparative Studies in Society and History* 15(1):21–50.

Lavely, William, and R. Bin Wong. 1998. "Revising the Malthusian Narrative: The Comparative Study of Population Dynamics in Late Imperial China." *Journal of Asian Studies* 57(3):714–748.

Lee, James Z. 2000. *The Political Economy of a Frontier: Southwest China, 1250–1850*. Cambridge, MA: Harvard University Press.

Lee, Sukhee. 2009. *Negotiated Power: The State, Elites, and Local Governance in Twelfth-to Fourteenth-Century China*. Cambridge, MA: Harvard University Asia Center.

Lerner, Daniel. 1958. *The Passing of Traditional Society: Modernizing the Middle East*. New York, NY: Free Press.

Levenson, Joseph Richmond, and H. Franz Schurmann. 1971. *China: An Interpretive History, From the Beginnings to the Fall of Han*. Berkeley, CA: University of California Press.

Levi, Margaret. 1988. *Of Rule and Revenue*. Berkeley, CA: University of California Press.

Levi, Margaret. 2002. "The State of the Study of the State." In *Political Science: The State of the Discipline*, ed. Ira Katznelson and Helen Milner. Washington DC: American Political Science Association, pp. 33–55.

Levitsky, Steven, and Lucan A. Way. 2010. *Competitive Authoritarianism: Hybrid Regimes After the Cold War*. New York, NY: Cambridge University Press.

Lewis, Mark Edward. 2007. *The Early Chinese Empires: Qin and Han*. Cambridge, MA: Harvard University Press.

Lewis, Mark Edward. 2009. *China's Cosmopolitan Empire: The Tang Dynasty*. Cambridge, MA: Harvard University Press.

Li, Changxian. 2013. *A Study of Song Bureaucracy (Songchao guanpinling yu hebanzhizhi fuyuan yanjiu)*. Shanghai, China: Shanghai Ancient Works Publishing House (Shanghai guji chubanshe).

Li, Guohong. 2009. *The Chronicles of the Five Shangshu Huang Kejian of Ming Dynasty (Ming wubu shangshu Huang Kejian nianpu)*. Fujian, China: Tong'an Literature and History Materials Committee (Tongan wenshi weiyuanhui).

Li, Hengfa, and Huaying Xie. 2011. *Jining Epitaphs Collection (Jining lidai muzhiming)*. Shandong, China: Qilu Bookstore Publishing House (Qilu shushe).

Li, Lillian M. 2007a. *Fighting Famine in North China: State, Market, and Environmental Decline, 1690s–1990s*. Palo Alto, CA: Stanford University Press.

Li, Tao. 1979 [1177]. *The Extended Continuation to Comprehensive Mirror in Aid of Governance (Xu zizhitongjian changbian)*. Beijing, China: Zhonghua Book Company (Zhonghua shuju).

Li, Tingji. 1970. *Li Wenjie Works Compilation (Li Wenjie ji)*. Taipei, Taiwan: Wenhai Publishing House (Wenhai chubanshe).

Li, Weiguo. 2007b. *Fiscal Revenues and Documentary Research (Songdai caizheng he wenxian kaolun)*. Shanghai, China: Shanghai Classic Archival Publish (Shanghai guji chubanshe).

Li, Weizhen. 1997. *Dami Mountain Hut Collection (Dami shanfang ji)*. Shandong, China: Qilu Bookstore Publishing House (Qilu shushe).

Li, Yunlong. 2018. "A Study on the Marriage and Heir Relations of Suzhou Shen Family in Ming and Qing Dynasty (Ming qing suzhou Shen shi jiazu hunyin yu jisi guanxi yanjiu)." M.A. Thesis, Suzhou University of Science and Technology.

Li, Zhiliang. 2003. *A Complete Study of Song National Officials (Songdai jingchaoguan tongkao)*. Sichuan, China: Bashu Press (Bashu shushe).

Li, Zhixian. 2002. *A Study of Yang Yan and His Two-Tax Law (Yangyan jiqi liangshuifa yanjiu)*. Beijing, China: China Social Sciences Press (Zhongguo shehui kexue chubanshe).

Li, Zude. 1995. *History of Chinese Currencies (Zhongguo huobi shi)*. Beijing, China: China Cultural History Collections (Zhongguo wenhuashi yeshu).

Liang, Fangzhong. 1989. *Collection of Liang Fangzhong's Economic History Essays (Liang fangzhong jingjishi lunwen ji)*. Beijing, China: Zhonghua Book Company (Zhonghua shuju).

Liang, Fangzhong. 2008. *Statistics on Households, Land, and Taxation in Chinese Dynasties (Zhongguo lidai hukou tiandi tianfu tongji)*. Beijing, China: Zhonghua Book Company (Zhonghua shuju).

Liang, Qiao. 1650. *Genealogy of Liang Clan in Zhengding, Hebei (Hebei zhengding Liang shi zupu)*. Hebei, China: Zhengding Liang Clan.

Liang, Qichao. 2009 [1908]. *Biography of Wang Anshi (Wang Anshi zhuan).* Beijing, China: Oriental Publishing House (Dongfang chubanshe).

Liang, Xinqi. 2012. "The Interaction between Family Construction and Local Society: A Case Study of the Ma Family in Tongzhou in Ming and Qing Dynasties (Jiazu jiangou yu difang shehui hudong—Mingqing tongzhou Ma shi jiazu de gean yanjiu)." M.A. Thesis, Jiangxi Normal University.

Licheng Cultural and Historical Documents Research Commission. 2010. *Licheng Cultural and Historical Documents (Licheng wenshi ziliao).* Shandong, China: Licheng Cultural and Historical Documents Research Commission.

Lipset, Seymour Martin. 1959. "Some Social Requisites of Democracy: Economic Development and Political Legitimacy." *American Political Science Review* 53(1):69–105.

Lipset, Seymour Martin, and Stein Rokkan. 1967. *Party Systems and Voter Alignments: Cross-National Perspectives.* New York, NY: Free Press.

Liu, Hongxun. 2009. *Si Su Mountain Hut Collection (Si su shan fang ji).* Beijing, China: Chinese Classic Ancient Books Database (Zhongguo jiben gujiku).

Liu, James. 1959. *Reform in Sung China: Wang An-shih (1021–1086) and His New Policies.* Cambridge, MA: Harvard University Press.

Liu, Pengbing. 2008. "Wang Daokun Literature Research (Wang Daokun wenxue yanjiu)." Ph.D. Dissertation, Fudan University.

Liu, Tingluan, and Jialan Sun. 2014. *A Comprehensive List of Shandong's Presented Scholars in Ming and Qing, The Ming Dynasty (Shandong mingqing jinshi tonglan, mingdai juan).* Shandong, China: Shandong Publishing House of Literature and Art (Shandong wenyi chubanshe).

Liu, William Guanglin. 2015. "The Making of a Fiscal State in Song China, 960–1279." *The Economic History Review* 68(1):48–78.

Lohmann, Susanne. 1994. "The Dynamics of Informational Cascades: The Monday Demonstrations in Leipzig, East Germany, 1989–91." *World Politics* 47(1):42–101.

Lu, Kejiao. 2009. *Scholar Lu Unpublished Manuscripts (Lu xueshi yigao).* Beijing, China: Chinese Classic Ancient Books Database (Zhongguo jiben gujiku).

Luo, Ergang. 2009. *History of the Taiping Heavenly Kingdom (Taiping tianguo shi).* Beijing, China: Zhonghua Book Company (Zhonghua shuju).

Ma Clan. 1870. *Biography of Ma Clan from Western Tongguan (Guanxi Ma shi shi xing lu).* Shaanxi, China: House of Filial Orders (Dun Lun Tang).

Ma, Debin. 2004. "Growth, Institutions and Knowledge: A Review and Reflection on the Historiography of 18th–20th Century China." *Australian Economic History Review* 44(3):259–277.

Ma, Debin. 2021. "Ideology and the Contours of Economic Changes in Modern China during 1850–1950." *CEPR Discussion Paper No. DP15835.*

Ma, Debin, and Jared Rubin. 2019. "The Paradox of Power: Principal-Agent Problems and Administrative Capacity in Imperial China (and Other Absolutist Regimes)." *Journal of Comparative Economics* 47(2):277–294.

Ma, Duanlin. 1986. *Comprehensive Examination of Literatures (Wenxian tongkao).* Beijing, China: Zhonghua Book Company (Zhonghua shuju).

Ma, Wu. 2013. "A Study on Wang Heng's Poetry and Prose (Wang Heng shiwen yanjiu)." M.A. Thesis, Jinan University.

Maddison, Angus. 2007. *Contours of the World Economy 1–2030 AD: Essays in Macro-Economic History.* New York, NY: Oxford University Press.

Mahoney, James. 2000. "Path Dependence in Historical Sociology." *Theory and Society* 29(4):507–548.

Malthus, Thomas Robert. 1992 [1806]. *An Essay on the Principle of Population; or, A View of Its Past and Present Effects on Human Happiness.* New York, NY: Cambridge University Press.

Mann, Michael. 1984. "The Autonomous Power of the State: Its Origins, Mechanisms and Results." *European Journal of Sociology* 25(2):185–213.

Mann, Susan, and Philip A. Kuhn. 1974. "Dynastic Decline and the Roots of Rebellion." In *The Cambridge History of China: Late Ch'ing, 1800–1911, Part I,* ed. John King Fairbank. Vol. 10. New York, NY: Cambridge University Press, chapter 3, pp. 107–162.

Mao, Hanguang. 1966. *A Study of the Politics of Great Clans in Jin, Northern, and Southern Dynasties (Liangjin nanbeichao shizu zhengzhi zhi yanjiu).* Taipei, Taiwan: Committee on Funding Chinese Academic Books (Zhongguo xueshu zhuzuo zizhu weiyuanhui).

Mao, Hanguang. 1981. "Examining the Centralization of the Tang Civil Bureaucratic Clans from Clans' Migration." *Collected Works of Institute of History and Philology at Academia Sinica (Zhongyang yanjiuyuan lishi yuyan yanjiusuo jikan)* 52(3):421–510.

Mao, Tse-Tung. 1965. *Selected Works of Mao Tse-Tung.* Vol. 1. Oxford, UK: Pergamon Press.

Marsden, Peter V. 1993. "The Reliability of Network Density and Composition Measures." *Social Networks* 15(4):399–421.

Mazumder, Soumyajit, and Yuhua Wang. 2021. "Social Cleavages and War Mobilization in Qing China." Working Paper.
  URL: *http://dx.doi.org/10.2139/ssrn.3622309*

McDermott, Joseph P. 2013. *The Making of a New Rural Order in South China: Volume 1: Village, Land, and Lineage in Huizhou, 900–1600.* Vol. 1. New York, NY: Cambridge University Press.

McNaughton, Arnold. 1973. *Book of Kings: A Royal Genealogy.* New York, NY: New York Times Book Company.

Meltzer, Allan H., and Scott F. Richard. 1981. "A Rational Theory of the Size of Government." *Journal of Political Economy* 89(5):914–927.

Migdal, Joel S. 1988. *Strong Societies and Weak States: State-Society Relations and State Capabilities in the Third World.* Princeton, NJ: Princeton University Press.

Migdal, Joel S., Atul Kohli, and Vivienne Shue. 1994. *State Power and Social Forces: Domination and Transformation in the Third World.* New York, NY: Cambridge University Press.

Miller, Harry. 2009. *State versus Gentry in Late Ming Dynasty China, 1572–1644.* London, UK: Palgrave Macmillan.

Miyazaki, Ichisada. 1992 [1953]. "Scholar-Officials in the Song Dynasty (Sōdai no shifu)." In *Complete Works of Ichisada Miyazaki (Miyazaki Ichisada zenshū).* Vol. II. Tokyo, Japan: Iwanami Shoten pp. 339–375.

Mokyr, Joel. 2016. *A Culture of Growth: The Origins of the Modern Economy.* Princeton, NJ: Princeton University Press.

Moore, Barington. 1966. *Social Origins of Dictatorship and Democracy: Lord and Peasant in the Making of the Modern World.* Boston, MA: Beacon Press.

Morby, John E. 1989. *Dynasties of the World: A Chronological and Genealogical Handbook.* New York, NY: Oxford University Press.

Murdock, George Peter. 1967. *Ethnographic Atlas*. Pittsburgh, PA: University of Pittsburgh Press.

Muzzuca, Sebastián. 2021. *Latecomer State Formation: Political Geography and Capacity Failure in Latin America*. New Haven, CT: Yale University Press.

Naidu, Suresh, James A. Robinson, and Lauren E. Young. 2021. "Social Origins of Dictatorships: Elite Networks and Political Transitions in Haiti." *American Political Science Review* 115(3):900–916.

Naito, Konan. 1992 [1922]. "A Summary of Tang Song Times." In *Selected Translations of Japanese Scholars' Research on Chinese History (Riben xuezhe yanjiu zhonguo shi lunzhu xuanyi)*, ed. Junwen Liu. Vol. 1. Beijing, China: Zhonghua Book Company (Zhonghua shuju), chapter 2, pp. 10–18.

Nanjing Military Academy. 2003. *The Catalog of Historical Wars (Lidai zhanzheng nianbiao)*. Beijing, China: People's Liberation Army Press (Jiefangjun chubanshe).

National Research Council. 2006. *Surface Temperature Reconstructions for the Last 2,000 Years*. Washington, DC: National Academies Press.

Ning, Ke. 2007. *A History of Chinese Economy: Sui, Tang and Wudai (Zhongguo jingji tongshi: Sui tang wudai)*. Beijing, China: Economic Daily Press (Jingji ribao chubanshe).

North, Douglass C. 1981. *Structure and Change in Economic History*. New York, NY: W. W. Norton.

North, Douglass C., and Barry R. Weingast. 1989. "Constitutions and Commitment: The Evolution of Institutions Governing Public Choice in Seventeenth-Century England." *The Journal of Economic History* 49(4):803–832.

North, Douglass C., John Joseph Wallis, and Barry R. Weingast. 2012. *Violence and Social Orders: A Conceptual Framework for Interpreting Recorded Human History*. New York, NY: Cambridge University Press.

Nunn, Nathan, and Diego Puga. 2012. "Ruggedness: The Blessing of Bad Geography in Africa." *Review of Economics and Statistics* 94(1):20–36.

O'Donnell, Guillermo. 1993. "On the State, Democratization and Some Conceptual Problems: A Latin American View with Glances at Some Postcommunist Countries." *World Development* 21(8):1355–1369.

Olson, Mancur. 1965. *The Logic of Collective Action: Public Goods and the Theory of Groups*. Cambridge, MA: Harvard University Press.

Olson, Mancur. 1982. *The Rise and Decline of Nations: Economic Growth, Stagflation, and Social Rigidities*. New Haven, CT: Yale University Press.

Ostrom, Elinor. 1990. *Governing the Commons: The Evolution of Institutions for Collective Action*. New York, NY: Cambridge University Press.

Padgett, John F., and Christopher K. Ansell. 1993. "Robust Action and the Rise of the Medici, 1400–1434." *American Journal of Sociology* 98(6):1259–1319.

Peng, Hui. 2015. "Biography and Chronology of Sun Piyang (Sun Piyang shengping jinianpu)." *Changan Scholarly Journal: Philosophy and Social Sciences Division (Changan xuekan: zhexue shehui kexue ban)* (6):6–11.

Peng, Kaixiang. 2006. *Rice Price from Qing Dynasty: Explanation and Re-explanation (Qingdai yilai de liangjia: lishixue de jieshi yu zai jieshi)*. Shanghai, China: Shanghai People Press (Shanghai renmin chubanshe).

Peng, Xinwei. 1965. *A Monetary History of China (Zhongguo huobi shi)*. Shanghai, China: Shanghai People Press (Shanghai renmin chubanshe).

Perkins, Dwight H. 1969. *Agricultural Development in China, 1368–1968*. London, UK: Aldine Publishing Company.

Perry, Elizabeth J. 1980. *Rebels and Revolutionaries in North China, 1845–1945*. Palo Alto, CA: Stanford University Press.

Perry, Elizabeth J. 1993. *Shanghai on Strike: The Politics of Chinese Labor*. Palo Alto, CA: Stanford University Press.

Peterson, C. A. 1979. "Court and Province in Mid- and Late T'ang." In *The Cambridge History of China: Sui and T'ang China, 589–906, Part I*, ed. Denis Twitchett. Vol. 3. New York, NY: Cambridge University Press, chapter 8, pp. 464–560.

Pincus, Steven C. A., and James A. Robinson. 2014. "What Really Happened During the Glorious Revolution?" In *Institutions, Property Rights, and Economic Growth: The Legacy of Douglass North*, ed. Sebastian Galiani and Itai Sened. New York, NY: Cambridge University Press, chapter 9, pp. 192–222.

Pines, Yuri. 2012. *The Everlasting Empire: The Political Culture of Ancient China and Its Imperial Legacy*. Princeton, NJ: Princeton University Press.

Platt, Stephen R. 2012. *Autumn in the Heavenly Kingdom: China, the West, and the Epic Story of the Taiping Civil War*. New York, NY: Knopf.

Pomeranz, Kenneth. 1993. *The Making of a Hinterland: State, Society, and Economy in Inland North China, 1853–1937*. Berkeley, CA: University of California Press.

Pomeranz, Kenneth. 2000. *The Great Divergence: China, Europe, and the Making of the Modern World Economy*. Princeton, NJ: Princeton University Press.

Pulleyblank, Edwin George. 1955. *The Background of the Rebellion of An Lu-shan*. New York, NY: Oxford University Press.

Qi, Xia. 1987. *Economic History of the Song Dynasty (Songdai jingjishi)*. Shanghai, China: Shanghai People's Press (Shanghai renmin chubanshe).

Qi, Xia. 2007. *Comprehensive History of Chinese Economy: Song (Zhongguo jingji tongshi: Songdai jingji juan)*. Beijing, China: Economic Daily Press (Jingji ribao chubanshe).

Qiao, Jitang, Luo Wei, Fupeng Li and Xuehui Li. 1996. *The Complete Biographies of Chinese Emperors (Zhongguo huangdi quanzhuan)*. Beijing, China: Industry and Commerce Press (Gongshang chubanshe).

Qiu, Zhangsong. 2004. "Textual Research on Wang Zongmu's Life (Wang Zongmu shengping kaobian)." *Eastern Archaeology (Dongfang bowu)* (3):79–93.

Quan, Hansheng. 2012. *Essays in Chinese Economic History (Zhongguo jingjishi luncong)*. Beijing, China: Zhonghua Book Company (Zhonghua shuju).

Queralt, Didac. 2019. "War, International Finance, and Fiscal Capacity in the Long Run." *International Organization* 73(4):713–53.

Rankin, Mary B., John King Fairbank, and Albert Feuerwerker. 1986. "Introduction: Perspectives on Modern China's History." In *The Cambridge History of China: Republican China, 1912–1949, Part 2*, ed. John King Fairbank and Albert Feuerwerker. Vol. 13. New York, NY: Cambridge University Press, chapter 1, pp. 1–73.

Rawski, Evelyn Sakakida. 1979. *Education and Popular Literacy in Ch'ing China*. Ann Arbor, MI: University of Michigan Press.

Ren, Jian. 2010. "A Study of Wang Guoguang's Court Memoir Compilation of Ming Dynasty (Ming Wang Guoguang si quan zou cao yanjiu)." M.A. Thesis, Shanxi University.

Rosenthal, Jean-Laurent, and Roy Bin Wong. 2011. *Before and Beyond Divergence*. Cambridge, MA: Harvard University Press.

Rowe, William T. 2007. *Crimson Rain: Seven Centuries of Violence in a Chinese County*. Palo Alto, CA: Stanford University Press.

Rowe, William T. 2009. *China's Last Empire: The Great Qing*. Cambridge, MA: Harvard University Press.

Rubin, Jared. 2017. *Rulers, Religion, and Riches: Why the West Got Rich and the Middle East Did Not*. New York, NY: Cambridge University Press.

Samuelson, Paul A. 1958. "An Exact Consumption-Loan Model of Interest With or Without the Social Contrivance of Money." *Journal of Political Economy* 66(6):467–482.

Scheidel, Walter. 2019. *Escape from Rome: The Failure of Empire and the Road to Prosperity*. Princeton, NJ: Princeton University Press.

Schelling, Thomas C. 1960. *The Strategy of Conflict*. Cambridge, MA: Harvard University Press.

Scheve, Kenneth, and David Stasavage. 2016. *Taxing the Rich: A History of Fiscal Fairness in the United States and Europe*. Princeton, NJ: Princeton University Press.

Schurmann, H. Franz. 1956. "Traditional Property Concepts in China." *The Journal of Asian Studies* 15(4):507–516.

Schurmann, H. Franz. 1966. *Ideology and Organization in Communist China*. Berkeley, CA: University of California Press.

Scott, James C. 2017. *Against the Grain: A Deep History of the Earliest States*. New Haven, CT: Yale University Press.

Searle, Eleanor. 1988. *Predatory Kinship and the Creation of Norman Power: 840–1066*. Berkeley, CA: University of California Press.

Selden, Mark. 1970. *The Yenan Way in Revolutionary China*. Cambridge, MA: Harvard University Press.

Shanghai Shudian Press. 2015. *Veritable Records of the Ming Dynasty (Ming shilu)*. Shanghai, China: Shanghai Shudian Press (Shanghai shudian chubanshe).

Shi, Zhihong, and Yi Xu. 2008. *Finance in the Late Qing, 1851–1894 (Wanqing caizheng)*. Shanghai, China: Shanghai University of Finance and Economics Publishing House (Shanghai caijing daxue chubanshe).

Shue, Vivienne. 1988. *The Reach of the State: Sketches of the Chinese Body Politic*. Palo Alto, CA: Stanford University Press.

Sima, Guang. 1937 [1086]. *Collected Works of Sima Guang (Sima wenzhenggong chuanjia ji)*. Beijing, China: Commercial Press (Shangwu yinshuguan).

Skinner, George William. 1977. *The City in Late Imperial China*. Palo Alto, CA: Stanford University Press.

Skinner, George William. 1985. "Presidential Address: The Structure of Chinese History." *The Journal of Asian Studies* 44(2):271–292.

Skocpol, Theda. 1979. *States and Social Revolutions*. New York, NY: Cambridge University Press.

Skocpol, Theda. 1985. "Bringing the State Back In: Strategies of Analysis in Current Research." In *Bringing the State Back In*, ed. Peter B. Evans, Dietrich Rueschemeyer, and Theda Skocpol. New York, NY: Cambridge University Press, chapter 1, pp. 3–37.

Slater, Dan. 2010. *Ordering Power: Contentious Politics and Authoritarian Leviathans in Southeast Asia*. New York, NY: Cambridge University Press.

Smith, Adam. 1986 [1776]. *The Wealth of Nations: Books I-III*. New York, NY: Penguin Press.

Smith, Paul Jakov. 2009a. "Introduction: The Sung Dynasty and Its Precursors, 907–1279." In *The Cambridge History of China: The Sung Dynasty and Its Precursors, 907–1279, Part I*, ed. Denis Twitchett and Paul Jakov Smith. Vol. 5. New York, NY: Cambridge University Press, Introduction, pp. 1–37.

Smith, Paul Jakov. 2009b. "Shen-tsung's Reign and the New Policies of Wang An-shih, 1067–1085." In *The Cambridge History of China. Volume 5, Part 1, The Sung Dynasty and Its Precursors, 907–1279*, ed. Denis Twitchett and Paul Jakov Smith. New York, NY: Cambridge University Press, chapter 5, pp. 347–483.

Smith, Paul Jakov, and Richard Von Glahn. 2003. *The Song-Yuan-Ming Transition in Chinese History*. Leiden, NL: Brill.

Sng, Tuan-Hwee. 2014. "Size and Dynastic Decline: The Principal-Agent Problem in Late Imperial China, 1700–1850." *Explorations in Economic History* 54:107–127.

Sng, Tuan-Hwee, and Chiaki Moriguchi. 2014. "Asia's Little Divergence: State Capacity in China and Japan Before 1850." *Journal of Economic Growth* 19(4):439–470.

Soifer, Hillel David. 2015. *State Building in Latin America*. New York, NY: Cambridge University Press.

Solow, Robert M. 1956. "A Contribution to the Theory of Economic Growth." *Quarterly Journal of Economics* 70(1):65–94.

Somers, Robert M. 1979. "The End of the T'ang." In *The Cambridge History of China: Sui and T'ang China, 589–906, Part I*, ed. Denis Twitchett. Vol. 3. New York, NY: Cambridge University Press, chapter 10, pp. 682–789.

Song, Jun. 1739. *Shangqiu Song Family History (Shangqiu Song shi jiacheng)*. Hunan, China: Shangqiu Song Family.

Spence, Jonathan D. 1996. *God's Chinese Son: The Taiping Heavenly Kingdom of Hong Xiuquan*. New York, NY: W. W. Norton.

Spence, Jonathan D. 2002. "The K'ang-Hsi Reign." In *The Cambridge History of China: The Ch'ing Empire to 1800, Part I*, ed. Denis Twitchett and John King Fairbank. New York, NY: Cambridge University Press, chapter 3, pp. 120–182.

Spruyt, Hendrik. 1994. *The Sovereign State and Its Competitors: An Analysis of Systems Change*. Princeton, NJ: Princeton University Press.

Stasavage, David. 2002. "Credible Commitment in Early Modern Europe: North and Weingast Revisited." *Journal of Law, Economics, and Organization* 18(1):155–186.

Stasavage, David. 2003. *Public Debt and the Birth of the Democratic State: France and Great Britain 1688–1789*. New York, NY: Cambridge University Press.

Stasavage, David. 2016. "Representation and Consent: Why They Arose in Europe and Not Elsewhere." *Annual Review of Political Science* 19:145–162.

Stasavage, David. 2020. *The Decline and Rise of Democracy: A Global History from Antiquity to Today*. Princeton, NJ: Princeton University Press.

Stone, Lawrence. 1965. *The Crisis of the Aristocracy, 1558–1641*. Oxford, UK: Clarendon Press.

Stone, Lawrence. 2017 [1972]. *The Causes of the English Revolution*. New York, NY: Routledge.

Strauss, Julia C. 2020. *State Formation in China and Taiwan: Bureaucracy, Campaign, and Performance*. New York, NY: Cambridge University Press.

Strayer, Joseph R. 1970. *On the Medieval Origins of the Modern State*. Princeton, NJ: Princeton University Press.

Sun, Guodong. 2009. *A Study of the Rotation of Tang Central Officials (Tangdai zhongyang zhongyao wenguan qianzhuan tujing yanjiu)*. Shanghai, China: Shanghai Ancient Book Publishing House (Shanghai guji chubanshe).

Sun, Kuang. 1814. *Compiled Works by Mr. Sun Yuefeng of Yaojiang (Yaojiang Sun Yuefeng xiansheng quanji)*. Zhejiang, China: Sun Yuanxing.

Szonyi, Michael. 2002. *Practicing Kinship: Lineage and Descent in Late Imperial China*. Palo Alto, CA: Stanford University Press.

Tackett, Nicolas. 2014. *The Destruction of the Medieval Chinese Aristocracy*. Cambridge, MA: Harvard University Press.

Tan, Xiping. 1891. *Fuping County Gazetteer (Fuping xianzhi)*. Shaanxi, China: Fuping County Government.

Tang Clan. 1990. *Tang Clan Genealogy (Tang shi jia pu)*. Tang Clan.

Tang, Wenxian. 1997. *Tang Wenke Court Documents Collection (Tang Wenke gong wen ji)*. Shandong, China: Qilu Bookstore Publishing House (Qilu shushe).

Tarrow, Sidney G. 1994. *Power in Movement: Social Movements and Contentious Politics*. New York, NY: Cambridge University Press.

Tawney, Richard Henry. 1966. *Land and Labor in China*. Boston, MA: Beacon Press.

Tian, Yuqing. 2015 [1989]. *Great Clan Politics in Eastern Jin (Dongjin menfa zhengzhi)*. Beijing, China: Beijing, China: Peking University Press (Beijing daxue chubanshe).

Tilly, Charles. 1975. *The Formation of National States in Western Europe*. Princeton, NJ: Princeton University Press.

Tilly, Charles. 1978. *From Mobilization to Revolution*. Boston, MA: Addison-Wesley.

Tilly, Charles. 1992. *Coercion, Capital and European States: AD 990–1992*. Hoboken, NJ: Wiley-Blackwell.

Tilly, Charles. 1995. *Popular Contention in Great Britain, 1758–1834*. Cambridge, MA: Harvard University Press.

Toghtō. 1985 [1343]. *History of Song (Song shi)*. Beijing, China: Zhonghua Book Company (Zhonghua shuju).

Truman, David. 1971. *The Governmental Process*. New York, NY: Alfred A. Knopf.

Turchin, Peter, Thomas E. Currie, Edward A. L. Turner, and Sergey Gavrilets. 2013. "War, Space, and the Evolution of Old World Complex Societies." *Proceedings of the National Academy of Sciences* 110(41):16384–16389.

Twitchett, Denis. 1970. *Financial Administration under the T'ang Dynasty*. New York, NY: Cambridge University Press.

Twitchett, Denis. 1979. "Introduction." In *The Cambridge History of China: Sui and T'ang China, 589–906, Part I*, ed. Denis Twitchett. Vol. 3. New York, NY: Cambridge University Press, chapter 1, pp. 1–47.

Twitchett, Denis, and Howard J. Wechsler. 1979. "Kao-Tsung (Reign 649–83) and the Empress Wu: The Inheritor and the Usurper." In *The Cambridge History of China: Sui and T'ang*

China, 589–906, Part I, ed. Denis Twitchett. Vol. 3. New York, NY: Cambridge University Press, chapter 5, pp. 242–289.

Vansina, Jan. 1966. *Kingdoms of the Savanna*. Madison, WI: University of Wisconsin Press.

Von Glahn, Richard. 2016. *An Economic History of China: From Antiquity to the Nineteenth Century*. New York, NY: Cambridge University Press.

Vries, Peer. 2015. *Averting a Great Divergence: State and Economy in Japan, 1868–1937*. London, UK: Bloomsbury Publishing.

Wakeman, Frederic. 1970. High Ch'ing, 1683–1839. In *Modern East Asia: Essays in Interpretation*, ed. James B. Browley. San Diego, CA: Harcourt, Brace and World, chapter 1, pp. 1–28.

Wakeman, Frederic. 1972. "The Price of Autonomy: Intellectuals in Ming and Ch'ing Politics." *Daedalus* 101(2):35–70.

Wakeman, Frederic. 1975. *The Fall of Imperial China*. New York, NY: Free Press.

Walder, Andrew. 1988. *Communist Neo-Traditionalism: Work and Authority in Chinese Industry*. Berkeley, CA: University of California Press.

Wallerstein, Immanuel. 1974. *The Modern World-System I: Capitalist Agriculture and the Origins of the European World-Economy in the Sixteenth Century*. Berkeley, CA: University of California Press.

Wang, Anshi. 2017 [1086]. *Collected Works of Wang Anshi (Linchuan xiansheng wenji)*. Beijing, China: Commercial Press (Shangwu yinshuguan).
URL: *shorturl.at/xFGMV*

Wang, Chaohong. 2006. *A Textual Research on the Composers of Ming and Qing Dynasties (Ming qing qujia kao)*. Beijing, China: China Social Sciences Publishing House (Zhongguo shehui kexue chubanshe).

Wang, Heming. 2008. *The Comprehensive Catalog of Chinese Genealogies (Zhongguo jiapu zongmu)*. Shanghai, China: Shanghai Ancient Works Publishing House (Shanghai guji chubanshe).

Wang, Na. 2007. "Kejia Family–Yu Clan in Tuochuan, Wuyuan (Kejia mingzu–wuyuan tuochuan Yu Shi)." *Huizhou Social Sciences (Huizhou shehui kexue)* (4):33–37.

Wang, Qiang. 2016. *Genealogy Manuscript (Chao gao ben jiapu)*. Jiangsu, China: Phoenix Press (Fenghuang chubanshe).

Wang, Shengduo. 2003. *A Monetary History of the Song Dynasties 960–1279 (Liangsong huobi shi)*. Beijing, China: Social Sciences Literature Archives (Sheke wenxian xueshu wenku).

Wang, Shizhen. 2009. *Yanzhou Recluse Four Categories Compiled Drafts (Yanzhou shanren sibu jigao)*. Beijing, China: Chinese Classic Ancient Books Database (Zhongguo jiben gujiku).

Wang, Tseng-yü. 2015. "A History of the Sung Military." In *The Cambridge History of China: Sung China, 960–1279, Part II*, ed. John W. Chaffee and Denis Twitchett. Vol. 5. New York, NY: Cambridge University Press, chapter 3, pp. 214–249.

Wang, Yeh-chien. 1973. *Land Taxation in Imperial China, 1750–1911*. Cambridge, MA: Harvard University Press.

Wang, Yianyou. 2014. *Study on Ming State Organizations (Mingdai guojia jigou yanjiu)*. Beijing, China: Forbidden City Press (Zijincheng chubanshe).

Wang, Yuhua. 2021a. "Blood Is Thicker Than Water: Elite Kinship Networks and State Building in Imperial China." Forthcoming, *American Political Science Review*.

Wang, Yuhua. 2021*b*. "State-in-Society 2.0: Toward Fourth-Generation Theories of the State." *Comparative Politics* 54(1):175–198.

Wang, Yuquan, Zhongri Liu, and Xianqing Zhang. 2000. *Comprehensive History of Chinese Economy: Ming Economy (Zhongguo jingji tongshi: Mingdai jingji juan)*. Beijing, China: Economic Daily Press (Jingji ribao chubanshe).

Wang, Zhe. 1981. *History of Finance in Historical China*. Beijing, China: Beijing Finance College Press (Beijing caimao xueyuan chubanshe).

Wasserman, Stanley, and Katherine Faust. 1994. *Social Network Analysis: Methods and Applications*. New York, NY: Cambridge University Press.

Weber, Max. 1946 [1918]. *Essays in Sociology*. New York, NY: Oxford University Press.

Wechsler, Howard J. 1979. "The Founding of the T'ang Dynasty: Kao-tsu (Reign 618–26)." In *The Cambridge History of China: Sui and T'ang China, 589–906, Part I*, ed. Denis Twitchett. Vol. 3. New York, NY: Cambridge University Press, chapter 3, pp. 150–187.

Wei, Qingyuan. 1999. *Zhang Juzheng and the Politics of Late Ming (Zhang juzheng he mingdai zhonghouqi zhengju)*. Guangdong, China: Guangong Higher Education Press (Guangdong gaodeng jiaoyu chubanshe).

Wilkinson, Endymion. 2000. *Chinese History: A Manual*. Cambridge, MA: Harvard University Asia Center.

Williamson, Henry Raymond. 1935. *Wang An Shih: A Chinese Statesman and Educationalist of the Sung Dynasty*. London, UK: Arthur Probsthain.

Williamson, Oliver E. 1981. "The Economics of Organization: The Transaction Cost Approach." *American Journal of Sociology* 87(3):548–577.

Williamson, Oliver E. 1983. "Credible Commitments: Using Hostages to Support Exchange." *The American Economic Review* 73(4):519–540.

Williamson, Oliver E. 1985. *The Economic Institutions of Capitalism*. New York, NY: Free Press.

Wittfogel, Karl. 1959. *Oriental Despotism: A Comparative Study of Total Power*. New Haven, CT: Yale University Press.

Wong, Roy Bin. 1997. *China Transformed: Historical Change and the Limits of European Experience*. Ithaca, NY: Cornell University Press.

Wright, Arthur F. 1979. The Sui Dynasty (581–617). In *The Cambridge History of China: Sui and T'ang China, 589–906, Part I*, ed. Denis Twitchett. Vol. 3. New York, NY: Cambridge University Press, chapter 2, pp. 48–149.

Wright, Mary Clabaugh. 1962. *The Last Stand of Chinese Conservatism: The T'ung-Chih Restoration, 1862–1874*. Palo Alto, CA: Stanford University Press.

Wu, Baipeng. 2012. *Compilation of Works by Wu Baipeng (Wu Baipeng ji)*. Beijing, China: Zhonghua Book Company (Zhonghua shuju).

Wu, Bangshu, and Shanqing Wu. 1924. *Genealogy of Wu Clan in Shanyin and Zhoushan Prefecture (Shanyin zhoushan Wushi zupu)*. Shanghai, China: Shanghai Library (Shanghai tushuguan).

Wu, Daonan. 2009. *Wu Wenke Court Documents Collection (Wu Wenke gongwenji)*. Beijing, China: Chinese Classic Ancient Books Database (Zhongguo jiben gujiku).

Wu, Guolun. 1830. *Danzhui Cave Manuscripts (Dan zhui dong gao xu)*. Osmanthus Fragrance House (Gui fen zhai).

Wu, Songdi. 2000. *China Demographic History: Ming Dynasty (Zhongguo renkou shi: Ming shiqi)*. Shanghai, China: Fudan University Press (Fudan daxue chubanshe).

Wu, Weijia. 2014. *A Study of Zhao Yongxian and Zhao Qimei, the Yushan Bibliophiles in Ming Dynasty (Mingdai yushan cangshujia Zhao Yongxian, Zhao Qimei fuzi yanjiu)*. Anhui, China: Anhui Normal University Publishing House (Anhui shifan daxue chubanshe).

Xi, Tianyang. 2019. "All the Emperor's Men? Conflicts and Power-Sharing in Imperial China." *Comparative Political Studies* 52(8):1099–1130.

Xie, Wenzhe. 2014. "Huizhou Merchants' Involvement on Jiangnan Cultural Activities in the Late Ming Dynasty: A Case Study on Wang's Family and Wang Dao Kun (Wanming huishang zidi dui jiangnan wenyi huodong de touru)." M.A. Thesis, National Jinan International University.

Xiong, Min. 2012. "A Study on the Relationship between Zhang Siwei and Zhang Juzheng (Zhang Siwei yu Zhang Juzheng guanxi yanjiu)." M.A. Thesis, Central China Normal University.

Xu, Jie. 2009. *Shi Jing Hall Collection (Shi jing tang ji)*. Beijing, China: Chinese Classic Ancient Books Database (Zhongguo jiben gujiku).

Xu, Xianqing. 1964. *Tianyuan Cabinet Collection (Tian yuan lou ji)*. Taipei, Taiwan: Guolian Book Publishing Company (Guo lian tushu chuban youxian gongsi).

Xu, Zhen. 2015. "A Study of Wei Xuezeng in the Ming Dynasty (Mingdai Wei Xuezeng yanjiu)." M.A. Thesis, South Central University for Nationalities.

Yan, Gengwang. 1986. *List of Tang Major Officials (Tang pushangchenglang biao)*. Beijing, China: Zhonghua Book Company (Zhonghua shuju).

Yang, Guoan. 2012. *State Power and Social Order (Guojia quanli yu minjian zhixu)*. Hubei, China: Wuhan University Press (Wuhan daxue chubanshe).

Yang, Haiying. 2018. "The Shanyin Family and the Ming and Qing Dynasties (Shanyin shijia yu mingqing yidai)." *Historical Research (Lishi yanjiu)* (4):37–54.

Yang, Lien-sheng. 1954. "Toward a Study of Dynastic Configurations in Chinese History." *Harvard Journal of Asiatic Studies* 17(3/4):329–345.

Ye, Qing. 2006. *Comprehensive China Fiscal History: Five Dynasties and Song Dynaties (Zhongguo caizheng tongshi: wudai, liangsong juan)*. Beijing, China: China Fiscal and Economic Press (Zhongguo caizheng jingji chubanshe).

Ye, Renmei. 2010. "Research on Xu Xuemo, a Literati in the Late Ming Dynasty (Wanming wenren Xu Xuemo yanjiu)." M.A. Thesis, Zhejiang University of Technology.

Ye, Xianggao. 1997. *Cang Xia Manuscripts (Cang xia ji cao)*. Beijing, China: Beijing Publishing House (Beijing chubanshe).

Ye, Zhi. 2011. "The Epitaph of the State Scholar Xi Gong and the Ruren Li Family found in Xiangyang (Xiangyang faxian guoshi Xigong, ruren Li shi muzhiming)." *Jiang Han Archaeology (Jiang han kaogu)* (3):128–131.

Yin, Xiujiao. 2014. "Textual Research on the Epitaph of Jia Sanjin in the Ming Dynasty in Zaozhuang (Zaozhuang mingdai Jia Sanjin muzhiming kaoshi)." *Haidai Archaeological Journal (Haidai kaogu)* 7:442–448.

Yu, Deyu. 2015. *Research on the Wu Family of Shanyin and Zhoushan (Shanyin zhoushan Wu shi jiazu yanjiu)*. Beijing, China: China Social Sciences Publishing House (Zhongguo shehui kexue chubanshe).

Yu, Xianhao. 2000. *A Complete List of Tang Prosecutors (Tang cishi kao quanbian)*. Anhui, China: Anhui University Press (Anhui daxue chubanshe).

Yu, Xianhao. 2003. *An Investigation of Tang Major Officials (Tang jiuqing kao)*. Beijing, China: China Social Sciences Press (Zhongguo shehui kexue chubanshe).

Yu, Ying-shih. 2003 [1956]. *The Relationship between the Great Clans and the Founding of the Eastern Han Dynasty (Donghan zhengquan zhi jianli yu shizu daxing zhi guanxi)*. Shanghai, China: Shanghai People's Press (Shanghai renmin chubanshe).

Yuan, Kexin. 2017. "A Study on Wang Xijue (Wang Xijue yanjiu)." M.A. Thesis, Shanxi Normal University.

Zang, Yunpu, Chongye Zhu, and Yundu Wang. 1987. *Government Institutions, Military Institutions, and Civil Service Examinations in Chinese Dynasties (Ming shilu)*. Jiangsu, China: Jiangsu Ancient Book Publishing House (Jiangsu guji chubanshe).

Zelin, Madeleine. 1984. *The Magistrate's Tael: Rationalizing Fiscal Reform in Eighteenth-Century Ch'ing China*. Berkeley, CA: University of California Press.

Zeng, Zaozhuang, and Lin Liu. 2006. *Complete Prose of Song (Quansongwen)*. Shanghai, China: Shanghai Lexicographical Publishing House (Shanghai cishu chubanshe).

Zeng, Zhen. 2012. "Song Yiwang Poetry Collection Corrections and Footnotes (Song Yiwang shiji jiaozhu)." M.A. Thesis, Xiangtan University.

Zhang, Dexin. 2009. *Chronicle of Ming Civil Positions (Mingdai guanzhi nianbiao)*. Anhui, China: Huangshan Publishing House (Huangshan shushe).

Zhang, Huiqiong. 2016. *A Study on Tang Shunzhi (Tang Shunzhi yanjiu)*. Jiangsu, China: Phoenix Press (Fenghuang chubanshe).

Zhang, Jian. 2008. "A Brief Discussion on the Value of 'Wang Daokun's Epitaph' (Luetan Wang Daokun muzhiming de jiazhi)." *Journal of Henan Institute of Education: Philosophy and Social Sciences Edition (Henan jiaoyu xueyuan xuebao: zhexue shehui kexue ban)* 27(1): 63–66.

Zhang, Jian. 2014. *Research on Huizhou Distinguished Literati Wang Daokun (Huizhou hongru Wang Daokun yanjiu)*. Anhui, China: Anhui Normal University Publishing House (Anhui shifan daxue chubanshe).

Zhang, Jiankui. 2015. *A Study of Celebrities in the Past Dynasties in Gansu (Gansu lidai mingren yanjiu)*. Gansu, China: Gansu Science and Technology Press (Gansu keji chubanshe).

Zhang, Jiayin. 1997. *Compiled Works by Mr. Julai (Julai xiansheng ji)*. Shandong, China: Qilu Bookstore Publishing House (Qilu shushe).

Zhang, Jie. 2018. "A Chronology of Yang Wei (Yang Wei nianpu)." M.A. Thesis, Lanzhou University.

Zhang, Shunhui, and Liangkai Wu. 1987. *Zhang Juzheng Works Compilation (Zhang juzheng ji)*. Fujian, China: Jing Chu Bookstore (Jingchu shushe).

Zhang, Siwei. 2009 [1593]. *Tiao Lu Hall Collection (Tiao lu tang ji)*. Beijing, China: Chinese Classic Ancient Books Database (Zhongguo jiben gujiku).

Zhang, Taisu. 2017. *The Laws and Economics of Confucianism: Kinship and Property in Preindustrial China and England*. New York, NY: Cambridge University Press.

Zhang, Taisu. 2021. *The Ideological Foundations of the Qing Fiscal State*. Book Manuscript.

Zhao, Chao. 2017. "A Study on Pan Sikong's Court Memoir (Pan Sikong zoushu yanjiu)." M.A. Thesis, Anhui University.

Zhao, Dingxin. 2015. *The Confucian-Legalist State: A New Theory of Chinese History*. New York, NY: Oxford University Press.

Zhao, Kesheng. 2009. "Family Etiquette and Family Integration: A Case Study of the Ge Family in Dongshan in Ming Dynasty (Jiali yu jiazu zhenghe: mingdai dongshan Geshi de gean fenxi)." *Seeking Truth (Qiushi xuekan)* 36(2):126–132.

Zhao, Shi'an. 1993. *Kangxi Renhe County Gazetteer (Kangxi renhe xianzhi)*. Shanghai, China: Shanghai Bookstore (Shanghai shudian).

Zhao, Yongguang. 1595. *Cangxue Study Full Collection (Cang xue xuan quan ji)*. Beijing, China: Zhao Yongguang.

Zheng, Zhenman. 2001. *Family Lineage Organization and Social Change in Ming and Qing Fujian.* Honolulu, HI: University of Hawai'i Press.

Zheng, Zhenman. 2009. *Lineage Coalitions and the State (Xiangzu yu guojia)*. Beijing, China: Joint Publishing (Sanlian shudian).

Zhu, Duanqiang. 2015. *Biography Series of Hundreds of Historical Celebrities in Yunnan: Envoy to Ryukyu Xiao Chongye (Yunnan baiwei lishi mingren zhuanji congshu: chushi liuqiu—Xiao Chongye)*. Yunnan, China: Yunnan People's Publishing House (Yunnan renmin chubanshe).

Ziblatt, Daniel. 2006. *Structuring the State: The Formation of Italy and Germany and the Puzzle of Federalism*. Princeton, NJ: Princeton University Press.

Zunhua. 2013. *Encyclopedia of Zunhua Cultural and History Documents (Zunhua wenshi ziliao Daquan)*. Hebei, China: Zunhua Chinese People's Political Consultative Conference (Zunhua renmin zhengxie).

INDEX

Absolute monarchy
    during Ming Dynasty, 133
    during Qing Dynasty, 183
    during Song Dynasty, 92
Acemoglu, Daron, 17, 22, 259, 261, 262
Advanced scholar, 69, 86, 170
Africa, 29
    centralized societies in pre-colonial
        era, 203
    chiefs in post-colonial era, 206
    chiefs in pre-colonial era, 203
    chiefs under colonial rule, 204
    decentralized societies in
        pre-colonial era, 203
    democratization in the 1980s, 206
    elite social terrain in post-colonial
        era, 205
    elite social terrain in pre-colonial
        era, 8, 15, 203
    elite social terrain under colonial
        rule, 15, 205
    varieties of states in post-colonial
        era, 207
Agricultural productivity, 76
Aisin Gioro (Manchu clan), 182
Alesina, Alberto, 261
Allen, Robert, 262
Altan (Mongol chief), 131, 139
An Lushan Rebellion, 49, 70, 71, 95
Analytic narratives, 25
Ancestor worship, 165
Anderson, Lisa, 216, 217, 261

Anderson, Perry, 19, 23
Aristocracy
    capital concentration, 78, 88
    compared with European nobility,
        40
    demise, 79
    origin, 40, 66
    reproduction, 40
    rise in late Tang, 77
Autumn tax, 75, 111

Bai, Ying, 196
Baldwin, Kate, 206
baojia (military conscription), 117, 118
Barkey, Karen, 214
Bates, Robert, 21, 23, 25, 172, 205, 206,
    260
Beattie, Hilary, 159, 160, 163, 166
Blaydes, Lisa, 213, 259
Bol, Peter, 83, 100, 127
Bossler, Beverly, 83, 87, 96
Bowtie network
    and state form, 11
    and state strength, 9
    and state-society relations, 12
    definition, 8
    durability, 17
    measurement, 39
Buddhist temple, 126
Bureau of Personnel Evaluation, 111
Bureaucratic rotation, 78
Burt, Ronald, 11

A NOTE ON THE TYPE

THIS BOOK has been composed in Arno, an Old-style serif typeface in the classic Venetian tradition, designed by Robert Slimbach at Adobe.

CPSIA information can be obtained
at www.ICGtesting.com
Printed in the USA
JSHW022226040423
39929JS00004B/4